HOW TO BUILD A
WOODEN BOAT

HOW TO BUILD A

WOODEN BOAT

David C. "Bud" McIntosh

Illustrations by Samuel F. Manning

WoodenBoat Publications, Inc.

1987

To Babe

I have had great help and support from
my family and the staff at WoodenBoat.
Beyond that, I take all the blame.

Published by WoodenBoat Publications, Inc.
Brooklin, Maine 04616

Copyright © 1987 by David C. (Bud) McIntosh
Third printing 1993
All rights reserved.
ISBN 0-937822-10-8
Library of Congress Catalog Card Number: 87-040010

Design by Sherry Streeter
Printed by Arcata Graphics
Jacket printed by New England Book Components

McIntosh, David C., 1907–1993
How to Build a Wooden Boat.
Includes index.
1. Boatbuilding.   2. Sailboats—Design and
construction.   I. Title.

VM351.M378   1987   623.8'207   87-40010

Foreword

When I was very young, I built for myself the best boat in all the world. It was a fat dory, designed to fit a secondhand sail, and not very impressive to other eyes. What matter? It was a brave thing and, to me, beautiful—and I have never since lost my vision of the Best Boat in the World—always just a bit beyond the present one, and always there to strive toward. Maybe this background will help explain the chapters that follow. I hope they convey some of the feeling of joy I have had from a lifetime of boatbuilding. I hope they may encourage you to gather a few ancient tools and natural materials and build for yourself the best boat in all the world—a thing of perfect beauty, which will guard and preserve you wherever you want to go on the vast ocean seas. The voyaging may be mostly in the imagination, and this, the best boat in the world, may seem less than that to other people. That really doesn't matter. It will be your own, born of study, toil, and sacrifice; and you'll get from it a continuing emotional experience almost unique in this modern world.

Critics may well point out the narrow scope of this book: what amounts to one builder's techniques (and prejudices?) applied to one very special (shall we say, limited?) type of boat. You won't find here complete discussion of your favorite hard-chined skipjack or lapstrake surfboat or sawn-frame schooner or featherlight canoe—any one of which, I'll grant, may be the best boat in the world. You can buy a book that treats all of these, and more, too, in one volume—a book written by a yacht designer of great skill and experience, who knows all about the parts of the finished boat; but that designer doesn't know (or perhaps can't be bothered to tell you) the basic techniques, the inch-by-inch marking, cutting, and fastening that get all of these parts together in the proper order.

Here, if you will pardon me, is where I come in. I am opinionated, lazy, plodding, timid about trying anything new, and I have built about 500 deadweight tons of sailing yachts—largely with my own hands, and perhaps half of them to my own designs. And over the past 50 years I have tried, earnestly and constantly, to borrow, steal, invent, or develop by trial and error the best and easiest way for me to perform each of the several different operations involved in the building of a wooden boat.

I apologize to all the old pros, who have their own different and very satisfactory ways to do the same things. I say only that these techniques have worked for me and that if you will stay with me patiently, I think I can, in the following pages, explain to you how I set up, frame, plank, and deck such a boat, with maybe a centerboard trunk and a rudder thrown in. MERRYWING, the boat shown in most of our illustrations, poses almost all the problems you are likely to meet up with, whatever you build, and I hope I can convince you that there's no great mystery to boatbuilding after all.

I'm sure that the boat of your dreams is the best and most beautiful boat in the world. If you don't go ahead and build it, you will miss one of the most exciting and satisfying experiences left to us today. You'd better get going!

—Bud McIntosh

Preface

I had heard about Bud McIntosh for years before I met him. Among the cognoscenti in the field of traditional wooden boats, his name was uttered with a special kind of awe: not the mystical kind, but the kind that is characterized by utter amazement. Here was an artist and craftsman, I heard, who could not only design and build beautiful boats but who could build them quickly and cheaply—in the best sense of that word. Here was a man who knew from experience how much and what kind of wood to use where, and how to fit it so well that it seemed to have grown in place. Moreover, here was a man who was remarkably erudite—well read, well spoken—but without an overbearing nature. It was the stuff of legend, all right, and I was certain that our fledgling magazine would find a way to do an article on this unusual man. But time and money passed quickly in the early days of *WoodenBoat*, and somehow that goal seemed to elude me.

One day, my friend Randy Peffer called to say that he'd just been to visit Bud; he'd discovered that the boatbuilder had been working on writing a book about boatbuilding, and that this was no ordinary work. I would see for myself, he told me, because he had put copies of a couple of chapters in the mail.

When they arrived, I read them eagerly, hoping that I might have come upon something new and useful for the magazine's readers, but expecting nothing special. After all, the builders of traditional wooden boats in this country had not, up to that time, been given to writing much at all, and certainly not with the clarity and style desired in magazine journalism. Yacht designers wrote about boatbuilding, and sometimes very well; historians did, too, and preserved thereby some very important information. But one did not hear much from the boatbuilders who trudged off to their shops every day to coax even more beauty from that most lovely of natural materials. Making a living at it was—and is—challenge enough; it would be difficult to find oneself inspired, upon arriving home at the end of the day, to sit down and write freely about it. I was, therefore, unprepared for the elegance of Bud McIntosh's writing.

Indeed, I was truly moved by a clarity and style which seemed unmatched in the literature of boatbuilding. Here, in one chapter, was a profoundly clear blend of solid experience, literary style, and a measure of wit and humor unlike anything I had ever encountered. I wasted no time in arranging to publish whatever Bud could write, whenever it could be written. And I dreamed that, if it could become a book, we would be the ones to publish it. That was 10 years ago.

The boatbuilder had been able to write, it turned out, because he had found himself suddenly rendered infirm by an injury to his foot. To prevent himself from being overwhelmed by boredom, he decided to begin writing about boatbuilding—from his own strictly practical point of view and experience—with little or no attention to the theoretical, except where it mattered absolutely.

Thus, the series of articles by Bud McIntosh began in *WoodenBoat*. There was a certain irregularity to it, and a certain absence of method to the order in which the chapters appeared, but we were happy. The material was being published, and the readers were finding it both informative and inspiring. For, in Bud they found a real educator—one who wasted little time on the nonessentials, and who encouraged his readers freely to see both the basic simplicity of each step in wooden boat building, and its relationship to the whole.

There was, however, an element not yet well expressed in the series: illustration. We had begun with a few photographs and a few sketches, but we knew we were not doing enough to convey directly the essence of what was being said. And it was not possible to assign just any illustrator to the task of bringing these ideas to the printed page, because a thorough understanding of the process was essential to conveying it.

Thus entered Sam Manning, a uniquely capable artist and writer, and an accomplished boatbuilder himself. We had worked before with Sam, and knew well his ability to translate abstract ideas into comprehensive drawings. He had demonstrated it clearly in numerous maga-

zine and book illustrations over the years, and he appreciated the simplicity and directness with which Bud approached this subject. When he consented to collaborate with Bud on the series, and to aim toward the publication of a book, we were thrilled at the prospect. Over the years, the collaboration between these two extraordinary individuals has yielded a body of work which we believe sets a new standard in the field.

It is by no means a text on building all manner of wooden boats; it is by no means a general treatise on the subject. Rather, it is an attempt to convey, in detail, the processes by which Bud McIntosh has successfully built so many boats over the years. It is an attempt to convey the spirit and the philosophy behind these processes. To the extent that it succeeds at this, the reader is treated to the rare experience of wisdom acquired firsthand—and to the inimitable pleasure of understanding what seemed to be complex and mysterious procedures.

This book is a celebration of the wisdom of one New England boatbuilder. In a culture where fewer and fewer items are constructed by hand, and where too little time is spent preserving *process* itself, and the lasting pleasures such process can bring, we are honored and proud to be able to offer it at last.

—Jonathan Wilson, Editor
WoodenBoat Magazine

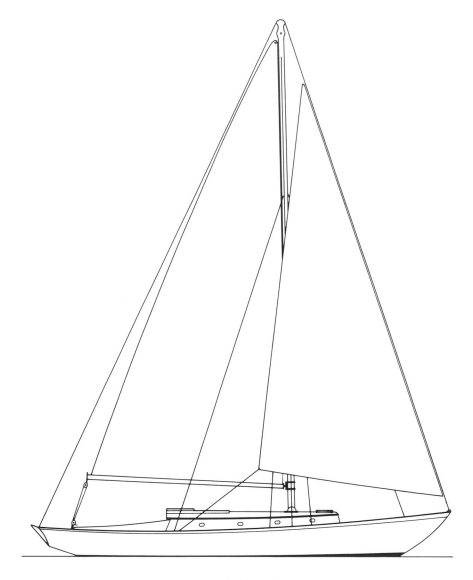

MERRYWING

Designed by David C. McIntosh
Sail plan redrawn by Dave Dillion

LOA 39′0″
LWL 27′6″
Beam 10′0″
Draft 5′6″

Contents

2-10-4 =
2' + 10" + 4/8"

		Stem	1	2	3	4	5	6	7	8	transom
Heights above and below LWL	Sheer	4-4-4	3-11-0	3-7-0	3-3-6	3-1-2	2-11-6	2-10-4	2-10-4	2-11-2	3-3-0
	profile		0-0-0	1-6-0	3-0-0	5-0-0	5-3-6	5-5-0	4-4-0	0-1-0	
	rabbet		0-2-0	1-4-0	2-4-2	—		4-3-0	2-0-0	0-1-2	
	butt 12		1-0-2	0-8-2	1-8-4	2-4-2	2-7-2	2-2-2	0-11-4	0-4-6	
	butt 24		2-5-2	0-1-4	1-0-0	1-6-4	1-8-0	1-4-0	0-6-0	0-8-6	
	butt 36			1-3-2	0-4-6	1-1-0	1-3-0	0-10-4	0-0-0	1-3-4	
	butt 48				0-9-4	0-5-4	0-9-0	0-3-4	0-9-0		
Halfbreadths from centerline	sheer	0-2-0	1-9-0	3-11-0	4-7-2	4-11-0	5-0-0	4-9-7	4-4-7	3-7-4	1-9-4
	profile		0-0-4	0-0-4	0-1-0	0-3-7	0-4-0	0-3-3	0-1-0	0-0-0	
	rabbet		0-2-0	0-2-0	0-4-0	0-6-6	0-6-3	0-3-5	0-3-0	0-3-0	
	24 A		1-8-0	3-4-0	4-5-0	4-11-0	5-1-0	4-11-0	4-5-2	3-5-4	
	12 A		0-1-2	2-9-5	4-0-6	4-9-2	5-0-0	4-10-0	4-2-4	2-7-4	
	LWL			1-10-1	3-4-4	4-4-2	4-7-2	4-3-1	3-0-4		
	12 B			0-6-0	1-11-4	3-1-4	3-5-6	2-9-0	0-11-0		
	24 B				0-7-4	1-4-4	1-6-6	1-1-4	0-2-4		
	36 B				0-1-0	0-6-6	0-8-7	0-7-0	0-2-0		
	diag. 1			0-4-4	1-2-0	1-8-2	1-10-0	1-6-0	0-7-2		
	diag. 2			0-1-1	1-11-4	2-5-2	2-7-0	2-3-2	1-4-2		
	diag. 3		0-7-2	1-10-4	2-9-6	3-4-0	3-5-3	3-3-2	2-4-0	1-0-0	
	diag. 4		1-4-2	2-9-6	3-11-4	4-8-2	4-10-7	4-7-0	3-8-6	2-5-0	
	diag. 5		2-0-0	3-5-6	4-6-2	5-2-1	5-4-4	5-3-0	4-8-0	3-7-0	

Offsets for sloop Merrywing. Read feet, inches, and eighths of an inch.

Chapter One

Laying Down

Our title would at first glance appear to suggest a confusion of bad grammar and bad taste. In truth it is an old, proper, and excellent definition of the first task in the art and craft of boatbuilding: the lofting process. In simple terms, the operation consists of drawing ("laying down") an accurate, full-sized picture on the floor, from which patterns are "taken off." The process is neither mysterious nor difficult, but there are some simple and essential truths. (In the learning process, there are one or two *shocking* truths, as well!)

When I was very young I held most naval architects in awe, and considered myself very smart indeed to have mastered the mechanics of lofting those sacred and untouchable drawings—waterlines, buttocks, magnificent diagonals, finally the body plan—and I crawled reverent miles on hands and knees, correcting tiny (and not-so-tiny) errors committed by men who had mastered the greatest and most thrilling of all arts: yacht design. It was an honor and a privilege to be chosen as one who would, however inadequately, bring this vision to being in wood, metal, paint, and whatever else the specifications called for (most of these items bought by the Designer at one-third off, and furnished to me, or our common victim, the Owner, at list price, as I finally learned)—and it was wonderful.

Time passed, my work improved, my knees and my faith became worn and battered, and I discovered a shocking truth: Practically anyone who can read the figures on a yardstick can lay down a body plan and a profile; and that's all you need to lay down, anyway. If the designer howls betrayal for some reason, there are two suggestions you can make about that set of lines and offsets. The polite one is that he take them back to his drawing board and correct them himself. If he can't develop a curved transom, he shouldn't expect you to do it for him. If he says you can't get the angles for the stem rabbet from the scale drawing, he needs further education. And finally, if this lofting were half as difficult as you have been led to suspect, some of us old pros would still be chopping dugouts out of tree trunks, and managing to make that look like quite a mystery, too.

So let's lay down what is strictly necessary, and no more; build a set of molds; make two-dimensional patterns of stem, sternpost, tail feather (the late Sam Crocker's term for the keel-of-the-counter, usually called the horn timber), and transom knee; and make the pattern for the ballast-shoe casting. This last item is the only difficult one of the four, and will be treated separately and at length later.

The basic grid

For this laying-down business you need a reasonably smooth floor, slightly longer than the boat and slightly wider than the total of maximum draft plus greatest freeboard—in the case of our example, 10 by 40 feet. You can manage on half this length or even less, but you'll have some confusion of lines-over-lines to cope with. If the floor is good enough, and the owners don't object, give it a coat of flat white paint, and work directly on that. If it's the floor of your living room, or as rough as my shop floor, cover it with light-colored sheathing paper (40 inches wide, 500 square feet to the roll, available at any lumberyard), which you spread out and let lie for 24 hours before you stretch and tack (or tape) it in place. Don't worry if the experts tell you this is all wrong, and that you'll never be able to do accurate work on a surface that changes dimensions every time a cloud goes by. You're going to have expert trouble from now on, anyway, and you might as well get used to it. (One of them used to haunt us with the threat that he'd get out his astrolabe and prolapse and show us the scientific way to figure out the shape we were seeking; and for a while we wondered that one small head could carry all he knew.)

Get yourself a 10-foot straightedge. A 4-inch strip off a ½-inch plywood panel makes a good one; or you can true up the edge of a dry board with your jointer. While you're at it, make a 6-footer and a long one—maybe 16 feet long. Stretch a string (nylon is best) the length of your loft floor, far enough from the edge to allow for the full draft of the boat, plus 2 or 3 inches. Do not chalk and snap it; instead, crawl along and mark where it lies at 3- or 4-foot intervals. Take up the string, mark this line with a good black number 2 pencil, using your 10-foot straightedge, and you have the load waterline, from which everything else develops. Using the same technique, mark the other full-length lines (three above, four below the load waterline, and exactly 12 inches apart) parallel with the load waterline. Now mark on the load waterline the locations of all the perpendiculars shown in the lines drawing—face of stem, station numbers 1 through 8, intersection of the sheerline projected through the centerline of the transom, and all the buttock lines you'll need on either side of station number 5. Draw these lines in, exactly at right angles to the load waterline. The safest way to do this is to erect station number 5 by the old high-school-geometry method of swinging intersecting arcs above and below the line, marking station number 5 through these intersections, and then working forward and aft (with your 50-foot steel tape) from station number 5 along the 36-inch load line and the 48-inch waterline. If your straightedge, joining these new marks, passes precisely through the corresponding marks on the load waterline, you will know your measurements were correct. All this is dull business, and perfectly obvious, I'm sure.

The diagonals for the body plan are only a bit more complicated (see Figure 1–1). Notice that in this design they all start at points where station number 5 (the centerline for the body plan) intersects the horizontal load line and waterlines, and they all pass through intersections of buttock lines with these same horizontal lines. Thus, diagonal D1 starts 12 inches below load waterline at centerline, and passes through the intersection of the 24-inch buttock and the 36-inch waterline; and diagonal D5 starts 36 inches above the load waterline and intersects the 12-inch load line 5 feet out from the centerline. Draw them all in, then, forward and aft of station number 5, and you are ready to start working from the table of offsets. The hard work is over, and the fun is about to begin.

The table of offsets

I have known bright people to whom a lines drawing resembled a cross section through a barrel of frozen angleworms, and meant but little more; and these same people thought of a table of offsets as something you might expect to come from the maw of a mad computer that had been fed on Pictish runes, rock and all. Both these conceptions are faulty and exaggerated. If you have managed (as I did, rather late in my childhood) to master the technique of drawing a line from 1 to 2 and so on in proper sequence to 87, and got for your diligence the picture of a nice horsie, you should have no trouble with a table of offsets. Any figure in any one of the little boxes simply tells you to start from a known point, proceed along a carefully labeled line for an exact number of feet, inches, and eighths of an inch, and there put a pencil mark. For *heights*, you start at the load waterline and measure up or down, as common sense and a glance at the scale drawing indicate. For *breadths*, you start at the centerline and measure out horizontally. For *diagonals*, you start where the diagonal starts (at the centerline of the plan) and measure along the line of the diagonal. When you've located and marked all these spots, you draw a fair curve (or sometimes a straight line) through them, and get, full-size, a line that I hope looks amazingly like the

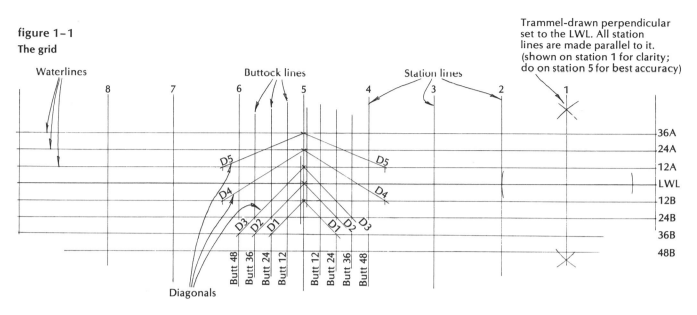

figure 1–1
The grid

Waterlines

Buttock lines

Station lines

Trammel-drawn perpendicular set to the LWL. All station lines are made parallel to it. (shown on station 1 for clarity; do on station 5 for best accuracy)

8 7 6 5 4 3 2 1

36A
24A
12A
LWL
12B
24B
36B
48B

D5 D5
D4 D4
D3 D2 D1 D1 D2 D3

Butt 48 Butt 36 Butt 24 Butt 12 Butt 12 Butt 24 Butt 36 Butt 48

Diagonals

corresponding line on the scale drawing. Occasionally some sadistic N.A. will take all his vertical measurements from a base line, or something he prefers to call the designed waterline, but he usually gives you a hint that you'd better watch out.

Now that the above is all clear in your mind, you are probably itching to get at the body plan and make the molds. For these, however, you need to know the exact height of the top of the backbone (keel, stem, stern knee, tail feather) where each mold stands, the corrected height of the sheer at each station, and the half-widths of the backbone, from the centerline to the rabbet, where the molds straddle it. So curb your impatience, and lay down just enough of the construction profile to show the shape of each piece of the backbone assembly, the line of the rabbet, the exact location of the shaft alley and rudderport, and the line of the sheer in profile. Indicate (and label, lest you mistake these lines for something else later) the positions of the principal fastenings in the backbone. If these are not shown in the scale drawing of the construction plan (as they certainly should be), demand them from the designer. Finally, lay off from one of the full-length horizontal lines (assuming it, for the purpose, to be the centerline of the keel in plan view) the half-breadths of the rabbet, for each station, as given in the table of offsets. The load line 36 inches above the load waterline is the best one to use for this particular half-breadth, because it's in the least-cluttered section of the floor. If you want to lay down the sheerline in plan view, use the waterline 12 inches below the load waterline for your theoretical center-

line, lest you measure yourself right off the side of the floor.

So much for the general plan of attack. Now let's choose weapons and carry it out.

The construction profile

Start with the rabbet line on the keel (see Figure 1-2). You will observe that this is a straight line from station number 3 to and through station number 6, and that the table of offsets therefore omits the height of the rabbet on stations number 4 and 5. This straight section of rabbet is the most important line of reference in the entire laying-down and setting-up processes, so get it right—and extend it to station number 2 forward, and to station number 7 aft. Use your nylon string all the way, and be sure. Now note that the top of the wood keel is exactly parallel to, and 3½ inches above, this straight rabbet line. Mark this in, all the way from number 2 to number 7; repeat the performance for the *bottom* of the wood keel, exactly 1½ inches *below* the line of the rabbet. This last line is also, of course, the top of the ballast keel. It might be worth your while to use a red pencil for these last two lines and all other *construction* (as distinct from *design* lines) details. Note, finally, that all the heights in the boat are based on the line representing the top of the wood keel: the stem, the stern assembly, the four principal molds, and, eventually, the underside of the cabin sole. Check the offsets, check your measurements, check your youthful exuberance, and *get it right*.

While your straightedge is still warm, and before we get to the subject of battens, mark

5

figure 1–2

Construction profile

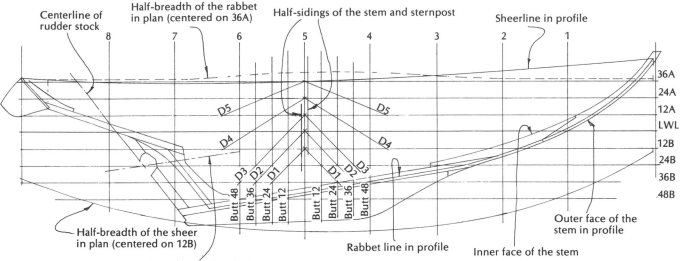

Centerline of rudder stock

Half-breadth of the rabbet in plan (centered on 36A)

Half-sidings of the stem and sternpost

Sheerline in profile

8 7 6 5 4 3 2 1

36A
24A
12A
LWL
12B
24B
36B
.48B

D5 D5

D4 D4

D3 D2 D1 D1 D2 D3

Butt 48 Butt 36 Butt 24 Butt 12 Butt 12 Butt 24 Butt 36 Butt 48

Half-breadth of the sheer in plan (centered on 12B)

Centerline of propeller shaft

Rabbet line in profile

Inner face of the stem

Outer face of the stem in profile

some more straight lines: the centerline of the transom; the profile of the tail feather, from its intersection with the transom, across the top of the sternpost; the lines of the rabbet on the tail feather; the centerline of the rudder stock from the deck to the heel of the sternpost; the centerline of the propeller shaft; the straight portion of the profile of the bottom of the ballast keel; the straight portion of the rabbet line on the sternpost. These straight lines, each joining two points exactly located (by measurements on the lines drawing or from the table of offsets), will precisely determine the starting points of the curves you are about to draw.

Now about battens. You'll be using these in practically infinite variety every time you turn around on this job, and for a long time to come, so you'd best start your collection now. You'll need two immediately, at least 22 feet long, about ¾ inch by 1 inch in section. These will overlap to mark the sheerline, here on the floor, and, later, on the planked-up hull. One of them will do for marking long planks. The curve of the stem requires a limber one, ½ inch square and at least 16 feet long. The rabbet on the sternpost, and the forward end of the ballast keel, must be marked with very limber battens indeed—straight-grained oak or ash, less than ⅜ inch square. These will do also for the body plan and molds, and at least two of them must be over 8 feet long. And when you come to the outline of the curved transom, you'll be an old hand at this business and be able to judge for yourself what's needed.

If you don't already have your ribband

stock, pick it out now (2-inch by 4-inch, 6-inch, 8-inch, 10-inch clear fir, if you can get it, at least half of it 22 feet long or better) and steal your battens out of it. Clear white pine is the best and most pleasant to use, but you'll not be likely to find a board over 16 feet long. Saw out half a dozen of them anyway, from 10 feet up, and about ¾ inch square. Build a batten rack on the wall, out of reach of young fishermen and your own big feet.

So now you are equipped to finish laying down the construction profile. Do the face of the stem first: height at the sheer from the offset table. All other points (measured horizontally on the waterlines from the forward perpendicular) are taken from the scale drawing. Start a fivepenny box nail at each point, pull your 16-foot limber batten in against this curved line of fence posts, ease it in or out where necessary to correct for slight errors (holding it in place with nails driven against, not through it), and mark. Move in and mark the rabbet line in the same way, with your batten flowing into and following the straight line previously marked. Now draw, on the floor, the inside face of the entire stem, the scarf joint, and the jog at the forward end of the wood keel. You will have to scale some of these dimensions from the plans. Go aft now and do the same job on the entire stern assembly—the main and outer sternpost, the tail feather, the knee to the transom, the completed rabbet line, the aperture for the propeller, and the bolt pattern.

If you are still able to bend over, mark the height of the sheer at each station (dimensions,

6

from the table of offsets, up from the load waterline), correct with long battens until fair, and mark. Do the same for the half-breadth of the sheer (working from the assumed centerline 12 inches below the load waterline—remember?) and for the half-breadth to the rabbet. Note that this width must be exactly 2 inches at the point where the rabbet leaves the keel and goes on to the stem, and exactly 2½ inches where the rabbet intersects the sternpost—these figures being the halfsidings, of course, of the stem and the sternpost, respectively. While you have them fresh in mind, draw them in as they must appear in the body plan: stem siding 2 inches forward of the station number 5 ordinate, and sternpost siding 2½ inches aft of it. Be very careful henceforth, when laying out half-breadths on the body plan, that you do not mistake one of these for your centerline. (Actually, when you get into the swing of it, you'll find that you match the 3-foot mark on your rule with the 36-inch buttock, or whatever, and ignore the centerline altogether except when laying off distances on diagonals. Thus you avoid errors and save yourself much crawling.)

Now for the molds

Now is the time to lay down the body plan, which gives the exact outlines of eight cross sections through the hull, and from which (after subtracting the thickness of the planking) you will derive the shapes of the eight molds. (See Figure 1-3.)

Start with station number 5. Find the point where the straight line of the rabbet in profile intersects the station number 5 ordinate. Get the half-breadth-to-rabbet distance from the line you laid off, above, from the 36-inch load line. Square out this distance, forward, from your point of intersection, and mark the spot. This one is sacred and final. Locate the uppermost (sheer) point in the same way—out, forward, from the intersection of the sheer profile with the station number 5 ordinate, to the distance shown on your plan view of the sheerline—or the breadth called for in the table of offsets, which should be the same thing. Be sure that this point is at the correct height above the load waterline, as taken at the station number 5 ordinate, and *not* as it appears so attractively before you where you squat 5 feet forward of station number 5. (I hate to belabor the obvious, but I have fallen into this error myself.) Now, working from the table of offsets, mark distances out on all horizontals; heights above or below the load waterline on all buttocks; and distances from the centerline on all diagonals.

Set up your row of fivepenny-nail fence posts, and with trembling hand, bend your best oak batten in to the curve.... Take a deep breath, calm yourself, make sure that *you* haven't made any mistakes in reading or marking those offsets, and proceed to move this or that nail to get a fair curve on the batten, bearing in mind that of all the offsets, the diagonals are most likely to be correct. When you are satisfied that the curve is fair and yet as near as possible to the original offset points, draw it in and go on to the next one, and the next, until you have all eight done, with no more help from me. I can do this whole body-plan job in less than three hours, which indicates not that I am a fast worker, nor even a very careless one, but simply that it's a quick and easy business after all.

figure 1-3

Sectional curves of the body plan and the principal fastenings of the backbone

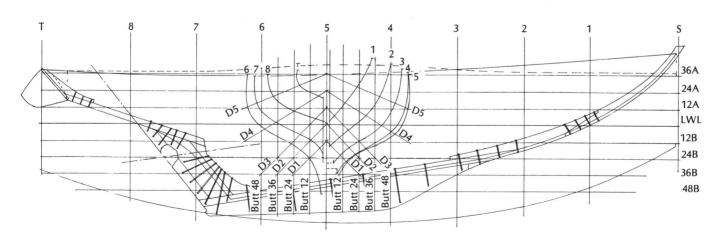

Chapter Two

The Making of Molds

Following the lofting process, you'll no doubt be anxious to set tools to wood and begin to shape your dream. Heaven knows you've anticipated it long enough! Well, the making of molds is as critical to the success of the project as lofting, since the molds are but perfect reproductions (in three dimensions) of the stations we've laid out on the body plan. Station number 1 becomes station mold number 1, and so on.

When the molds are all set up, and especially when the ribbands are bent over them, you'll have the distinct pleasure of seeing before you the shape you've longed for, all these weeks and months of planning. Keep in mind, though, that although the shape is permanent, the structure is not. As planking goes on, ribbands come off, and when planking is done, the molds come out. But by this time, of course, the hull will be built and you'll be feeling like ten million dollars. (It used to be a million, but inflation changed all that.)

Materials

For molds, we always use white pine round-edged box boards, 1¼ inches thick, which come wide and crooked, withstand any amount of nailing, and cost less than any other lumber we can get. Run the batch through a surface planer. Pick out the straight ones and saw them for cross spalls—4 inches wide, one for each mold, and *absolutely straight* on one edge. Saw out another 40 to 50 running feet of 4-inch stock, also absolutely straight, and a like amount 2 inches wide. You'll need great quantities of this stuff in the setting-up process, so don't worry about extravagance. Lay in six or seven pounds of eightpenny common nails, a 2-foot steel square, a good hammer, a good crosscut saw, a set of dividers with a soft, soft pencil for one leg (set the gap to the thickness of the planking), a good bandsaw (or a better sabersaw than I've ever owned), and you're ready to begin work. (You can, of course, do all this cutting out with an assortment of good handsaws, but it sure takes longer!)

Marking and putting together the half-molds

To make the number 5 mold, first subtract from the laid-down body plan outline the thickness of the planking, using the dividers to mark short arcs, at about 6-inch intervals, from the rabbet to the sheer. Now mark a line square across the centerline exactly 3½ inches above the rabbet height, to represent the top of the wood keel (and, of course, the flat at the bottom of the mold). Take a wide and crooked board, about 7 feet long, and lay it on the half-section so that it covers all the inside-of-planking marks from the rabbet to a point above the load waterline, and extends at its lower end past the centerline and the top-of-keel mark. This positioning is shown in Figure 2–2. Now, very carefully, turn that board over, toward the center of the drawing, as if it were hinged to the floor along its upper edge. If you have not already seen the next operation, the results of which are shown in Figure 2–3, you're going to think boatbuilders must be somewhat primitive in their thinking, but don't be too hasty; this is undoubtedly the greatest invention since the wheel.

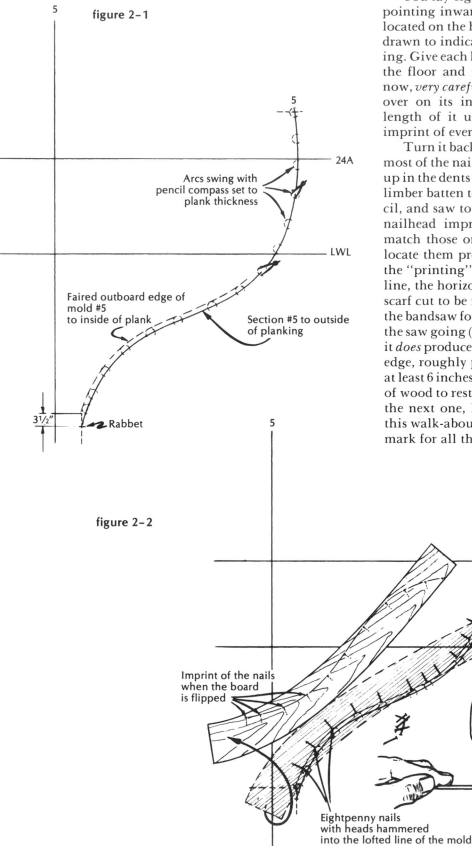

figure 2-1

5

5

24A

Arcs swing with
pencil compass set to
plank thickness

LWL

Faired outboard edge of
mold #5
to inside of plank

Section #5 to outside
of planking

3½"

Rabbet

figure 2-2

5

5

24A

LWL

Imprint of the nails
when the board
is flipped

Eightpenny nails
with heads hammered
into the lofted line of the mold

You lay eightpenny nails flat on the floor, pointing inward, each with its head precisely located on the high points of the arcs you have drawn to indicate the inside line of the planking. Give each head a hammer-tap to set it into the floor and make it stay in position. And now, *very carefully indeed*, turn the board back over on its invisible hinges—and walk the length of it until you think it has felt the imprint of every one of those nailheads.

Turn it back again, and you'll discover that most of the nails are clinging to it. Stand them up in the dents their heads have made, spring a limber batten to the curve, mark it with a pencil, and saw to this line on the bandsaw. The nailhead impressions on the cut edge will match those on the floor, and enable you to locate them precisely where they were during the "printing" process. Now mark the centerline, the horizontal cut at the bottom, and the scarf cut to be made at the upper end. Back to the bandsaw for these cuts; and, while you have the saw going (some builders don't do this, but it *does* produce fuel for the stove!), cut the inner edge, roughly parallel with the outer, leaving at least 6 inches of width all the way, and plenty of wood to rest on the keel. (And when you do the next one, having become convinced that this walk-about printing process really works, mark for all those straight cuts before you tip

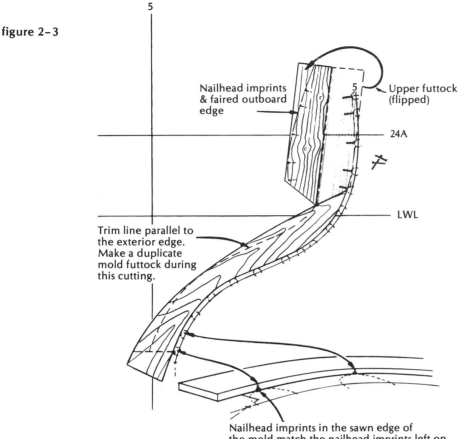

figure 2-3

5

Nailhead imprints & faired outboard edge

5

Upper futtock (flipped)

24A

LWL

Trim line parallel to the exterior edge. Make a duplicate mold futtock during this cutting.

Nailhead imprints in the sawn edge of the mold match the nailhead imprints left on the floor. Helps reposition the seam futtock.

the board over to get at the clinging nails.) Back to the floor with it, for a moment, to mark *on the floor* the scarf line for the upper section. Take the piece up, trace an exact duplicate of it on another piece of mold stock, go through the whole positioning-printing-scarfing process with the second piece of the mold (allowing it to extend about 6 inches above the sheer), mark a duplicate of this second piece, and then tack the two pieces of this half-mold in their proper positions on the floor. And when you tack them (two eightpennies in each), consider that there will be a 4-inch cross spall with its upper edge at the 2-foot waterline, a cleat 8 inches wide across the bottom, and a doubling piece to join two parts of the half-mold. Keep your tacks clear of all these.

Fit the doubling piece, keeping it below the place where the spall will land, and fasten it with plenty of eightpenny nails. Now, with the mold still tacked in place, mark on both the face and the edge the sheer, spall, and LWL heights.

Now for the other half. Pull the four tacks, turn the half-mold over, doubling side down

and with a wood scrap of the same thickness under each end, so that it will lie comfortably. Saw out the traced duplicates and tack them back-to-back with their already joined mates on the floor (as shown in Figure 2-4). Join them with a doubling piece, and transfer all edge-marks from the first half-mold to the mirror duplicate. Separate them, tack the first half to the floor through the original nail holes, and drive a nail (fence-post style) on the 24-inch load line, and to the left of the centerline exactly as far as the first half-mold lies to the right of it. Lay the second half in position against the nail, and check to see that it matches the proper heights at the keel, load waterline, and spall. Tack it to the floor.

Completing and setting up the mold

Now to join the two halves. The cross spall is the key to accuracy in the setting-up process, and must be applied on this and all the other molds at exactly the same height (top edge at the 24-inch waterline) and exactly level across.

11

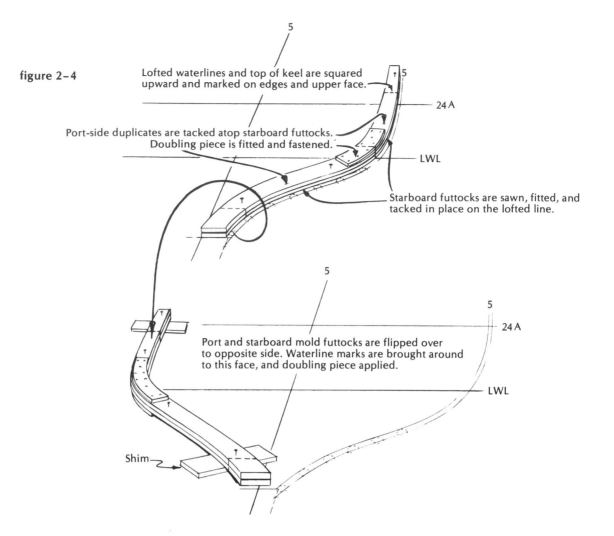

figure 2-4

Lofted waterlines and top of keel are squared
upward and marked on edges and upper face.

5

24 A

LWL

Port-side duplicates are tacked atop starboard futtocks.
Doubling piece is fitted and fastened.

Starboard futtocks are sawn, fitted, and
tacked in place on the lofted line.

5

5

24 A

LWL

Port and starboard mold futtocks are flipped over
to opposite side. Waterline marks are brought around
to this face, and doubling piece applied.

Shim

Cut it to length, fasten it to each mold with five nails, and mark the centerline (squaring up from the floor) on the top edge and the exposed face. Go to the bottom, and fit and fasten a wide cross-cleat, with a straight lower edge to bear on top of the keel. Mark the centerline on the face of this cleat. Now fit a 4-inch vertical post, flat on the floor, bearing against (under) the cross spall and the top edge of this cleat, and off center so that one edge lies exactly on the vertical centerline. Check to make sure that the cross spall is precisely at the 24-inch height at its midpoint, and fasten this post in place. As shown in Figure 2-5, brace the mold diagonally with two 2-inch pieces from the top of the centerpost (under the spall) out to the mold below the doublings, and it's finished, ready to be raised up and make way for the next. Write the number "5" all over it in big black letters, because you'll be peering at it from strange angles when you get to planking.

You could make each half of the number 1 and number 2 molds out of single boards. The forwardmost mold will need a second cross spall, about at the sheerline, fastened with

screws so that it can be removed temporarily in the setting-up process. Number 5 will stand on the keel with its after face on the station line, which requires that its contact surface with the keel must be beveled upward, or else be 3⅞ inches above the rabbet, instead of the 3½-inch height that is proper for mold numbers 3 and 4. Lacking wide and crooked stock, you may have to use three pieces in each half of the big molds. When measuring for the height of bearing surface (landing place on stem, sternpost, tail feather) on the other molds, allow for a little more height than the construction profile shows. It's easier to fit wedges under them than to cut more wood away.

With the molds out of the way, you should now take off exact profile patterns of all the pieces (except the keel) that will make up the backbone of the vessel. Use pine boards or cheap plywood, and the same tip-over, nail-head, walk-about technique to mark the shapes that you used for the molds. These are much more complicated than the mold prints, of course, since you must get, in one operation, the shapes of both edges, the line of the rabbet, and the scarf lines. So place the nailheads carefully, lay the stock tenderly, and do a quiet double shuffle over all. Turn it over, mark the curves (including the rabbet line) and straight cuts, saw to the outlines, and return the pattern to the floor. Tack it in place and mark, on the exposed face, waterlines, load lines, stations, thickness of stock—and the name of the boat, if you've got that far. (You realize, of course, that the name must never be mentioned aloud, near the boat, until the moment she starts down the ways. Fortunately, the evil spirits that lurk need to know the name of the vessel in order to work their spells, which take time to prepare; but it's a well-known fact that they can't read. This may illuminate some aspects of the snobbery of education.)

Well, back to business. The sternpost template must show the centerline of the propeller shaft and the shape of the aperture, because you'll bore the first and cut the second before assembling the members of the backbone. Do not delude yourself into the belief that you can omit a template for the tail feather, just because it's a parallel-sided five-by-seven with one simple cut at the after end and a hole through it. Do your thinking and make your mistakes on the template, before you start cutting a valuable piece of timber.

Incidentally, this whole operation of mold-building and template-shaping should be completed in 24 man-hours. Since the boat, ready to sail, will represent about 4,000 hours' labor, it might be worth squandering three or four more at this stage, trying to find any mistakes the designer might have made. Believe me, he can make them. As for me, I'm heartily sick of this stage, and will leave you scrabbling about while I try to make sense out of the next one.

figure 2–5

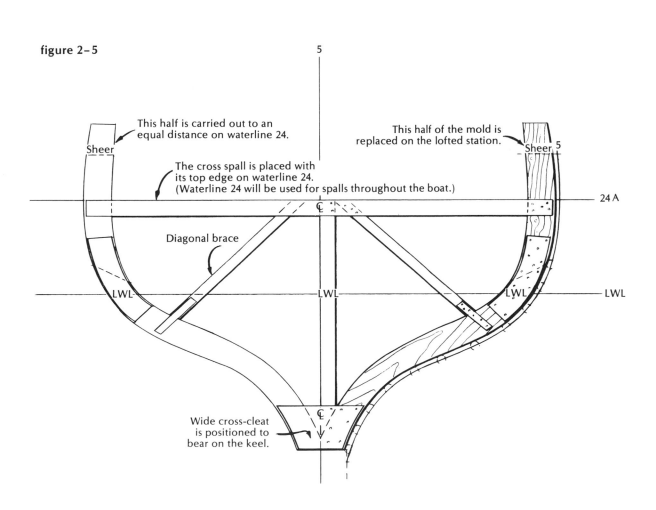

This half is carried out to an equal distance on waterline 24.

Sheer

This half of the mold is replaced on the lofted station.

Sheer 5

The cross spall is placed with its top edge on waterline 24.
(Waterline 24 will be used for spalls throughout the boat.)

24 A

Diagonal brace

LWL   LWL   LWL   LWL

Wide cross-cleat is positioned to bear on the keel.

Chapter Three

The Ballast Keel

One of the most fascinating and heartwarming things about the boatbuilding business is the universally friendly helpfulness of the many visitors we have. They are not, for the most part, people with, as you might say, an axe to grind—or a plane to be adjusted, or even a check to press into our embarrassed hand as down payment on a new design. Not at all. They come because they like us, and they like the smells around the shop that speak of cedar shavings, wood preservatives, and certain little creatures who have discovered good digging under the boiler.

These visitors are not ignorant. They are keen students of yacht design and boatbuilding, ever willing to help with a bit of friendly advice, or a quick demonstration of how Manny (whose shop they visited on last week's day off) fits a beam in less than half the time we're likely to need for the same job. And when they say, "Do you *really* think this stuff is fit for planking"—or, "My gahd, don't tell me you're still using *iron* keels and *galvanized* bolts!"— we feel properly grateful and almost at a loss for words. Almost, but not quite.

Therefore, having arrived at the subject of ballast keels, and in full awareness of my vow to avoid contention concerning matters of design, I'd like to attempt to justify that hunk of weight, to describe what it's made of and why it's shaped the way it is.

Outside iron

There are still some who, steeped in the lore of Friendship sloops, sandbaggers, Brixham trawlers, and seasickness cures, maintain that all ballast should be inside, anyway. I have given up fighting the battle of sail-carrying power ("After all—admit it—if you want to go to windward, you turn on the engine"), and have even stopped pointing out that lead inside is fully as expensive as lead outside, and terribly dangerous if the boat rolls completely over. I even dare suggest that some of those encapsulated-birdshot ballast systems in the plastic boats will bear watching, too. All I do now is give the inside-ballast man a flatiron and suggest he hit the bench with it, twice—once with his hand on top of the iron, and once with his hand underneath. If you have never run a boat aground and feel completely confident that you never will, then this demonstration does not apply; but if you are half as timid and bumbling as I am, you'll be happy in the thought that the weight is already at the bottom of the pile.

So we'll put the ballast outside and keep the bilge airy. But why iron? You can melt lead yourself, in an old iron bathtub over burning automobile tires, and ladle it into a wooden mold. If a foundry casts a lead keel for you, in a sand mold, you need only provide the wooden

figure 3-1

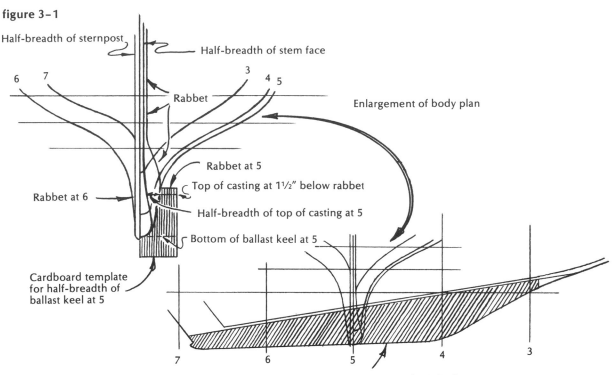

Half-breadth of sternpost

Half-breadth of stem face

6 7   3   4 5

Rabbet

Enlargement of body plan

Rabbet at 5

Top of casting at 1½″ below rabbet

Rabbet at 6

Half-breadth of top of casting at 5

Bottom of ballast keel at 5

Cardboard template
for half-breadth of
ballast keel at 5

7   6   5   4   3

Profile of the ballast keel in the loft plan

pattern and more money. The weight can be lower, less bulky, more easily located at the correct fore-and-aft position. It won't rust. The bronze bolts through the lead shoe are more reliable than the steel bolts you'd use through iron (and just to be cautious, I'll include stainless steel in my doubts). And, as someone always points out, you can take lead ballast off anytime, sell it for scrap, and get your money back.

In the face of all this undisputed evidence in favor of lead, what can we say in favor of iron? Well, first, it's less expensive, if compared to the foundry's price for a lead keel, or if you add your own extra labor cost in making a negative pattern or mold and doing your own melting and pouring—which, incidentally, can be somewhat hazardous, if you get careless; I have scars to prove it. But cost is a poor argument. The best money in the boat is the money that buys outside ballast, so don't begrudge it. Get the best material, and get enough. In my case, get iron. Design the boat so that only iron can hit those adamantine ledges—and slide smoothly off, undistorted. Design it, furthermore, so that you don't have to carve out large mounds of outside deadwood, where vile worms will dwell soon after you scrape the paint off.

Think how strong the boat must be, with stem, sternpost, and all points between tied directly to that unyielding base. Neither thrust of mast nor two-point support from a storage cradle will ever bend that foundation.

The solid pattern method

Whether your design calls for lead or iron, slabsided or streamlined, someone has to make a pattern for it. Patternmaking is a craft that demands a very high degree of skill, precision, and ingenuity—if you're dealing with something like a matched pair of water-jacketed engine manifolds, or a massive frame whose finished dimensions must be accurate to tiny fractions of an inch. But such skill is not essential to the making of a ballast-keel pattern, and you have to make a pattern anyway—so let's get at it.

If your design calls for the simplest form—parallel-sided for the greater part of its length, tapering very slightly from top to bottom to give the pattern "draft" so it can be lifted out of the sand—then the problem is very simple. You can make the pattern solid, preferably of white-pine timber sawn to the maximum thickness required at the top of the casting. Pile it up, and

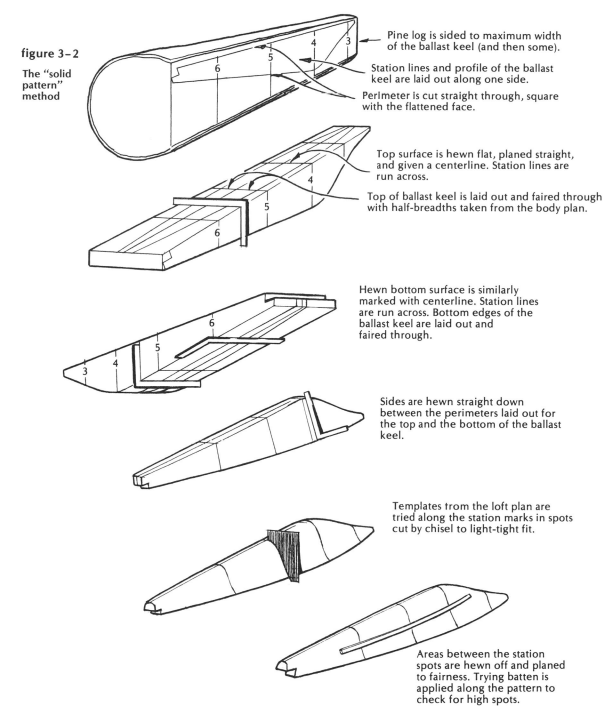

figure 3-2

The "solid pattern" method

Pine log is sided to maximum width of the ballast keel (and then some).

Station lines and profile of the ballast keel are laid out along one side.

Perimeter is cut straight through, square with the flattened face.

Top surface is hewn flat, planed straight, and given a centerline. Station lines are run across.

Top of ballast keel is laid out and faired through with half-breadths taken from the body plan.

Hewn bottom surface is similarly marked with centerline. Station lines are run across. Bottom edges of the ballast keel are laid out and faired through.

Sides are hewn straight down between the perimeters laid out for the top and the bottom of the ballast keel.

Templates from the loft plan are tried along the station marks in spots cut by chisel to light-tight fit.

Areas between the station spots are hewn off and planed to fairness. Trying batten is applied along the pattern to check for high spots.

cut it to the profile you laid down on the floor. Taper the pattern for draft by running it through a single-surface planer, with a batten tacked along its lower edge. Double the thickness of the batten, of course, when you turn the pattern over to do the other side. (Or lacking a surface planer, you can do this tapering by hand plane. A taper of ¼ inch to the foot is enough.)

Taper the ends of the pattern as necessary, and shape the entering edge as shown in the lines drawing. If your designer has been paying attention to the findings of the tank-research men, he will be very fussy about this, probably demanding a curve like a snubbed parabola, rather than the flat-with-rounded-corners, full half-round, or blunt knife-edge that were considered proper by various designers at various times during the past hundred years. Laminar flow, width and location of maximum chord, acceleration of water particles, minimization of the areas of turbulence—these are all sud-

17

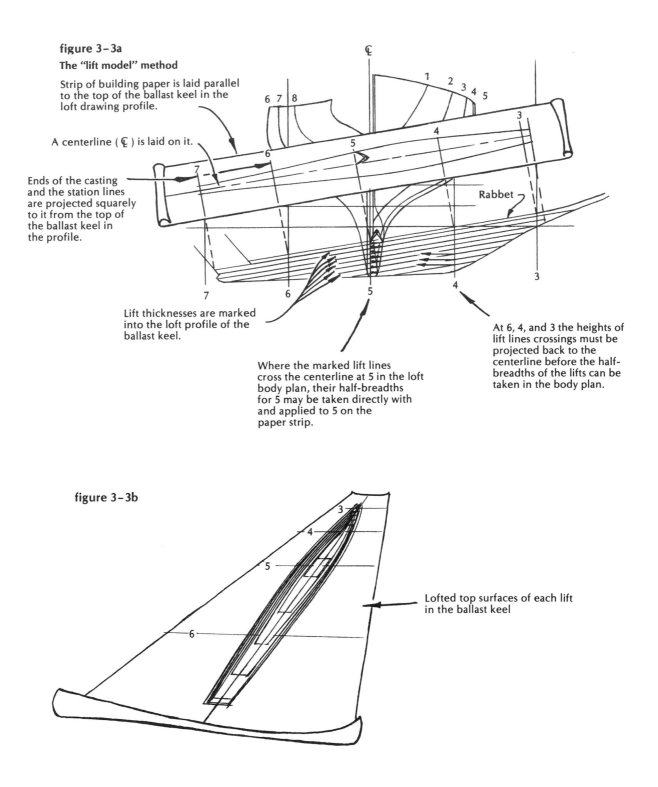

figure 3-3a

The "lift model" method

Strip of building paper is laid parallel to the top of the ballast keel in the loft drawing profile.

A centerline (℄) is laid on it.

Ends of the casting and the station lines are projected squarely to it from the top of the ballast keel in the profile.

Rabbet

Lift thicknesses are marked into the loft profile of the ballast keel.

Where the marked lift lines cross the centerline at 5 in the loft body plan, their half-breadths for 5 may be taken directly with and applied to 5 on the paper strip.

At 6, 4, and 3 the heights of lift lines crossings must be projected back to the centerline before the half-breadths of the lifts can be taken in the body plan.

figure 3-3b

Lofted top surfaces of each lift in the ballast keel

denly very much to be considered, and you can be sure that your designer had them in mind when he shaped those lowermost waterlines.

For the moment, let's ignore the problem of core prints, lifting eyes, and surface finish, and discuss instead the building of a more compli-

cated pattern—for instance, the one required for our example.

There are at least three ways to do this job. The first and most primitive (and by far the most difficult, in my opinion) is to start with an enormous baulk of timber and whittle it to

figure 3-3c

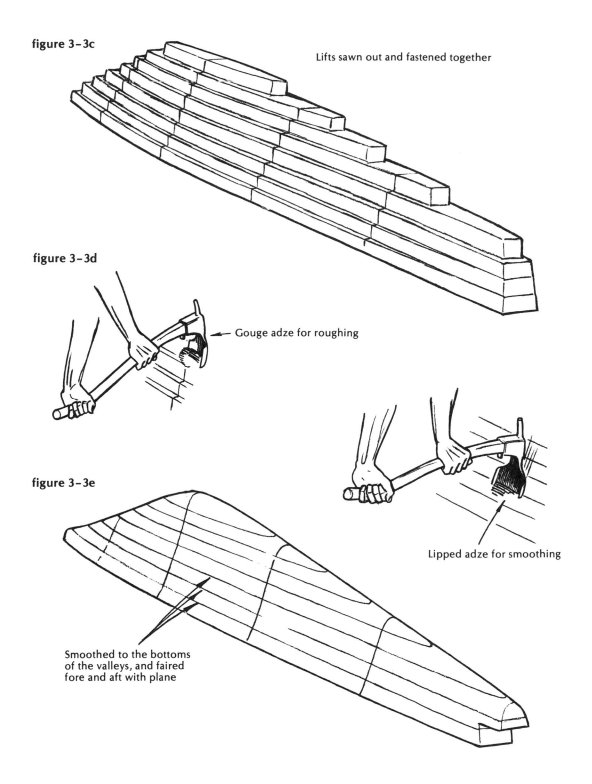

Lifts sawn out and fastened together

figure 3-3d

← Gouge adze for roughing

Lipped adze for smoothing

figure 3-3e

Smoothed to the bottoms of the valleys, and faired fore and aft with plane

shape, using templates lifted from the section lines in the body plan as guides. (Figure 3-2 illustrates this method step by step.) An old-time sparmaker, good with broadaxe and adze, could possibly do an acceptable job by this method. So could Michelangelo.

The lift model method

Instead, suppose we build this pattern as if it were a lift model—using layers of 2-inch plank, sawn to shape, pinned together, and faired off with adze and plane, as shown in

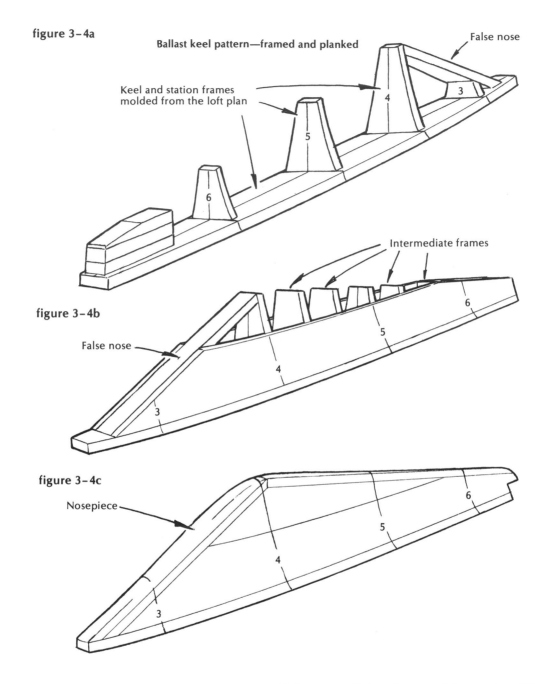

figure 3-4a

Ballast keel pattern—framed and planked

False nose

Keel and station frames molded from the loft plan

4

3

5

6

Intermediate frames

figure 3-4b

False nose

6

5

4

3

figure 3-4c

Nosepiece

6

5

4

3

Figure 3-3. This makes much more sense. This method will eat up a lot of good pine plank, and will require some additional lofting and much hand planing, but it's simple, foolproof, and entire satisfactory (and the molders in the foundry can ram the pattern to their hearts' content and never dent it a bit).

Back to the lines on the floor, then. Tack down a fresh piece of building paper—longer than the pattern you're going to make, clear of the casting in the body plan, and parallel to the keel. Draw a centerline on this strip, exactly

parallel to the top of the casting (Figure 3-3a). Mark this line where each station ordinate crosses it, and at each end. Draw a line square across at each mark. Now lay off and pencil in the half-siding of the rabbet line in the plan view, and extend it all the way to the after face of the sternpost. You will not use this rabbet line in shaping the pattern, but it will serve as a guide to the lines you are about to develop inside it. Each one of these lines will represent the top surface of one of the lifts that will make up the pattern.

20

Go back to the body plan; intersect each station line 1½ inches below the rabbet height at that station; take these widths out from the centerline; then lay down this line in plan view, as you just laid down the rabbet line. This line you have just drawn, of course, represents the top of the casting, and the top of such deadwood as may be used to continue the shape of the casting all the way aft. Now go through this process again to get the shape of the top of the second slice down from the first exactly the thickness of the stock you are using. (This thickness is purely arbitrary and depends solely on what you can get. Probably 1⅞-inch thickness is the likeliest.)

You will, of course, note that the forward and after ends of each lift are determined by their intersections with the profile, except at the top of the forward end of the pattern, where the lifts are cut off square to butt against a small fairing piece. All lifts will have the same half-siding at the line of the rudder stock, even as their points of intersection move progressively forward (Figure 3–3b).

Continue this laying down, then, until the ninth, tenth, or whatever slice appears as a short little pad at the toe of the profile, and prepare to reproduce all these flats, double, in wood. You can use the nailhead walk-about system for printing the half-width and centerline, and develop the other half with measurements and a batten on the other side of the centerline. Be sure that the centerlines are exactly right, and mark at least one station on each lift so that you can locate them in their proper fore-and-aft positions.

Saw the lifts out right to the line. Pile them up, upside down, holding each lift to the one below it with glue and plenty of 3-inch number 12 screws. The pattern should now look like Figure 3–3c—corrugated, but showing promise. All that remains to be done is to work the pattern down to the lines until it is perfectly fair and smooth, when it will be ready for core prints and three coats of shellac.

Right now, with this rough thing confronting you, you need a shipwright's lipped adze and some confidence in the use of it. If you can't find an old adze, complete with handle, order a new one from your ship chandler and fit a handle yourself. (I know of one book on boatbuilding that discourages any amateur's hopes of mastering this tool; but the text's accompanying drawing, depicting this strange and wonderful instrument, shows the handle in backward. If the author attempted to use it like that,

he comes by his pessimism naturally.) Actually, a good adze is one of the easiest of all tools to use; it is precise, powerful, fast, and far safer to use than a hammer. So get one—or three or four assorted sizes and shapes, if you can; Figure 3–3d shows how a gouge adze is used for roughing, and a lipped adze for smoothing—and practice with it for a few minutes. Sit down, holding the end of the handle so it is anchored in your left hand against your tummy. Lift the handle with your right hand and chop down gently. Cut across the grain, seldom with it. Slide your left hand down your front as the cut moves down the timber.

But shun the broadaxe, my son, because that *is* a tool that's hard to master. I can still recall the dismay I felt, at the age of six years, when my father gave me my first real chopping axe and told me that you have to start really young if you're ever going to be a good axeman. A fine thing to spring on me at that late date! There I was, practically grown up, and just starting to learn. And I was right. I never did become a good axeman, but I can cut out wooden gears for an alarm clock with an adze. So can you, by the time you've got that pattern roughed off to the hand-plane stage.

The frame-and-plank method

I promised three ways to make this pattern. The third way is to build it like a boat—framed and planked, as in Figure 3–4.

The top of the pattern should be cut from 2-inch pine plank, just as you laid out and cut the first lift in the above process. Mark the centerline and stations on its under face, and lay it upside down on at least three horses. This represents your keel, so be sure it's straight. Clamp the plank to the horses so it will stay that way from now on.

Go to the body plan, and there lay out the shapes of the stations in way of the ballast. From these you will make up solid bulkheads, cut to shape from heavy pine boards. Each one will be 2 inches short at the top and bottom, and ⅞ inch scant in width on each side. The top edge of each will be cut to the angle of the drag (downward slope aft) of the keel. Set these upon the upside-down top so they are centered exactly, toe-nailed in place, and braced at the correct angle.

Now fit, brace, and fasten a false nose, as shown in Figure 3–4a, so it is roughly parallel with the forward profile of the ballast casting and about 6 inches aft of it. You must cut off the

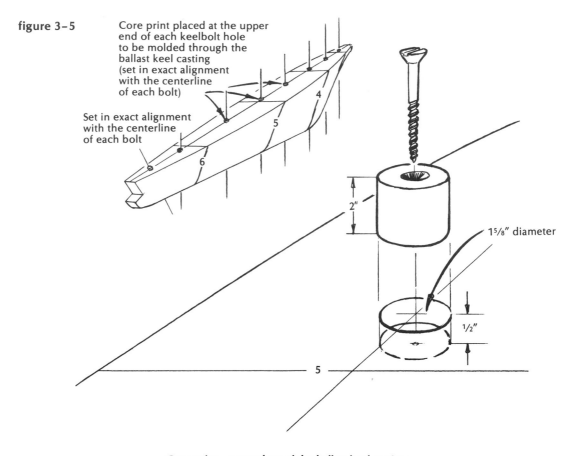

figure 3-5

Core print placed at the upper end of each keelbolt hole to be molded through the ballast keel casting (set in exact alignment with the centerline of each bolt)

Set in exact alignment with the centerline of each bolt

4

5

6

2"

1⁵/₈" diameter

¹/₂"

5

Core print—upper face of the ballast keel casting

These produce 1¹/₂" depressions in the top face of the sand mold to receive the pipe cores extending upward from the lower part of the sand mold during the casting process.

number 3 bulkhead to allow the passage of this false nose from the underside of the plank top to the straight line determined by the bottoms of the bulkheads on stations number 4 and number 5. ("Bottom" here means, of course, the true lower ends, which are at the moment facing upward as this pattern is being assembled.) This false nosepiece will be straight sided, and its taper determined by widths at its intersections with the number 3 bulkhead and the plank that forms the inverted backbone. Allowance must be made, of course, for the beveling of that plank, as shown on station number 2 of the body plan, and for the ⁷/₈-inch boards that will be bent around, outside the frames and the nosepiece, to constitute the side planking of this pattern (Figure 3-4b).

Before planking, however, you must fit intermediate frames a foot apart, between the station frames already in place (Figure 3-4b).

These either can stand plumb to the backbone, or be raked to match the station frames. To get their shapes, you will, of course, work to two curves, determined by battens bent around the station frames, top and bottom. When you fasten them in place, align their center marks exactly to a straightedge tacked to the lower ends of the station bulkheads.

Now to plank the sides of this pattern: Start with a straightedged board, about 10 inches wide and 16 feet long, and clamp it to the number 4 bulkhead, with its lower edge up 3 to 4 inches from the backbone. Do the same on the other side with an identical board. Pull the forward ends together until you can clamp across and squeeze the false nose between them, with their lower forward corners almost touching the backbone. Go aft, and pull the after ends together. The lower after corners should be just clear of the backbone, if your guess at

figure 3-6

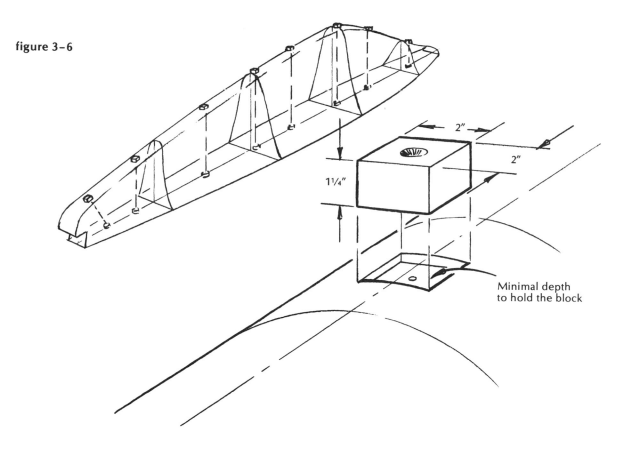

2"

2"

1¼"

Minimal depth
to hold the block

Core print—on the lower face of the ballast keel pattern

These produce depressions in the lower part of the sand mold to
accommodate the square head of the sand core, which aligns the
pipe core within the sand mold.

number 4 was right. This is, of course, too much to expect; so loosen the clamps at number 4, and move the clamped-together after ends up or down as may be necessary.

The purpose of all this double-action bending is to maintain equal pressure on both sides of the bulkheads, and thereby avoid pushing anything out of place. Now set your dividers as wide as they will go, and scribe lines on these two boards exactly equidistant, at all points, from their final resting place on the backbone. Reverse the clamping-on process, and saw one out. Theoretically, the other one should be an identical twin; if a great discrepancy appears, try to find out where you went wrong.

Bevel the edges of the boards to fit against the backbone; reclamp; mark for alterations in the fit, and for the cuts to be made flush with the forward face of the false nose and in the same plane as the bottom ends of the bulk-

heads; take it all apart again, and alter and cut; reclamp, and fasten the boards to the bulkheads with 2-inch number 12 screws. The second boards, which will cover the remainder of the sides, go on next. Dress off the edges so they are exactly straight, right to the nosepiece, and fit to them the 2-inch plank, which will eventually be rounded off as the underside of the pattern. Cut its forward end flush and in line with the forward face of the nosepiece (Figure 3-4c).

Now build up the laminations of 2-inch plank, against the line of the false nosepiece, until you have enough material to make the shaped entering edge and toe of the pattern. When fastening these one to another, bear in mind the shaping that is to be done, and try to keep the screws clear of the danger areas. Use a drawknife, planes, and Stanley "Surform" wood rasps for this final shaping, getting the contours from plywood templates taken off the

figure 3–7a

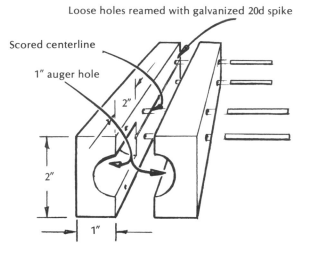

Loose holes reamed with galvanized 20d spike

Scored centerline

1″ auger hole

2″

2″

1″

20d spikes, shanks (bright)
driven flush into tight holes

figure 3–7b

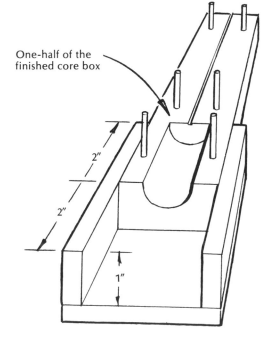

One-half of the
finished core box

2″

2″

1″

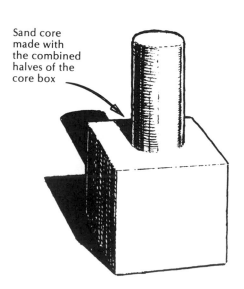

Sand core
made with
the combined
halves of the
core box

lines on the floor. Cut the after end to the exact line of the rudder stock, leaving the jog at the bottom as shown in the construction plan.

We still have to fit core prints and lifting eyes, make a core box for the bolt heads, and apply the final finish.

Core prints and the core box

The core prints, of course, leave their marks in the two parts ("drag" and "cope") of the sand mold that will be packed and rammed around this pattern at the foundry. (This explains the use of heavy scantlings for patterns. Foundrymen will not accept a pattern made of thin plywood, which will bulge inward under the pressure of the ramming.) These prints must match exactly the cores they are to accommodate—in this case, standard 1-inch iron pipe, which measures $1^{5/16}$ inches outside diameter. For the top prints, therefore, plane out a 2-foot length of round stock, of this diameter, and cut it into 2-inch lengths.

Turn the monster right-side up, and lay out the locations of the bolts, as shown on the construction plan. (In this design, all bolts are on the centerline, and all but the aftermost one are square with the line of the keel.) Bore a shallow hole, about $1/2$ inch deep and $1^{5/16}$ inches diameter, at each mark; tap one of your round pegs into each pit, and fasten the peg with one 3-inch number 12 screw right down

figure 3-8

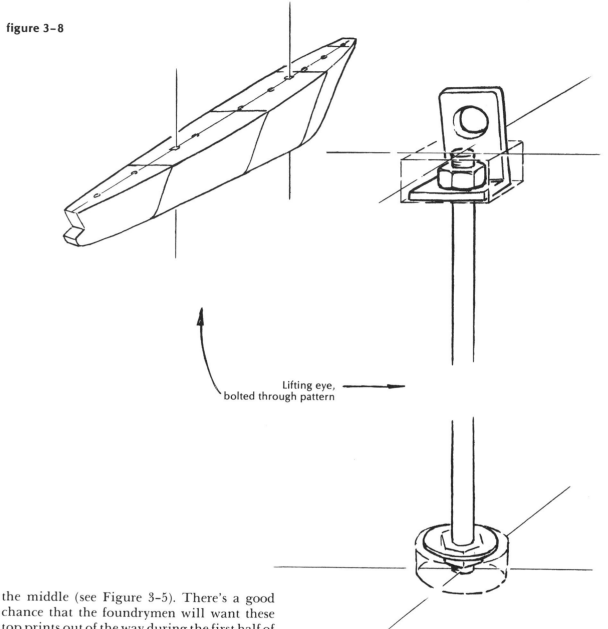

Lifting eye, bolted through pattern

the middle (see Figure 3-5). There's a good chance that the foundrymen will want these top prints out of the way during the first half of the molding, and the screw fastenings can be removed and later replaced without tearing anything up.

Now turn the pattern over and fit the bottom prints (Figure 3-6). These are blocks 2 inches square, to take the square cores which will form the pockets for the bolt heads, and, of course, center the lower ends of the pipes. They must stand up straight on the hillside—that is, their sides must be precisely parallel to the line of the bolts—and they must be carefully located, on the centerline, directly under the top prints. If you start with stock 1¼ inches thick, you will have enough wood left after fitting to the slopes.

Now for the core box. Cut two pieces of pine exactly 1 by 2 inches, and about 8 inches long. Cut a groove about ¹/₁₆ inch deep by ⅛ inch wide lengthwise down the center of one face of each piece. The easiest way to do this is on a table saw. Clamp the two pieces firmly together, groove to groove, with their edges matching exactly. Start the worm of a sharp 1-inch wood auger in the double groove, and bore lengthwise (with the worm following the groove) a distance of 2 inches. Without disturbing the

25

figure 3-9

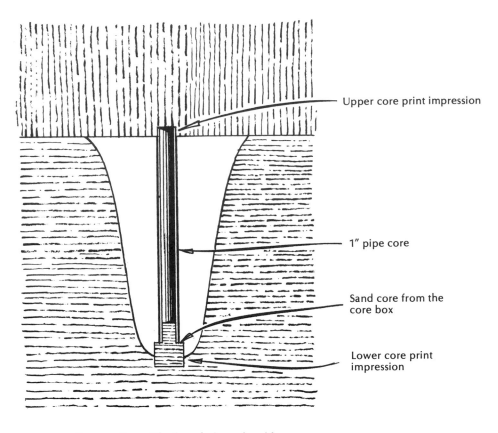

Cross section of the founder's sand mold

clamps, drill four ³/₁₆-inch holes squarely through the two pieces to take slip-fit pins. Remove the clamps and spin a headless 20-penny galvanized spike through the pin holes in one of the two pieces. Cut lengths of *plain* 20-penny spikes for the pins, 1½ inches long, and drive them through the tight holes in the other piece (Figure 3-7a). Clamp the two pieces together and build a wall 4 inches high around the bored end, made up in two parts that separate on the same plane as the first two pieces. (See Figure 3-7b.) Take the core box apart, smooth all the inside surfaces, shellac, smooth some more, fill any crevices with beeswax, shellac again, and it's done.

The foundryman will very likely snort and tell you he has a much better core box in the core room, but don't let that bother you. If you hadn't brought this one, you would have been treated to a demonstration of shocked pity for your ignorance. Quite seriously, though, if you don't know much about this business, make friends with the foundry boss and watch the molders at work. Theirs is a fascinating art, and they'll teach you some things you'll need to know hereafter about patternmaking.

And, although they won't expect it, they'll be happy to see the pair of lifting eyes you are about to install in the top of your pattern. Remember, however, that if one of these eyes pulls out, after the crane has lifted the pattern clear, and the heavy end drops down and ruins a day's work, you will wish you were not around to hear the comments. So install the eyes this way: Bore a ⁷/₁₆-inch hole all the way through the pattern, from top to bottom; countersink at the bottom to take a washer and ³/₈-inch nuts; countersink at the top so that, with the top of a ³/₈-inch threaded bolt just flush, there'll be room to drop over it an upset shackle

figure 3-10

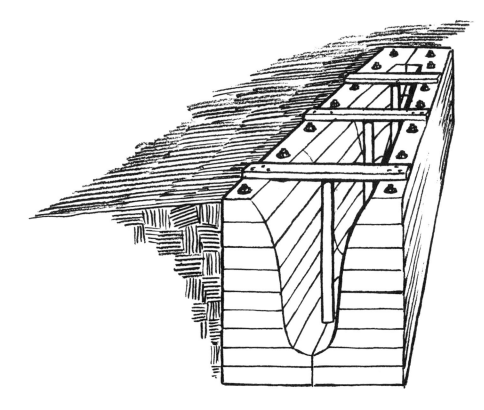

Open female ballast keel mold for lead

made of $^1/_8$- by $^3/_4$-inch flat stock, with a hole drilled through its crown, and a full nut to hold it on (or buy a pair of $^3/_8$-inch eye nuts). This assembly is pictured in Figure 3-8.

Female mold

A female mold, shaped, rounded, and flared, into which you can ladle your own bathtub lead, is built by the same contour system as described in the second method above, but reversed, with wooden walls, well-bolted top and bottom, surrounding the grand canyon, whose sides you will pare smooth with an adze, gouges, round-faced planes, and a disc sander. Make the mold in two halves, split vertically, so you can lay each on its side and really get at it for shaping—and so you can get it off the casting without breaking it to bits. Set the mold level, on a base that will support all those tons

without subsiding or leaning. Use dry hardwood dowels for bolt-hole cores. Set the dowels in shallow holes at the lower end, held by well-fastened cleats around the mold at the top (see Figure 3-10). Remember that the dowels will try very hard to float when the lead is poured. Paint the cores and the interior with something that will prevent charring of the wood. We once used ordinary waterglass, on somebody's recommendation, and it certainly didn't do any harm.

If I were doing the job, I'd pile and pack sand all around that mold, so that if it sprang a big leak, or a lot of small ones, I wouldn't lose the whole damned shooting match.

Right now (never mind what I said at the beginning of this chapter), I'm beginning to think fondly of a good sailing dory with beach stones under the middle thwart. I heard somewhere that the pink ones are the heaviest.

27

Chapter Four

The Backbone: Keel and Sternpost

Your designer probably calls for a white oak keel, properly air dried. This is good; he could have been much more specific, and gotten us all in trouble. He might have inherited from his Naval Construction days one of those little electric moisture-content indicators, and gotten all excited about what it told him. (Although, confidentially, I've watched him read the shielded dial, nod with satisfaction, and mark "OK" on a timber that had been swaying to the summer breezes three weeks before.) He might even have been able to recognize white oak when he saw it, although this is unlikely. But he has fulfilled his duty by the book, and said, "white oak, properly air dried." We can take it from there.

Good timber

The keel for the boat in our example will spend most of its life in the water, and will never, except by awful accident, lose much of its moisture. It should therefore be at its maximum size when fitted to the ballast casting (lest, if dry, it swell its normal 5 percent, hang out over the metal, and strain the floor-timber fastenings), and should be kept at that size, throughout the building process, by liberal doses of sealer. I favor a mixture of linseed oil and kerosene, with a slug of Cuprinol for luck. If the wood will take a pencil mark, it's dry enough. If it's too wet for that, use a rase knife, which marks the wood by scoring it.

And if you can't get white oak, the wood most favored by designers and builders, what then? Longleaf hard pine, if dense and heavy, is as good in almost every respect, and somewhat better for a boat that's going into southern

figure 4-1

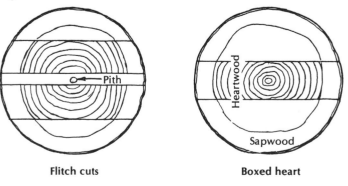

Flitch cuts · Boxed heart

29

figure 4–2

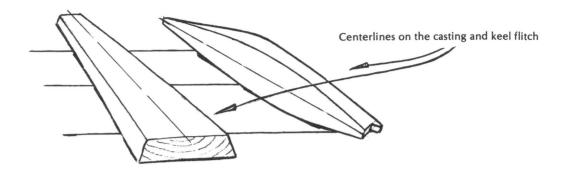

Centerlines on the casting and keel flitch

waters. "Spar-quality" Douglas-fir (which becomes "Oregon pine" on its way to the boatyard) is magnificent timber, good enough for any part of a boat except bent frames and fancy trim. If you were in England you'd sigh with ecstasy over a bit of American elm, which we use for flooring horse stalls. And then there are other varieties of oak, which we won't mention by name, but which get whiter and whiter as they travel from the mill to the shop. I could bear the thought of teak, if someone gave me a piece. If I were in Norway, or Australia, I'd ask a local builder what he'd use in his own boat and do likewise.

A flat keel such as this one—5 inches deep and 14 inches wide at mid-length—should come out of the log entirely clear of the heart, and lie small-face down. This gets you away from possible cup shake, porous pith, and the tendency to check open at the ends, where stem and sternpost must attach with absolute integrity. Figure 4-1 shows the "flitch" cuts that yield the best timber for the keel. Obviously, the tree that produces this off-the-side timber will be much bigger than you'd need if you were satisfied to take a boxed-heart keel. (Just as obviously, there will be a twin on the other side, which gives you a choice, and the problem of what to do with the second keel. If you share my passion for good timber, you'll buy it,

figure 4–3

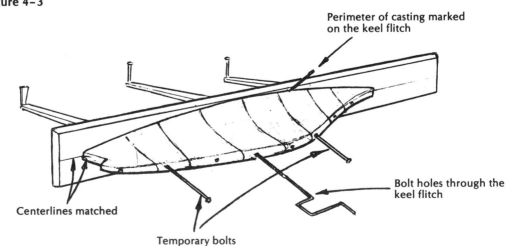

Perimeter of casting marked on the keel flitch

Bolt holes through the keel flitch

Centerlines matched

Temporary bolts

figure 4–4a

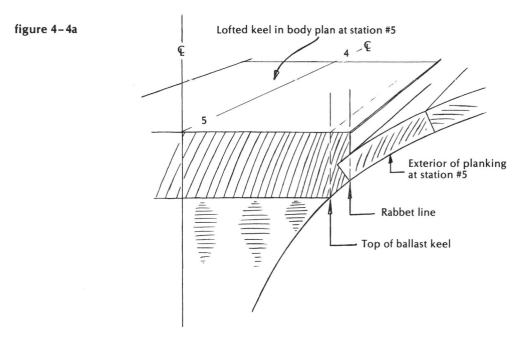

Lofted keel in body plan at station #5

₵

4

₵

5

Exterior of planking at station #5

Rabbet line

Top of ballast keel

along with all the other full-length pieces out of that log. You never know when you might want to build another boat—and clear toerail stock 22 feet long is hard to find on short notice.)

Marking method

Let's mark this keel and cut it to shape, before we take up the various problems and possible alternatives in the other pieces of the backbone.

I assume that the ballast casting has arrived, or has been revealed behind the bathtub, and

figure 4–4b

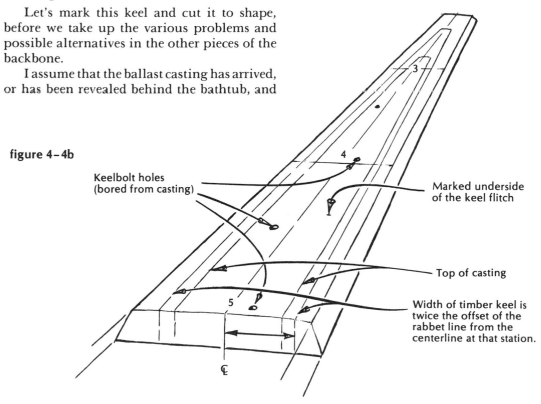

Keelbolt holes (bored from casting)

Marked underside of the keel flitch

Top of casting

Width of timber keel is twice the offset of the rabbet line from the centerline at that station.

₵

3

4

5

figure 4-4c

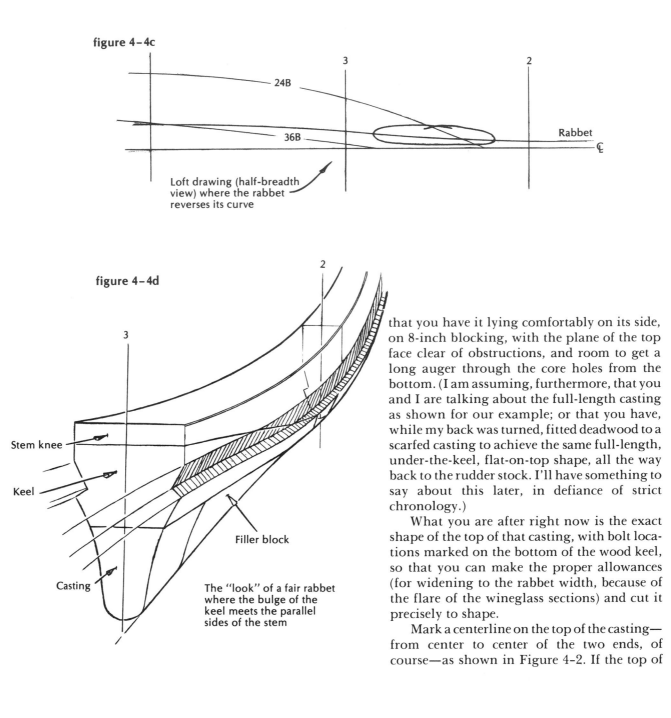

24B

3   2

36B   Rabbet

                                           ℄

Loft drawing (half-breadth
view) where the rabbet
reverses its curve

figure 4-4d

2

3

Stem knee

Keel

Casting

Filler block

The "look" of a fair rabbet
where the bulge of the
keel meets the parallel
sides of the stem

that you have it lying comfortably on its side, on 8-inch blocking, with the plane of the top face clear of obstructions, and room to get a long auger through the core holes from the bottom. (I am assuming, furthermore, that you and I are talking about the full-length casting as shown for our example; or that you have, while my back was turned, fitted deadwood to a scarfed casting to achieve the same full-length, under-the-keel, flat-on-top shape, all the way back to the rudder stock. I'll have something to say about this later, in defiance of strict chronology.)

What you are after right now is the exact shape of the top of that casting, with bolt locations marked on the bottom of the wood keel, so that you can make the proper allowances (for widening to the rabbet width, because of the flare of the wineglass sections) and cut it precisely to shape.

Mark a centerline on the top of the casting—from center to center of the two ends, of course—as shown in Figure 4-2. If the top of

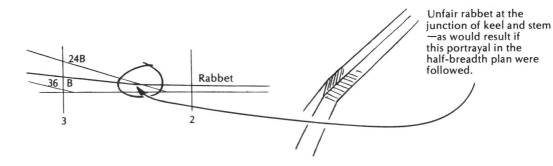

24B

36 B   Rabbet

3   2

Unfair rabbet at the
junction of keel and stem
—as would result if
this portrayal in the
half-breadth plan were
followed.

32

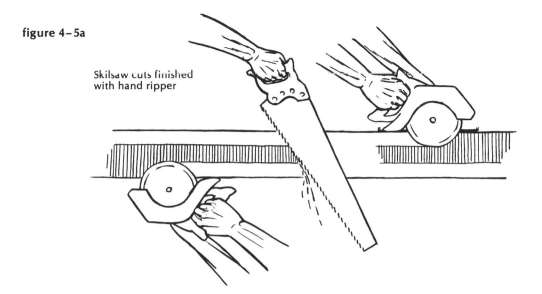

figure 4-5a

Skilsaw cuts finished
with hand ripper

the casting shows a slight discrepancy in width on either side of this line or through the middle, ignore it, and don't tell the owner. It's too late for tears, and the lack of perfect symmetry won't do any harm. (We always judged the timbre of an owner by the way he phrased the inevitable question at the end of his first season. It might be "Why does she sail even better on the starboard tack?", but it was more likely to come out "Why the ---- is this thing slower with the wind on the left-hand side?" We never came up with a really good answer, but we propounded some wonderful theories concerning the strange behavior of sails, and the clockwise rotation of objects in the Northern Hemisphere.)

Now mark, with great care and consideration, a centerline on the lower face of the wood keel. Get from the loft floor the "expanded" locations of the stations, and square them across on this lower face. Gather rollers, peaveys, a toe jack, wedges, bar clamps, and friends, and get the wood against the ballast, solidly, with centerlines matching, and precisely located fore and aft. Think hard, and then bore two bolt holes, one at each end of the casting by way of core holes, through the wood keel, as shown in Figure 4-3. If the casting was cored with 1-inch pipe, it's likely that your $7/8$-inch auger is the tool to use, unless you've done a painful lot of reaming. Make up two temporary $3/4$-inch bolts, and set them up through keel and casting. Now you know that nothing will shift, and you can proceed to mark the outline of the casting on the wood, and bore the other bolt holes. Measure for the lengths of all keelbolts (bearing in mind, and allowing for, the extra lengths needed at the

figure 4-5b

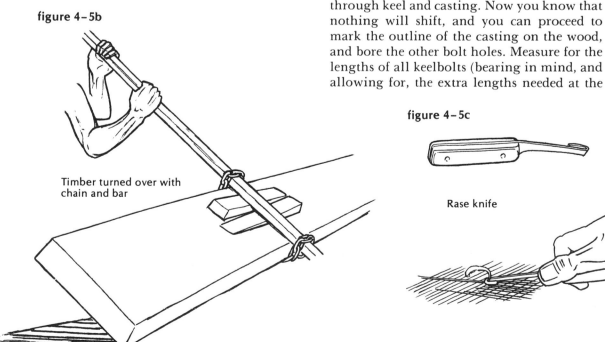

Timber turned over with
chain and bar

figure 4-5c

Rase knife

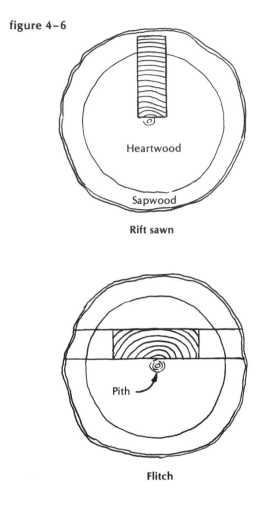

figure 4-6

Heartwood

Sapwood

Rift sawn

Pith

Flitch

match the top of the casting; bolt holes have been bored; and the corrected line (to the width of the rabbet) has been drawn in way of the casting, and continued forward to join with and fair into the rabbet as marked on the stem (Figures 4-4a, 4-4b). You will have noticed, long ago, when laying out this half-breadth of rabbet on the floor, the slight reverse in its curve just before it reaches the stem (Figure 4-4c), and the manner in which it straightens out and follows the parallel sides of the stem thereafter (Figure 4-4d). Pardon me if I seem to doubt your aptitude in the spatial relationships test. I know of three designs, one of them widely built to, all of them done by designers who should have known better, and all of which contain this glaring fault—the assumption that the rabbet line can show an abrupt change in direction as it leaves a swelled keel and encounters a parallel-sided stem. I built one of these boats, when I was very young, and it was a painful and costly experience. I hadn't then learned to think like a garboard (that has an unflattering connotation) or to look for possible errors in every set of plans that came along. I finally got smart; and you are expected to become so, now that I've told you how.

The keel is cut

So we have a fair line to cut to, but a thick timber to cut through. Take your portable electric saw, with its sharp, well-set 8-inch blade at full cutting depth (2³/₄ inches, that is) and check to see that the blade stands precisely square to the shoe. Try a practice run, around a similar curve, to learn the proper allowance to make from the guide mark on the front of the shoe. You'll want to leave the mark, but just barely. Cut with the wide part of the shoe inside. Don't push too hard; have a small assistant sweeping and blowing ahead of the cut. When you've gone the length, both sides, get out your extra-long ⁵/₃₂-inch drill, and shoot holes down through the saw kerf and out the other side—one at every station, one or two between, 1 foot apart at the forward end, where the reverse comes. Turn the timber over. (If you can't do this with a peavey, chain a 6-foot bar to it, as shown in Figure 4-5b. Take the slack out

after and forward ends, where they must reach through the stern knee and forefoot, respectively), and order them *now*, if they are to be made of galvanized steel. Take out the temporary bolts, lay the timber bottom-up, and mark for the outline cut, which will be exactly in the vertical plane of the rabbet line. Perhaps we should rephrase that, and get the horse in front of the cart where he belongs: The flaring sides of the casting, if continued smoothly upward to the height of the rabbet as shown in the body plan, will dictate the width from the centerline to the rabbet at each station throughout the length of the keel. Join these points with a fair curve, and you are ready to cut. If the rabbet width does not agree exactly at all points with the widths originally laid down, don't worry too much about it. Later on, you can alter the lower ends of the molds, within reasonable limits, to allow for this shrinking or swelling of the casting.

Now, the bottom face has been marked to

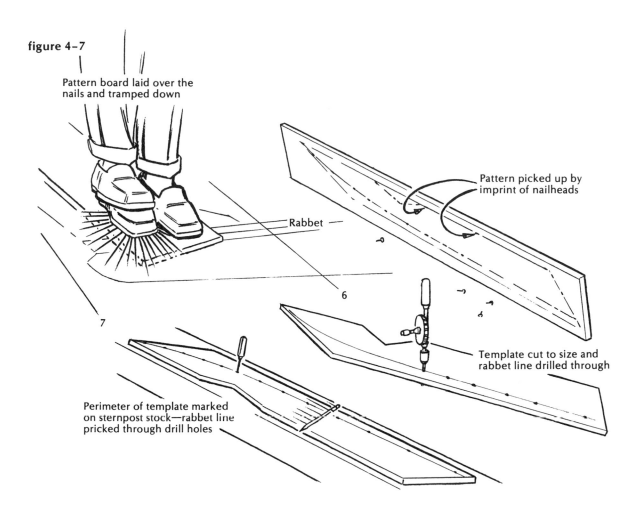

figure 4-7

Pattern board laid over the nails and tramped down

Rabbet

Pattern picked up by imprint of nailheads

6

7

Template cut to size and rabbet line drilled through

Perimeter of template marked on sternpost stock—rabbet line pricked through drill holes

of the chain by driving wedges under it.) Stand tenpenny nails in the postholes you just punched through, spring a batten to them, and mark for the cut. Your saw should follow the bottom kerf with no more than ⅛-inch error either side. (And what if the keel is 6 inches thick, and the saw cuts don't meet? Pray that they line up, and finish the job with your handsaw.)

Set your locking bevel to the angle between the perpendicular station ordinates and the top of the keel, on the laid-down profile, and transfer the station marks up the sides and across the top of the keel. Run a true centerline along the length of it, using string, a straightedge, and a rase knife, so that you'll be able to find the line through the sawdust and sealer. Look to the profile, and score the rabbet line (Figure 4-5c), but stop short of the forward end until the stem (whose lower-end rabbet is also left unfinished) is in place, and you can flow a true curve through the intersection. Leave this now and

consider the remaining members of the backbone—stem, sternpost and its knee, and the tail feather.

And now, the sternpost

The sternpost, like the keel (and for the same reason), should be cut from a timber that is not thoroughly seasoned. The perfect cut, as shown in Figure 4-6, would have through its middle a radius from the center of the log, with the growth rings crossing it almost at right angles—"rift sawn," or "edge grain," in the purest sense—clear of the heart on one edge, and stopping inside the sapwood on the other. It is unlikely that you would find an oak butt big enough to provide this ideal sternpost, which must come from rather less than the half-diameter of the log. The next best choice is a flitch like the keel, off the side of the log, well clear of the heart. I would avoid a boxed-heart timber if possible.

35

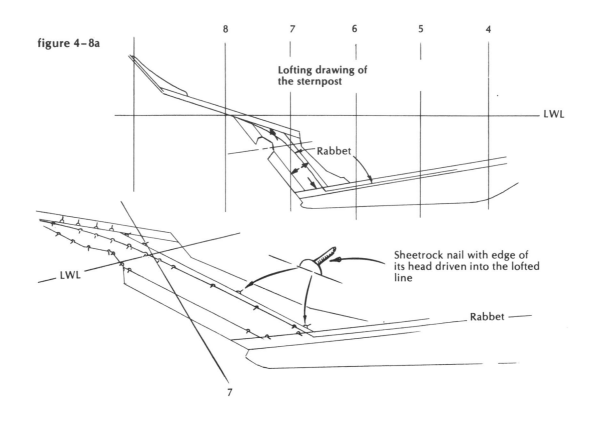

figure 4–8a

8 7 6 5 4

Lofting drawing of
the sternpost

LWL

Rabbet

LWL

Sheetrock nail with edge of
its head driven into the lofted
line

Rabbet

7

figure 4–8b

Boring from both directions, freehand

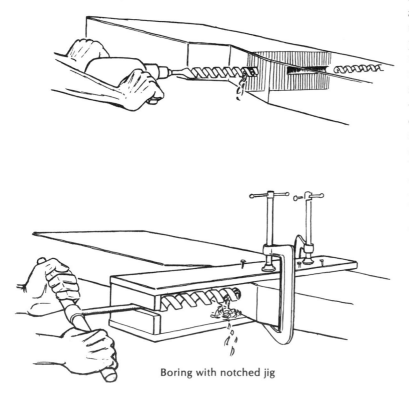

Boring with notched jig

The problem of transferring a rabbet line from a pattern is solved thus: Drill small holes clear through the pattern at 6-inch intervals along the penciled rabbet line; prick the timber through these holes in the pattern while it is in place, for marking the outline. Saw the timber to shape, plane all faces square and exactly to the marks, then place the pattern on the reverse side, and prick through the same holes (Figure 4-7). You will, of course, use a batten to draw a curve through all these pricked spots on both sides to guide later on in cutting the rabbet. (The casual "saw-to-shape" above will have been done with the 8-inch portable saw, just as you did when you cut the keel. One cut in the propeller aperture is inaccessible to this treatment, however, and you'll need to make this one with a series of overlapping auger holes, square through, just clear of the line. Clean off the rough points with an adze and a plane.)

Let's bore the shaft alley before we go on to making the stem. You will have transferred, from the sternpost pattern, the line of the shaft in profile—marked on both faces of the timber and squared across its forward and after edges (see Figure 4-8a). The shaft line terminates on the aft face of the sternpost in way of the propeller aperture, where you can prick-mark its

36

figure 4–8c

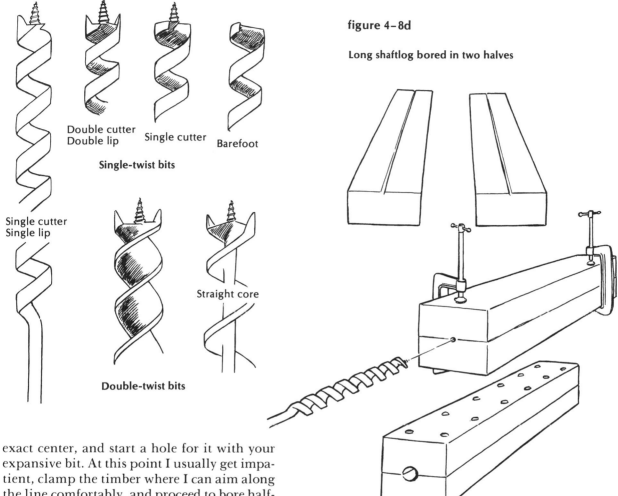

Single cutter
Single lip

Double cutter
Double lip

Single cutter

Barefoot

Single-twist bits

Straight core

Double-twist bits

figure 4–8d

Long shaftlog bored in two halves

exact center, and start a hole for it with your expansive bit. At this point I usually get impatient, clamp the timber where I can aim along the line comfortably, and proceed to bore halfway through it, freehand, with a barefoot auger (if I happen at the moment to have an electric drill with enough torque to handle it). Then I flip the timber over, cut enough of a flat (with gouge and chisel) to start a hole on the forward face, and bore back through the tunnel. This is a bare 15 inches of hole, and no great feat. You may feel better boring more slowly by hand with an auger whose shank is running in a notched guide, precisely located by a straightedge, in line with the desired shaft hole (Figure 4–8b). With such a guide, you should be able to bore true, all the way through from the aft to the forward face, in one operation. Turn the boring tool with a 3-foot cross handle, or a 30-inch pipe wrench. But if you are using a worm auger (which has a lead screw) instead of a barefoot one, beware: it will crawl to the

starboard every time. (Figure 4–8c depicts the variety of drill bits available to the boatbuilder.)

While we're on this subject, let me tell you the only easy way to make a long shaftlog, bored exactly on center from end to end. Plan the log in two halves, one above and one below the centerline of the shaft. Score both halves, dead center, full length, on their contact faces (Figure 4–8d). Clamp them very firmly together, groove to groove, and follow the groove from end to end with the worm of a ship auger. Don't worry about splines, feathers, glue, or outing flannel when you join these together. Oak casks don't leak; neither will these, if you put enough bolts through them.

Chapter Five

The Backbone: Stem, Rabbet, and Frame Sockets

The stem

I'd like to read from my Ode to the Black Locust, but fortunately it's still all in the head, and hazy at that. The subject is the Stem. Out front every time; first to take the brunt, whatever that is; symbol of Man's conquest of the unknown; stark in the cresting seas, the boiling sun, the creaking frosts of high latitudes. And not always up to facing these responsibilities, either, unless it's a pretty good piece to start with, and capped at the top to keep fresh water out of the end grain.

So, for the stem, you want the best cut out of the best tree that ever grew. This is where the old pro has the advantage over you. For years, he's been pushing choice bits of timber under the shop—crooked, curved, too rough-looking to suit the visiting N.A.s—waiting for that slack spell when he'll build one for himself, or for a friend who's going winter fishing. He might even have a piece of black locust, grown to the sweep, clear of the heart, and seasoned all the way through. A piece of really good, genuine white oak, grown and seasoned as above, is not to be sneered at. Dense hard pine would do, but you'd likely have to accept

straight grain. Just don't give up the search too easily. And if all else fails, you can cold-laminate the whole length, on a form, with no scarf, out of ¾-inch hard mahogany—and with plenty of through-rivets to quiet my doubts about the glue. We'll consider this possibility later.

Let's assume that you plan to make the stem in two pieces, as shown in the present plans. It's permissible to shift the location of the scarf up or down, to suit your timber. Don't shorten the scarf, or I'll be disappointed. Don't put jogs, hooks, or keys in it. Keep the lower end of the scarf below the waterline. Make the whole assembly of three pieces, as shown in Figure 5–1a, if necessary. Leave plenty of wood on top of the keel, far aft enough to take that forward-most ballast bolt with plenty to spare. You can cut all these parts, even some portions of the inside curves, just as you cut the keel and the sternpost; although with these lighter-weight and easier-to-carry timbers, a big bandsaw does it with less fuss. Dress off the matching faces of the scarfs with great care, square to the sides and right to the template outlines, light-tight when you put them together. Use a rabbet plane across the grain in the corners, and a

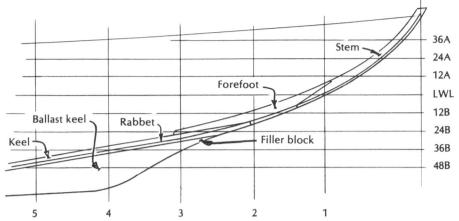

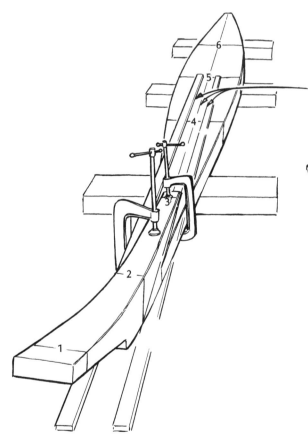

Alignment of forefoot and keel is established by laying a long straight-edge along the side of the forefoot timber. Distance away from the centerline aft should be that of the half-siding of the timber.

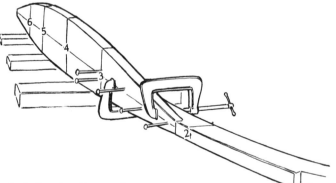

Joining it all together

My first move, at this point, is to set the wood keel level, on timbers, and fit the forefoot (lower part of the stem) to it. Use a tackle from overhead, unless you have a strong and patient helper to hold it while you scramble for clamps. You were probably timid in cutting the end of the keel and the matching jog in the forefoot, so you'll probably need to make saw cuts up the joint—several of them—before the reference lines (marked on each piece at station 3) match up. Set your clamps so that they tend to pull the two pieces together lengthwise, tightening the scarf as you tighten them. As shown in Figure 5-1a, check with a long straightedge against each side of the forefoot to points 2 inches off center, back on the keel top. Now, if you have absolute confidence in your clamps, you can lay the assembly on its side, counter-

smoothing plane and a foreplane in the open stretches. Transfer waterlines, sheerline, and station lines to all four faces of each piece they cross; prick in the rabbet line (but do not mark it yet) on both sides, as you did on the sternpost. Lay them out on the full-sized lofting, and notice what happens to the height of the sheer when you change the angle of that scarf at the fore end of the keel.

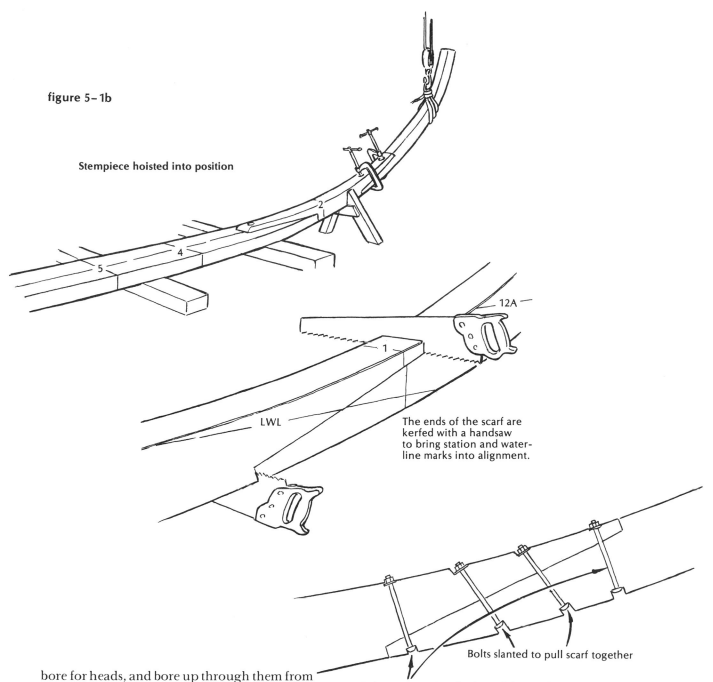

figure 5–1b

Stempiece hoisted into position

12A

1

LWL

The ends of the scarf are kerfed with a handsaw to bring station and waterline marks into alignment.

Bolts slanted to pull scarf together

Bolts set normal to the face of the scarf

bore for heads, and bore up through them from the bottom of the keel. The two forwardmost counterbores must be nicely calculated for depth, to allow for final fairing and shaping of the keel. For strength, the ideal is to set the heads barely below the surface (not enough to hold an honest bung) in order not to remove too much wood by counterboring. You can thicken epoxy resin with sander dust and get a paste that will stick to anything, anywhere—including the sunken bolt heads. Note the angle of the bolt holes, as shown in Figure 5-1b. They are laid out to range forward of a line perpendicular to the top of the forefoot, so that they will tend to pull the stem aft, against the end of the forefoot, as the nuts on top are tightened. Bore half of them square to the joint, if you want to, but never on a line that will

bring them out at right angles to the top of the forefoot. Start them all dead center at the bottom, but angle all but the end bolts alternately port and starboard—enough to come out at the top 1 inch off center. Square off a flat, with gouge and chisel, to take a washer and a nut, where each bolt hole breaks through at the top. Notice the bolts through two floor timbers, to be put in later. Lay out the fastenings with care, to avoid interference with these floors. For material, use silicon bronze, 1/2-inch diameter, for these wood-to-wood scarf bolts—and 7/8-inch galvanized steel, of course, for the aftermost bolt, which passes through the iron bal-

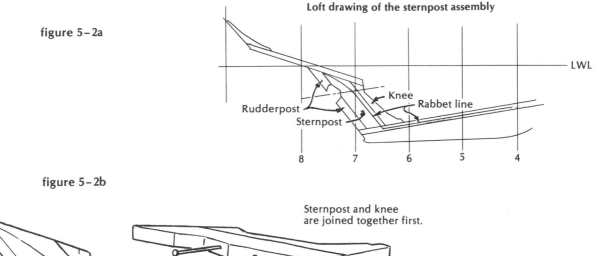

Loft drawing of the sternpost assembly

figure 5-2a

LWL

Rudderpost

Knee

Rabbet line

Sternpost

8   7   6   5   4

figure 5-2b

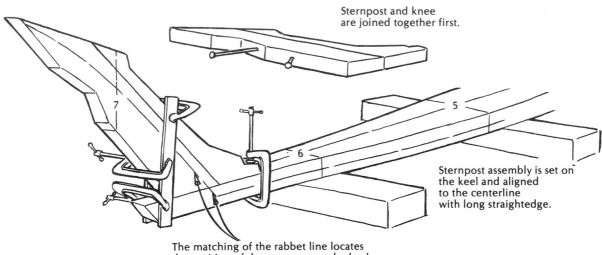

Sternpost and knee
are joined together first.

Sternpost assembly is set on
the keel and aligned
to the centerline
with long straightedge.

The matching of the rabbet line locates
the position of the sternpost on the keel.

figure 5-2c

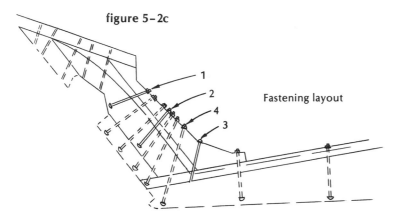

Fastening layout

last casting. Remember that a giant (the outside ballast keel) will plant one foot on this scarf and try to tear the planks and the stem away from it, with a strength that might produce 9,000 pounds of pull, so it's wise to keep this earnestly in mind when you're putting these parts together.

Very well, then. Stand it up, unclamp, soak the contact surfaces with your favorite poison, reassemble, drive the bolts, and set them up with nuts and washers. Counterbores should be 1 inch deep, and bolt heads can be made by threading on a standard full-depth hex nut of the same bronze as the bolt.

Hoist the top piece of the stem, and sag it into place on the forefoot with two clamps to hold it there. Run your saw blade through the butt joint at the top and bottom of the scarf, and let it slip down (with, maybe, someone on a stepladder gently tunking it at the top) to make an airtight fit. The load waterline marks should run together as reference marks when fitting is complete. Lay out the lines of the bolts; counterbore for same (½-inch bronze); bore end holes to center, and the two in between aimed to port and to starboard, and slant them all as before— to pull the two pieces together when the bolts come tight.

Sternpost next. This is a tricky bit of business, because you must fasten it first to its knee, then—knee and all—to the wood keel, while leaving room for the bolts from the ballast, and for the fastenings from the outer sternpost. Take a good look at Figure 5-2. Bolts 1 and 2

figure 5-3

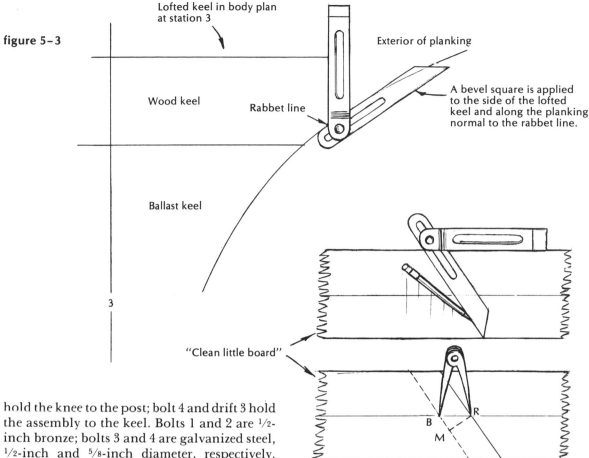

Lofted keel in body plan at station 3

Exterior of planking

Wood keel

Rabbet line

A bevel square is applied to the side of the lofted keel and along the planking normal to the rabbet line.

Ballast keel

3

"Clean little board"

hold the knee to the post; bolt 4 and drift 3 hold the assembly to the keel. Bolts 1 and 2 are $\frac{1}{2}$-inch bronze; bolts 3 and 4 are galvanized steel, $\frac{1}{2}$-inch and $\frac{5}{8}$-inch diameter, respectively. Locate and mark the after end of the rabbet line on the keel from the profile drawing, and bring the rabbet line already drawn on the sternpost to that mark (Figure 5–2b). Check that things are in correct fore-and-aft alignment by using a straightedge to the side, just as you did with the forefoot. Clamp as best you can, and have your helper support it tenderly as you lay the whole assembly on its side once more. Pray, and bore. Bolt and drift.

How good are drifts?

Drift, did I say? The word is out at last, and open to suspicion and attack. Drifts will be coming up (or if you care to be precisely literal, going down) very frequently from now on; so I'll say grace over the pork barrel right now, and sanctify all our meals for the next six months. We've had drift trouble. Once we tried boring for them a sixteenth scant, according to the book—in hard, dry oak, mind you—and had them fold like spaghetti before they were halfway home. We cured this by using a slightly worn $\frac{1}{2}$-inch auger for a fat $\frac{1}{2}$-inch galvanized rod—and reamed the floor timber with a new barefoot auger, so that there'd be a

fighting chance of driving the drift all the way. The head swelled nicely to fill the clinch ring, no fear. The big trouble comes from the owner. "For goodness' sake," says he (or words to that effect), "you don't really think those things will hold, do you?" So we start one for him (with no grease on it), hand him a hammer (not the best-balanced one we own), and invite him to drive. That's all it takes. Half an hour later, he has been converted to drifts; we saw off the battered remains, and tell him these things really get set after they've been in the wood a few months. Drifts are good fastenings. But don't use cast-iron clinch rings; they're brittle and they'll burst at the last blow, every time. Flat steel washers can take it, so use them instead.

Cutting the rabbet

Here we are now, with keel, stem, and sternpost assembly fastened together and lying on its side, waist high, with room around it. This is the backbone of your boat, and now,

figure 5-4

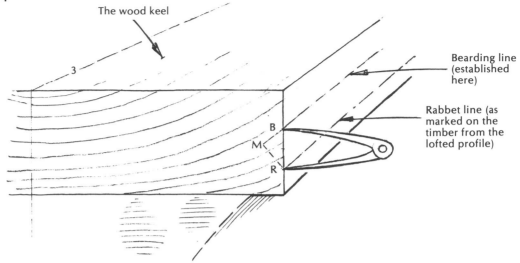

The wood keel

Bearding line (established here)

Rabbet line (as marked on the timber from the lofted profile)

B

M

R

3

before you set it up in final position for building the boat, is the time to cut the plank rabbet and frame sockets. This operation terrifies some amateurs; and I've even known pros who dared not do it before the molds were up. Be not afraid; it's simple. Be not timid about it, either, comforted by the thought that you can always increase the angle and finish to full depth as you go along. The frame sockets derive their precise depth and angle from the rabbet cut, and you'll compound a windy night with a rainy morrow if you lack bold confidence. So get a clean little board—say, 4 inches wide, 18 inches long, straight on both edges—and a bevel gauge, a pencil, a steel tape, and the lines drawing of this boat. We'll try to lay and cut this rabbet.

Draw a straight line down the middle of the board, parallel to the edges, as shown in Figure 5-3. This represents a horizontal line along the flat side of the stem or the sternpost (any load or water line), or it represents just as well the vertical side of the keel at any station mark. And I mean vertical, allowing for the drag of the keel, and not simply square with its top. Go now to the body plan in your lofting on the floor, and set your bevel gauge to the angle made by the intersection of the outside of the planking and the side of the keel at the rabbet mark for station number 3. Transfer this angle to your board—edge of board to centerline—and mark the point of intersection "R" (for rabbet line—representing, on your board, the outside of the planking). Square in from this angled line, at "R", the thickness of the plank-

ing you intend to use (in this case, $15/16$ inch). This new point, labeled "M" (for middle line), represents the inside corner of the rabbet cut, and is a cinch to locate in this view (body plan), but not so apparent when you look at the side of the keel, as in the profile. But we'll dig to it, unerringly. Draw a line from this point, parallel to the "outside of the planking" line— exactly $15/16$ inch from it, of course—and note the point of intersection with the centerline (side of keel), which you label "B" (for bearding line). The distance from "B" to "R" is what you get from all this, and nothing more. Measure it. I get $2^{1}/16$ inches. Measure up from the rabbet line—along the vertical station line, on the side of the keel—exactly this distance, and make a mark. Now go through this whole process for all the other stations along the keel. You'll find that "B" is somewhere above the top of the keel, at station number 6 and beyond. Clamp or nail a square block flush with the edge of the keel at station number 6, and mark the correct height for "B" on it (see Figure 5-4).

So far, so good. A fair line through these points (marked with a batten, of course) will give you the bearding line (see Figure 5-4.) Don't mark it yet. Finish up the stem, by using waterlines instead of body plan section lines. You are now working in a horizontal plane, but the method is exactly the same. Take the angle at the sheer from the full-size half-breadth you laid out on the floor long ago. Get the angles at the load waterline, 12-inch and 24-inch waterlines, from the half-breadth plan in the scale drawing of the lines (Figure 5-5).

44

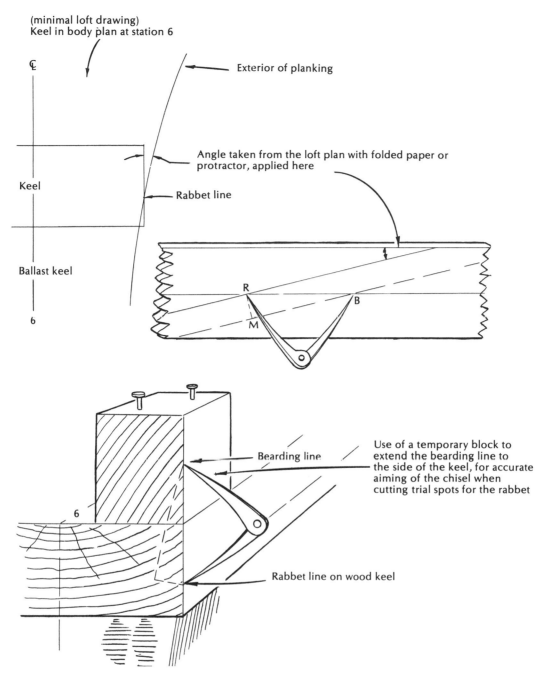

(minimal loft drawing)
Keel in body plan at station 6

℄

Exterior of planking

Angle taken from the loft plan with folded paper or protractor, applied here

Keel

Rabbet line

Ballast keel

6

R

B

M

Bearding line

Use of a temporary block to extend the bearding line to the side of the keel, for accurate aiming of the chisel when cutting trial spots for the rabbet

6

Rabbet line on wood keel

You'll be told that this is impossible, but pay no heed—angles stay the same, even though the scale of the drawing changes. Develop the distances from "R" to "B" on your board, just as you did it for the vertical stations, and lay these distances off *along the horizontal lines*—never at right angles to the rabbet line. You'll get a nice check for accuracy at the load waterline, because you already have a mark on station number 1, only inches away. Go back to the sternpost, and do what you can from the waterlines provided. Here's the place to be timid. Save most of the marking and cutting here until you have the molds set up, battens to go by, and adze in hand. This is not merely the safest way, but also the easiest.

Out with your battens, then, and mark the bearding line. It should be a fair, logical curve, with no abrupt changes. Cut yourself a gauge stick—exactly the thickness of the planking, about 2 inches wide, 1 foot long, and square at both ends. Sharpen your 1/4-inch and 1 1/2-inch chisels.

Now lock your bevel gauge to that first angle you took at station number 3, and stand the gauge alongside the station mark, so that its blade represents the garboard plank (Figure 5-6). Start a chisel cut just clear of the rabbet line, and precisely at right angles to that line of the bevel blade. Start another cut near the bearding line, and try to visualize the point "M" waiting for you down there in the heart of

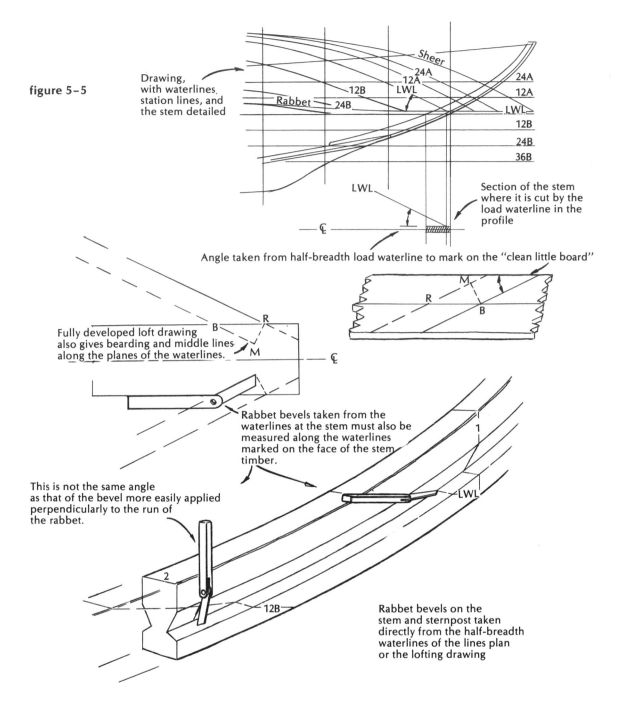

figure 5-5

Drawing, with waterlines, station lines, and the stem detailed

Sheer

24A
12A
LWL
24A
12A
LWL
12B
24B
36B

Rabbet
24B

LWL

Section of the stem where it is cut by the load waterline in the profile

Angle taken from half-breadth load waterline to mark on the "clean little board"

M
R
B

Fully developed loft drawing also gives bearing and middle lines along the planes of the waterlines.

B
R
M

Rabbet bevels taken from the waterlines at the stem must also be measured along the waterlines marked on the face of the stem timber.

This is not the same angle as that of the bevel more easily applied perpendicularly to the run of the rabbet.

1

LWL

2

12B

Rabbet bevels on the stem and sternpost taken directly from the half-breadth waterlines of the lines plan or the lofting drawing

the oak. The cut from the bearding line to "M" will, of course, be parallel to the line of the bevel blade. Make the cut wide enough, fore and aft, to take your gauge stick—and keep cutting, with many trials for depth, until the stick is flush at the rabbet, resting firmly at the bearding line, and butting square against the face where the lower edge of the garboard will bear. You have found "M". You'll be quicker on the next spot, and the next—until you have proved the rabbet at every station, and at every checkpoint on the stem (Figure 5-7). Now finish cutting the rabbet between spots. I usually rough out most of the wood with a big chisel, and finish with a rabbet plane. Friends will

urge using a power saw and a router to speed it up, but I'd stick to hand tools, myself. Those bevels change very subtly, and take some watching and feeling out.

Sockets for the frames

Shall we cut the boxes for the frames? This is something more than a formal invitation to the dance. No one is going to change my mind on this question, but you may waver to arguments from the opposition. The Herreshoff boats, the Concordia yawls, and Bill Simms's ocean racers are all built with frames fastened to floor timbers only. This is a mighty trium-

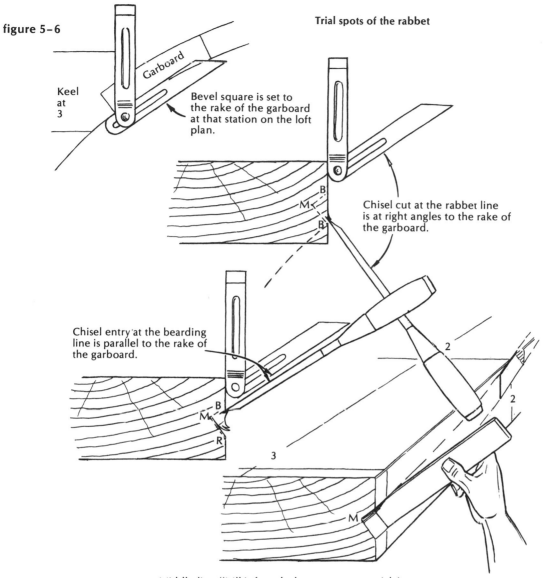

figure 5-6

Trial spots of the rabbet

Keel at 3

Garboard

Bevel square is set to the rake of the garboard at that station on the loft plan.

Chisel cut at the rabbet line is at right angles to the rake of the garboard.

Chisel entry at the bearding line is parallel to the rake of the garboard.

Middle line "M" is found when your gauge stick is flush at the rabbet line, rests firmly at the bearding line, and butts square against both faces of the rabbet.

virate to go against. There are those who will tell you this boxing-in of frame heels is a sheer waste of time, an open invitation to dry rot, a poor subterfuge to hide the lack of properly fitted (and properly numerous) floor timbers. With this I disagree, maintaining steadfastly that direct fastening of the frames to the keel is a fine thing, adding tremendously to the strength of the boat, and fully justifying all the time it takes. So make up your mind; but as long as you're with me, you may as well learn to mark and cut frame sockets. There's a trick to it.

Run to your table saw and cut out two or three frame heel facsimiles (gauges 1 and 2 shown in Figure 5-8). For this boat, they will be 1 5/8 by 1 3/4 inches, with sides exactly square to faces, and about 1 foot long. Make them of hardwood, because they'll be treated roughly. Saw their ends square. Set your locking bevel to the rake of the station marks down the sides of the keel. Mark, on the flat side of the keel above the bearding line, the exact center of each frame—one 6 inches to each side of the station mark, and another 18 inches to each side. Be sure to take these distances not along the sloping run of the keel, but rather, parallel to the waterline—square to the station marks on the sides. Be precise about this. You'll mark the other side by the same system, and you want to wind up with matched pairs. Mark one forward

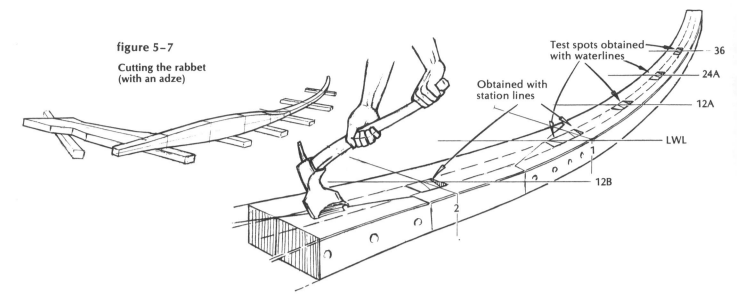

figure 5-7

**Cutting the rabbet
(with an adze)**

Test spots obtained
with waterlines

36

24A

Obtained with
station lines

12A

LWL

1

12B

2

of station number 1, and one aft of station number 6. There'll be no more boxes forward of station number 1, and those aft of station number 6 can wait until you've finished the rabbet there, with the keel up.

Start with a frame between stations number 4 and 5. Mark a plumb line, with a pencil and pre-set bevel, on the flat above the bearding line, half the frame width aft of the center mark—in this case, ⅞ inch. Now lay one of your marking pieces against the back rabbet, as if it were the rabbet gauge, and with its after edge precisely in the same plane—square athwartships—as the vertical line marked on the keel. Mark each side where it bears against the back of the rabbet. Hold it still, and slide its twin down the inner face to contact with the keel. Mark the line of contact, which gives the necessary depth of the cut at that point. Slide the first piece up ½ inch clear of the middle line, and mark across its bottom edge. This is all very simple so far. Mark for the forward edge of the cut—up on the flat side of the keel—and pro-

ceed to remove most of the wood inside the marked socket outline with a ⅞-inch auger, boring exactly square to the surface of the back of the rabbet (which is how the frame will naturally lie). Count the turns, and you'll soon learn just how many will give you the proper depth—which will be 1½ inches, leaving ⅛ inch for cleaning up with the chisel. Square the socket, also with a chisel, to a good drive fit for your marking piece.

Now move to the mark on the stem forward of station number 2. Mark your vertical line, ⅞ inch aft of the frame center, on the flat above the bearding line. Hold the marker against the back rabbet, as before, with the after edge in an imaginary athwartships plane that passes through that vertical line. Use a square from the side of the stem, at the line, to touch the edge of the marker at the top. Now sight along the side of your marker, and notice (and mark) the direction the cut must take, in order that the frame may stand plumb when in its socket. This line leans away aft at the top, and bears no

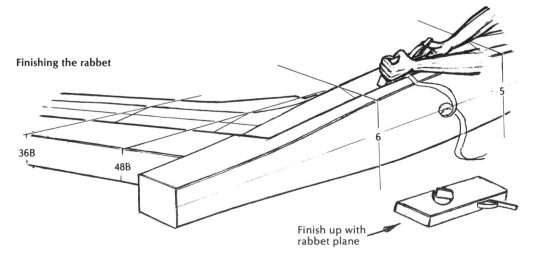

Finishing the rabbet

36B

48B

5

6

Finish up with
rabbet plane

48

figure 5-8

Sockets for frames

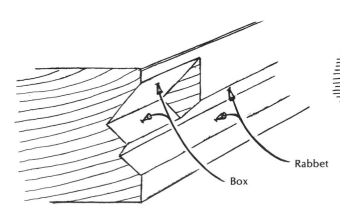

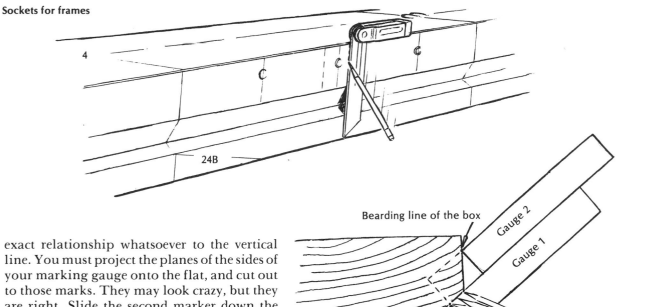

Bearding line of the box

Gauge 2

Gauge 1

Mark alongside

½"

Rabbet line of the box

exact relationship whatsoever to the vertical line. You must project the planes of the sides of your marking gauge onto the flat, and cut out to those marks. They may look crazy, but they are right. Slide the second marker down the inner face of the first one, as before, parallel to the rabbet, and touching the flat of the stem with its inner, lower edge. Mark that line. Mark around the bottom and sides of your marker on the back rabbet, with its corner at the bearding line. Believe those marks, even if they happen to look all wrong. Bore square to the back rabbet, clean out the socket with a chisel, and try the marker for a fit. I trust that it fits well and stands true, and that you now know how to mark frame sockets. Every one will be a separate problem; every one must be projected from the flat sides of your marker. Once you get the routine established, you'll mark one in two minutes, and cut it in ten. Six to the hour—but don't hurry the first few.

Turn it over and finish the backbone's other side, and we'll set her up in the next chapter.

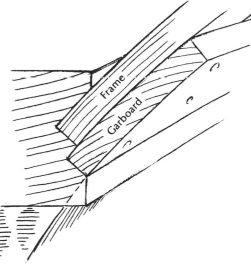

Frame

Garboard

Rabbet

Box

Chapter Six

The Backbone: Tail Feather and Transom, Molds, and Sheer

Getting it upright

Let's assume that this keel is on its side, with stem and sternpost in place, and with ballast keel bolted on. Chain a timber to the exposed side and stand it upright to rest on two wide 10-inch blocks—one way aft, and the forward one at the toe of the ballast casting. The vessel is obviously down by the head. Secure it at the after block so that it cannot possibly slide backward or tip sideways. Now clamp a straightedge from the side of the sternpost to a temporary upright on the keel, forward, so that its top edge is exactly parallel to the designed waterline as marked on the sternpost and the stem (see Figure 6–1a). Go to the lofted profile, on the floor, and determine how much the top of the keel rises from, say, station number 6 to station number 4, and be sure that the straightedge approaches the keel by the same amount in the same length. This, then, is your built-in water level. Jack up the forward end of the casting until the straightedge is truly level, and build up under the ballast keel with firm blocking. You'll wedge up three times before you

overcome the settling of the blocking when the weight comes on it. Be patient and get it right, or you'll be in a mess from now on. Level the top of the keel athwartships, and brace it; plumb the sternpost, and brace it with diagonals, from the floor to the after face so that they'll be well clear of the rabbet. Now stretch a tight line from a midpoint on the after face of the stem at the sheer, all the way back to the middle of the sternpost at its highest (aftermost) point. Hang a plumb bob from this line to hit the top of the keel just aft of station number 3, where the centerline of the keel is still visible (Figure 6–1b). Push the top of the stem sideways, as necessary, until the plumb bob hangs exactly over the centerline, and secure it there, preferably with a horizontal brace from the top of the stem to the side of the shop. Brace it from forward also, trying to estimate and overcome its tendency to droop. You'll have a final check on this height when you have established the plane of the cross spalls on the molds and can project it to the 24-inch waterline marked on the stem.

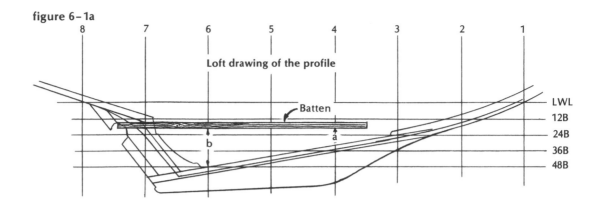

figure 6–1a

8 7 6 5 4 3 2 1

Loft drawing of the profile

Batten

LWL
12B
24B
36B
48B

b   a

Fitting the tail feather

We've still got the tail feather to fit before the molds go up, and the transom frame must be in place before the ribbands go on. Let's get these two settled.

There are those who will argue that the tail feather as I show it is all wrong and criminally weak as compared to the old system, wherein the central member butts against the after face of the sternpost and is locked there by the twin horn timbers (Figure 6-2a).The old system is good indeed, especially if you bring the top of the post all the way up and tie it to heavy deckbeams. The system I show gets worse and finally becomes very poor as the angle between the sternpost and the tail feather approaches 90 degrees—as, for instance, in a normal power-boat or a motorsailer. But it is a perfectly good system in the present instance, where the joint amounts almost to a long scarf, so long as the bolts are big enough and properly located. It has to be strong. The backstay pulls upward at the end of the counter, and this normal load of a ton or so can increase to a frightening amount when a sea breaks into the foot of a big jib. But don't worry about that joint. The mast will explode before it pulls apart.

So much for that argument. Here we have a flawless piece of timber, 5 inches deep and 7 inches wide, which must be bored for the rudderport, rabbeted on both sides, and fitted at its after end to the transom frame.

Start with the rudderport. Same auger, same technique as for the shaft hole—we are *not* going to thread a tube through the timber in the usual way, and therefore we need only be sure of proper clearance for the 1½-inch rudder stock through the wood. You can line the port

Leveling the backbone assembly by use of the lofted waterlines

Spirit level

Sticks cut to lengths a and b   4

24B
7

36B

5

6

48B

with a thin-walled copper or lead tube to keep the worms out, if you want to do the best possible job. You will eventually make a pattern for a bronze casting, which will be tapped to take the bronze-pipe rudderport and stuffing box, and which will be bedded and through-bolted to the top of the timber. Save this job for later.

Now the rabbet. Get the angles from station number 8 on the body plan; note that the rabbet lines are exactly 5 inches apart, to match the width (and therefore the rabbet lines) on the sternpost. Study the cross section in Figure 6-2b, and if your courage is good, make both cuts with your portable power saw—from aft to a point 15″ forward of station number 8, no more. Save the rest of it until you have molds and battens to guide your chisel.

And finally, you are ready to make the cuts at the after end to receive the transom frame (Figure 6-2c). Get out the transom knee first—its profile from the construction plan on the floor, cut from 4-inch stock—and place it in position atop the tail feather. Cut off the tail feather in line with the after face of the knee, but be sure to leave a jog at the bottom in way of the rabbet that matches the mitered ends of the planking-to-be, and simply carries the face of the rabbet across the transom. Note also that the bottom of the transom frame is in one piece across the end of the tail feather, and must be allowed for when you locate the knee and make that cut. A pad on the after face of the knee, from the top of this piece to the underside of the deck, provides a straight line for the transom planking to bear on.

Clamp the tail feather to the top of the sternpost, and sight it like a gun—right down its centerline to the middle of the keel just forward of station number 5 (see Figure 6-2d).

Drop a plumb bob from station number 8, and check its horizontal distance from station number 7 on the sternpost. Cut a narrow straightedge (³/₄ inch by 1⁵/₈ inches) and push it down through the rudderport to the keel. This proves the angle of the rudderport, gives the line to which the outer pieces of the sternpost will come, and will eventually support the skeleton pattern of the rudder, complete with the shape of the aperture and the location of the pintles. Put it aside for future use and bore those two forwardmost bolt holes, from the top of the propeller aperture up through the tail feather. Counterbore, as shallow as you dare, for the heads of ⁵/₈-inch bronze bolts. Square off on top for washers and nuts. Poison the contact surfaces and drive the bolts. Fit a post from the floor to support the tail feather, just forward of the transom, and brace it strongly with diagonals to the floor.

If you are sensible and methodical, you will now fit and fasten the two pieces of the outside sternpost (above and below the shaft hole). These will of course be tapered from the forward to the after edge, and grooved for the rudder stock and forward face of the rudder. Use ¹/₂-inch bronze for all these remaining bolts. Plan locations of the three sets of gudgeons, and keep your drifts and bolts clear of them.

Bolt the transom knee in place—and be sure it stands absolutely true athwartships.

figure 6-1b

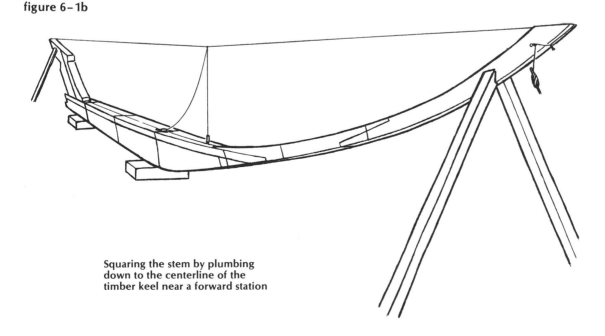

Squaring the stem by plumbing down to the centerline of the timber keel near a forward station

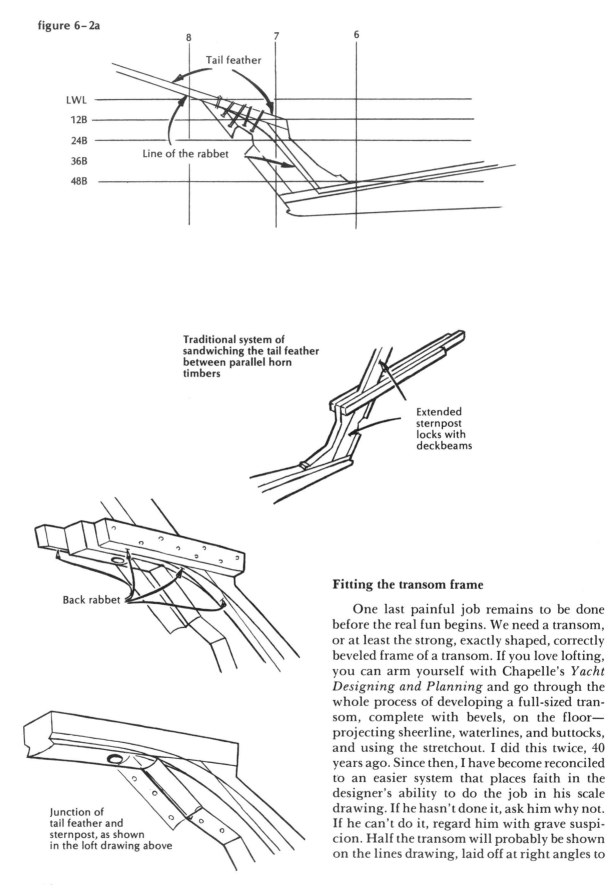

figure 6-2a

8   7   6

Tail feather

LWL
12B
24B
36B
48B

Line of the rabbet

Traditional system of
sandwiching the tail feather
between parallel horn
timbers

Extended
sternpost
locks with
deckbeams

Back rabbet

Junction of
tail feather and
sternpost, as shown
in the loft drawing above

Fitting the transom frame

One last painful job remains to be done
before the real fun begins. We need a transom,
or at least the strong, exactly shaped, correctly
beveled frame of a transom. If you love lofting,
you can arm yourself with Chapelle's *Yacht
Designing and Planning* and go through the
whole process of developing a full-sized transom, complete with bevels, on the floor—
projecting sheerline, waterlines, and buttocks,
and using the stretchout. I did this twice, 40
years ago. Since then, I have become reconciled
to an easier system that places faith in the
designer's ability to do the job in his scale
drawing. If he hasn't done it, ask him why not.
If he can't do it, regard him with grave suspicion. Half the transom will probably be shown
on the lines drawing, laid off at right angles to

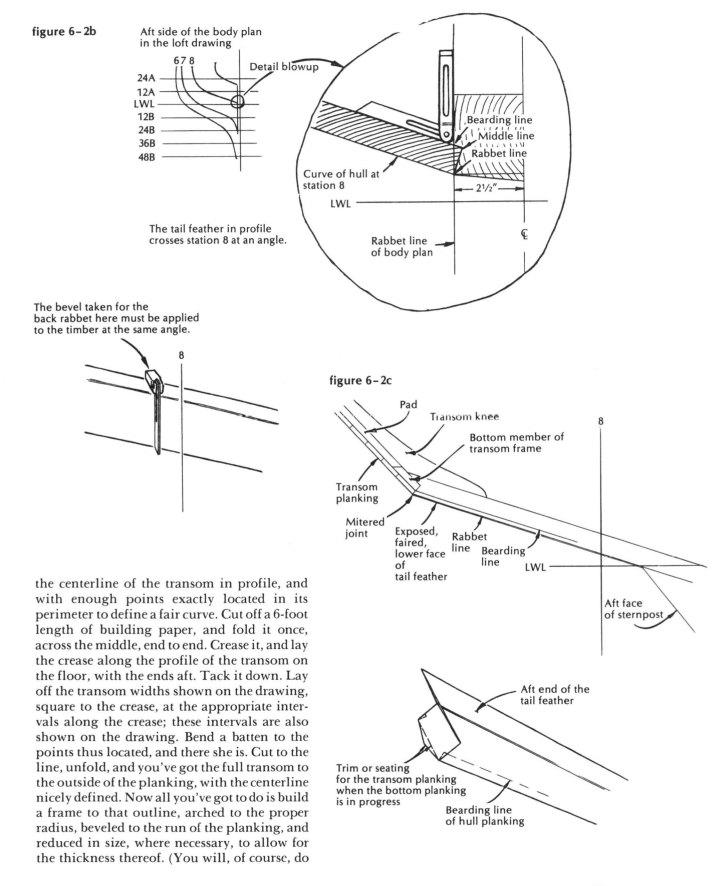

figure 6-2b

Aft side of the body plan in the loft drawing

Detail blowup

24A
12A
LWL
12B
24B
36B
48B

6 7 8

Bearding line
Middle line
Rabbet line

Curve of hull at station 8

2½"

LWL

Rabbet line of body plan

₵

The tail feather in profile crosses station 8 at an angle.

The bevel taken for the back rabbet here must be applied to the timber at the same angle.

8

figure 6-2c

Pad
Transom knee
Bottom member of transom frame

8

Transom planking

Mitered joint

Exposed, faired, lower face of tail feather

Rabbet line

Bearding line

LWL

Aft face of sternpost

Aft end of the tail feather

Trim or seating for the transom planking when the bottom planking is in progress

Bearding line of hull planking

the centerline of the transom in profile, and with enough points exactly located in its perimeter to define a fair curve. Cut off a 6-foot length of building paper, and fold it once, across the middle, end to end. Crease it, and lay the crease along the profile of the transom on the floor, with the ends aft. Tack it down. Lay off the transom widths shown on the drawing, square to the crease, at the appropriate intervals along the crease; these intervals are also shown on the drawing. Bend a batten to the points thus located, and there she is. Cut to the line, unfold, and you've got the full transom to the outside of the planking, with the centerline nicely defined. Now all you've got to do is build a frame to that outline, arched to the proper radius, beveled to the run of the planking, and reduced in size, where necessary, to allow for the thickness thereof. (You will, of course, do

figure 6-2d

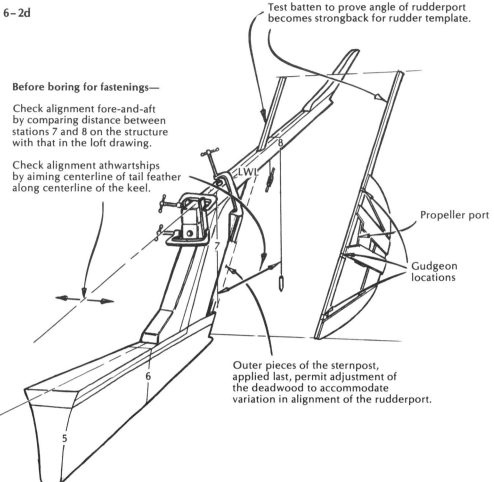

Test batten to prove angle of rudderport becomes strongback for rudder template.

Before boring for fastenings—

Check alignment fore-and-aft by comparing distance between stations 7 and 8 on the structure with that in the loft drawing.

Check alignment athwartships by aiming centerline of tail feather along centerline of the keel.

LWL

8

7

6

5

Propeller port

Gudgeon locations

Outer pieces of the sternpost, applied last, permit adjustment of the deadwood to accommodate variation in alignment of the rudderport.

all this in the best locust, white oak, black walnut, or dense hard pine you can get your hands on. This is the place where the rot starts first.) The transom frame is pictured in Figure 6-3a.

Begin with some bandsaw work. Swing an arc on a board to a radius 1 inch less than that given on the plans (to allow for the thickness of the transom planking) and long enough to reach across the full width of the transom. Saw this out, and use it as a pattern to mark at least two curved beams of 2-inch stock, which will temporarily bolt to the outside of the frame and hold it in shape until the transom planking replaces them. Now comes the tough one. You need a slab 1½ inch thick, about 7 inches wide and 30 inches long, sawn (or bent) to that same radius, which will make the bottom piece of the frame across the end of the tail feather. (Lacking a big, single chunk, or the means to saw something of this thickness, you can build it up

with four layers sawn from 2-inch stock, doweled and glued edge to edge.) You will save yourself time and frustration if you now prepare an arched bed, on which you can assemble and clamp the various parts. Saw two boards to a radius 3½ inches less than that of the finished transom—to allow for the thickness of the transom (1 inch) and its frame (1½ inches) and the slats mentioned below (1 inch)—and separate them a distance slightly more than the height of the transom. Tack 1-inch slats square across them, one to take a centerline, two on each side to support the vertical members and joining knees.

Fit the various parts together, face down, on the bed, as shown in Figure 6-3a, and apply the full paper pattern you made earlier for the final outline. (The paper pattern represents the *outer* face of the transom and includes the hull planking in its outline. For this particular boat, the pattern, if used for the inner face of the transom—i.e., for the shape of the transom frame—makes things come out about right. In other words, the plank thickness and the transom bevel just about cancel each other out. But be careful about using this simplistic approach on other designs—sometimes it doesn't work. Another technique that might not work is that of ignoring the difference in expanded transom widths over the projected ones. The designer's plan shows projected widths, and I've assumed, because there's not much curve in this transom, that these can be used for making up the paper pattern. If your boat has a significantly radiused transom, you'll have to be more precise here as well.)

Saw the individual pieces of the transom frame to the line, with a standing bevel sufficient to add wood enough for fairing in the finished bevel when the molds have been set up. The rough bevel along the bottom of the transom can be taken directly from the junction of the transom and the tail feather in the loft drawing. The bevel along the sides can be

approximated where the transom joins the sheer on the half-breadth view in the loft plan. Finished beveling will come later. Reassemble. check with the pattern, pin the corner knee to the bottom and side pieces, and bolt your two temporary beams across from side to side to hold the true arc and tie everything together. Mark the vertical centerline on these cross-beams. Fit the 1½-inch by 4-inch vertical pad up the middle, the two intermediate vertical timbers, and the pair of big scab cleats that tie the sides to the bottom piece. Figure 6–3a shows all this better than I can describe it.

Now cut a notch at the bottom of this heart-shaped transom frame to fit the angle at the end of the tail feather, and just wide enough in the forward face to match the rabbet lines (Figure 6–3b). Practice with a scrap piece until you understand the requirements. Hoist the frame into place now, clamp and bolt it dead center to the knee (Figure 6–3c), and prepare to square and brace it. To square it, you need a heavenly reference point. By eyeball estimate, project an

figure 6–3a

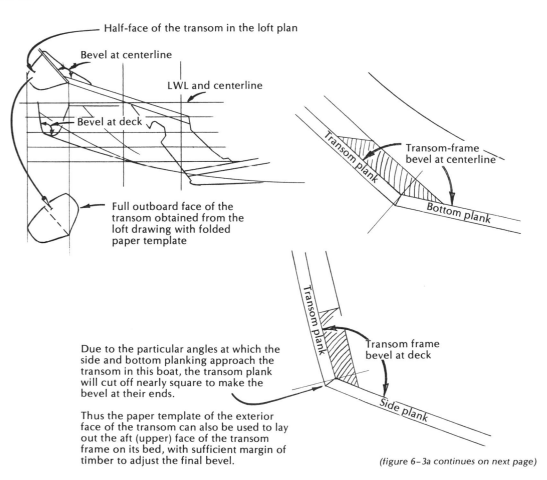

Half-face of the transom in the loft plan

Bevel at centerline

LWL and centerline

Bevel at deck

Full outboard face of the transom obtained from the loft drawing with folded paper template

Transom-frame bevel at centerline

Transom plank

Bottom plank

Transom plank

Transom frame bevel at deck

Side plank

Due to the particular angles at which the side and bottom planking approach the transom in this boat, the transom plank will cut off nearly square to make the bevel at their ends.

Thus the paper template of the exterior face of the transom can also be used to lay out the aft (upper) face of the transom frame on its bed, with sufficient margin of timber to adjust the final bevel.

(figure 6–3a continues on next page)

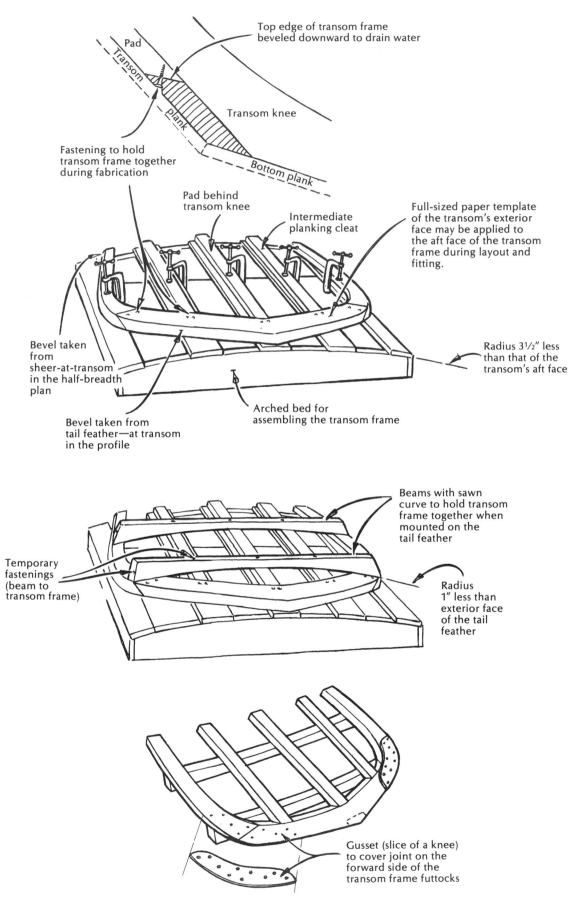

Top edge of transom frame beveled downward to drain water

Pad

Transom

Transom plank

Transom knee

Fastening to hold transom frame together during fabrication

Bottom plank

Pad behind transom knee

Intermediate planking cleat

Full-sized paper template of the transom's exterior face may be applied to the aft face of the transom frame during layout and fitting.

Bevel taken from sheer-at-transom in the half-breadth plan

Radius 3½" less than that of the transom's aft face

Arched bed for assembling the transom frame

Bevel taken from tail feather—at transom in the profile

Beams with sawn curve to hold transom frame together when mounted on the tail feather

Temporary fastenings (beam to transom frame)

Radius 1" less than exterior face of the tail feather

Gusset (slice of a knee) to cover joint on the forward side of the transom frame futtocks

58

figure 6–3b

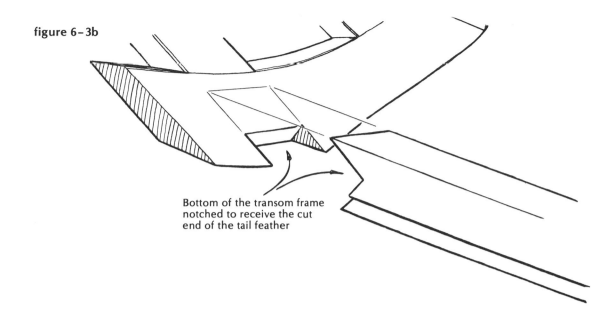

Bottom of the transom frame
notched to receive the cut
end of the tail feather

imaginary line from the top of the transom knee, square to the line of its raking profile, and up to the roof of the shop. Plumb up from the center of the keel in this general neighborhood, and drive (and bend) a nail there, to hold the ring in your long steel tape. The nail must center exactly over the middle line on the keel (see Figure 6-3d). Now swing the tape from side to side of the frame, and brace the frame from the floor, so that the twin points on the two edges are equidistant from the skyhook. If

the boat you are building has an almost plumb transom, you can, of course, do this squaring from the center of the stem, or from the center of the cross spall on one of the molds. You can also square a raking transom from a point on a true centerline on the floor, extended well astern of the boat. But this is not always an easy line to lay off, through all those piles of blocking. Stretch your tight line from the top of the stem to the top of the transom knee; check once more with the plumb bob to the centerline of

figure 6–3c

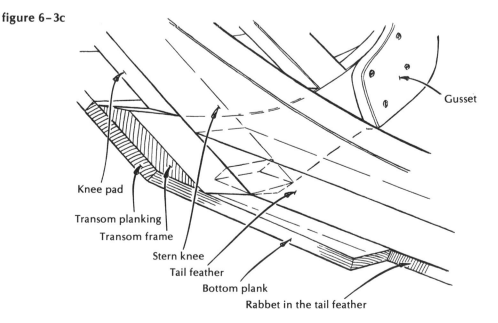

Gusset

Knee pad

Transom planking

Transom frame

Stern knee

Tail feather

Bottom plank

Rabbet in the tail feather

figure 6-3d

Horning a transom

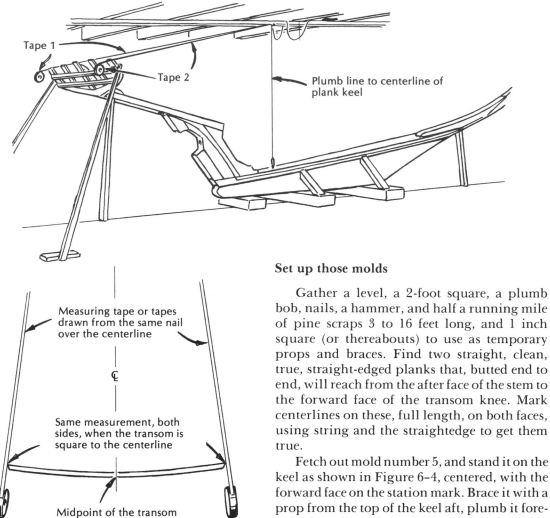

Tape 1

Tape 2

Plumb line to centerline of plank keel

Measuring tape or tapes drawn from the same nail over the centerline

₵

Same measurement, both sides, when the transom is square to the centerline

Midpoint of the transom

Set up those molds

Gather a level, a 2-foot square, a plumb bob, nails, a hammer, and half a running mile of pine scraps 3 to 16 feet long, and 1 inch square (or thereabouts) to use as temporary props and braces. Find two straight, clean, true, straight-edged planks that, butted end to end, will reach from the after face of the stem to the forward face of the transom knee. Mark centerlines on these, full length, on both faces, using string and the straightedge to get them true.

Fetch out mold number 5, and stand it on the keel as shown in Figure 6-4, centered, with the forward face on the station mark. Brace it with a prop from the top of the keel aft, plumb it fore-and-aft, and hold it level athwartships with two posts to the floor. Measure from the top of the cross spall to the rabbet line, exactly on station, and make sure that this agrees with what you laid down on the lofting floor. Set up mold number 4, then number 3, checking the height to the spalls and keeping the forward faces of the molds on the station marks. Brace these from number 5, well clear of the centerline on the tops of the spalls. Toe-nail the bottoms of the molds to the top of the keel lightly; brace number 5 forward, so that you can remove the braces to make way for number 6, which will stand with its *after* face on the station line. These four molds establish the plane of the spalls, which is of course precisely 2 feet above the load waterline. Set up number 8 on the tail feather, with its after face on the station mark;

the keel and tail feather, and brace strongly against sideward movement. You may by this time wish you'd picked a double-ended boat with a fine, simple stem at the back end, as well. I would understand and sympathize. Transoms demand thought, firmness, and constant vigilance in their handling or they'll fool you, every time. But this one is locked, for the moment.

If you have a bell to ring, or a rocket to shoot off, now's the time. You are about to set up the molds and see your boat full-size in three dimensions.

figure 6-4

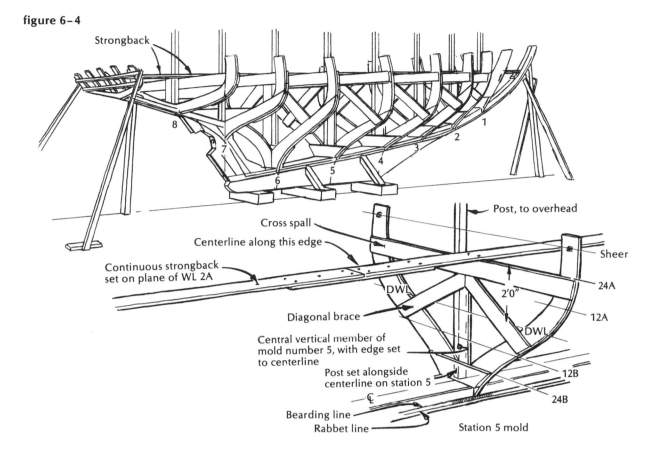

Strongback

Cross spall

Centerline along this edge

Continuous strongback
set on plane of WL 2A

Post, to overhead

Sheer

DWL

2'0"

24A

12A

Diagonal brace

DWL

Central vertical member of
mold number 5, with edge set
to centerline

Post set alongside
centerline on station 5

12B

24B

Bearding line

Rabbet line

Station 5 mold

set up number 2 on the stem, forward face to the mark. Stretch a tight string from the stem to the transom knee, touching the tops of all the spalls, and mark the stem and the knee precisely where this line intersects them. You will probably need to adjust the heights of the last two to agree with the plane established by the first four. You may find to your dismay that the mark for the 2-foot load line on the stem does not exactly agree with the string you stretched. Try to figure out what went wrong, and correct it; *but keep those cross spalls in line.* If you raise or lower one or two out of that flat plane, you will perpetuate worse errors than the most careless designer could commit in fairing lines and scaling offsets. With this cross spall plane sacred and unbroken, you know that the sheer marks on the molds are right; you can extend the plane, by string, straightedge, or eyeball, and measure up to spot the height of the sheer on the transom—and on the stem, too, if any doubt exists. Finally, you can lay a fine strongback down the middle, and tie everything together square and true, thus:

Lay the longer of the two centerlined planks fore-and-aft on the spalls; bevel its forward end

to fit the slope of the stem; fasten it securely to the stem, centered exactly, underside on the corrected 2-foot load line mark. Let's assume that its after end reaches 2 feet beyond the number 5 cross spall. Bring its centerline to the center of station number 5 spall. Plumb the mold fore-and-aft again with your level to the vertical post. Use your big steel square to set the cross spall precisely at right angles to the centerline on the under face of the strongback, and clamp it. Finally, drop the plumb bob from the centerline to the keel top, and tie the strongback to the side of the shop so that it cannot budge off center. Anchor your long steel tape on the after face of the stem, dead center, just above the strongback, and measure to the two sides of the mold at the height of the spall. If these agree, it must be square to the centerline. Now, butt the other section of the plank to this one; cut it to length to fasten to the stern knee; join the two at the butt with a wide board cleat. Hang the missing molds in place; plumb, square, and fasten all of them. Tie the strongback to the shop wall every 8 feet and put a special tie, high up, on station number 1—and she's almost ready for ribbands.

Prove the sheer

For my sake, if not yours, let's define and prove the sheerline with light battens. This is a process shrouded in mystery, mentioned in whispers outside the shops of the incompetent, accepted wordlessly as the final touch of the Master Craftsman—if you happen to like the way it came out. We've all heard of that taciturn genius who spends a day making minute adjustments to the batten, viewing it from his stepladder, allowing in his subconscious for perspective, haze, highlights—and finally achieving a line of ineffable grace, which even looks good when she's out of the shop. I'm not in that class. I decided long ago that the designer probably liked to have the sheer come out about the way he marked it on his drawing. This assumption takes most of the glamour out of the business, but saves a lot of time and soul-searching. If the molds are at their proper heights and spacing, and the sheer marks, taken from the loft floor, are clean and accurate on them, there's not much need for inspired guessing. Start a batten at the stem, with its bottom edge at the mark, and wrap it around as far as it will go. Don't pull it lengthwise and cause it to flatten its curve between molds. Tap another batten over it, top edge to the marks, and go the rest of the way aft. Measure up from the plane of the spalls for the height on the transom. If the curve has humps and hollows, go back to the floor and try to find your mis-takes. After all, you are the one who laid her down. If some expert (other than the designer) tells you it ought to tip up more quickly up front, don't just knuckle under. Tell him you'd like to see a half-dozen of his boats in the flesh, in order to study his individual style...and mark the sheer as it shows in the plans.

The line of the tuck

One more line should be determined and marked now, before the clutter gets too thick. I call this the "line of the tuck," for want of a better name. It marks the division between two different areas of planking, and it's important to get it in there, with a good ribband to follow it, just to establish squatter's rights and keep others from encroaching on the territory. Choose a long, flat batten, 1 by 1½ inches, say, and start it at the point where the rabbet line crosses the joint between the sternpost and the tail feather. Run it forward as if roughly parallel to diagonal number 2 in the lines plan, to cross mold number 3 about 9 inches above the rabbet line, and thence straight (without side-wise distortion) to the back rabbet on the stem (see Figure 6-5). If you pulled a string tight between these two endpoints, and outside the molds, you would get much of the same line— the shortest distance, or the nearest thing to a straight line between the points. Mark the molds at the crossings.

figure 6-5

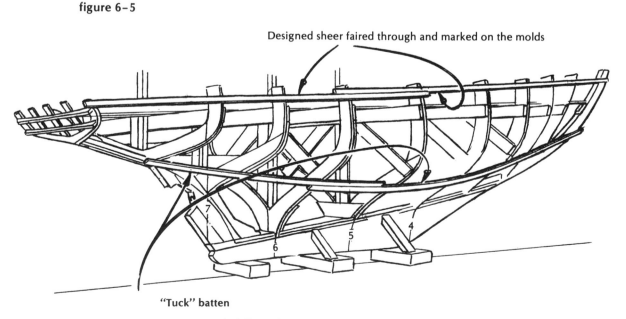

Designed sheer faired through and marked on the molds

"Tuck" batten

Approximately follows diagonal 4. Establishes run of bottom plank

figure 6-6
Cutting the remaining frame sockets

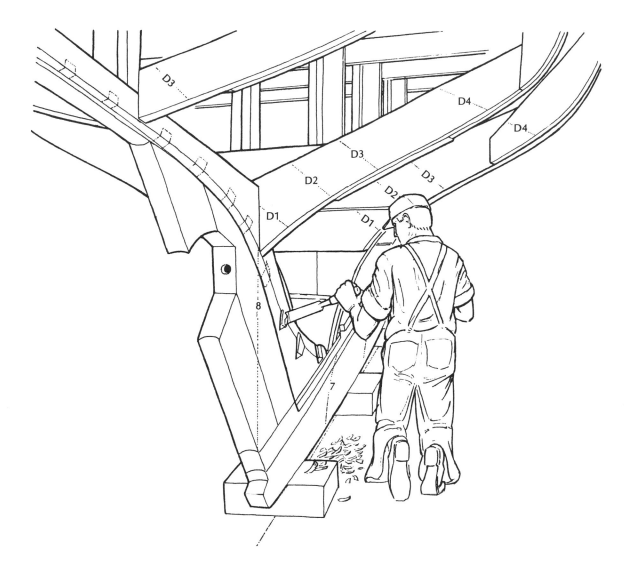

Finishing the rabbet

Go aft, now, and study the problem of the unfinished rabbet at the after end of the keel, up the sternpost and around the curve to the tail feather. Use plenty of battens to simulate planking. Twist a thin board from mold number 5 to the sternpost, to see where the garboard will lie. Cut with special care and caution at the top of the sternpost, where the angles change very abruptly. The battens will tell you what to do, if you are patient with them. Use your adze on the back rabbet on the keel and up the sternpost; use a chisel to cut the face of the rabbet all the way.

Finish this chore by cutting all the remaining frame sockets in the keel, knee, and tail feather (see Figure 6-6). These last will angle aft, in order to lie in a true vertical plane athwartships. Clamp a matched pair in place, apply square and plumb line, and study them. You'll get the point.

Bevel the transom frame. Bring the battens past it from mold number 5, and make saw cuts, in line with the battens, all around the edges of the frame. Cut to the bottom of the scores with an adze, a chisel, and a plane. Leave the final and exact cutting to be done one jump ahead of the planking crew.

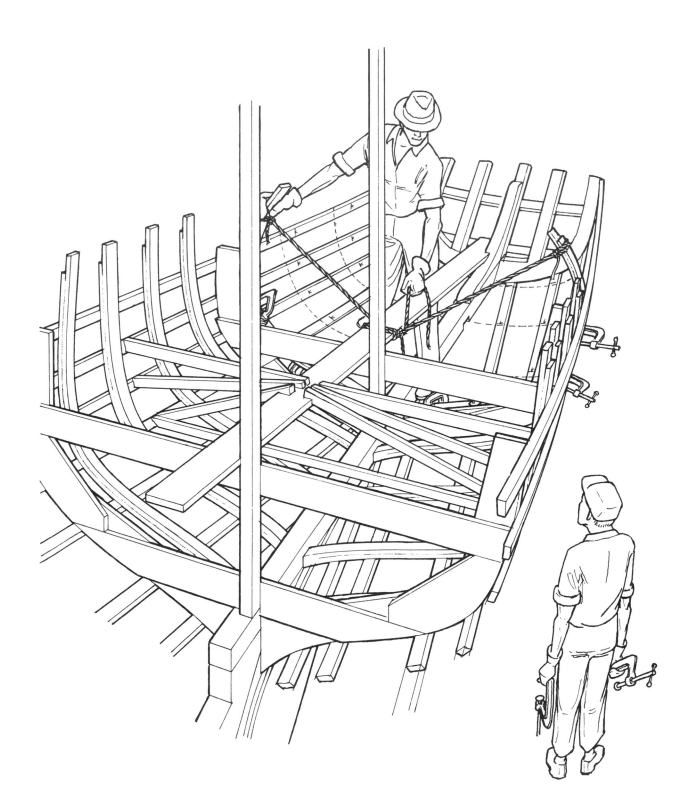

Chapter Seven

Ribbands and Timbering Out

And now to put on the ribbands. We always use clear fir, 1⁵/₈ inches thick and a bit wider than that. Half of these we leave solid (at least while they are young, green, and flexible); the others are cut with a saw, flat, right up the middle, stopping a foot short of the other end. They recuperate between boats, in the darkness under the shop floor, and last for years. You can use two layers of green spruce, and consider them expendable, if the fir is hard to come by; but watch them with suspicion between molds. Fasten the ribbands to stem and transom with one 2¹/₂-inch number 14 screw; use the same wire, ¹/₂ inch longer, for the softwood molds.

These ribbands have one purpose only, and that is to hold the bent frames precisely to the shape of the hull, at the inside of the planking, until the planking can take the job over. Their arrangement, therefore, is governed by two considerations: first, to get them on fair, as easily as possible, and spaced closely enough to do their job; and second, to hang them so that they follow somewhere near the line the planks will take, and can be removed one by one, as the planks go on, without leaving a great area of unsupported frames at one end of the hull. Study the problem with the aid of a long batten draped around the molds. Think of Great Circle courses and barrel staves. Look at the body plan on the lines drawing, and consider each diagonal as a ribband. They are spaced twice as far apart as the ribbands should be, but their arrangement is about right.

Hanging the ribbands

Start the first one just below the 36-inch load line on the stem. Drape it in a gentle sweep, to cross mold number 5 barely clear of the load waterline, and up the transom frame just below the line of diagonal 5. This will, of course, be done in two halves, with the butt end screwed to the transom frame, for the second. The after half should lie fair, against and above the forward one, where they lap by each other. Fasten an exactly similar pair on the other side of the boat. Check to be sure the molds still stand, undistorted, in the true athwartships station plane. You understand, of course, that you do *not* bevel the molds where the ribbands land. Just hit the forward corners in the forebody, the after corners aft of amidships. Shoot the screw fastenings into these corners, square to the run of the ribbands.

I like to have the uppermost ribband just clear of the sheerline, to remain in place there until the sheerstrake is fitted and fastened. You must bevel the forward end to fit against the flat of the stem above the top of the rabbet. Be sure its inner surface is in line with the back rabbet. Always work in matched pairs, keeping them as nearly as possible at the same height, each side, on every mold they cross. Where the ribbands lap past each other and end, forward or aft of amidships, they will tend to flatten out in the last bay they cross. Even them up with clamps, and edge-fasten them; back off the screw ½ inch, in the last mold they reach.

The final job in this setup is to brace the ribbands, down in the hollow of the wineglass, against the outward thrust of the frames. Use 1–inch-square pine props, up from the floor, butted square against the ribbands halfway between molds (see Figure 7–1). Experiment with a thin slat, jammed into a frame socket, bent outward to the flat of the bilge; and notice where the pressure comes. Hold the tuck ribband true at all costs. There's no sadder sight in a boatshop than frames leaning stiffly away from their sockets—unless it's the same frames straining the ribbands inward at the turn of the bilge. You can do something about it, up there, as you'll learn in framing. Down below, the ribbands must do the job on their own.

Now, about those frames...

Clean out the braces, pile the firewood, round up your crew, and get ready for the big day. I feel that we've come a long and tedious way, with too many side excursions; but pretty soon, now, she's going to start to look like a boat. You are going to enjoy two, or three, or four of the happiest days of your life. You are going to put in steam-bent frames; you'll breathe vapors as sweet as honey, and shout with relief as those old bad doubts retreat...and take up new residence in the pile of planking stock. You'll know how J. Keats felt when he first looked into Chapman's Homer. And though the too, too solid flesh of your hands threatens to melt, thaw, and resolve itself into cooked meat, you'll still have (let's see, now: seven bays at four each; add four more in the counter; three forward of mold number 1, double it)—70 golden nuggets of pure happiness, when the timber goes *chunk* into the heel socket, and you ride it down and mold it to shape against their ribbands. Some fun, I assure you. This is Mardi Gras, breakthrough—the only quick and easy process you'll encounter in this whole business of boatbuilding.

Before we get going, I would like to discuss in my usual unpleasant way some of the bad advice, incorrect assumptions, and plain ignorance that show up in practically every treatise on steam-bending techniques—and in about half the designs and completed boats you'll see.

The first and perhaps worst mistake is based upon the pernicious fallacy that Too Strong is better than Too Weak. The Designer, urged on by the Owner, specifies frames built of wood 2¼ inches square (by God, *this* one is going to be built to last). The Builder, who is an ingenious chap, if long-suffering, uses super-steam, snake oil, and compression straps, and bends that timber in so that it touches all the ribbands (or perhaps one should say, "so that all the ribbands touch *it*"—there will be just the tiniest suggestion of a hollow at each clamp); this way, there will be very little slivering on the outside of the bends, even at the tuck and the turn of the bilge. It's a beautiful thing, that curved piece of flawless oak...and a beautiful thing it continues to be, when the boat is planked with fine, dry mahogany (extra thick, of course) and caulked tight in the good, old-fashioned way. (None of that sissy stuff with a wheel on this boat.) The boat is launched, and swells, and swells; they take her out and drive her (she was built to take it); and maybe she grounds out on a bar one day and pounds a few times before the flood makes enough to kedge her off (but she was built to take that, too). And then, in a week or two, she starts to leak. So she's hauled out for examination, and someone finally discovers that one seam at the turn of the bilge has, for some strange reason, opened up, and you can pull the caulking out with your fingers. That's easy to cure: drive in three strands, smooth off, put her back in the water...and this time they install that most wonderful of all inventions, an Automatic Bilge Pump. Ten or twelve battery charges later (or the end of the yachting season, whichever comes first) she's hauled again, the offending plank is removed, and the impossible truth is revealed. Several of those magnificent frames have broken clean off, right on the line of the fine, one-piece bilge stringer. (The bolt holes are only ⅜ inch, but the ⅞-inch counterbores for the heads may have a slight weakening effect.) Put in sister frames (half the thickness of the original ones), replace planks (be sure to use good, dry stock to butt against the soaked planks—this makes for a very interesting development at the ends), and maybe the other side won't let go until next year.

If you think this is an exaggeration, examine

figure 7-1

Ribbands in place

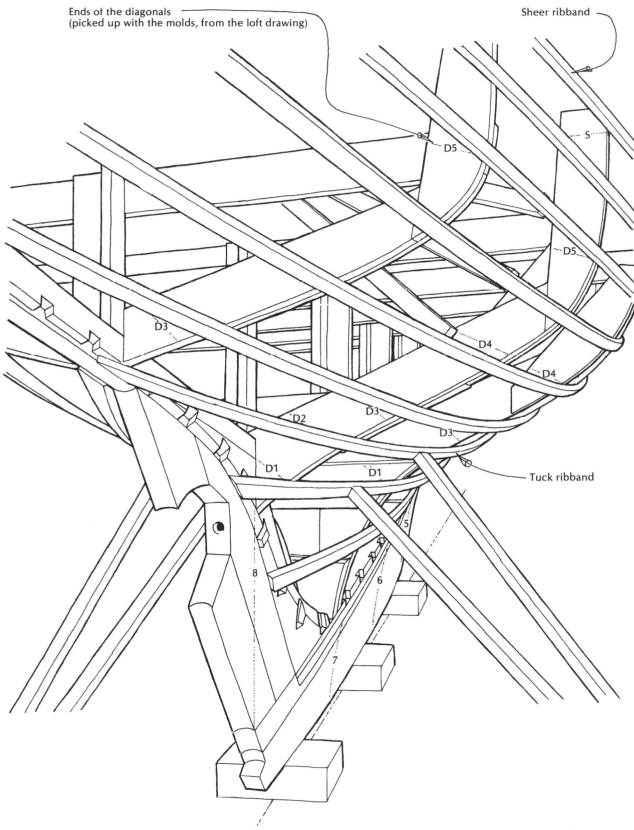

Ends of the diagonals
(picked up with the molds, from the loft drawing)

Sheer ribband

D5

D5

D5

S

D3

D4

D4

D3

D2

D3

D3

D1

D1

Tuck ribband

5

8

6

7

some old Navy liberty boats, or yachts built by the master craftsmen of European yards. The frames are such as no small boatyard could afford to match—standing square across, beveled inside and out, with the greatest dimension athwartships. They are scientifically correct and lovely to behold. They are shaped from oversized stock, which had been bent on a slab with a compression strap on the outside of the curve, and cooled in place. The wood fibers had to make a violent and painful readjustment under duress, and they didn't like it. Unfortunately, most of them are badly cracked or have broken clean off. If you want to know why this happened, hearken to the voices of the salty ones: "Do you [of course, you don't!] realize what it's like, driving to windward in the Fastnet, with the wind force 7?" Or, "Just watch one of these slam into the landing stage with 50 men aboard, and you won't wonder." If you suggest, timidly, that you've seen a heavily laden seine boat flexing her topsides in and out against the pilings half a foot every roll for hours on end, or have watched an old Down East lobsterboat twisting her tired length over the short seas as fast as her mighty 1947 Buick can push her—and nary a broken timber or open seam in either of them— you'll be treated to a diatribe on clam baskets and the men who build them. Why, those farmers couldn't bend a real frame if they tried all winter!

The point I'd like to make (and I seem to have spent considerable time getting to it) is this: in bent frames, even as in ski bindings, women's voices, alcoholic drinks, and the tethers that hold the heroine to the railroad trestle, too weak is usually better than too strong. When that frame is shaped in place it should have no regrets or hypertensions, no nervous dread of cold drafts or needle pricks on its Southern exposure. It should be relaxed, serenely confident, as it starts in its half-century of service.... Sometimes those skinny fellers'll fool you. They may not look like much, but they're withy, real withy. And don't feel too bad when that Constant Visitor sneers at your efforts and tells you that Manny Lucas *never* has to laminate his timbers to get them in. As Sam Crocker used to point out, with patient forbearance, you'll probably have to wait 20 years to prove you're right, but it'll be worth it.

So much for super-frames and the men who can bend them. Let's consider the Annual Ring theory, which appears in every good discussion of steam bending.

The theory, and the reason supporting it, are simple: bend the frame so that the annual rings, when viewed end-on, run as nearly as possible parallel to the line of the planking, because the frame bends most easily in this plane, and because fastenings driven through the annual rings at right angles (that is, in line with radii from the center of the tree) are least likely to split the frame. It is therefore very smart to use square frames, so that you can always present the proper face to the ribbands. The only trouble with this bit of advice is that it is almost completely wrong, as well as being impossible to follow more than 20 percent of the time, even with square frames, which only a trained naval architect would specify, anyway. It contains one tiny bit of truth—that one out of five frames will actually bend slightly more easily (although with no less likelihood of breaking) than a piece of wood from the same plank which has the rings at 20, 30, or 45 degrees to the plane of the planking. As for resistance to splitting—surely anyone who has ever spent two days on a farm knows that oak stove wood is always cleft straight through the heart, in line with the medulary rays. Any fastenings driven on these radial lines are *most*, rather than *least*, likely to split the frame. So what do you do? Forget the whole business, and take them as they come!

Then there's the Percentage-of-Moisture theory, which tells you to get that oak stump to steambox before the leaves begin to fade. This advice appears at first to be sound and reasonable. Surely a piece of dead-green stock, so limber it will almost bend in cold, is likely to give less trouble than one that's fully air dried, hard and stiff as an iron bar? Strangely enough, this conclusion is also wrong—at least in the light of my own experience, which covers thousands of bent frames, and the use of frame stock that had seasoned from 10 minutes to 10 years. The dry stuff (at least a year on the sticks, for 1½-inch or 2-inch plank) seems to require shorter steaming time, and bends more easily and with less breakage. It is admittedly much more difficult to work before it is steamed, and rough on drills after it has cooled and hardened again, but that is all you can say against it.

And now, what magic lubricant do we apply to this frame stock before it goes into the box, or add to the water in the boiler, so that the wood becomes pliable as rubber and tough as whalebone? Frankly, I don't know! I have tried linseed oil and kerosene. Others swear by permanent antifreeze, creosote, bag balm, and one or two more that I won't mention in a book that might fall into the hands of small children. All these treatments work wonders—if you have really straight-grained white oak to start with, plenty of screeching-hot wet steam to cook it in, and the speed of a sleight-of-hand artist to get it bent to shape before it knows what's going on. Unfortunately, the timbers you forget to paint, subjected to the same steam and speedy treatment, also bend very nicely, and the only real differences you are likely to notice are: (1) the treated timbers are darker in color; and (2) you are in somewhat less danger of sliding off and breaking your neck with the untreated ones. (The hot oil does make things a bit more exciting if you lose your gloves.)

I don't use any of these treatments. But I have not the slightest doubt that someone could (if he hasn't already done so) develop a boiling process involving a good wood preservative, perhaps a fiber-softening ingredient, in a solution that would go higher than 212 degrees; this might be worth investigating. However, plain steaming, at atmospheric pressure, with no tricks or additives, seems to work satisfactorily; and I suspect I am no more likely to try anything else in this direction than I am to investigate the possibilities of rock elm or some other substitute for white oak. I know about glued laminates, and I assure you that the cost would be enormously greater than the cost of our good bent-frame system. And don't try to convince me that putting edge-glued strips around the bulkheads is the answer. I have built strip-planked

figure 7–2

Three types of frames needed

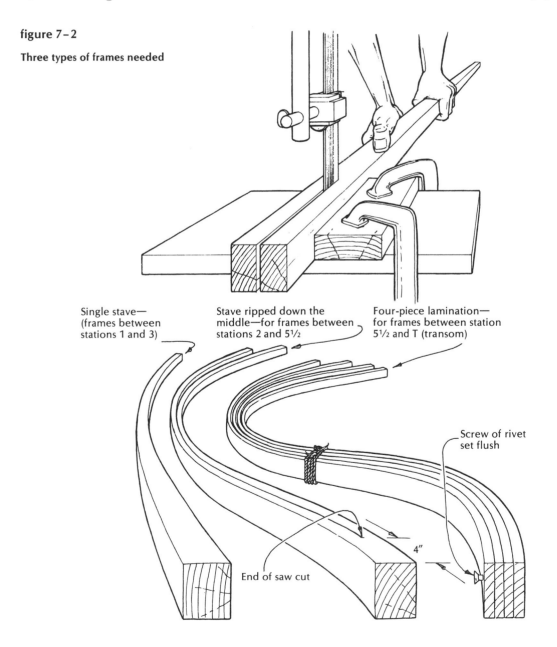

Single stave—
(frames between
stations 1 and 3)

Stave ripped down the
middle—for frames between
stations 2 and 5½

Four-piece lamination—
for frames between station
5½ and T (transom)

Screw of rivet
set flush

End of saw cut

4"

boats, cross-planked deadrise boats, lapstrake boats, plywood boats—and I still prefer the type of construction we are describing here.

So, let's get a few things together, and bend the frames. I've promised you great joy, and so far I've come up with nothing but grief.

Getting out the frames

First, of course, you've got to get out the frames. In this particular boat they will finish $1\frac{7}{8}$ inches by $1\frac{5}{8}$ inches, and will be sawn most economically out of rough 2-inch plank. Slice them off $1\frac{3}{4}$ inches thick, starting just inside the sapwood and as nearly as possible parallel to the outside of the tree—that is, if the plank tapers, work in from both edges. Don't skimp on length. Any one of them, in its proper place, should reach at least 2 inches above the sheerline. The frames that are going in away aft should be a foot longer than that. If the rough plank is sawn oversize, trim the frames on your table saw to a scant 2-inch width. Dress off all four sides in a surface planer to your finished dimensions.

Inspect them carefully, choose ends, and square the butts. (You might also make sure that the top ends are even enough so that you'll be able to hit them true with your mallet.) And now, with your thinnest saw, set very lightly and filed sharp, split every one of those frames dead center, edgewise, from the top to within 4 inches of the square butt end (see Figure 7-2). You will have taken out, I hope, a bit less than $\frac{1}{8}$ inch of the original $1\frac{5}{8}$-inch thickness. If you want to be properly methodical, you can mark all these frames with numbers to your own system, so that you'll know where each one is supposed to go in the boat. (It's embarrassing to get one all bent in and discover that it stops below the sheerline.)

Three pairs of frames will need special treatment. These are to go at the after end of the tuck, where the reverse curves at the butt ends of the frames are most severe; that is, two pairs immediately forward of station number 6, and one aft of it. The best way to make these up is simply to lay together four pieces, each $\frac{3}{8}$ inch thick by $1\frac{7}{8}$ inches wide, and tack the butt ends together with a pair of $1\frac{1}{2}$-inch screws. Tie a string around the bundle halfway along the length of the frame. Some sharp mathematician will point out that this assembled butt is $\frac{1}{8}$ inch thinner than the regular frames, and I will counter with the fact that this frame is exactly the same as they are at the top, where the sheer

clamp demands uniformity. If you insist on perfection, and have read to this point before cutting the sockets for the frames, you can make those six sockets $\frac{1}{8}$ inch shallower.

If you want to be absolutely sure that you won't lose one of these special frames by breakage, make up four spares. They may come in very handy farther aft.

There's one more thing I feel obliged to add here, but it should be in very small print, so that only the desperate few will notice it. It's this: I once knew a man who couldn't get any white oak for his frames, and used some tough, young, fast-grown oak of another variety instead. He pointed out, in his defense, that 85 percent of the boats and yachts on this coast are framed with this other variety, and most of them are doing tolerably well; and furthermore, you show a piece of this oak to one of those smart young architects and he smells it and says, "That certainly is a beautiful piece of white oak" (with the bark still on it, mind you); so what are you supposed to do? Tell him he ought to work in a boatyard for a year, and learn the facts of life? Don't be ridiculous. Congratulate him on his sense of smell, and let it go at that.

So if you can't find any good white oak, remember that there is another kind, known (though not to botanists) as gray oak. In North America it grows on, I think, 57 different types of stump (in England only one, strangely enough), but it's all gray by the time it gets to the boatshop. And if you, like the man I'm speaking of, can get some young, heavy, fast-grown oak of this variety, and sozzle it with some potent bug juice after you get it bent into place—don't worry too much about its ancestry. There are many others in the same boat with you, if I may be permitted to coin a phrase.

Of course, if you turn pro, and contract to use only genuine white oak in the boat you are to build, that's a different matter altogether. You should not take advantage of their ignorance, however thickly and obnoxiously it may be displayed. If you don't know how to recognize *Quercus alba* when you see it, ask almost any farmer or sawmill man. Don't bother the botanists. They'll draw you pictures of round-lobed leaves, and have you taste the acorns, which are sweet.

Bending the frames

Let's assume, then, that you've got your frames ready to cook, and get on with the business. If you haven't already done it, make up and install that steam-box bulkhead, complete with pusher and cross rack, just far enough in to take your longest frame. No sense wasting steam. Lay the frames on edge, so that the laminations can hang apart. Separate the tiers with cross sticks at the open end of the box. Don't push them back any further than necessary, or you won't be able to see them 'mid the encircling gloom, and it's no fun fishing around in there. Don't try more than a dozen in the first batch, unless you own more clamps than I think you do. You'll need four on each frame, and you'll not want to stop and fasten, when things are going really well, just to get clamps free. Close the door on the steam box, whoop up the fire, note the time when the steam starts coming through strong, and assemble your gear.

Inside the boat, laid out on the strongback, you'll have a big mallet, a good claw hammer, the stone-crusher shown in Figure 7-3, a can of eightpenny nails, some cotton gloves—and, eventually, yourself, shod with non-skid rubber, trying to rally from a knock on the head. (Young fellers do get a little worked up, first time they try it, and tend to forget they aren't really sitting on a cloud.) You might also have with you a piece of black crayon, and while away the hour marking where the frames are to be spaced on the ribbands. Throughout most of the length of the boat they will, of course, stand plumb in profile—that is, parallel to the nearest mold, from heel socket to sheer ribband. Forward of mold number 2, and aft of number 7, we'll start to compromise with this ideal; but right now we won't worry about that problem.

Outside the boat, your assistant festoons the ribbands with all the C-clamps you can buy, borrow, or steal, and provides himself with two heavy carpenter's hammers (one for each side of the boat, and damned lucky if either one of them is in reach when he needs it) and a better pair of gloves than you've got. He may decide to make himself a short gaff for hooking the frames out, after he's groped for a few with his wrist exposed. There are some special boatbuilding terms that are used to describe this experience, but I think we can afford to omit them here.

If we've forgotten anything, it's too late now. They've been cooking an hour, with the box huffing and puffing and spewing out great gouts of ink-black water. Take your stand on the ribbands just forward of mold number 5, and call for the first frame timber. Your helper should fetch it at a dead run, shove it to you butt-first over the top ribband, and then dive to the keel with hammer in hand. You start the

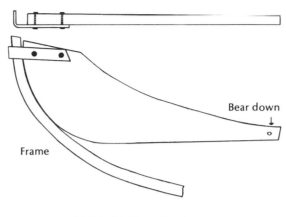

figure 7-3

McIntosh's Stone-Crusher

butt into its socket, crawl up the ribbands with your big mallet, and belabor the upper end until your helper cries "Hold, enough"—and drives the butt sideways in the socket, while you are riding the frame down to the ribbands. It bends quite easily to the shape, but you know perfectly well that it's only waiting for your foot to slip. All this has taken about 30 seconds.

Right now the serious business begins. It is not enough merely to bend it out until it touches all the ribbands, and there fasten it to await the planking. It and its three companions will inevitably distort the fair curve of the ribbands between the molds, and cause a flat spot, ugly to look at and difficult to plank. Someone is going to get all excited here and point out that molds should never be more than 2 feet apart. I know one good boatbuilder who uses no molds at all, and others who couldn't turn out a good job if they made a mold for every frame in the boat. Take my word for it: if you know how to work the timbers, you can keep them fair with this 4-foot spacing. You've got to over-bend each frame, manipulate it, shape it with your hands, feet, and the stone-crusher, until it stops fighting and relaxes into place. And the way you do it is this: the outside man clamps the frame to the ribband just below the turn of the bilge, and then you pull the head of the frame inboard all you dare, and half a foot more (see Figure 7-4). Hold it 10 seconds, let it go outboard to take a clamp on the next ribband up, and repeat the extreme bend and holding. (You'll learn eventually to bear down on the top as you pull it in, to increase the amount of the bend and move it upwards on the frame.) Continue to move upward, ribband by ribband, breaking it in each time, until you end up with the bending tool at the very head of the frame. The frame should be by this time completely tractable, so that one clamp only, to the ribband just above the turn of the bilge, will almost hold it in place. Of course, you leave at least four on it, until you have time to fasten to the ribbands. I hope that you have remembered through all this excitement to keep it lined up at those black crayon marks. As a last act before you leave it, nail the head of the frame to the uppermost ribband, right at your crayon mark.

And what if the frame refuses to take this punishment—being bent to 6-inch radius, when it needs only to fit a curve three or four times bigger? If it won't take the quick turn without showing signs of distress, you don't want it in your boat. Throw it out and try another. But if it *does* take it—then it's a good, tough frame, well adjusted within itself, and quite able to withstand all the flexing and shocks it's likely to get in the next 30 years. And it accepts those ribbands as guides, not captors, in assuming its final shape, so that the curves of the planking fore and aft will remain fair.

Now, this bending should have been easy to do (I hope much easier than trying to describe it). If it wasn't easy, there's something wrong—poor stock, steam not hot enough, too much time lost somewhere. The same rule should apply throughout this business of boatbuilding—and possibly in broader fields of endeavor, if you want to get philosophical about it. If it comes hard, try to figure out where you've gone wrong. (It might be the designer, too, you know. Invite him to come up and demonstrate. You and he might be somewhat surprised at the results.) But hang onto this thought: if it's done properly, it should be easy.

Use up the rest of this first batch here in the middle of the boat—forward and aft of station number 5—to develop your speed and skill. These big frames are the easiest to fit, since they require very little twisting. There is the further advantage that a frame you break here may still be long enough to reach the sheerline if you go two stations forward with it. Remember to keep the boiler full and driving until the last timber is out of the box. Take the clamps off, one by one, and substitute for each of them a 3-inch number 12 steel screw—for which you drill a $^3/_{16}$-inch hole—through ribband and frame from the outside. Always try to drive those screws precisely in the middle of the frame, because this is the one spot you're not supposed to hit with the plank fastenings. You'll break your pre-

cious tapered drill every time you let it fall into one of these hidden gopher holes. Finally, before you start another batch, check all these newly bent frames to make sure they are still touching the ribbands above and below the reverse curve, 'way down low. They have a sly tendency to lift away here as they cool off.

It should be safe now to go aft and consider the special problems in the counter. These short frames aft of the sternpost might appear at first glance to be the easiest of all to fit, but they are not. They can get you into bad trouble if you don't watch out. They'll try to straighten out by pulling the bilge ribbands insidiously upward; and you'll realize, too late, with the topsides all planked, that she looks starved in the flanks. You can try to blame it on the designer (the transom does look too big, it's true), but you'll be wrong. You gave up too soon. You let the clamps take part of the burden, instead of fighting it out to total victory with your bare hands. (You think I've forgotten your gloves? Oh, no. You shook off the right-hand one early so that you could hang on to the mallet handle long enough to drive the frame down the inside curve to the heel socket.) And maybe you had some foolish notion that you could twist this frame and haul the head aft, so that it stands plumb in profile, and follows those crayon marks up the ribbands to the sheer. An attempt to do this would impossibly complicate an already difficult situation. Forget your ideals. Let the thing lie almost as it wants to, leaning drunkenly forward from the bilge up. Pull the top of that frame in, and hold it 'til your arms crack, and your foot is paralyzed; and then, having let it fall out against the ribbands at the turn, tie that top with rope, across to the strongback, with enough tension to pull the frame clear of the sheer ribband (see Figure 7-5).

You will have noticed in the midst of this struggle that the extra foot of length on the frame was a great help to you. You may also have had the fleeting thought that three or even four laminations (totaling the full thickness of the two-layer frames, of course) would have been much more pleasant to handle. Why not? It's far better to have them go in with only moderate strain on their fibers and your muscles. The butt ends of at least three pairs, as you remember, are already prepared for that extreme turn at the after end of the tuck. If you have doubts, or troubles, fit all the frames, between station number 7 and the transom, in four layers each. Easy does it, every time.

One more point, before we go up front

figure 7–4

Bending the frames into place

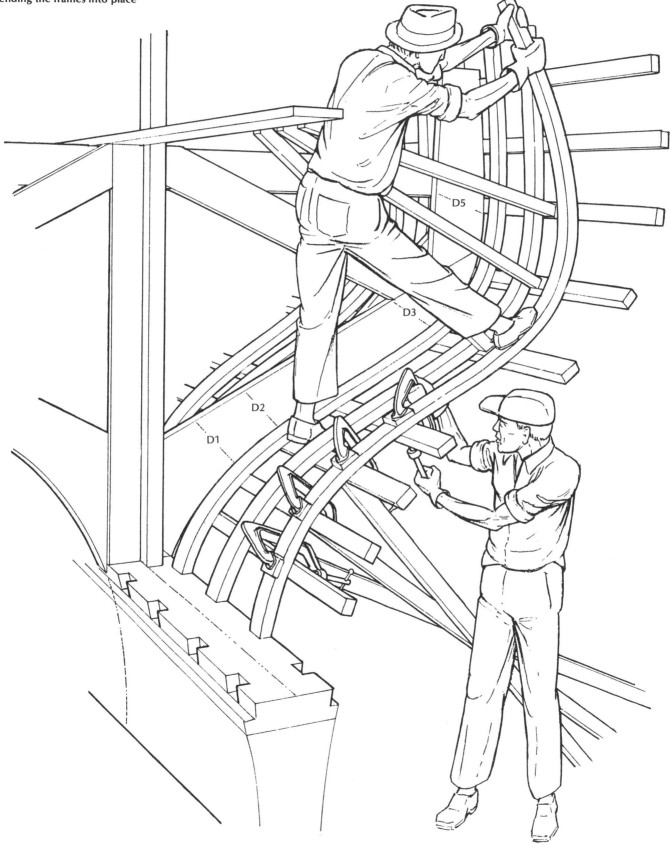

figure 7–5

Bending stubborn frames aft

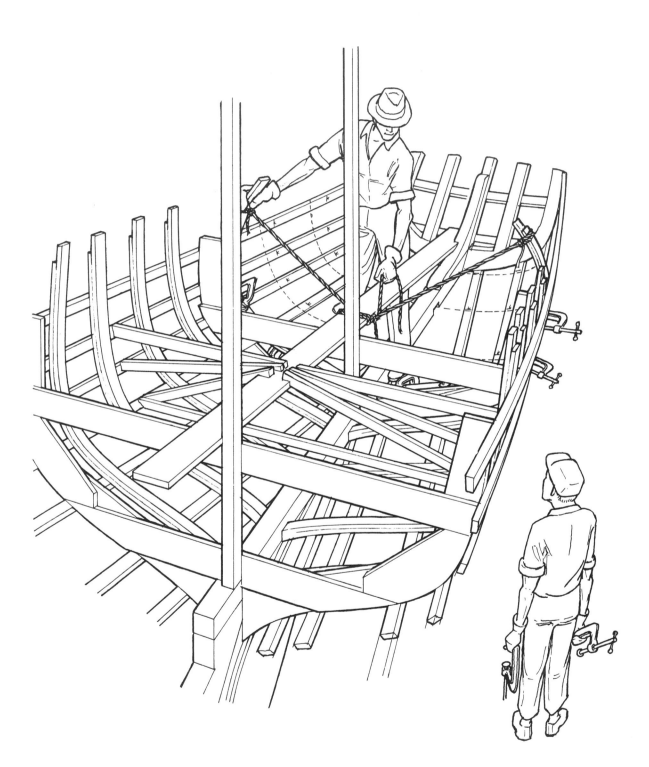

("forward," to you purists) to discuss the problems there. In this matter of allowing the frames to lie naturally, with their heads leaning toward the bow, try (as they will try) to have this effect increase gradually and evenly as you work aft. The second frame aft of station number 7 could start the trend; it is permissible also to increase the distances between frames at the bilge as those distances decrease at the sheer. And, of course, match them up port and starboard, and tell all your visitors you meant to do it that way, and that you've got authority to back you up.

The same spirit of moderation and compromise should guide your hand up forward. You'll be able to hold the line aft of the number 2 mold, but beyond that you'll encounter an increasing desire in the frame heads to lean aft. Don't fight them too hard. Better to allow a slight laxity in posture than to have them present a hard and unyielding corner to the planking. And shape them, before clamping, just as earnestly as you shaped the frames in the stern.

Remember, when you are bending those three terrible pairs aft (the one just forward of mold number 7, and the next two aft of it) that the ribbands that form the tuck are sacred and must not be forced outward. Better to have no frame there at all than to allow a bulge in the fair curve of the plank line.

Fastenings

And now to fasten these frames to the foundation. I hope you will by this time feel that those sockets were worth cutting if only to locate and hold one end of the frame while you worked on the rest of it. I think you will get great satisfaction and reassurance from the act of fastening them; you'll *know* it's good; and never mind how it looked on the construction plan. If you estimate that each of these connections will take a 500-pound load, and count only the frames between stations number 2 and number 7, you still come up with a figure of 20,000 pounds, which is a nice little start toward supporting 6,500 pounds of ballast and keeping the garboard seams tight. And all free, you might say—since your critics will maintain that the floor timbers do all the work, anyway.

Those same critics will shake their heads in shocked disbelief if you follow my advice and fasten each frame heel with two hot-galvanized 20-penny spikes. Drill $^3/_{16}$-inch holes for them, angled out and down, and countersunk so the heads will be out of the way when you fair the frames off flush with the back rabbet. Back on the tailfeather, and up the stem, where there is less wood to hit, use 10-penny nails, or $2^1/_2$-inch number 8 bronze nails. Pay no attention when the Voice of Doom gets going on the subject of electrolysis. If the two metals are not in actual contact with each other, and are buried and bunged in sound wood, they'll manage a peaceful coexistence in spite of all the agitated experts.

Now, while you are (having bent the last frame) in the full flush of pride and victory, you would do well to get down on your knees with an adze, planes, a slice, battens, thin boards, a big hammer, and a punch, and fair off the frames and the back rabbet to make ready for the garboard. You'll want a clear conscience when you face the next operation.

*"But put a timber and jack under each bilge...
and the ocean drops right out of her garboard seams."*

Chapter Eight

Floor Timbers

The glossary will say something like this: "Floor timber—an athwartships member, usually of wood, used to tie the heels of the frames to the keel." This definition comes close to being the ultimate in oversimplification. The floor timbers provide a base for the engine bed, intermediate shaft bearings, and a mast step. They tie the two halves of the boat together down where it really counts. They take in hand the enormous wringing strains of the ballast keel, and transfer these loads smoothly and subtly to the main fabric of the hull. They connect a flexible keel to the longitudinal rigidity of the topsides. They even provide support for a platform to walk on. Unfortunately, they are not always provided in sufficient numbers, styles, and sizes to do this work in a satisfactory manner.

Various types of floors

I can think of seven different forms in which this member can appear, each one with certain virtues of its own (Figure 8-1).

There's the simple plank-on-edge, suggested by the above definition, which can go before, abaft of, on top of, or between the frames. In its best form this simple floor is shaped from a "grown crook," with long arms up the inside of the planking. You are most likely to find it in a primitive boatyard where the builders live close to the forest and time is not of the essence—and you can well envy them their pile of sweeps and knees, because we can't improve on them a bit with all our refined techniques.

There's the metal floor—forged from wrought iron or steel, or cast in bronze, or welded in web form from bar and angle stock.

figure 8–1

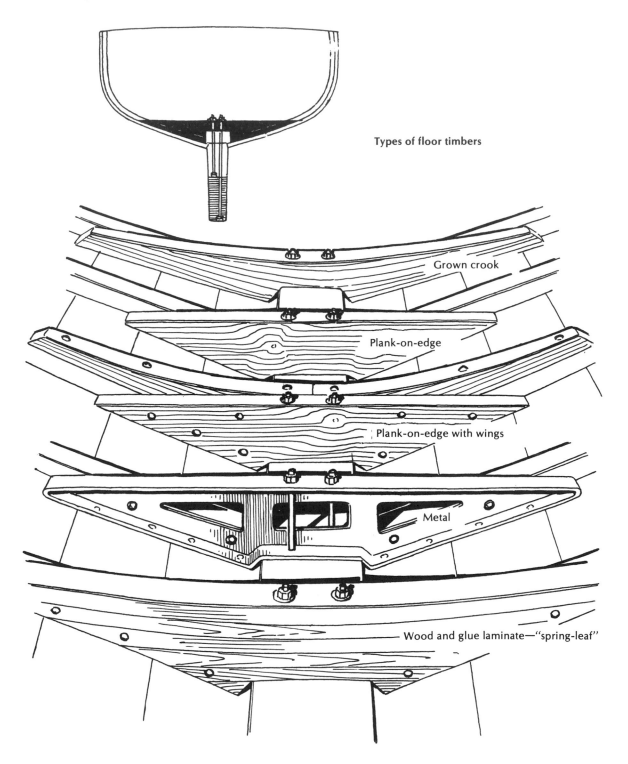

Types of floor timbers

Grown crook

Plank-on-edge

Plank-on-edge with wings

Metal

Wood and glue laminate—"spring-leaf"

This usually is used up forward, where an honest plank floor would stand too high and spoil the headroom. It's a pretty thing, and very expensive; but it sometimes fails to do its job. I'll have more to say about this later. (Once upon a time, there was a special rating rule in the Great Lakes which for some reason penalized inside ballast, as distinct from structural members. One boat appeared with a 600-pound bronze fairing piece on the lower end of the rudder stock; another used, in the refrigeration system, bronze tubing with a 2-inch-thick wall. Needless to say, the designers of these boats went wild with metal floors. In my innocence I contracted for and built one of them, and the old scars act up when I think of it. I have suffered since from the failings of three others that came here in mid-career and drooped their chins, as it were, on my doorstep, asking to be made whole again—and I learned a lot about floors from them.)

And there's the spring-leaf floor (Figure 8-2), built up of glued laminations, saturated and sealed with super-epoxy, light, stiff, strong, and guaranteed not to delaminate as long as the moisture content stays the same. It is also frightfully expensive, but worth every nickel if you are building a three-ply featherweight to the quarter-ton rule. Such a boat is outside my experience and beyond my desire. However, if my boat won't get there the same day, it'll make it the same summer, fortified by massive, heavy, perhaps crude floors that'll never let a garboard swing open.

Let's contemplate some of the stresses that occur in a sailboat with outside ballast. We'll stand the boat on edge and drop her off the top of a 6-foot sea that hits beam-on.

Look at "Knockabout, 1900" (Figure 8-3). This boat probably leaked very little in its youth, even when driven hard. But despite splendid workmanship and tender loving care, the fastenings and joints would eventually work loose and allow for cruel leaking. Caulking would aggravate the trouble; the only cure would be more and bigger floors, with bigger bolts through them. And don't tell me you can fiberglass the bottom and make her as good as new. You've got to stop that wiggle first.

Now look at "Sam Crocker, 1939" (Figure 8-4). This is much better. (We were building *Fomalhaut* then, and trying to learn all we could from Sam Crocker; there was a lot he taught us—one lesson having to do with that particular keel-floor-ballast configuration. It seems that even he had had secret doubts as to its ultimate indestructibility, so when he started

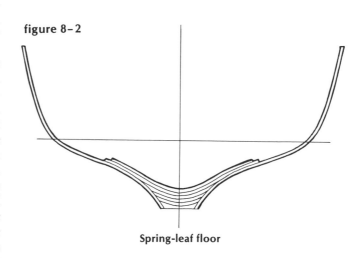

figure 8-2

Spring-leaf floor

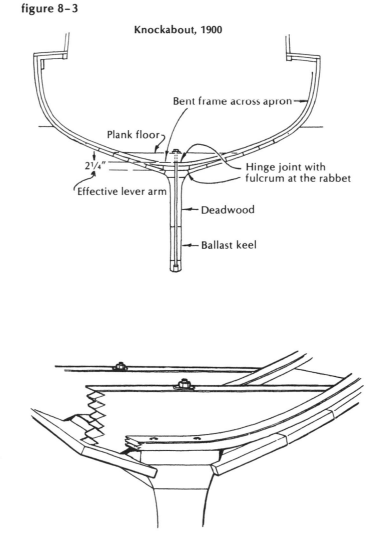

figure 8-3

Knockabout, 1900

Bent frame across apron

Plank floor

2¼"

Effective lever arm

Hinge joint with fulcrum at the rabbet

Deadwood

Ballast keel

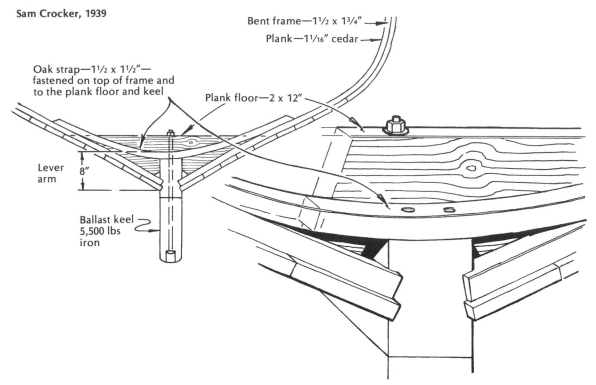

figure 8-4

Sam Crocker, 1939

Bent frame—1½ x 1¾"

Plank—1¹¹/₁₆" cedar

Oak strap—1½ x 1½"—
fastened on top of frame and
to the plank floor and keel

Plank floor—2 x 12"

Lever
arm   8"

Ballast keel
5,500 lbs
iron

across country, after the 1938 hurricane, on the trail of one of his 30-footers, he counted the successive trenches her keel had gouged. His heart sank lower and lower as he approached the 50 mark—and there the little so-and-so sat, leaning against an oak tree. "Christmas!" said Sam. "She hadn't even squeezed the putty out of the garboard seam!" He told of another case in which they hadn't, for some reason, boxed the frames into the foundation; that boat always leaked a little when they drove her hard, and they couldn't cure it.)

If we accept the garboard (in the rabbet) as the fulcrum in this diagram of forces, then the lever arm to the top of the keel is at least four times as long in the second instance as in the first. Add the greater depth of floor, the thicker bolt, the boxed-in heel, and the bent timber across the keel and atop the frames, and you have a very strong structure, perfectly suited to a stand-up keel.

Now look at the third case, illustrated in Figure 8-5. This shows the usual molded keel, wide in the way of the outside ballast, tapering both ways to the siding of the stem and stern-post, and only as deep in profile as necessary to provide an adequate junction for frames, floors,

planking, and ballast shoe. A plank-on-edge floor will do nicely here—drift-fastened to the keel, heavily fastened to the two or three planks that cross its ends. But it would be far more effective if it had tapering arms that reached almost to the turn of the bilge, strongly secured to eight or nine planks on a side and directly attached to the ballast keel, if possible. This line of thought (or yearning?) has led me to design and use, in my latest half-dozen big boats, what you might call a composite-construction floor. It's not difficult to shape, it's enormously strong, it allows easy access to the keelbolt, and it spreads the bolt load across the entire width of the wood keel.

The composite construction floor

Start with a piece of ½- by 4-inch steel long enough to reach almost across the top of the wood keel in the way of a ballast-keel bolt. Make a pattern for a vertical plate, or web, comfortably smaller than the width down there in the ditch. Get your friendly metalworker to cut this out of ³⁄₈-inch plate and weld it across the forward edge of the first piece, to stand plumb, as in Figure 8-6.

Drill the bottom plate for the keelbolt; drill at least five holes on each side of the centerline in the vertical plate; drop the assembly down to the top of the wood keel, with 2 inches of threaded keelbolt coming up through the cross plate. Shim it ⅛ inch clear of the top of the keel, turn a nut on finger-tight, and proceed to fit the wings—sawn to shape out of the toughest white oak or locust that ever grew, scribed to fit snugly against the inside of the planking, and extending out and up at least to the underside of the cabin sole. Clamp to the plate and drill the wood to match the holes in the plate. Mark where the wings lie on the planking, and punch lead holes out through to lead the screws that will go from the planking into the wings.

Take the whole business apart; apply zinc-rich paint to the metal; set the athwartships plate on a fine bed of canvas gasket and tar-and-oakum grommet, but don't tighten the keelbolt nut until everything else is bolted and screwed together. That last ⅛ inch (with roofing tar squeezing out around the edges) will take up all the slack. The final move is to fit and fasten a fine timber across from tip to tip, at the height of the underside of the cabin sole. You can spike and screw-fasten the ends as shown, or you can fit a metal plate on each side and through-rivet to tie things together.

I think you'll be satisfied with one of these floors in every other bay (say, 24 inches apart) and view with pleasure the chance you have to install worthwhile fuel and/or water tanks below the cabin sole—but be sure you can get them out without disturbing the joinerwork. You might want to check a keelbolt after 20 years, or you might have to clear the limbers, or convince a surveyor that there's still a sound boat down in that hole.

Before we finish comparing timbering systems, look at Figure 8-7, which shows typical big-ship double-sawn frame-with-keelson construction.

New bootstraps

I'd like now to consider some of the responsibilities of the floor timbers, how they can fail in their duties, and what can be done to get them out of a bind.

There is a subject dear to my heart best described as The Case of the Shrinking Garboard. This crops up most frequently in "planked-down," "ditch-keel" powerboats like Old Novis, but I've known the phenomenon to occur in an ancient Crowninshield schooner

figure 8-5

"Third case"

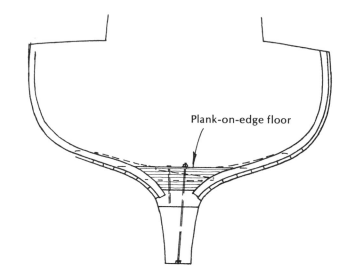

Plank-on-edge floor

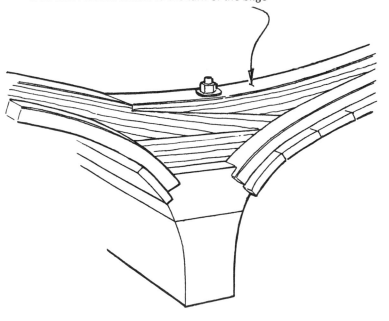

—but more effective if it had tapering arms that reached almost to the turn of the bilge

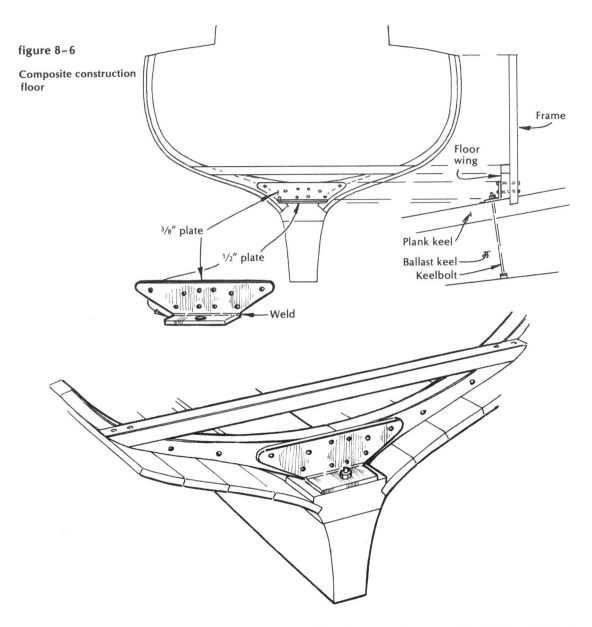

figure 8-6

Composite construction floor

Frame

Floor wing

³/₈" plate

½" plate

Plank keel

Ballast keel

Keelbolt

Weld

and a classic fantail-stern launch. The opening move is always the same. "Have you got any real good oakum?" asks the owner. "My garboards have shrunk something awful. 'Course, they're original—been on there 15 years—can't expect them to last forever—anyone knows you can't do a real caulking job with cotton...."

So you tell him you think she needs new bootstraps more than she needs further prying apart. (Garboards don't shrink, all evidence to the contrary notwithstanding. Keels sag under the weight of engines; and if the frame-butts let go their grip of the foundation, there's bound to be a gap above the rabbet. You can't blame the trouble on floor timbers, because they were not provided in any great quantity when the boat was built.) If you are as foolhardy as I have

been known to be, you will tell him to bring her up, and you'll put her on the railway; and if he'll tear up four feet of cockpit floor down the middle, you'll fix her.

So you haul her out, with water in her up to the flywheel, and not a drop runs out of the old basket. But put a timber and a jack under each bilge, just aft of the engine, and take half her weight off the car—and the ocean drops right out of her lovely garboard seams. While she's up thus, rake out the lovely mess of cotton, oakum, and roof tar from the garboard seams, and let her down again. Chances are those garboards have miraculously expanded (or something has happened, anyway) so now the open seam looks almost respectable. All you need worry about is keeping it that way when she's

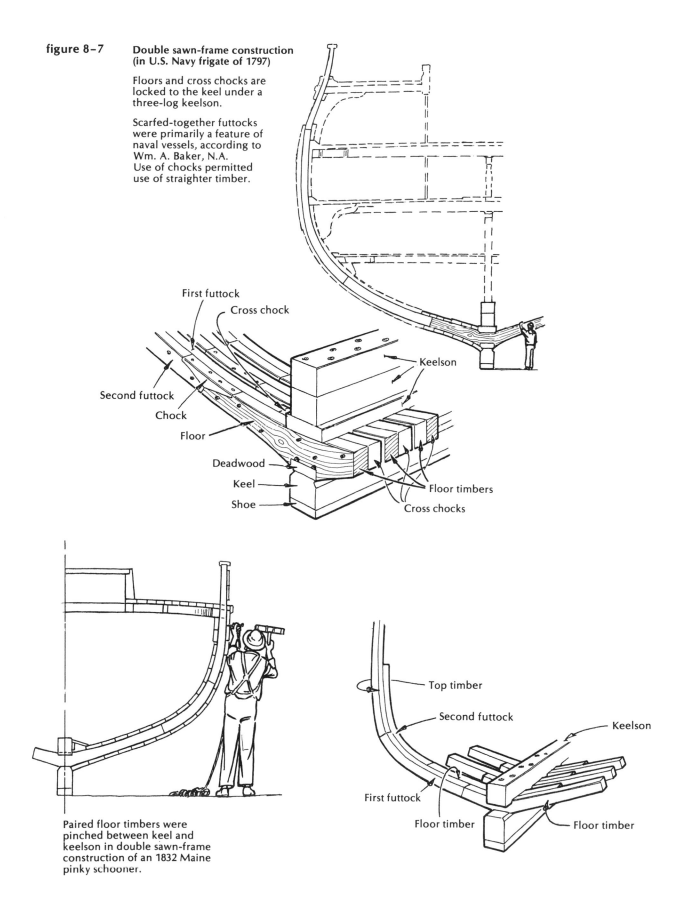

figure 8-7 **Double sawn-frame construction (in U.S. Navy frigate of 1797)**

Floors and cross chocks are locked to the keel under a three-log keelson.

Scarfed-together futtocks were primarily a feature of naval vessels, according to Wm. A. Baker, N.A. Use of chocks permitted use of straighter timber.

First futtock

Cross chock

Keelson

Second futtock

Chock

Floor

Deadwood

Keel

Shoe

Floor timbers

Cross chocks

Paired floor timbers were pinched between keel and keelson in double sawn-frame construction of an 1832 Maine pinky schooner.

Top timber

Second futtock

Keelson

First futtock

Floor timber

Floor timber

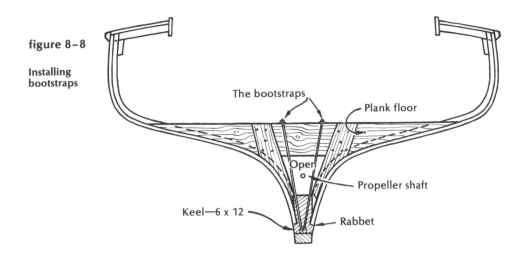

figure 8-8

Installing
bootstraps

The bootstraps

Plank floor

Open

Propeller shaft

Keel—6 x 12

Rabbet

supported by water instead of by railway.

Here's where the bootstraps are applied. First, look at Figure 8-8. That timber sitting on edge across the ditch is brand-new to this old boat, and is one of three, judiciously spaced between the sternpost and the forward end of the cockpit. I call it a floor timber for lack of a better name. Bore a hole down through it, far enough off the centerline to clear the propeller shaft. Continue the hole down through the keel. Cut and thread bolts to reach from countersunk heads on the bottom of the keel to the top of this cross piece. Do the other two likewise; fasten earnestly from the planking into these pseudo-floors; fit vertical cleats, wedges, and fillers down each side of the ditch, bolted to the crosspiece at the top, fastened to the planking below. Tighten the nuts on the bootstraps 'til she squeaks in pain. Caulk that fine small garboard seam and shove her back in. You shouldn't have missed more than one tide.

(We did Brooksy's gramp's boat this way one morning. She was strip-planked, and not too old, and sat on the railway tighter'n a you-know-what in flytime until we jacked her a little—whereupon 1,000 miles of hairline seam appeared in view, oozing water every damned inch. We put the bootstraps to her, as above, and shoved her back in to adjust herself. Saw Gramp a week or two later looking kind of morose, and felt obliged to inquire how she was doing. "She stinks!" he said. "Used to be you pumped enough water through her to keep her sweet, but not any more. That gurry just sets in the bilge and rots." Ah, well...some days you can't do anything right.)

With all these pictures of flat-floored powerboats around, this is a good time to consider another special responsibility of the floor timbers—or perhaps what happens, in this type of boat, when they're too small and too few.

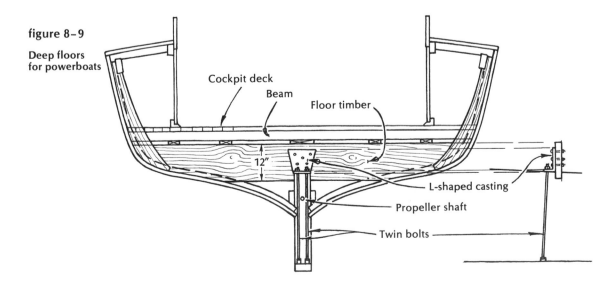

figure 8-9

Deep floors
for powerboats

Cockpit deck

Beam

Floor timber

12"

L-shaped casting

Propeller shaft

Twin bolts

figure 8–10

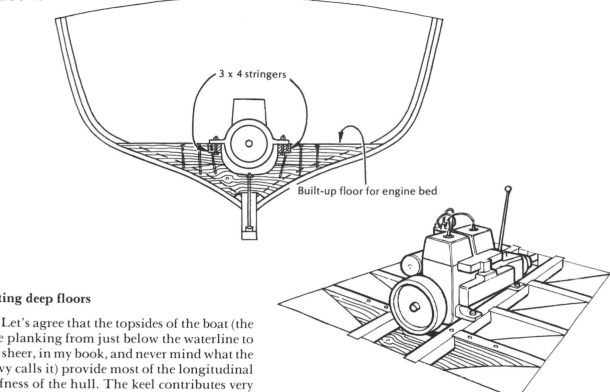

3 x 4 stringers

Built-up floor for engine bed

Fitting deep floors

Let's agree that the topsides of the boat (the side planking from just below the waterline to the sheer, in my book, and never mind what the Navy calls it) provide most of the longitudinal stiffness of the hull. The keel contributes very little to this (unless, of course, we are considering a heavily built dragger, with considerable deadrise even in the after sections), and the great need is to transfer this topside strength to the rest of the fabric, including the keel. This is one of the main functions of the floor timbers. Go to any graveyard of old lobsterboats, and you'll see what I mean. If they've sat long without careful shoring under the bilges and transom, they'll likely show a dimple at the top of the sternpost and a kink in the keel where it rests in the forward-most crossbeam of the cradle. The bilges may sag a bit, like the jowls of middle age; and in a planked-down boat there will be a definite coming-together of the sides above the shaft alley.

You may argue at this point that the boat was designed to float in water, and not sit up there in the weeds. True enough; flexibility is a great virtue if you don't have too much of it, and they all have to leak a little or they wouldn't be boats—but what if you hit the sand a few times while running an inlet, or get caught in the surf along the beach? You'll feel better if you know the garboards aren't likely to pop out of the rabbet on the third bounce, nor the sternpost to come up through the deck, nor the propeller shaft to go so much out of line that the engine is lost.

You can take arms against this sea of troubles thus: Fit long floors clear across the flat, as in Figure 8-9. Make them as deep as you can; bolt a vertical member at each end, pinned to the sheer clamp, where possible; fasten them solidly to the backbone with drifts and L-shaped castings locked to the twin bolts in the deadwood. The athwartships strength of these deep floors will hold the topsides and centerline structure in their proper relationship. The floors provide a perfect base to support the timbers of the cockpit floor frame. And they add 207 pounds to the weight of the boat, and 15 years to its useful life, and reduce its speed by $9/10$ knot. You may question the accuracy of these figures, but it won't do any good to tell me about it.

While we're still aboard this powerboat, let's consider the engine bed and the floors that support it. Remember that the mighty thrust of the propeller must be transmitted from engine to bed to floors to hull, and that the whole assembly will be subject to violent lurches and possible sudden stops. You're not concerned merely with a weight of 500 to 1,500 pounds sitting serenely upright. Someday it will tilt 45

figure 8–11

Cure for strained and leaking garboards

These wooden floor timbers with wings are set between existing frames with their bronze floors.

The wooden floors and their wings are heavily fastened to the hull plank.

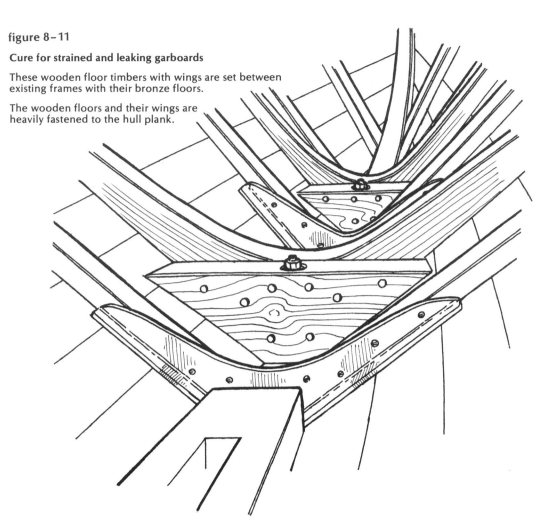

degrees and drop 6 feet in the trough between seas. The usual plank-on-edge engine bed won't stand such treatment without strong lateral support. As shown in Figure 8–10, this support can be provided by adding to the height of the floors, outboard of the engine mounts. Or you can fit one-piece floors, scooped out to take the crankcase, and land the engine mounts on flat stringers notched into the floors. This system allows you to use through-bolts in the engine mounts, because the lower ends of the bolts are in the clear below the stringers.

If you tie all these members to each other, and to the keel and frames and planking, and anything else you can think of, then you can feel fairly certain that the bed won't wrack or loosen. And if you are installing two engines side by side, make these floors high and plenty where they cross the keel; lock the engine-bearing stringers into partial bulkheads before and abaft the engines, and don't allow the weight to bear on the frames and the planking. (I've seen three-year-olds with double hernias.)

Adding timbers with "wings"

Let's now take a good look at the front end of a long-snouted sailboat. She's got a fine pedigree, metal floors up forward, and a frantic owner. He has read all about inadequate mast steps and outside strapping in the Herreshoff manner, but he's not quite sure what to do, because she leaks—not too badly at rest if the rigging is slack, but fearfully indeed when she's under sail. She's a $50,000 deathtrap that's worth just what the gear will bring on the second-hand market—unless, of course, we can think of a cure, preferably quick and inexpensive.

Let's try to analyze the trouble.

Obviously, the garboard seam (or much less likely, the joint between the keel and stem) opens when the mast pushes down and the shrouds pull up. It's customary to blame this phenomenon on a mast step that's too short. No one would dare blame it on a weakness of those magnificent cast-bronze floors, or the builder's refusal to box the frames into the foundation. "Completely useless, and just another rot-pocket," he'll tell you. Maybe the mast step *is* a bit on the limber side; but if it were a cast-iron bar twice as long, it wouldn't change things much. The shrouds are still going to pull the frames and planking away from the keel unless there's a very strong, non-stretching tie to hold them there. (And it takes only $1/16$ inch of slackness in a 3- to 4-foot length of seam to cause a leak that'll scare you to death.)

Believe it or not, the cure for this dreadful state of affairs is relatively simple. The most difficult part of the project is to convince the owner that you have to rip out all that lovely ceiling and joinerwork, and leave him with 6 inches less headroom up front. Turn a deaf ear to his wails and fit some real floor timbers—between frames, bolted strongly through the keel or stem as may be, fitted with wings—up the inside of the planking as far as you dare (see Figure 8-11). Fasten from the planks into the floors as if your reputation depended upon it, as indeed it may. Recaulk, hard, the garboard seam and two or three plank seams above it. Say a prayer, shove her in, and try her out. You may have gained a satisfied customer and a friend—if you managed to replace most of the joinerwork intact and didn't charge him for it.

Tangs and tie-rods

There's yet another way to hold these parts together. It's somewhat akin to the bootstrap technique described 'way back there for the salvation of old powerboats, and has the great virtue of taking up practically no room at all. It's all done with simple tangs and tie-rods. Figure 8-12 makes it perfectly obvious: Fasten the tang to a frame or rivet it to the inside of the planking; drill all the way through the stem, as nearly as possible in line with the tang; counterbore for the nut and rivet the tie-rod up and through the tang end; turn on a nut, and tighten down. The longer the tangs, the better. The more of them you apply, the better. The bronze floors can stay right there to impress surveyors, and the garboards will hold the new caulking.

Having read this far, you may have the feeling that old boatbuilders spend most of their declining years repairing their own and others' mistakes. This is not the whole truth. We go on making more mistakes, but we don't usually make the same ones all over again. Profit by our examples and warnings, and try to do better.

And that's about all I have to say, right now, about floor timbers.

figure 8–12

Curing strained garboards by use of tangs and tie-rods

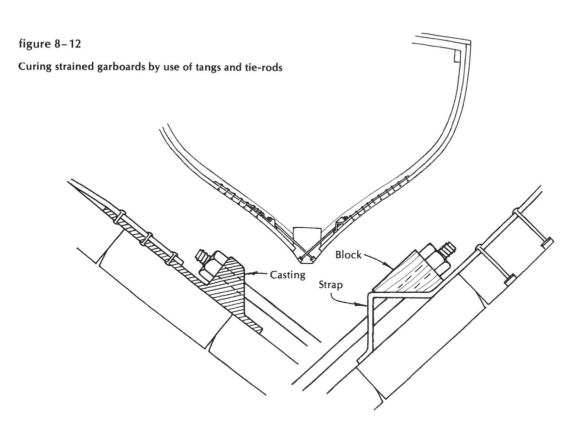

Block

Casting

Strap

Chapter Nine

The Planking Process: From the Sheer Down

So there she is, set up, timbered out, rabbet faired, ready for planking. *This* is the biggest single job, and probably the most difficult for the beginner—not because there's anything very complicated about it, but because much of it depends on judgment, eye, and the unconscious skill of hand that you gradually acquire without knowing it. The old pro loves to fit planks because he can do it without thinking, and it's his great talent, with a sort of timeless rhythm to it, which clothes and defines a thing of beauty.

What we're talking about here is, of course, real planking in the ancient, classical manner: fair-seamed, tapered, fitted and through-fastened to the timbers, smoothed fair, and caulked. Learn this, and you are welcome to try edge-nailed strips, battened seams, cold-molded laminates, or chicken-wire-and-fiberglass. (I hope you will sometime try a lapstrake job, because that is beautiful indeed.) But for now let's get on with the problems of smooth planking, which keeps the water out, and the people in, better than anything else I know of, and delineates (at least for you, the builder) the most beautiful shape that man has managed to create.

So, first, you need to know what shape the individual planks will be, before you worry about how to mark, cut, bevel, hang, and fasten them off. This boat we are dealing with is in some ways the most difficult and complicated shape one is likely to encounter, with wineglass sections throughout, great area below the tuck, extreme variations in girth, long counter, and plank ends mitered to the cylindrical-section transom, but that is all to the good. I'm sure that if I can explain it, you can understand it, and you may as well know the worst at the beginning. It's like swinging two bats when you come up to the plate.

Lining out the sheer planking

Well then. If you will allow yourself to view the hull of our 39-foot sloop in two distinct

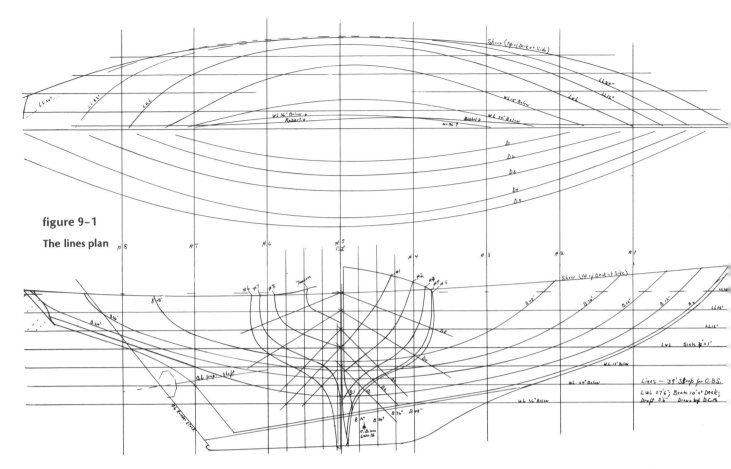

figure 9–1

The lines plan

parts, separated for our purposes approximately along diagonal D2 in Figure 9–1 (and if we're lucky, also along what has been referred to elsewhere as the tuck ribband), you will dimly discern that I have distinct approaches in mind for these areas. The areas, one above and the other below this ribband, are for our purposes completely independent of each other. Kindly ignore the lower one, and bear with me as I attempt to line out the planks that will clothe the area between this special ribband and the sheer.

The simplest way to do this (and entirely satisfactory, if you have skill and time enough) is to line out with a batten, by eye, the lower edge of the proposed sheerstrake, cut a plank to that shape, fasten it in place, and repeat the whole process over and over till you get there—in this case, to the flat of the bilge, where I hope you're planning to put in the shutter. This method is slow, laborious, and lends to irregularities, but it works.

I prefer a somewhat more precise system, which is based on the following assumptions: Ideally, all seams are to be fair curves from bow to stern; all planks are to taper exactly the same amounts from the widest point in the middle to their narrowest points forward and aft. Thus, if we have 17 planks, all exactly the same width on station number 5, we should have 17 planks exactly the same width at station number 3, and

at station number 7, and anywhere else in the length of the boat. This is a simple enough proposition. Find the length, find the girths at each section, divide these varying girths equally into the same number of parts, and you've got it—the shape of the Ideal Plank, which, repeated the proper number of times, will cover the area beautifully. What we want, then, is to get this information into precise, convenient, and graphic form, so that the man getting out planking can determine in a moment the exact width of any plank at any place in its length, at or between stations (e.g., proposed butts).

And the way we do it is thus: Measure the distances between stations along a sort of Great Circle course from stem to transom—say, along the ribband that lies between diagonals D4 and D5 on the body plan of the lines drawing. These dimensions will increase as you go away from the middle of the boat. Write them down thus:

Stem to #1	46″	#5 to #6	48″
#1 to #2	50″	#6 to #7	49½″
#2 to #3	49½″	#7 to #8	50″
#3 to #4	48½″	#8 to transom	53″
#4 to #5	48″		

Now find a clean board about 6 inches wide and 6 feet long, and joint one edge straight. Starting a few inches from one end, lay off these

90

figure 9-2

Plank layout by use of a diminish board

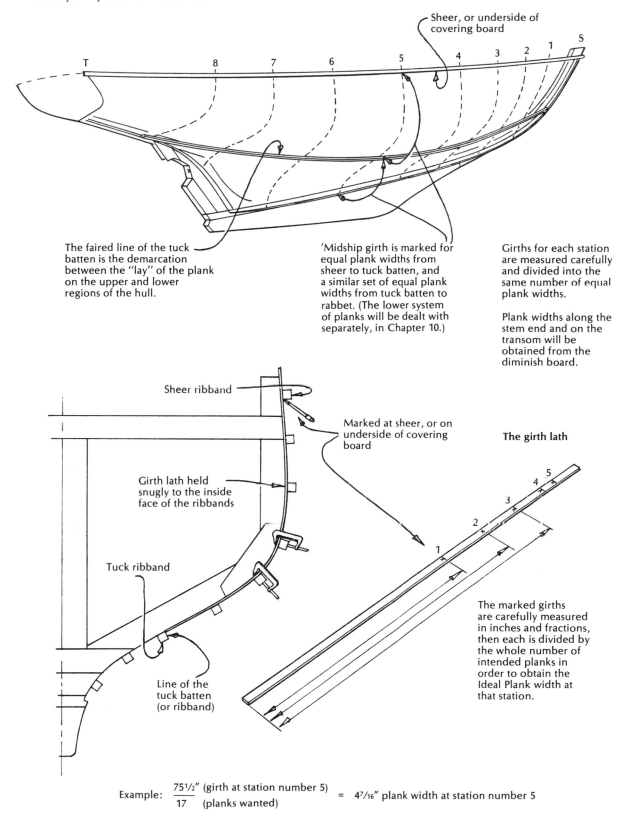

Sheer, or underside of covering board

T 8 7 6 5 4 3 2 1 S

The faired line of the tuck batten is the demarcation between the "lay" of the plank on the upper and lower regions of the hull.

'Midship girth is marked for equal plank widths from sheer to tuck batten, and a similar set of equal plank widths from tuck batten to rabbet. (The lower system of planks will be dealt with separately, in Chapter 10.)

Girths for each station are measured carefully and divided into the same number of equal plank widths.

Plank widths along the stem end and on the transom will be obtained from the diminish board.

Sheer ribband

Marked at sheer, or on underside of covering board

Girth lath held snugly to the inside face of the ribbands

Tuck ribband

Line of the tuck batten (or ribband)

The girth lath

5 4 3 2 1

The marked girths are carefully measured in inches and fractions, then each is divided by the whole number of intended planks in order to obtain the Ideal Plank width at that station.

Example: $\dfrac{75\frac{1}{2}" \text{ (girth at station number 5)}}{17 \text{ (planks wanted)}}$ = $4^{7}/_{16}"$ plank width at station number 5

figure 9–3

Plank layout by use of a diminish board

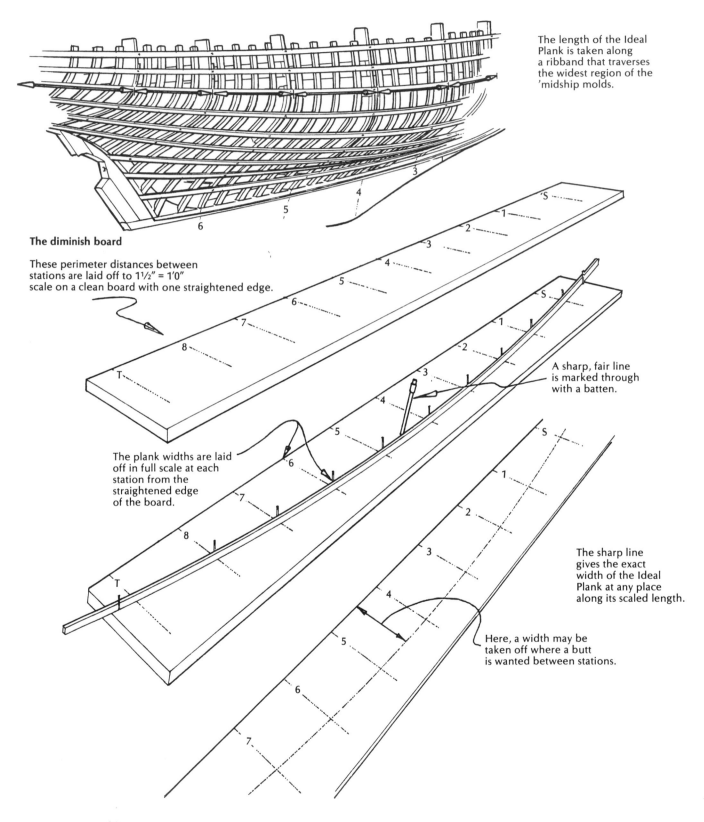

The length of the Ideal Plank is taken along a ribband that traverses the widest region of the 'midship molds.

The diminish board

These perimeter distances between stations are laid off to 1½" = 1'0" scale on a clean board with one straightened edge.

The plank widths are laid off in full scale at each station from the straightened edge of the board.

A sharp, fair line is marked through with a batten.

The sharp line gives the exact width of the Ideal Plank at any place along its scaled length.

Here, a width may be taken off where a butt is wanted between stations.

92

distances, consecutively, to a scale of 1 1/2 inches equals 1 foot (1/8 inch equals 1 inch), and label each mark clearly (and, of course, correctly). So you will end with a mark labeled "transom" exactly 4 feet 7 1/4 inches from your starting point labeled "stem."

Leave this board now and find a limber lath, about 1/8 inch thick, 3/4 inch wide, and 8 feet long. This is a marking stick to get the girths. As shown in Figure 9-2, bend it inside the ribbands, with its lower end resting on the top edge of the special tuck ribband, close alongside the number 5 mold and snug against the insides of the ribbands. Mark the lath exactly at the height of the sheer mark on the mold. Get the other six station girths in the same way, being very careful to measure exactly from the top of that critical ribband to the sheer mark. Don't get the labels mixed. You will have to do a bit of guesswork on station number 1, because the magic line has entered the rabbet before reaching the station mark; and the girths at the points called "stem" and "transom" cannot be measured at all.

Now measure the girths, subtract from each the thickness of the deck (1 inch in this example), and write down the results in inches and quarters. (For purposes of illustration, we're using only the girth at station number 5, which is the greatest, measuring 75 2/4 inches.)

It is now time to decide how many planks (and, of course, the maximum width of each one) are to be used to cover this space. A workable rule of thumb on widths goes like this: Maximum width of a plank should not be less than four nor more than five times the thickness of that plank. If we apply this rule here (based on 15/16-inch thickness of stock), we want no less than 4-inch width at station number 5, where the girth is greatest. A monumental effort in fourth-grade arithmetic indicates that 17 planks, each 4 7/16 inches wide, will come somewhere near to filling this gap. So we divide each of the six other girths by 17, to get the width of each plank at each station.

Now comes the moment of truth. Go back to the board with the intervals marked on it in 1 1/2 inches-to-the-foot scale. Draw a line square across the board at each station, stem, and transom mark. Now measure along each of these cross lines, from the straight edge of the board, the width of plank obtained in the process of dividing each corresponding girth by 17. Now we have a series of marks, arcing from station number 1 upward to greatest height at number 5 and back down to a mark on the ordinate

labeled number 8. Drive a small nail firmly at each of these points. Find a flawless pine or spruce batten about 1/2 inch square and 7 feet long. Bend it around inside, and touching, the vertical nails, and hold it against them with three or four nails driven snugly against the inside face of your batten. The result (see Figure 9-3) should be a fair convex curve, requiring no local forcing of the batten to make it touch all of the marks. If any great discrepancies show up (a point more than 1/4 inch away from the line the batten wants to follow), you'd better check your arithmetic. Pull down the ends of the batten beyond the number 1 and number 8 ordinates until it exerts no pressure at these two points, and accept its decision as to the correct widths at the end ordinates—stem and transom. When you are satisfied that the curve is correct and fair, mark a sharp line on the board the full length of the outside of the batten. Pull the nails, and there she is—the true width of the plank that, repeated 17 times between sheer and tuck, should fill the space watertight.

With this diminish board you can now determine the correct width of any plank at any point between the ordinates. Suppose a plank butt is to come in a bay whose center is 18 inches forward of station number 4. In the longitudinal scale used on the diminish board, 1/8 inch on your rule equals 1 inch on the full-sized hull; therefore, measure on the board 2 1/4 inches (18 divided by 8) from the number 4 ordinate toward number 3, and take at this point the correct width (from the edge of the board to the curved line) of the butt end of the plank you are marking.

Let's mark and fit a few, before we face the day of reckoning that awaits us when we must go down below—down to the garboard, and the stealers, and the awesome bevels in the tuck, where your knees give out, and you hang upside-down like a nuthatch on a fence, trying to think of some way to clamp and edge-set a plank that's too hot to handle anyway.

Fitting the forward port sheerstrake

Arm yourself with a handful of fivepenny box nails, scribers, a light hammer, a crosscut saw, a bevel gauge, a half-dozen C-clamps, and a spiling staff, which is a thin board, 4 to 8 inches wide and as long as the longest piece of planking stock you propose to use. If this spiling board has a gentle S-curve in its length, it will do fine for the forward planks on the topsides; aft of amidships you'll need one with a gentle

figure 9-4

Scribing the sheerline

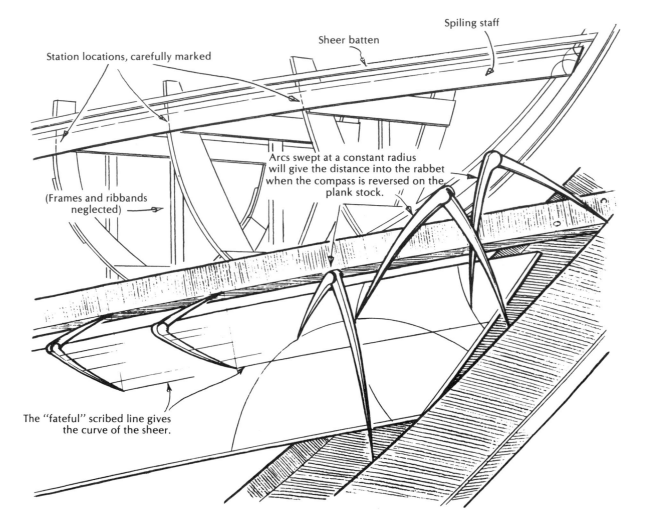

Station locations, carefully marked

Sheer batten

Spiling staff

Arcs swept at a constant radius
will give the distance into the rabbet
when the compass is reversed on the
plank stock.

(Frames and ribbands
neglected)

The "fateful" scribed line gives
the curve of the sheer.

concave curve the length of its top edge. Before you're through, you'll have short, narrow (and very thin) boards, which have been used and planed off and used again until you get to know them like old familiar faces. (I have one long, crooked cedar board that's been in use for 25 years, and it is so thin you can barely pick it up by the middle.)

Set up the staging planks on high horses, oil drums, what-have-you—so that the sheerline is waist- to shoulder-high on you. Tack a long, true batten to the stem, molds, and transom so that its lower edge delineates the exact line of the sheer.

Now get the spiling board into place—its forward end almost touching the rabbet and down 2 or 3 inches from the middle of the sheerline right up to the batten, and its after end probably too low. Try to adjust it (*without*

springing it edgewise) so that you can, with the dividers locked at one setting, run the whole length of it with a pencil line that will be equidistant at all points from the edge of the batten. (See Figure 9-4.) Before you draw the fateful line, however, be sure the patient is comfortable—twisted to lie snugly against the frames, relaxed all the way. (You want the sheerstrake to be *cut* to fit, not edge-bent to fit. With three or four strakes all around her—and under your belt, as it were—you can experiment with edge-setting as much as you want to; but get these binders on first.) Very well, then: Draw this line, representing the top edge of the sheerstrake, keeping the legs of your scribers at right angles to the line of the batten. Now, very precisely, note (on the spiling board) first, the extra distance to be added to the plank to reach the rabbet line; second, the location of all stations (molds) for the purpose of marking widths to the lower edge; third, the location of the butt. I like to start the sheerstrake from the stem with the longest plank available, for reasons that will be apparent shortly.

So now, as shown in Figures 9–4 and 9–5, we have on the spiling board the exact curvature of the top edge of the sheerstrake, from the stem rabbet to the butt, carefully marked in the middle of a bay some 20 feet aft of the stem; and we have notations of the locations of all the molds so far covered. This, with the diminish board, provides all the information we need. Therefore we can now take off the clamps, carry the spiling board tenderly to the three horses where lies the raw plank (1 inch by 10 inches by 21 feet, probably mahogany), and mark the shape of the forward half of the sheerstrake, port side.

Set your dividers at about ¼ inch greater span than was used to mark the line on the spiling board. Use this span as a guide in placing the spiling board on the stock, and then, with the sharp leg of the dividers on the line, swing short arcs with the pencil end on the stock. Do this at 12-inch to 18-inch intervals along the entire length of the line you're transferring (see Figure 9–5). Now mark on the new plank all the other information you've got on the spiling board: the exact spot where the top edge of the plank will hit the rabbet line at the stem; the location of each station where the plank will cross it; and the location of the butt-

cut (which will, of course, come midway in the farthest-aft bay that the plank will reach). Now put the spiling board aside, and drive a nail (fivepenny box, one tap) at the top of each of the short arcs you marked. Bend a batten against these nails (see Figure 9–6), and you should be able to draw a line along it exactly parallel to the one on the spiling board, and representing the top edge of the sheerstrake. Now get from the diminish board the exact widths indicated at each of the stations marked on the plank; lay off these widths, and the width at the butt (obtained by scaling to the right spot on the diminish board, and measuring directly from it); tap in a nail at each mark, lay the batten to them, and draw a line, which will be the bottom edge of the sheerstrake.

And now to cut this plank. The men of old did it with a hand ripsaw, and no fuss about it. Some moderns use a big bandsaw with a wide blade that won't wander. Others use an electric-powered circular handsaw, which you very likely possess—and a very good way this is, too, if you can follow the line accurately, freehand, or will take the trouble to tack a guide-batten at exactly the right distance from the line to be sawn. I use this last system if I'm dealing with a plank more than 24 feet long. But for anything shorter than that (and it can be very curved indeed) I always use the old slow tablesaw, with an 8-inch or 10-inch blade, and a wide extension table stretching away beyond it for 16 feet—and,

figure 9–5

Laying out spiling on plank stock

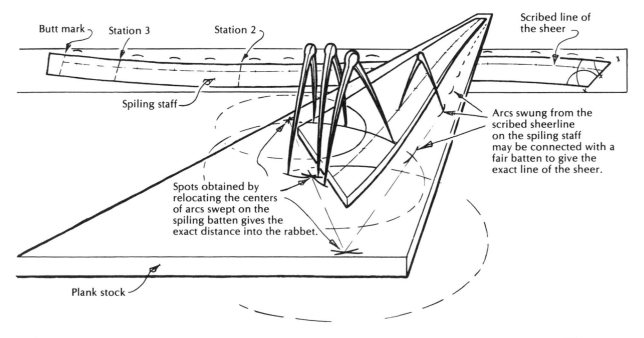

Butt mark   Station 3   Station 2

Scribed line of the sheer

Spiling staff

Arcs swung from the scribed sheerline on the spiling staff may be connected with a fair batten to give the exact line of the sheer.

Spots obtained by relocating the centers of arcs swept on the spiling batten gives the exact distance into the rabbet.

Plank stock

figure 9–6

Sheerstrake, ready to cut

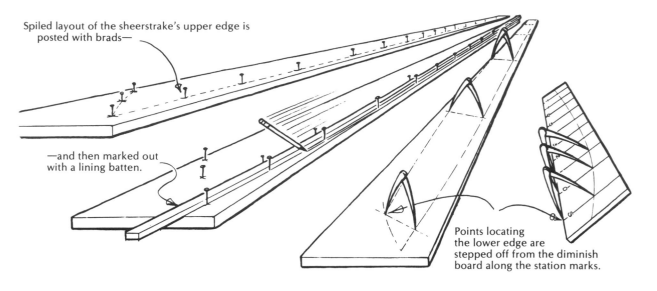

Spiled layout of the sheerstrake's upper edge is posted with brads—

—and then marked out with a lining batten.

Points locating the lower edge are stepped off from the diminish board along the station marks.

of course, a roller 8 feet in front of the saw and a support 10 feet beyond that. With a little practice, a sharp saw properly set, and relaxed confidence, you can with this system make a smooth, fair cut very quickly and with great precision. Do not shrug this off with the thought that you'll cut safely outside the line anyway, and work it down to size with your plane. Maybe you can afford the time and the muscle, but you must be highly skilled indeed to end up with a curve as fair as the curve that this saw can cut for you—right to the edge of the pencil line, needing only one pass with a good plane from end to end of the plank. So learn to saw a line, and learn to set and file that saw. And never, *never* fasten a plank on a boat if it has humps and hollows on its exposed edge. That way madness lies....

Go ahead then, and cut. Dress off the lower edge fair and true—and square. With your bevel gauge, get the angle between the sheer batten and the rabbet at the stem, mark and cut the forward end of the plank, and STOP right there, curb your eagerness, and go mark out an exact mirror duplicate of this port plank. But do not cut out this twin plank until you've tried the first one in place.

Now's the great moment. Pick up the plank about at its balance point, lay it up against the frames, and move it horizontally until the nearest station mark lines up with the corresponding mold. Clamp it to the nearest frame, with the top edge ¾ inch below the batten; go forward,

and swing the end in to the stem. If it's within ½ inch of the rabbet, clamp it lightly to the forewardmost frame, then to the stem; go back and lightly clamp the after end (beyond the buttmark, if it reaches) at the right height under the sheer batten. Tap the butt end with a heavy hammer, gently, until the forward end fetches into the rabbet. Beware that it has not slid up the slope of the stem beyond its proper height. (For deck thickness, remember?) If it's a good fit in the rabbet, tight inside all the way and showing a ¹⁄₁₆-inch outgauge, clamp it tight. If the fit is not good, swing the end out and plane it as necessary. Swing back and clamp; tap ahead again; proceed to put a clamp on every frame, being very careful to keep that top edge at its proper distance below the sheer batten. When planking from the sheer down, I always put the clamps on the forward face of the frame, under the plank, and inside out—that is, with the threaded part inside the boat. This arrangement keeps them out of the way of the fastenings, which are always staggered according to a fixed pattern—the lower one toward the after edge of the frame, the upper one forward. Do not try to get away with any shortcuts, such as clamping to every other frame, because the two laminations of the frame must be snug together, and the face of the plank must be tight to the frame, before a screw-fastening can be put in properly.

Fastening the sheerstrake

All set, then? Get out your ½-inch counterbore, with a tapered drill to fit 2-inch number 14 screws, and proceed to fasten off, ¾ inch up from the bottom edge and 1 inch down from the top. Counterbore about ⁵⁄₁₆ inch deep—no more. This act will do things for your morale, and you have to get those clamps free before you can do anything else, anyway. (The principal difference between a professional and an amateur boatbuilder, I think, is not that one does a better job than the other, or gets more for his pains, but simply that the pro has finally managed to acquire almost enough clamps, and has been forced by bitter necessity to learn more ways of making them work.) You will have come up against this truth while struggling to get that forward end tightly in place without hopelessly obscuring the target that your drill must hit.

And why, you may ask, did we fasten this plank with screws, when we're supposed to be using copper rivets? Simply for this reason: When you come to bolt through the sheerstrake and the frame heads to hold the sheer clamp in place, you'll find that about half the bolts will go best where you've already driven plank fastenings. Screws you can take out, to make way.

Right now, before you forget it, mark on this sheerstrake with bright red chalk the bays where the chainplates will go (see Figure 9-7). This is sacred ground, and no plank butts can be allowed to happen hereabouts until you're down at least eight strakes.

figure 9-7

Butts mated by use of the severed end

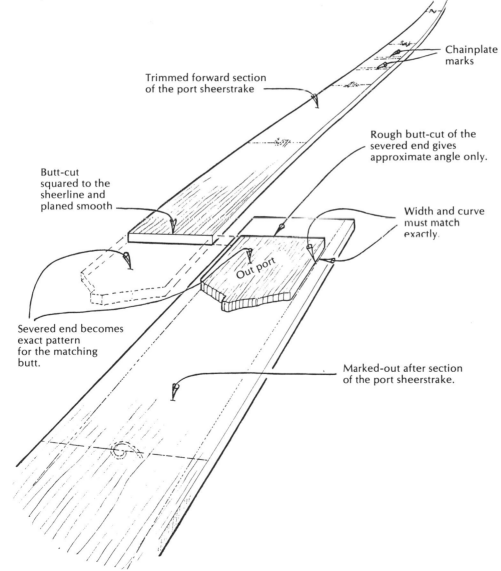

Trimmed forward section of the port sheerstrake

Chainplate marks

Rough butt-cut of the severed end gives approximate angle only.

Butt-cut squared to the sheerline and planed smooth

Width and curve must match exactly.

Out port

Severed end becomes exact pattern for the matching butt.

Marked-out after section of the port sheerstrake.

figure 9-8

Fitting sheerstrake to transom

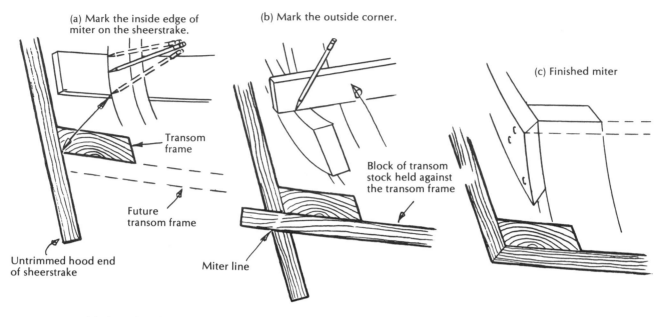

(a) Mark the inside edge of miter on the sheerstrake.

(b) Mark the outside corner.

(c) Finished miter

Transom frame

Future transom frame

Untrimmed hood end of sheerstrake

Miter line

Block of transom stock held against the transom frame

Fitting the aft port sheerstrake

Ignore, now, the temptation of that twin plank all marked to cut, and make ready to fit the after part of the port sheerstrake, as shown in Figure 9-7. I hope that the plank you have just fastened on extends at least 6 inches beyond the butt-cut (to be cut square with the top edge, up from the lower edge, with a sharp handsaw) that you are about to make. This waste end is your secret weapon. Mark it "out port" and save it. Now clamp a spiling board from the butt to and beyond the transom frame (I'm assuming that you have stock long enough to make the distance in one piece), and repeat all the business you went through on the forward plank: scribe for the top edge; mark the station locations and the after end at the transom; indicate the exact distance to the butt from the end of your spiling board; transfer all this information to the piece from which the plank will be cut; lay off the widths, for the bottom edge curve, from the diminish board; and finally, lay that "out port" waste piece on the marks just as it would have overlapped the new plank if it had not been sawn off. This waste piece gives you the exact width and, more important, the exact curvature of both edges that the new plank must have to match the first one. You also get from it, theoretically at least, the right line to saw for this matching butt end. You will use this trick over and over as you continue the planking, so you'd best get it clear in your mind right now. This is the most useful of all aids in getting the butts fair; and if you think that's an easy thing to do, or not very important anyway, just you wait until you've had to work a real humpy one down with a rabbet plane, and then tried to fit the next plank to the irregular curve and the out-of-square edge that you ended up with. If you're going to get clear around her with a strake a day, from now on you can't afford to have those curves anything but fair and sweet from end to end.

Having settled this, let's hang the plank. Shave the butt end to fit tight, clamp along and swing in to the transom frame, get the top edge on the marks, and look at the butt. Chances are two to one that the fit is not perfect. So run your well-set crosscut saw up the joint, go aft, and tap the plank ahead. Repeat until the joint is airtight; then mark at the transom frame for the miter cut (see Figure 9-8a). The inner line will obviously lie along the outer edge of the transom frame; the outer line is determined by laying a piece of 15/16-inch stock against the transom frame, under your plank end, and marking where the outside surfaces of each intersect (Figure 9-8b). If this isn't clear, to hell with it. Anyway, the cut will be roughly at 90 degrees to a tangent to the transom frame at the edge (Figure 9-8c). And be *sure* that the plank is really at the right height on the transom (you can sight from the plane of the cross spalls, and measure up to the height given in the offsets) before marking. Probably you'd best take the whole plank off again before you make this cut, because it's a very awkward thing to do (what with your hand trembling, and your eyes trying to see both sides of the plank at once), and the plank may need just the least bit of backing out at its after end. "Backing out" means hollowing (or, down in the wineglass sections, rounding off) the inner face of the plank to lie snugly for its entire width against the curved frame. You can use a short bit of ¼-inch-square lead bar, bent to the right curve, as a guide in the hollowing process, or you can use the guess-and-try method, which works fairly well after you've practiced for a few years.

And oh, my friend, if you value your sanity, do not forget to mark out a twin to this plank before you fasten it in place. I have seen a man jump on his hat and knock off for the day when he remembered this too late. Have you corrected the bevel on the transom frame where the plank lands? All right, then: clamp it in place again, and fasten off.

Fitting a butt block

We've still got the butt block to fit. I'm beginning to wonder if we'll ever get a sheerstrake clear around her.

The butt block should be a piece of black locust (or white oak, black walnut, or even dense mahogany) overlapping the adjacent planks, above and below, by about ⅜ inch, and with ends about that much short of touching the frames forward and aft of the butt. The block should be little, if any, thicker than the plank stock, and it should be fitted exactly to the hollow and twist of the inner surface of the planking. Hold it in place with C-clamps inside-out on the high corners; drill for three fastenings in each end, 1 inch back from the butt, and two more in each plank, a third of the way in from the edges and halfway from butt to frame (see Figure 9-9). Drill for 1¾-inch number 14 screws, counterbored 5/16 inch deep, for the end fastenings, and for number 8 copper rivets to take the back ones. Ream those end holes (through the planks only) with a ¼-inch drill, lest you start to split. And now take the clamps off, soak the contact surfaces and the ends of the block with strong poison, reclamp, and fasten. By now you'll know why butts cost money, and why the pros like to use long stock.

Getting out more planking

Now for "out, starboard, forward," which has been waiting all this while. Saw it out, run your plane the length of the lower edge (if the shaving breaks, find out why), and go to the pile of planking stock. Choose a piece 3 or 4 feet shorter than the one you've just shaped, and proceed to mark the *top* edge of this second plank from the *bottom* edge of your sheerstrake. Lay off the widths to match the sheerstrake widths, line out the bottom edge with a batten, and saw out. Dress off the edges fair, mark a twin; then use the lower edge of this second plank to mark the top edge of yet a third one, which will be short enough to butt perhaps two bays forward of the forward chainplate. Repeat the process to get the line of the lower edge, saw out and mark the twin. Now you have five planks ready to bevel, back out, hang, and fasten, all on the strength of the original spiling. This is Proliferation. If you could only mark those after planks the same way, life would be beautiful. It is not entirely ridiculous

figure 9–9

Butt block

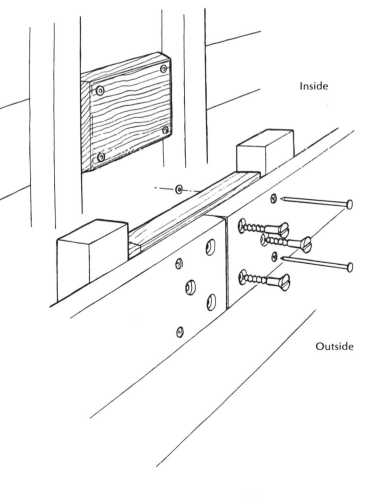

Inside

Outside

figure 9–10

Seam bevels

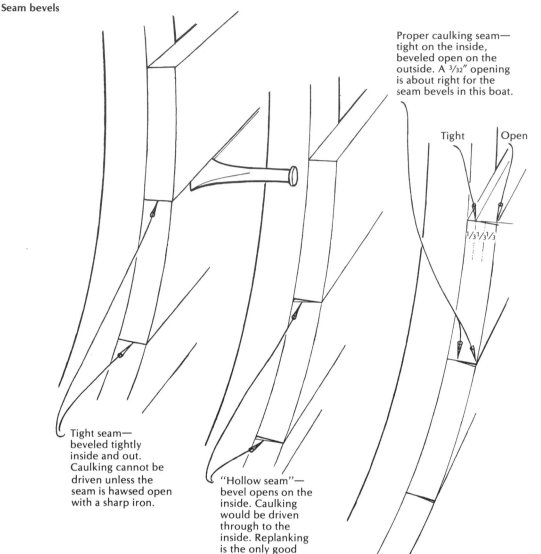

Proper caulking seam—tight on the inside, beveled open on the outside. A ³/₃₂″ opening is about right for the seam bevels in this boat.

Tight   Open

¹/₃¹/₃¹/₃

Tight seam—beveled tightly inside and out. Caulking cannot be driven unless the seam is hawsed open with a sharp iron.

"Hollow seam"—bevel opens on the inside. Caulking would be driven through to the inside. Replanking is the only good solution.

to hope, however, that after you have finished these three strakes all around (spiling for each of the after ones—the second and third of which will be in two lengths each), you can take another long spiling from forward, and go through the whole happy business all over again.

But right now, with a plank ready to go next to another plank, you are faced with two important problems: First, how to fit the seam; and second, how to squeeze the two together while you fasten the second one in place. At this stage, high on the topsides, both jobs are relatively easy to do; but the techniques are basic, and you may as well learn the whole business now as wait until things become more complicated.

Seam bevels

In beveling, what you're aiming for is to have all the seams open the same widths on the outside, and light-tight on the inside (see Figure 9-10). Ideally, with planking of this thickness, the opening for caulking should not be over ¹/₈ inch anywhere on the boat, and preferably a bit less than that. A joint that is tight both outside and in can be caulked, and is forgivable but not to be praised. A joint that is tight on the outside and open inside is a terrible thing in the sight of God and man, and can never be forgiven. (Judged on these grounds, and others, of course, very few of us old pros can hope for much in the Hereafter, but there's a very slick system of caulking a seam endwise that sure worked *wonders* on the last shutter I fitted.)

To proceed: the bottom edge of the sheer-strake was left exactly square, as it came from the saw. I always leave the open edge of every plank square, and do all the beveling on the edge of the plank that is to fit against it. Therefore, since the frames are practically straight up here, you need only plane a uniform outgauge of about 3/32 inch the whole length, and the seam should be right. But before we go through the business of edge-setting this plank into place, let's consider the more complicated situations that will soon arise, and how to handle them.

Look now to Figure 9-11, which shows two cross sections: one from the sheerstrake down past the turn of the bilge, and the other through the reversed bend in way of the tuck. This drawing is not to scale, and merely illustrates the general characteristics of the plank seams in these two areas. Working down from the sheer, then, we see that plank number 2 in the drawing must be beveled off on the outer edge to about 87 degrees. The third plank, landing where the frame has begun to curve, needs no bevel at all, either way, at this point. But the fourth one needs cutting down on the *inside* edge, in order to keep the seam uniform with those above it. This need for ingauge, reverse bevel, or whatever you want to call it, increases progressively as we approach the hardest part of the bilge curve, reaching a maximum of 16 degrees (106 degrees minus 90 degrees) on the top edge of plank number 6. The bevel starts the other way on plank number 7—and by the time you've gotten down on the flat, you'll be back to the 87-degree outgauge that was necessary on plank number 2.

Now consider the other half of Figure 9-11—the section through the tuck. We plank *up* from the garboard, leaving the top edge of each plank square as we fit it, making the planks narrower (and out of slightly thicker stock, if we have it) as we come into the quick turn. The cutback of the *outer* edge reaches a maximum of 23 degrees (90 degrees minus 67 degrees) on the lower edge of number 17, which of course is fitted to the square top edge of number 18. (Remember that these planks are entirely fictitious, and are not intended to bear any except family resemblance to actual planks.) Now, the painful part of all this is that the bevel on any given plank must be constantly changing, from bow to stern, if the seams are to be constant, uniform, and caulkable. Therefore you've got to learn to take bevels, and develop a feel in your planing hand so

figure 9-11

Plank bevels—from inguage to outgauge

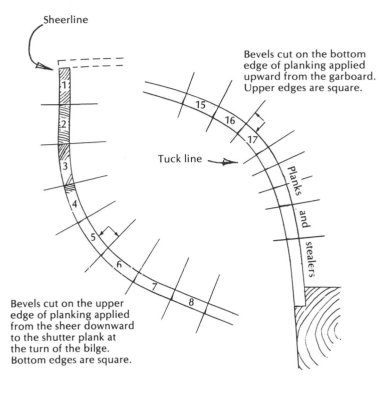

Sheerline

Bevels cut on the bottom edge of planking applied upward from the garboard. Upper edges are square.

Tuck line

Planks and stealers

Bevels cut on the upper edge of planking applied from the sheer downward to the shutter plank at the turn of the bilge. Bottom edges are square.

that you can roll the bevel from one spot to the next without abrupt transitions. You'll do a lot of cutting and trying to the first few planks you fit. (I'm still doing a lot of cutting and trying, after some 40 years of it, but I'm beginning to catch on.) The problem hasn't changed in 2,000 years, which is one of the things that make boatbuilding a fascinating business.

Pay no attention to that business with degrees, and make yourself a planker's bevel (see Figure 9-12). Take a bevel every 2 feet, and mark the angle on your bevel board.

Cheating with the spiling batten

If you are not using good crooked round-edged boat boards, which provide shapes to match your spilings, then you must be using straightedged stock—medium widths from 6 to 12 inches, say, with 8-inch and 10-inch boards making up most of the batch—and you'll be shocked, if not dismayed, at the curves you must fit to. If they are cut to precise shape, they will run to terrible waste and too many butts; therefore, you can be allowed some discreet cheating. Bend them edgewise—but not too much. Let the spiling batten do the thinking for you. Use one about 4 inches wide and not too shaggy, so that it will bend edgewise evenly; force it up in the middle, tenderly, and clamp it in place. Set your scribers to the widest necessary gap, and mark the line; if you run off the edge before you get to the ends, reset the scribers to just under the end widths of the batten, and mark these inner lines at the ends, overlapping the original line. As shown in Figure 9–13, mark on the batten, exactly, the two settings you've used, even though the overlapping lines will show how much alteration must be made when you shift from the wide gap to the narrow one. Now, when you place the spiling batten on the stock to be marked, spring its middle slightly *down*,

thereby making the top-edge line (which you are about to transfer, with your little arcs at 18-inch intervals) yet more nearly straight than it appears on the unsprung batten. The batten has recorded and allowed for the stresses that the plank will undergo—and kept the bending mostly within the middle third of its length, so that the ends, which can't be forced much anyway, are cut very nearly true to the actual shape required.

And don't forget to mark (on the new plank) where the butt comes on the one above it. This is the doubtful part of the curve, and should be laid out with care. And after you get one of these sprung on, put on the burrs and head up the

figure 9–12

Taking bevels

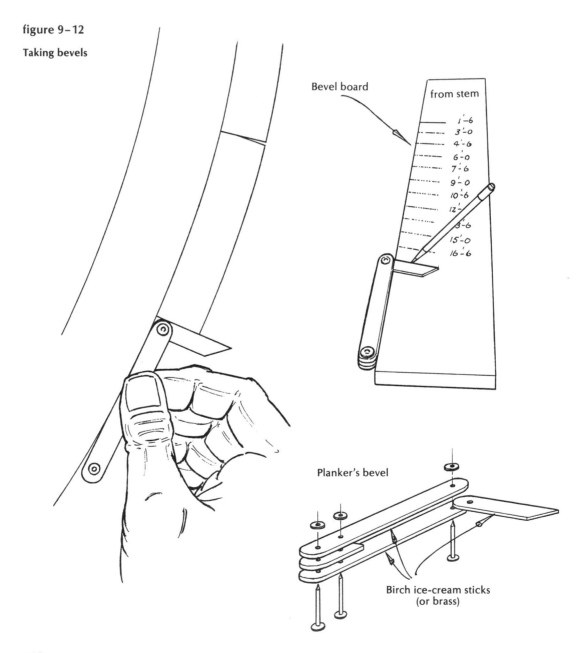

Bevel board

from stem

1′-6
3′-0
4′-6
6′-0
7′-6
9′-0
10′-6
12′-
3′-6
15′-0
16′-6

Planker's bevel

Birch ice-cream sticks
(or brass)

figure 9-13

Edge-setting the spiling batten to get a
more comfortable fit of edge-set plank

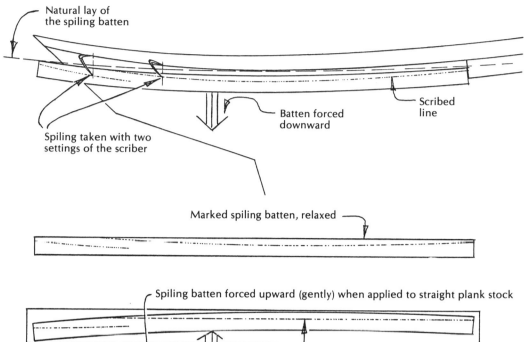

Natural lay of
the spiling batten

Batten forced
downward

Scribed
line

Spiling taken with two
settings of the scriber

Marked spiling batten, relaxed

Spiling batten forced upward (gently) when applied to straight plank stock

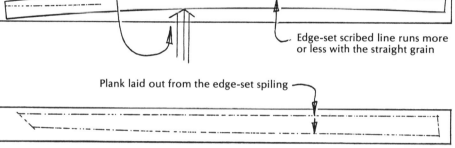

Edge-set scribed line runs more
or less with the straight grain

Plank laid out from the edge-set spiling

Edge-set fitted plank has minimal cross grain.
Ends are well fitted and relaxed.

rivets on the lower edge, or it will try to make itself look like a clapboard when you drive the fastenings into the next one below. If you don't want to take time for this riveting, or can't find a victim to hold the dolly, fasten the lower edge with screws. Quiet your conscience with the thought that a few days in the good salt water will relax that plank as if it had grown there.

It would be cruel to interrupt at this point, when everything is going well, and suggest that you shift to the garboard. So go ahead and plank her down to the flat of the deadrise. And if you go one plank too far, where it's starting to turn the other way, you'll be sorry. Shutters are bad enough, even with everything in your favor.

One other thing. As you sit inside the hull in the late afternoon, admiring the graceful sweep of the planking, you will suddenly note with horror that some of those seams, light-tight (or nearly so) when you fitted them, now look, against the window, wide enough so you could recognize friends passing by—even though, when you examine them closely, you can't get a thumbnail into the crack. I remember Sam Crocker on this subject, back in the 1930s, when I'd been trying, unsuccessfully, to keep him away from the dark side of the boat. "I know these seams are all right, and *you* know they're all right, but *please* get a little cotton into 'em before the owner shows up, because *He Doesn't Know Anything.*" So we did.

Chapter Ten

The Planking Process: From the Garboard Up

Now that the upper part of the hull is planked, it's time to plank up the bottom, starting with the lowermost plank called the garboard.

Put aside the diminish board, grab a batten, flex your knees, and get down where you can contemplate that section of boat below the tuck ribband. Now, you could close in this section with planks that run thus—narrow enough so that they can easily be shaped to fit the hollow of the wineglass, and not too hard to fit (see Figure 10-1).

It's perhaps worth noting that the German-built Concordia yawls and the Swedish Folkboats are lined out thus, and they must be acknowledged as splendid jobs of boatbuilding. I won't bring arguments for or against this narrow-plank approach except to say that if the work is done perfectly, this system is satisfactory; but if it is not done perfectly, somebody is going to have a bad time a few years later trying to recaulk those frail, sharp ends where they run out on the keel rabbet. Of course, the great Nat Herreshoff used to build this whole thing up out of deadwood, spring a colossal batten keel to the top of it, and start the planking from there—and his boats are still doing very nicely, thank you, some 40 or 50 years after they were put together.

But we are going to do this my way, and let the chips fall where they may.

Plank layout, using stealers

Suppose we draw the map again, and this time divide it into four equal tapering strips (see Figure 10-2). What could be simpler than to fit four planks to these lines, and be done with it? Well, one trouble is that the planks would be unnecessarily narrow at the forward end, with four thin and hard-to-caulk ends running out in the rabbet. The more serious difficulty, however, is that the three upper planks at least would be impossibly wide from station number 3 aft; and if you shaped them out of 3-inch stock, they would still not fit into that reversed curve, as you can tell (see Figure 10-3).

If you make them one-half that width, you can get them out of 1¼-inch stock; and if you make them one-fourth the width, you can use standard 1-inch lumber. (You will, I hope, have held out 60 to 80 board feet, random widths and lengths, of good fat ones when the rest of the planking stock went through the surface planer.)

The problem, then, is to have fewer planks

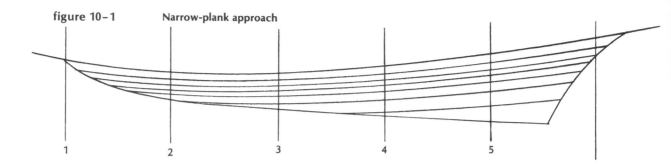

figure 10-1   Narrow-plank approach

at the forward end (two, each 4½-inches wide at station number 2) and at least twice as many aft, where the hollow is greatest. You can accomplish this proliferation by fitting stealers, or by a system of butting two against one, or by a combination of the two devices. I know that some experts—naval architects among them—think of "stealer" as a bad word, connoting shiftiness, if not incompetence, in the builder, and a thing not to be tolerated in real yacht work. Chances are good that they feel the same way about flat frames and wrought-iron fastenings. If you agree with the experts, line her out any way you want to; otherwise, let's get at it.

Draw the picture again, and start with the garboard; but this time let its top edge (back to the first bay forward of station number 3) be the next line up—halfway from rabbet to ribband. The remainder of the garboard can be left as drawn, because we are not yet up to the region of great curvature. So the second plank becomes a stealer, starting at S1 (see Figure 10-4), proceeding normally for 4 feet, and there (at S2) being cut down to half its width—which it retains all the way back to the sternpost. Its missing upper half is filled in with stealer S2, which in turn goes to the sternpost.

Now start another plank from forward—full width up to your ribband line, and aft to the first bay aft of station number 2—where we cut it down to half width, get the bay aft of number 3, and halve it again—running this line all the way aft. Fill up with stealer S3, which goes to the sternpost in a fair line and

represents the middle of the third plank as originally drawn.

Now we are up in difficult territory, where we need really narrow planks to fit that quick turn in the tuck.

Start again at the bay aft of station number 2, go back to the bay forward of number 4, and halve it—running this line fair to the sternpost. This is the top edge of the number 3 plank. Start the new stealer at S5, halve it at S6 (the bay midway between number 4 and number 5), and go aft. Finally, fit the last stealer, from S6 aft. So, you end up with eight planks at the sternpost. If the greatest girth aft (from the rabbet on the keel to the line of the ribband between number 5 and number 6) is 36 inches, then theoretically the garboard at this point is 9 inches wide; the next five planks are each 4½ inches wide; and the remaining two are each 2¼ inches wide. I assure you that I'm almost as confused as you are at this point, and I suspect that the pattern I have described is slightly more complicated than the one I followed when I planked this particular boat. You should, however, be able to figure out, from the above, the general scheme of attack.

This is as good a place as any to discuss the shifting of butts. First, there's the classical, by-the-book pattern, which usually goes thus—"Butts on adjacent strakes to be separated by not less than three bays; butts in the same bay to be separated by at least three planks"—and there it stops. How many bays between if there's a strake between, or two strakes between? The commonsense approach is to scatter them

figure 10-2   Four equal tapering strips

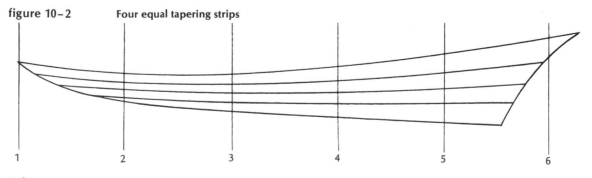

as widely as you can, with the lengths of stock you've got, and still keep them in the region of least twist. Fit and fasten the butt blocks as if your life depended on their integrity, as indeed it may. Down below the tuck they must be hollowed precisely to fit the round and twist of the inner face of the planks. The butt blocks at the stealer ends should be wider than normal, to spread the load over more area. And if you meet a butt that really fights back, fasten it with 1/4-inch bronze carriage bolts at the ends. Counterbore for the heads as little as you dare (not enough for proper bunging), and fill them flush with a proper filler. One final word: *Always* caulk butts...even if they fit so beautifully that you can't see the joint, and it seems a crime to touch them with an iron. If they're not caulked, and filled flush with seam compound, they will inevitably show a hairline crack in the paint, full width of the butt joint, before the summer's ended. You will undoubtedly be using some modern miracle seam filler that has 50- or 80- or 100-percent elasticity guaranteed forevermore, but the grim mathematical truth still stands: 100 percent of nothing is still nothing. Bear this in mind when bedding rails, molding, winches. Don't try to squeeze the compound all out the first time around. Let it set a day or two, maybe, and then tighten up fastenings and clean off the sticky stuff. It's a sad, strange truth that most yacht owners aren't very bright about such matters. They get far more excited about a few beads and blobs in sight than they do about a complete absence of sealer where it ought to be.

Fitting the garboard plank

You can make the garboard in one piece, if you have a good, tough plank 10 inches or wider at the butt end, and 33 feet long. If you have to do it in two lengths, that's all right too, as long as you fit the butt block properly. Clean

best 20-foot spiling board, and clamp it into place, tapping it and gentling it, slacking off and readjusting, until it settles down in complete comfort, and within scriber distance of the rabbet, of course (see Figure 10-5). Draw that line with the scribers plumb vertical (beware as you go up the curve at the forward end, lest you relax into an attitude at right angles to the line of the rabbet) and put all pertinent information on the board before you move it: the exact locations of all station marks, the bay where the stealer starts, and the required widths at 2-to 4-foot intervals. Since this garboard is to fill one-fourth of the space to be covered, the arithmetic involved isn't too complicated, even for me. You can, if you wish, tack a cross staff at the after end to mark the line of the cut to the sternpost rabbet; be sure at least to indicate the spot on your spiling board that corresponds exactly with the after end of the keel rabbet. And if the spiling does not reach all the way to the stern rabbet, don't worry. We'll take another way. (See Figure 10-6.)

Place the spiling board on the stock, and be very careful to leave enough room at the after end to reach the sternpost rabbet all the way up. Transfer the line as usual; transfer notations of widths, and mark exactly on the line the locations of station numbers 1 and 2. Now, mark, cut, and fit an exact pattern (out of thin pine, 1/4 inch by 6 inches, and about 6 feet long) for the forward end of the garboard, starting somewhere between station numbers 1 and 2, and reaching a bit higher on the stem rabbet than the proposed top of the garboard. This will be good practice, and it will teach you, painfully, the importance of holding those scribers exactly plumb at all times. Now, while this pattern is still tacked in place, mark station number 1 on its lower edge, to correspond exactly with the same mark on your original spiling, and on the plank you've started to lay out. Lay the pattern to the line, station marks

figure 10-3

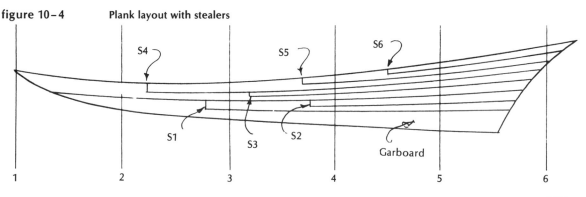

figure 10-4   **Plank layout with stealers**

107

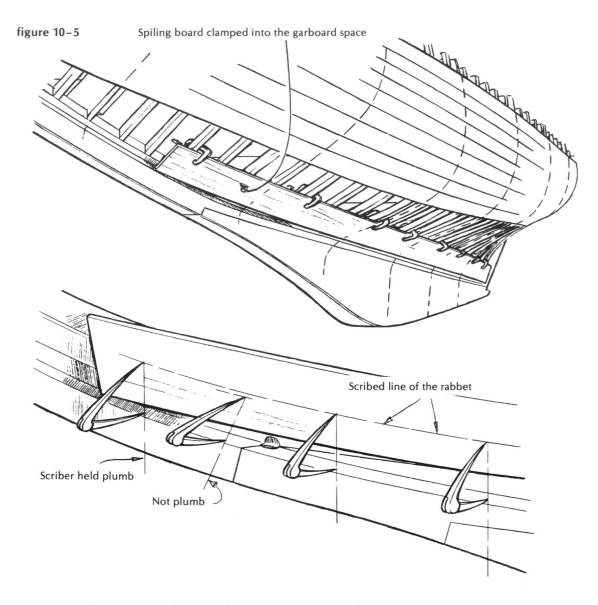

figure 10-5   Spiling board clamped into the garboard space

Scribed line of the rabbet

Scriber held plumb

Not plumb

together, and mark around it to finish out the shape of the forward end of the garboard in the rabbet. Lay off the widths to the top edge and mark; then saw out (probably using a hand ripsaw on the last 3 feet at the forward end, lower edge) and plane the top edge, leaving it square. Take the bevels and dress off the lower edge accordingly, and mark a twin to this one before you move another damned inch. Try to round off the inside face of the plank to fit the reverse curve of the frames...say a short prayer, and try her on. If the stock is good, tough wood, not too terribly dry, it will go on cold—that is, without preliminary steaming. If it seems determined never to submit or yield, cook the after 10 or 12 feet for half an hour. (I'm assuming that your steam box, like mine, is too short to take the whole length.) Clamp it any way you can think of, in and down, using bar clamps

aft, hooked into a bolt-hole counterbore under the forefoot; a stick-and-clamp system to get the lower edge tight against the back rabbet; edge-sets and wedges to tighten down where nothing else will work. Don't be afraid to give her a tunk with a big hammer now and then. Does wonders for the fit.

Unless you are very good indeed, or very lucky, there'll be a few spots in this plank where the fit could be improved. Probably the garboard seam shows tight on the outside, in places, and you don't know how much gap there may be on the inside. The after end, which lies in the rabbet on the sternpost, may not present a good consistent seam, or may be reluctant to go all the way in because the back rabbet needs fairing off. And the inner face of the plank will likely need more rounding off at the top, to allow good contact with the frames and the back rabbet on the keel. Spend plenty of time analyzing, marking, and describing (on the face of the plank) these necessary corrections; take the plank off, and make the alterations.

Inside stopwaters

Have you put in the inner stopwaters, where the rabbet crosses the joint between the keel and the sternpost, and between the keel and the forefoot? If not, do it now. The plank might fit, this time. I always install these inside stopwaters with the thought that (1) they are assumed by all yacht designers to be infallible; (2) they may do some good, at that; and (3) they can't do any harm. Then, after the planking is on and caulked, I put another set in, right through the center of the true rabbet line, and cut off flush with the outside of the planking. Caulk right across the ends, and *that* joint shouldn't weep. (See Figure 10-7.)

To put in stopwaters, then: use a sharp spur auger, 1/2 inch diameter, with a good worm that will follow the seam. Start right up against the center face of the rabbet, bore through until the

figure 10-6

End shape of the garboard established by template

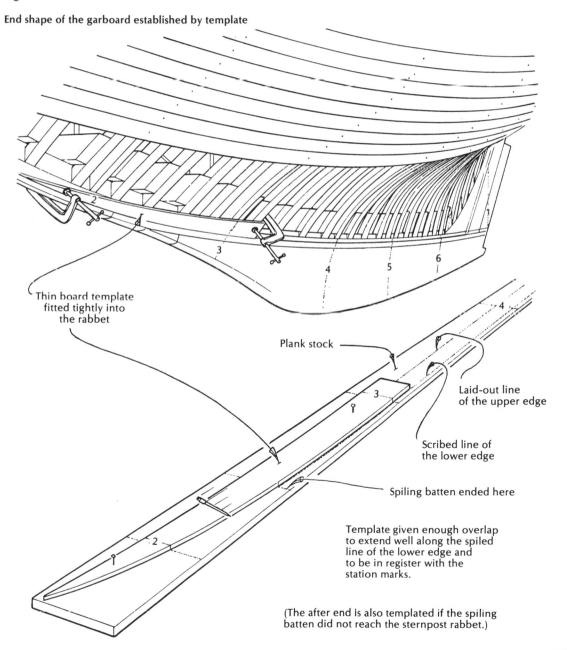

Thin board template fitted tightly into the rabbet

Plank stock

Laid-out line of the upper edge

Scribed line of the lower edge

Spiling batten ended here

Template given enough overlap to extend well along the spiled line of the lower edge and to be in register with the station marks.

(The after end is also templated if the spiling batten did not reach the sternpost rabbet.)

figure 10-7

Installing inside stopwaters

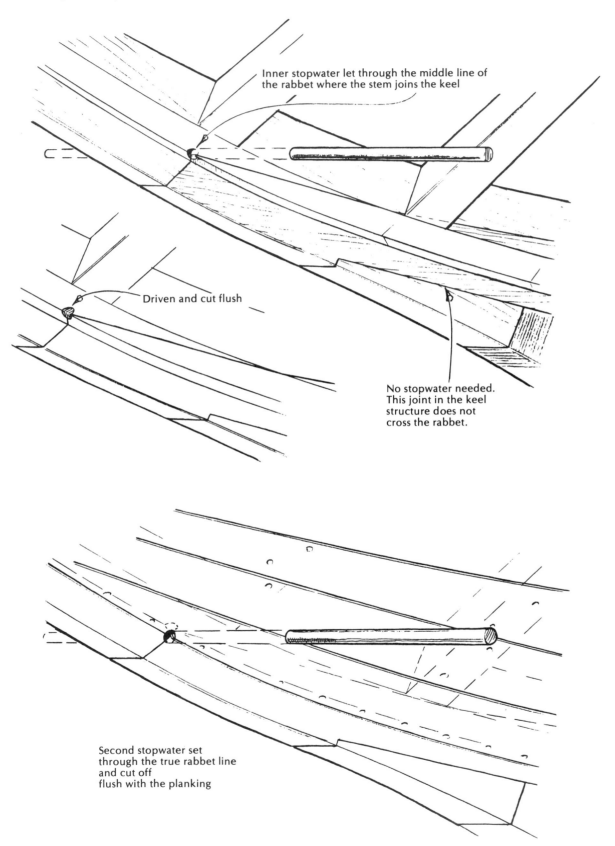

Inner stopwater let through the middle line of the rabbet where the stem joins the keel

Driven and cut flush

No stopwater needed. This joint in the keel structure does not cross the rabbet.

Second stopwater set through the true rabbet line and cut off flush with the planking worm shows on the other side of the backbone, and bore back from there to clean out the hole. With the same auger, bore a hole through a scrap of hardwood about an inch thick. This is a die, through which you are going to extrude a dowel. Saw out a 2-foot length of straight-grained white pine heartwood, a bit over $\frac{1}{2}$ inch square. Start your auger on the end of this stick as if you meant to bore a hole right up the middle, and, of course, quit as soon as the spur cutters have defined the perimeter of the intended dowel. Now plane it down—eight sides, then 16—and try the end in your hardwood die. Work it down evenly until you can drive it through the die, barely compressing the outside fibers in passage. You now have good stopwater stock, which you may proceed to drive into the holes you've bored in the ship's backbone. Cut the ends flush with a fine-toothed saw or a very sharp chisel.

Try that garboard again. If you're satisfied with it this time, fasten off: three screws into the keel in each bay (and stagger them all you can up and down); screws about 3 inches apart up the stem and up the sternpost; one screw, top edge, forward, into each frame; one screw, aft edge of frame, halfway down to the rabbet. This will do for a start. After the floors are in, you'll have a chance to do some real fastening. And when you've finished fastening the other garboard and suddenly realize that you've used some $20 worth of bronze on those two planks, you may wonder if maybe those old wrought-iron addicts might have had something after all!

To drive those screws you will, at worst, have used a good screwdriver bit in a good ratchet bit-stock. If you have begun to suspect that there might be an easier way, try the same type of bit (with the square shank cut off) in your $\frac{1}{2}$-inch-chuck electric drill. Once you've attuned your trigger finger to the music, this does very well. The trick, of course, is to let off the switch at *exactly* the right instant, so that the screw will fetch up snug when the chuck comes to a dead stop—with no momentum left to jump the bit out of the slot (or break off the screw head). Some get it, and never miss; some don't, and should go back to the hand bit-stock before they do any more damage.

Fitting the shutter plank

Once upon a time, a smart young man left the home farm in New Hampshire and went to the big city, where he made out well. Deciding to give his old mother a real treat, he took her to see Niagara Falls, at that time considered to be one of the wonders of the world. Mother looked, sniffed, said "Hmm," never batted an eye. The son, feeling a bit let down, especially considering train fare out and back, and hotel bills, said, "Gosh sakes, Ma, don't you think it's kind of wonderful, 'way all that water comes to the edge, and falls over, and drops clear'n to the bottom?" Mother looked again, and thought a minute, and said, "Well...what's to hinder?"

So why don't you plank her up to the tuck, and switch to the topside diminish pattern, and continue until only one small gap remains open; and then we'll fit the shutter, with all due ceremony, including shutter grease. You'll fasten the screws down low, where you'd lack room to swing a riveting hammer; change over to number 8 copper nails (which take a $\frac{3}{8}$-inch counterbore and follow a $\frac{9}{64}$-inch drill), as soon as you can. Of course, you can use screws all the way if you want to, but they must be long enough to reach almost through the inner lamination of the frame. I prefer rivets, which pull everything together, last forever, cost about one-eighth as much, and never break off. But you may well decide, after setting burrs, clipping off, and heading up 4,000 or so rivets, that an all-screw program would have been money well spent.

And one more thing. As you approach that happy place where the shutter is to go, stop and consider how you are coming out. If you're three planks away, you still have time, by discreet adjustments of their widths, to cover up accumulated errors, and make that shutter plank look as if you'd really meant it to be that size, right from the beginning.

Years ago, we had a regular visitor who always pronounced the word *shudder*—whether from ignorance or intent, we never knew. We sometimes entertained a nasty suspicion, however, that he had in either case hit upon a great truth—not that there aren't plenty of perfectly straightforward ways to fit this best of all planks.

The simplest and most obvious one, of course, is to wrap a piece of plank stock around the outside, shore it against the opening, and mark from the inside. This works very well on the flat aft sections of some boats, but not well at all around a full bow involving a lot of twist. A possible refinement of this system is to use a piece of thin pattern stock—say, $\frac{1}{4}$ inch thick—which can be easily twisted and tacked in place,

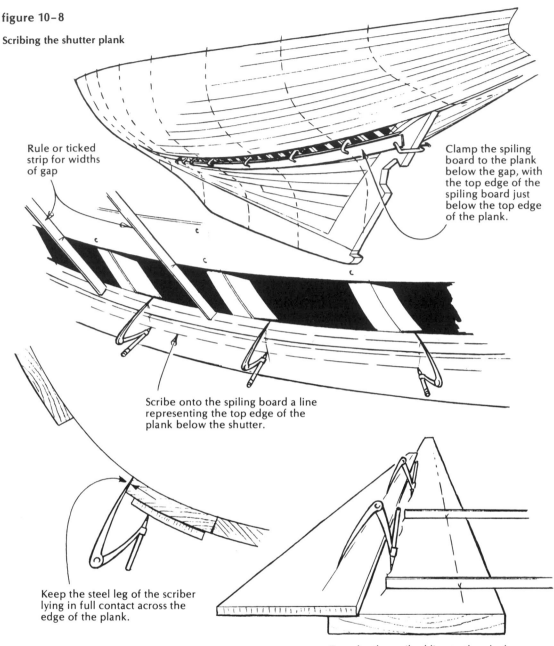

figure 10-8

Scribing the shutter plank

Rule or ticked strip for widths of gap

Clamp the spiling board to the plank below the gap, with the top edge of the spiling board just below the top edge of the plank.

Scribe onto the spiling board a line representing the top edge of the plank below the shutter.

Keep the steel leg of the scriber lying in full contact across the edge of the plank.

Transfer the scribed line to the plank stock in your normal fashion.

marked, cut, and proved right, before the real plank is marked from it.

The second method—which you might call the textbook, or classical method—works this way: Tack a spiling board to the frames down the middle of the gap to be filled; set your dividers, and scribe lines representing both edges of the proposed shutter. These scribed lines may cross and recross each other, but this makes no difference as long as you know which is which. To transfer this shape to the uncut plank, you proceed as in a normal spiling,

except that you mark two edges instead of one, and allow no change in the spread of the dividers. It helps your confidence if you take actual measurements of the gap at one or two points and find that the widths derived from your double spiling are indeed correct. This system works very well on a relatively wide and straight board, but it is very unhandy for a long, narrow, curved gap requiring a piece of spiling board cut to shape, tacked together, and ruined for further legitimate use (except for the corresponding shutter on the other side of the

112

boat). You may feel that this is an easy sacrifice and at this point hope fervently that you never have to look at a spiling board again; but the pro has to think ahead to the next boat.

The third system, about to be described, is the one I now use exclusively, no matter what the shape, size, or location of the shutter plank. It ruins no spiling boards, requires no sixth-sense allowances for parallax, height of eye above the horizon, or thickness of pencil marks. And it's my own, my very own, and therefore dear to me. (See Figure 10–8.)

Take a spiling board slightly longer than the plank you're going to fit, and with a top edge shaped something like the lower edge of the shutter gap. Clamp this board to the plank below the gap, with the top edge of the spiling board just clear of (below) the top edge of the plank. Now shorten the pencil leg of your dividers so that it is about an inch shorter than the steel leg. Adjust for the necessary gap (as Abe Lincoln said about the proper length for a man's legs, "Just long enough to reach the ground"), and scribe on the spiling board a line representing the top edge of the plank below the shutter. You will realize and beware the dangers that lurk about this act as soon as you start to draw that line, and discover that you can move it up and down at will by raising and lowering the apex of the dividers. Keep that steel leg lying in full contact across the edge of the plank.... So now you have a line (to be transferred eventually, of course) that represents the lower edge (out) of the shutter plank. The top edge will obviously be far enough above it, at any given point, to touch the edge of the plank above the gap. Therefore, take your good steel tape and measure that gap, at 8-inch, 12-inch, 15-inch intervals as seems necessary, and write these measurements on the spiling board, being very careful, of course, to note the exact point where they were taken. All that remains now is to transfer that line to the plank stock in your normal fashion. (You will, of course, have noticed that in this transfer process your spiling board has to be adjacent to, not on, the plank you are marking.) Mark the widths from it as written on the spiling board, and connect these points with a line drawn to a batten.

There's a bit of forgotten business needing attention here. The exposed edges of the final planks above and below the shutter should have been dressed to a slight outgauge (not over 1/16 inch), to ensure that the shutter will fit tightly when it hits bottom.

When you saw out the shutter, be bold, and cut right to the edge of the pencil line. Take bevels as accurately as you can, and plane out-gauge on both edges. Then, with your plane, just knock off the inner corners of the plank edges, at about a 45-degree angle, so that they'll be less inclined to dig in and bind when you drive the plank in. Cut the forward end to fit the stem rabbet (and this cut had better be at exactly the right place); cut the butt end just where the spiling board calls for it; get a big wooden mallet, and drive the forward end in against the rabbet and the frame. It should be tight enough to hang there patiently while you drill for, and drive, one screw into the stem near the top edge of the plank. Now lift the butt end up onto the horse, and clamp to the outside of it, right out in line with the squared-off end, a tough piece of 1- by 8-inch oak, with the clamp at the upper corner of the plank, but so arranged that it will enter the bay without bumping. The cross staff should show about an inch above the top edge of the plank, and at least 13 inches below it. This is your secret weapon for twisting shutters. A few trials will show where the push should be applied on this lever arm in order to twist the plank just the right amount as it swings up to its final resting place. Leave someone to guard and adjust the shore, and go forward with your mighty mallet to work the plank in. Don't be afraid of it; work back and forth over a 6-foot span; clamp the butt end as soon as you can to a piece of wood lying fore-and-aft inside the frames. Drive the plank home (Figure 10–9), fasten it to the frames, fit and fasten the butt block to the end; get out the next piece of shutter, fasten its forward end to this butt block, and proceed as before, until you can say to deaf ears, but with some satisfaction, "There, by God, that's done." And as for that shutter grease: it comes in a bottle with a ship on it, and will do you a lot of good right about now. Save a good slug, though, for the end of the riveting, which is next in order.

Riveting

For this job you need, first, a burr-setter. If you can buy one, it will probably be labeled Riveting Tool. You can make a satisfactory one from a 4-inch length of hard steel tube, 1/4-inch inside diameter; or you can drill a 3/16-inch hole lengthwise, and about an inch deep, in the end of a piece of 3/8-inch rod. If you are lucky, the burrs will fit just tightly enough so that they need driving, and will stay in place until the rivets are headed up. (See Figure 10–10.)

So you set the burr down tightly against the

113

figure 10–9

Fitting the shutter plank

wood, and then with your end cutters nip off all the excess nail you can get hold of. You are not likely to cut it too short. If the burrs are a loose fit, rock the cutters sideways as you increase the pressure on the handles. This motion spreads the end slightly and helps to keep the burr from popping off before you get to it with a riveting hammer. You may well decide that end cutters are not quite tool enough to handle number 8

wire. Try the smallest set of bolt-cutters you can find, but wiggle the handles up and down as you bring them together, to get that spreading effect over the burr.

And now to head up. For this you need a special dolly, which must be slender, to reach the nailheads where they lie in the depths of their $3/8$-inch bung holes, and yet heavy enough to hold them from flinching while somebody hammers lustily on the other end. A machinist friend might taper the end of a 2-inch steel shaft, and even round off the sharp edges on the other end, to make you a real deluxe model. Or you can drill and tap a hole in the end, thread and screw in a stub of ³/₈-inch steel rod, and file this to a slight taper. The real problem is to find someone at once devoted and tough enough to hold Dolly, who starts out a lissome 17-pounder in the morning and ends the day weighing just under 85 pounds. And don't think there's an easy answer, such as trimming her down to 8 pounds.

On the other end of the rivet you need a hammer. We use a moderately light machinist's (ball peen) hammer, with a 12-inch handle. We have perhaps a half-dozen of these around the shop, all looking about the same.

Five of them are just good enough to throw at stray cats; the sixth one will almost swing itself without any help. If we ever lose that one, we'll join the rest of the world and use screws all the way. So, if your hand threatens to drop off after the first five minutes, and the rivet end seems to be a very small and shifty target, try another hammer. Maybe you aren't entirely to blame. Try to develop a rhythmic pattern. Hit the end gently, twice, with the round face of the hammer; hit the wood beside it twice, vigorously, with the flat face, to pull the rivet tight; switch back to round, and head it up. You don't have to be too gentle with number 8's. Your big problem is the man outside with Dolly. Try to keep him thinking of untracked waters, undream'd shores, and what fun it's going to be when we get sailing.

figure 10–10

Tools for riveting

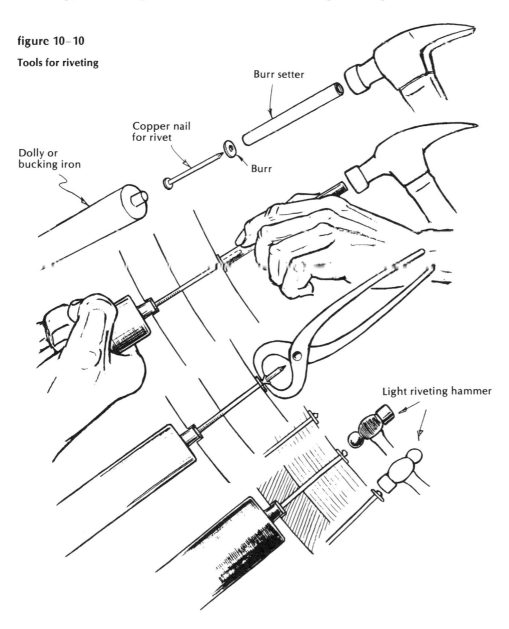

Burr setter

Copper nail for rivet

Burr

Dolly or bucking iron

Light riveting hammer

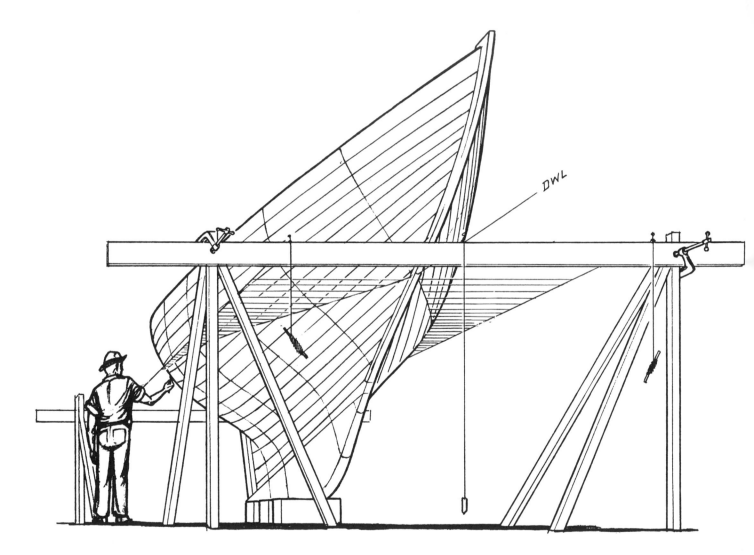

DWL

Chapter Eleven

A Smooth and Fair Hull

This will be a short chapter for me, and a long two weeks for you. You are going to plank the transom, bung the fastenings, smooth the hull, caulk, smooth some more, and mark the waterline; and you're going to do these things before you take the molds out, or you'll be sorry. I always reverse the procedure, and have all these things to do with shores and staging in the way. But I assume that you have a flawless character, and neither postpone the tedious nor reach greedily for the next payment before it is due. So keep your itching hands off those molds, and do what I tell you.

Bunging, fitting, and fairing

First, start someone bunging. This job may appear to be on a sub-kindergarten level, since it involves only round pegs and round holes, but there's more to it than meets the eye (see Figure 11–1). A small dab of integrity goes into each one of the 5,000 counterbores, along with the glue and the bung. You ream the glue into the hole with a tiny brush, start the bung with the grain in line, drive it true to the bottom of the hole, and *never* bruise it with an impatient hammer. Clip the excess off with a very sharp chisel, using the heel of your hand as a mallet.

Make the first cut ⅛ inch out, to see how the grain slopes; approach it from the opposite side, if necessary, for the final cut. Don't bung the sheerstrake.

Plank the transom next. You'll meet with powerful arguments in favor of three layers of ³⁄₈-inch plywood, glued together, or laminations of thin mahogany, bent in cold and set in glue. I still prefer to do the job in one thickness, with stock that has been steam-bent and dried on a form, and fitted, plank by plank, from the bottom up. I can get a better fit, in far less time, and have no worries about hidden gaps where rot could start. The individual planks can be held in place with a reasonable number of large, durable fastenings, instead of a multitude of small ones. The miter seam can be flooded with poison and caulked snug. The planks can be planed and sanded to shape with no fear of working through the outer layer. Five small problems hold less terror than two very large ones.

Whatever you use, however, the method of fitting is the same. You need to know the exact shape of that line where the inner face of the planking intersects the outside edge of the transom frame—the inner corner of the miter joint, that is (see Figure 11–2). You get this shape by

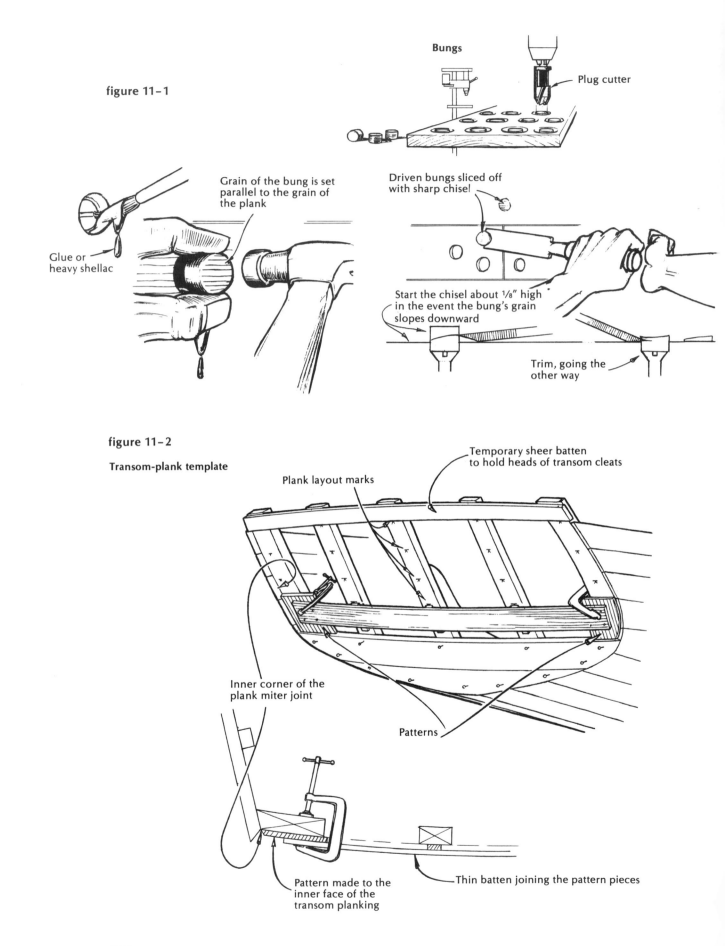

figure 11-1

Bungs

Plug cutter

Grain of the bung is set parallel to the grain of the plank

Glue or heavy shellac

Driven bungs sliced off with sharp chisel

Start the chisel about ⅛" high in the event the bung's grain slopes downward

Trim, going the other way

figure 11-2

Transom-plank template

Temporary sheer batten to hold heads of transom cleats

Plank layout marks

Inner corner of the plank miter joint

Patterns

Pattern made to the inner face of the transom planking

Thin batten joining the pattern pieces

fitting a skeleton pattern to the line—using a thin piece each side, and joining the two with a third, bent around the 'thwartships curve and tacked to the two with small brads. This pattern will later be placed on the inside, concave face of the pre-bent stock (see Figure 11-3), and you must therefore drive those brads flush so that the pattern can back into place on the piece to be marked. From the line thus obtained you cut outward, at the proper angle, and proceed to correct it until it fits. You have the consolation of knowing that you can lengthen it out, so long as you are still below the turn of the bilge, by dressing off the lower edge of the plank. Above the turn, in the region of the tumblehome, you have to be right the first time. Finish off at the top with a plank wide enough to crown to the underside of the deck at the center. Fasten each plank temporarily, before fitting the next; drill for all fastenings (which will be 2-inch bronze screws), take the planks off, and saturate all end grain with your favorite poison before assembling them finally in place.

Go forward now and prepare to fair off the sides of the stem in line with the planking. The lines drawing or offset table will give the widths of the face at the profile. Mark the two lines, as given, from the stem head to the ballast casting; note and mark the flat, if any, to be left at the top of the stem; make saw cuts at 6-inch intervals into the corners of the stem, right to the line of the planking (see Figure 11-4). These cuts should come exactly to the half-siding lines on the profile face. If the cuts fail to reach those lines, move the lines out. Your straight saw blade, touching the planking, will tell you how much to take off. You should be able to remove most of the excess wood, between saw cuts, with your adze. Use a big chisel and mallet in the awkward places. Finish off with a smoothing plane, and be glad you didn't attempt this shaping before you set up the backbone. She might have come out with a pinched nose, which is a horrible thing indeed.

While you are in the mood, do the same fairing job on the sternpost (see Figure 11-5). This member tapers from 5-inch siding at the rabbet to 2-inch siding at the line of the rudder. Shape a flat wedge, of soft wood, 1½ inches thick at one end and tapering to a point in the distance from the rabbet to the after edge of the post. Tack this to the flat of the sternpost, thick end at the rabbet, and use it as a depth guide for parallel cuts made with your electric hand saw—set for ½-inch depth of cut, of course.

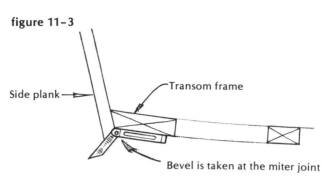

figure 11-3

Side plank

Transom frame

Bevel is taken at the miter joint

Template transcribed to pre-bent plank stock

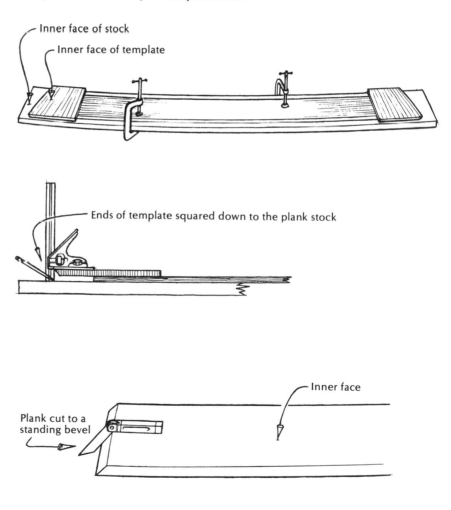

Inner face of stock

Inner face of template

Ends of template squared down to the plank stock

Inner face

Plank cut to a standing bevel

figure 11-4

Fairing off the stem

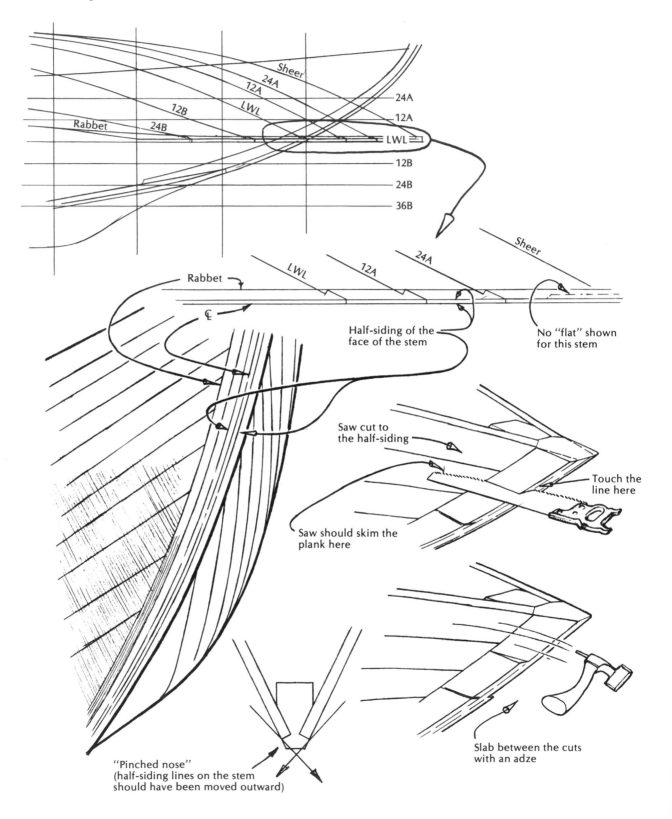

Sheer

24A

12A

12B

LWL

Rabbet

24B

24A

12A

LWL

12B

24B

36B

Sheer

24A

12A

LWL

Rabbet

℄

Half-siding of the
face of the stem

No "flat" shown
for this stem

Saw cut to
the half-siding

Touch the
line here

Saw should skim the
plank here

Slab between the cuts
with an adze

"Pinched nose"
(half-siding lines on the stem
should have been moved outward)

120

figure 11–5

Fairing the sternpost

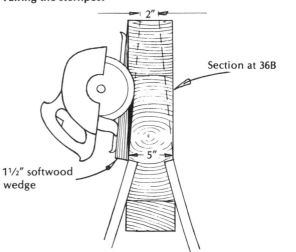

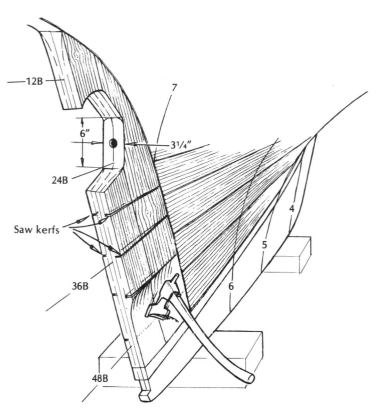

Stay well below the line of the propeller shaft with these cuts, adze off the excess wood between saw cuts, and plane the surface fair. Shape and fair off around the propeller aperture with all the artistry you can muster, remembering that the base of the stuffing box (which you'd better have on hand, to check my figures) will require a flat area 3 1/4 inches wide and 6 inches high. Otherwise, take off as much as you dare, and round off what's left as slick as a mackerel.

And now to plane the planking fair. You need, for this job, four smoothing planes, about 60 hours of uninterrupted effort, perfect patience, extreme caution, sensitive fingertips, tough knees, great endurance—and a system. I can make some suggestions as to the last item. The rest is up to you. Have a loaded gun at hand to use on anyone who approaches with a power tool.

The idea here is not simply to achieve a smooth surface. Any apprentice painter can do that, given enough time and sandpaper. What we are after is a surface perfectly curved, everywhere, both lengthwise and up and down. Fortunately, good wood tries to bend in such a curve, so that you need worry only about preserving, not shaping, the fore-and-aft line of the planks. The crosswise shaping is the difficult part. You are dealing with a curved surface made up of a series of more or less equal flats, each tangent to the curved line you must uncover (see Figure 11–6). The midpoint on each flat is already at this line, and must not be touched. Now, if you plane another flat, exactly tangent to the curve, at each seam, so that there

figure 11–6   Planing off the hull—longitudinally

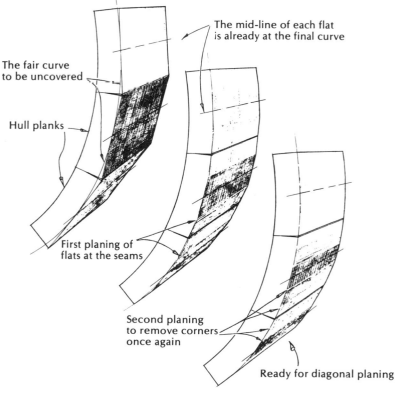

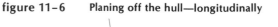

The mid-line of each flat is already at the final curve

The fair curve to be uncovered

Hull planks

First planing of flats at the seams

Second planing to remove corners once again

Ready for diagonal planing

121

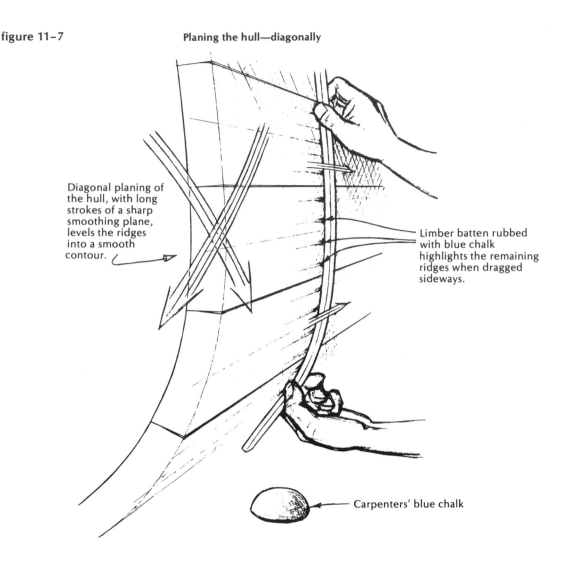

Diagonal planing of the hull, with long strokes of a sharp smoothing plane, levels the ridges into a smooth contour.

Limber batten rubbed with blue chalk highlights the remaining ridges when dragged sideways.

Carpenters' blue chalk

will be twice as many as before, and still all equal in width at any given girth—then the plank edges, as well as the midpoints, will be at the line. Chalk alternate flats, if you have trouble keeping track of their outlines, and then very carefully plane off the corners with yet another set of flats—ending up with four times as many as at the start, and all of the same width. Now take your best smoother, sharp as a razor, and plane diagonally, with long strokes, to remove the remaining ridges (see Figure 11–7). Cut shavings thin as gossamer. Lead the plane by the nose, rather than push it. Remember that the middle line of each flat should, theoretically, be untouched in this diagonal planing. Lose the centerlines, and you've lost control.

That's the theory. It's precisely the same technique as you'd use to shape a round spar from a square timber—make it 8-sided, then 16-sided, then 32-sided, and sand it the rest of the way. Of course, the geometry breaks down, in certain places, on the hull surface. The planks are not precisely equal in thickness—you will have been properly timid, in spots, and left too much wood on the flats. So you warm your left hand, place it flat (vertically) on the planking, and slide it up and down, with fingertips touching. They'll detect a ridge so small that you can't see it on the raw wood. Shave it off tenderly, because it will loom up like a small mountain when sunlight starts to slant across its gloss-painted surface. Rub blue chalk on a limber batten, bend it to the line of the frames, and rub it sidewise, fore and aft, to mark the high spots (see Figure 11–7). Shine a light beam, at night, tangent to the curves, and mark the humps it shows you. Don't get impatient. Don't get overconfident and decide to speed up the job. And don't sand the surface yet, because you are about to caulk the seams, and this operation will rough it all up again.

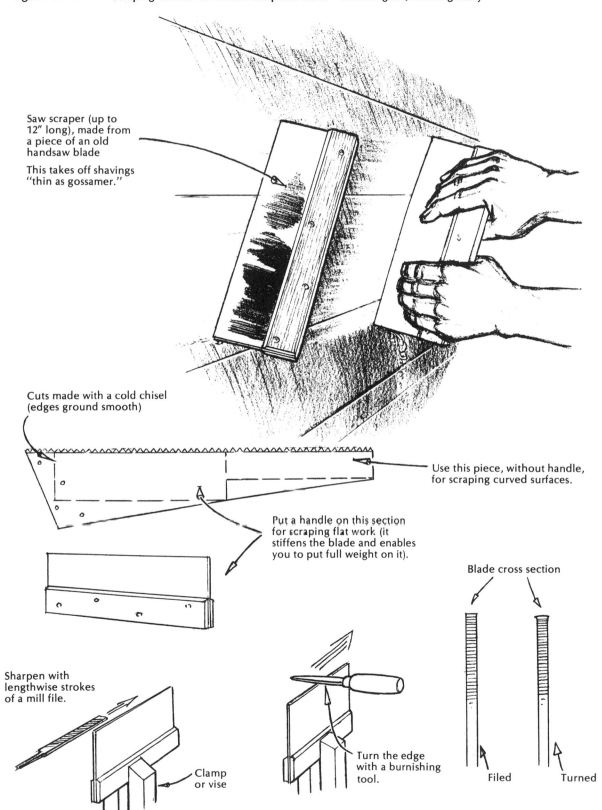

Saw scraper (up to 12" long), made from a piece of an old handsaw blade

This takes off shavings "thin as gossamer."

Cuts made with a cold chisel (edges ground smooth)

Use this piece, without handle, for scraping curved surfaces.

Put a handle on this section for scraping flat work (it stiffens the blade and enables you to put full weight on it).

Blade cross section

Sharpen with lengthwise strokes of a mill file.

Clamp or vise

Turn the edge with a burnishing tool.

Filed   Turned

Caulking

As a caulker, you are required by tradition to examine the plank seams with a highly critical eye, wonder audibly where that feller learned his trade, and finally allow as how you've saved worse jobs than this one. What you are about to undertake is, in short, a very important operation, requiring great skill, long experience, and absolute integrity. So you'll be told, anyway. There'll be much shaking of heads, and grim warnings about how those seams'll spit it out every time if it ain't druv just so. And as for using cotton instead of oakum, and rolling most of it in with a wheel—you'd better leave her setting right on the bank, boys, because she'll never be safe at sea.

Don't let them bother you. More boats have been ruined by overcaulking than have been lost for the lack of it. You can do a perfectly satisfactory job on this new boat. You don't need a live-oak mallet with tempered steel rings on it. You need two "boat pattern" caulking irons, one of which you file to a moderately sharp edge for opening too-tight butt seams. You need six pounds of plain unspun caulking cotton. This comes in one-pound rolls made up of three parallel strands, which can be split down the middle to fit the smallest seams. (Twisted cotton and plumber's wicking are useless. I further question the virtues of the new, revolutionary, no-cotton compounds

which are alleged to end your caulking problems for periods of up to four years. This seems to offer very little improvement over the old system, which is good for at least 20.) Finally, if you dare to do the job my way, you need a caulking wheel (Figure 11-9). This can be as crude or elaborate as you want to make it, so long as it consists of a 2½-inch metal disc, about ¹⁄₁₆ inch thick, set into a slot in the end of a wooden handle and free to revolve on a fixed axle. You'll hold it in both hands and lean half your weight on it, so it must be strong. The one I use is bushed with roller bearings, and has gone 50,000 miles in the last 40 years without an oil change. Moreover, the seams it has caulked have remained tight, with a fine no-spitting record.

You will, of course, caulk butts, hood ends, and garboard seams in the approved way, with caulking iron and mallet (see Figures 11-10, 11-11, and 11-12). Best of all, catch an expert in the act, and watch him for a few minutes. He'll tell you seven years of observation and practice might bring you to his level, and he's probably right; but don't give up in dismay. Your good new wood will swell and come tight, even if your mallet rings off-key.

Marking the waterline

There are 15 different ways of marking the waterline. They range from the friendly muskrat in the calm pool, through a perfectly level hull above a perfect floor, to an engineer's transit, and (for all I know) a laser beam operated by an all-knowing computer. The right and proper way is this:

Get the hull reasonably level athwartships. This isn't necessary, but it helps. Get two straight-edged boards, somewhat longer than the beam of the boat. Center them athwartships, one forward, one aft, at the height of the desired paint line (2 inches high aft, 3 inches forward?); level them precisely while clamping them to braced posts at their ends; stretch strings *damned* tight each side fore and aft, just touching the planking about amidships (see Figure 11-13). Measure the height to the sheer both sides to check whether the hull and your straightedges agree to what's level. You have now established a perfect plane, and need only mark it on the boat's skin. Line up the string and the top of the straightedge by eye; bring the pencil point to that line, and mark the hull. When the reach in gets too long for you, you'll need a sharp-eyed assistant to squint across the

figure 11-9

Caulking wheel

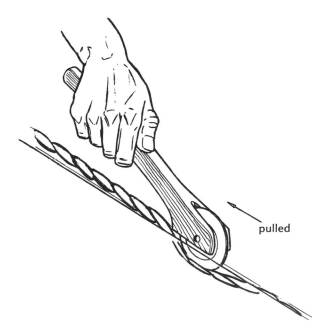

pulled

124

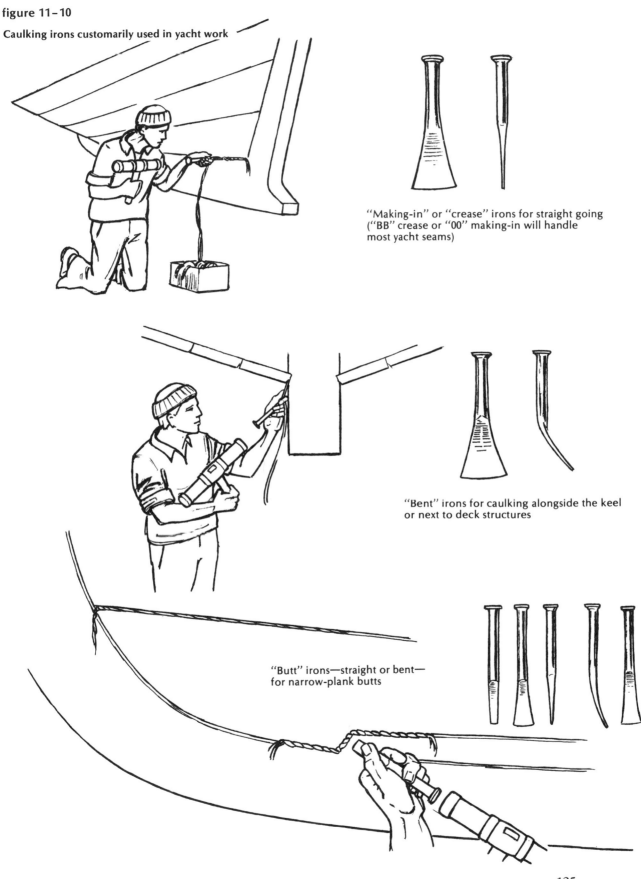

figure 11-10

Caulking irons customarily used in yacht work

"Making-in" or "crease" irons for straight going ("BB" crease or "00" making-in will handle most yacht seams)

"Bent" irons for caulking alongside the keel or next to deck structures

"Butt" irons—straight or bent— for narrow-plank butts

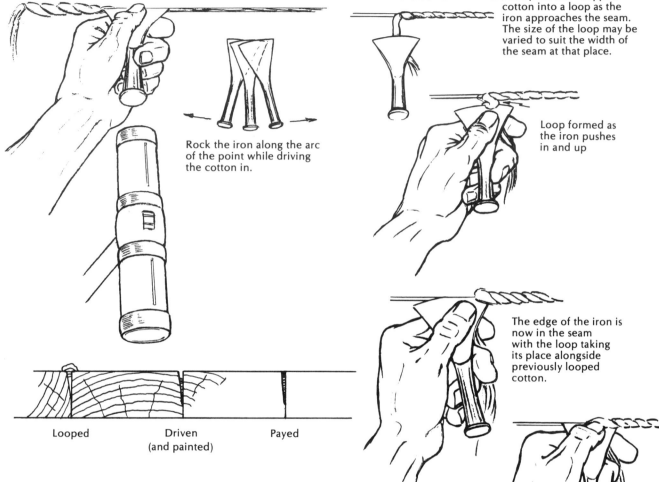

figure 11-11

Driving the looped cotton home (working from right to left)

Rock the iron along the arc of the point while driving the cotton in.

Looped | Driven (and painted) | Payed

figure 11-12

Applying unspun cotton by "looping" or "gagging"

Nip the extending end of the cotton strand(s) between the iron and the forefinger, or between the iron and the hull, and push the "trapped" cotton into a loop as the iron approaches the seam. The size of the loop may be varied to suit the width of the seam at that place.

Loop formed as the iron pushes in and up

The edge of the iron is now in the seam with the loop taking its place alongside previously looped cotton.

Note the position of the last two fingers. They're under the shank of the iron, and they rotate it against the index and the middle fingers.

Tension of the cotton rope is controlled by passing it through the fingers.

The loop is tapped into place and another loop is started. The cotton is driven home with a crease iron after several feet of the seam have been gagged this way.

"Looping" or "gagging" the loose cotton strands (one or more together) permits the caulker to vary the bulk required to fill the seam at that particular place. He doesn't gag too far before testing the pack by driving it home. The ring of the mallet against the iron tells him whether the pack is too tight or too loose.

plane and tell you where to mark—and you should end up with pencil marks about a foot apart, from stem to sternpost.

Now take a perfect softwood batten, about ½ inch square, and tack it with its top edge to those marks (see Figure 11-14). Sight along it for dips and hollows. Finally, cut a smooth and delicate groove in the planking, hard against the top edge of the batten. Use a rase knife, if you are fortunate enough to have one, or a rounded-off saw blade.

You are now face to face with your conscience. Obviously, you want the visible topsides to be as fair and smooth as can be; your zeal and young muscles may allow you to view the lower area with equal enthusiasm—and the same hand-sanding technique you'll use above. I confess that I have become reconciled in my

figure 11–13

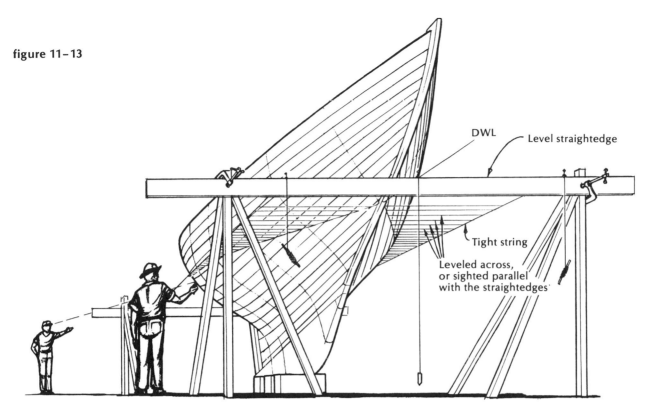

DWL · Level straightedge

Tight string

Leveled across,
or sighted parallel
with the straightedges

The plane of the designed waterline is established between two strings drawn
tightly between straightedges leveled to the DWL at bow and stern.

figure 11–14

Scribing a waterline

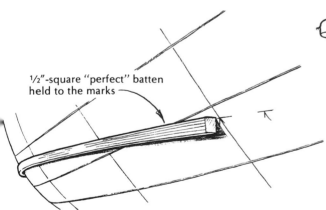

½"-square "perfect" batten
held to the marks

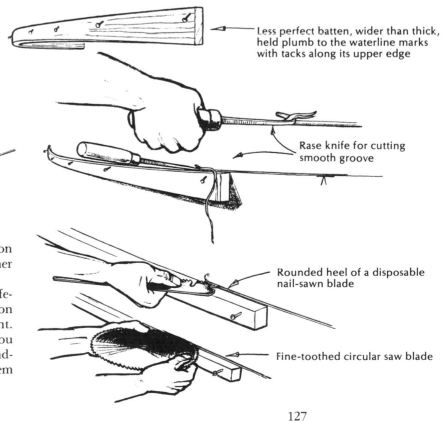

Less perfect batten, wider than thick,
held plumb to the waterline marks
with tacks along its upper edge

Rase knife for cutting
smooth groove

Rounded heel of a disposable
nail-sawn blade

Fine-toothed circular saw blade

old age to the fairness you get with a soft pad on
a disc sander, but I hope you are made of sterner
stuff.

Prime it now, maybe? It'll look more life-
like with the waterline defined, and the cotton
in the seams needs a good soaking with paint.
The prime coat will show up humps that you
missed with your fingertips. Wrap your sandpaper around a long block, and rub them
down.

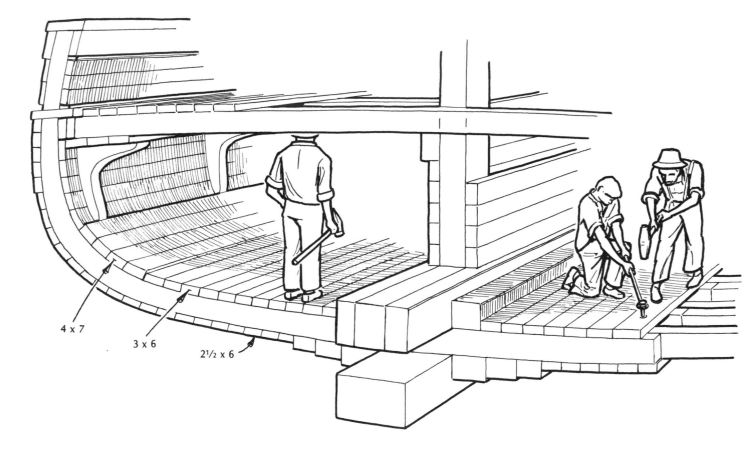

4 x 7

3 x 6

2½ x 6

Ceiling employed in the lumber schooner *Clipper City*, built in Manitowoc, Wisconsin, 1854, by W.W. Bates. Drawing courtesy of the Manitowoc Marine Museum.

Chapter Twelve

Ceilings

You have, I'm sure, lost that innocence which would direct your eyes Heavenward (toward the underside of the overhead, that is) at the mention of the word "ceiling." You know as well as I do that we're talking about the lining of the hull, the planking on the inside of the frames that stiffens, protects, covers up some rough work—and complicates my life with questions and uncertainties.

My trouble is, I have suddenly realized that the inside planking occurs in far greater variety and purpose than the outside skin, which is a very simple thing indeed. Consider, now:

Lo, the poor Indian split thin cedar slats to spread weight over the bottom of his birch. We lined our lapstrake rowboats up to the risers with light stuff, held with tiny screws, to protect against casually tossed grapnels and clam hods (and we tried with incomplete success to intercept small eels and crabs that headed for the gaps and ripened unseen).

At the other extreme, big cargo vessels were lined with timber at least as thick and as strong as the outside planking, through-fastened to it with alternate trunnels, caulked hard to stop slip and contain bulk cargo or stone-and-gravel ballast. The new schooner might even be lucky enough to get a first cargo of Turks Island salt, pickling her hold against rot for years to come. (I realize that this belief has been jeered at and given scant approval by most of our modern wood teck-nicians, and I suppose we should grieve at the folly of those pathetic millions of seamen who, since the dawn of shipbuilding, have believed that salt is good for wood, even as it saves the nets and the beef and the bait.) Pickled wood is good.

Let's agree that our present concern is with wooden boats larger than those open skiffs and somewhat smaller than a coasting schooner—in fact, our own ideal 'round-the-world ketch, or cutter, or yawl, or cat, or whatever it happens to be this week. This unique and flawless double-ender (or counter-stern schooner, as the case may be) sits there, in our mind's eye (or even in the flesh), planked and decked, and crying to be made complete as sanctuary and preserver 'midst the alien oceans' vastnesses. In short, 'bout time to do the joinerwork, or we'll never get the cussed thing fit to move aboard of. So let's cut the guff, and make some awful decisions, to wit:

figure 12-1

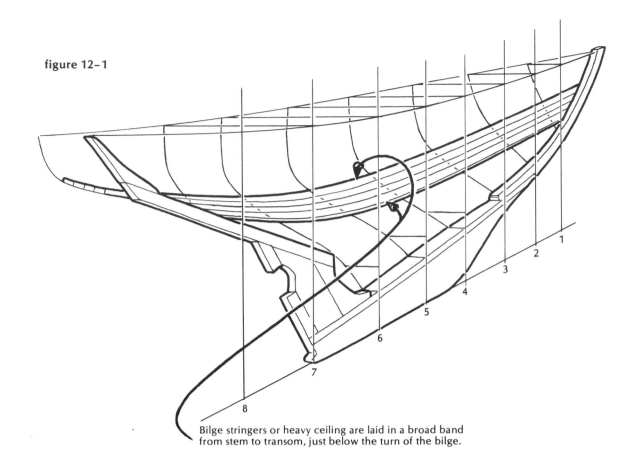

Bilge stringers or heavy ceiling are laid in a broad band from stem to transom, just below the turn of the bilge.

Should we ceil her entire, sheer clamps to floor timbers, end to end, above and below a bilge clamp? Or should we fit now our mightily structured bulkheads right out to the skin, fastened strongly to frames and planking (with, of course, light and lovely ceiling between, to protect unwary buttocks from splinters)? Should this ceiling be laid with gaps between strips for ventilation? Of the same thickness throughout? Sprung and/or spiled to shape? Go for aesthetics, or strength, or both?

Or even skip the whole damned business, as Mr. Herreshoff would have us do: no ceiling, no bilge clamp, no grand chimneys between frames, where incautious wristwatches slide down to lodge on butt blocks, and cockroaches can lurk by day. Frankly, I don't go for this idea. I want ceiling, and I want it for many more reasons than its obvious function of hiding my rough work from the pitying eyes of those fussy, fancy builders.

So here we go.

I like to start out with a broad band of heavy ceiling (same thickness as the planking) from end to end of the vessel, top edge just below the turn of the bilge, up to 2 feet wide, lying com-fortably with no great edge-bending, at a nice height to take the framing of the bunk flats, the cockpit floorbeams, and the downthrust of the bulkheads (see Figure 12-1). Lay it in strips three times as wide as they are thick; fasten it to the frames with flush-head screws, and never, ever, bore for large bolts through the frames. Eight strips measuring 1 by 3 inches, or $1\frac{1}{4}$ by $3\frac{3}{4}$ inches—you can butt them on timbers, or scarf the joints if time is not of the essence. Bevel the uppermost top edge, and the lower strip's bottom edge to the thickness of the lighter ceiling that will go above and below this heavy band. If your hull is broad and flat-floored (like a Friendship sloop, for instance), you may need to make those strips half as wide in order to bend that fine hook shape below the bilge. Edge nail (as in strip planking) between frames. Or if you will, and fine sweeping stock is at hand, spile the pieces to shape, as wide as you wish.

What you have achieved thus is a fine, springy stiffener, with no "hard" line to local-ize a severe stress athwartships in a frame or lengthwise in the planking. I have seen half a dozen frames in a row broken right off under a

130

heavy bilge stringer. They were coerced into holding that point, no matter what, and their strength was their undoing. If they'd been allowed to pant, and flex, and pass the load to a less vulnerable spot, they might have survived to fight another day. (See Figure 12–2.) I've also seen frightening bulges where rigid bulkheads, installed before the ceiling, refused to allow any adjustment in the fore-and-aft run of the planking, and the short sections of ceiling aggravated the hinge-joint effect of the rigid bulkhead. (See Figure 12–3.)

Some hard choices await you now. You'll climb aboard with a running mile of light ceiling, less than half the thickness of the heavy band, maybe with exposed corners chamfered. A voice loaded with authority will tell you to space these ¼ inch apart for ventilation, and especially, to start the topmost strip a full ½ inch below the sheer clamp (see Figure 12–4). This last would be very important if by some awful accident of misguidance you fitted the sheer clamp tightly to the underside of the deck, English fashion, or even imitated the mighty men of Friendship, with a great plank around the sheer. Obviously, no air could escape at the top of the chimneys between

figure 12–2

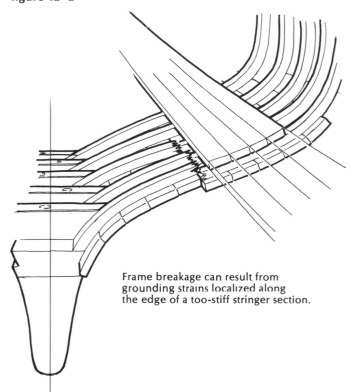

Frame breakage can result from grounding strains localized along the edge of a too-stiff stringer section.

figure 12–3

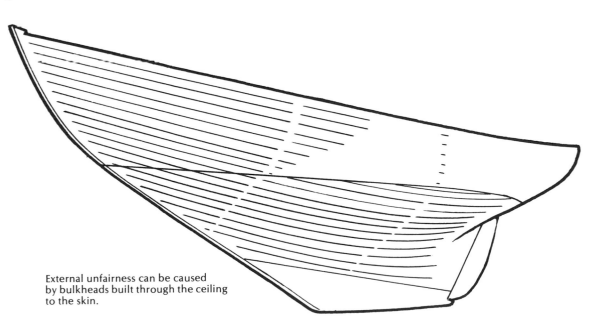

External unfairness can be caused by bulkheads built through the ceiling to the skin.

figure 12-4

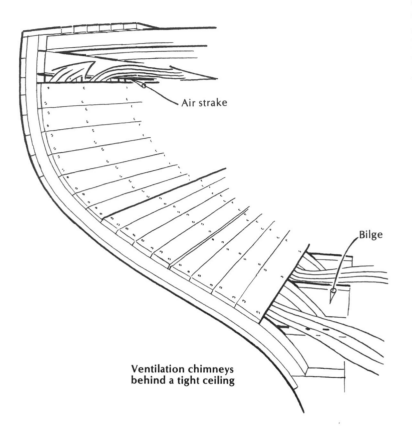

Air strake

Bilge

**Ventilation chimneys
behind a tight ceiling**

frames, and the whole beautiful ventilating system would be ruined. (Waldo Howland invented this system back in the 1930s, when we were both somewhat younger and more daring. He arranged to warm the topsides of the vessel whenever the sun shone forth; this caused the air inside the planking to rise and flow over the sheer clamp, drawing damp and chilly vapors from the bilge.)

The question of air spaces between strips is perhaps debatable. I'm agin 'em, on the grounds that leaky chimneys don't draw well, sawdust and dimes fall through the cracks, and it takes longer to fit and fasten strips precisely spaced apart than jammed inevitably together. And if she's rolling badly, with water in the bilge, maybe some of it will stay behind the ceiling instead of swishing through to soak your blankets.

We can even, I think, develop this thought further, in the usually one-sided debate between wood and glass. We know, of course, that the new glass boats can't leak (except through the shaft alley, and where the deck meets the sheer,

and a few other spots), but they can, and do, suffer from a phenomenon vulgarly known as sweating. In cold Northern waters, abetted by the fumes from an alcohol stove, this process can start little rivers down the inside of the hull, to be absorbed by bedding and breeks and wall-to-wall carpeting; the inmates squish about as in a swamp, and rush all movable fabrics to hang in open air whenever possible. Wooden walls, on the other hand, do not sweat much (nor leak either, Hamlet, though by your smiling you seem to say so), and if we have this good-smelling ceiling between us and our wooden walls, we may yet have one advantage to crow about.

So here you are, down below, with ceiling stock reachable, half a million 1¼-inch skinny bronze ringed nails in a can, electric drill to punch ¹⁄₁₆-inch lead holes into the hard oak frames, and a pocket full of fivepenny box nails to tack strips temporarily in place. And don't you move another damned inch until you've fitted blocking for the chainplates. If the plates are to be the simple outside variety, this blocking will be sawn to shape, same thickness as the frames, closely fitted up behind the sheer clamp to the underside of the covering board. Mark for the location of the plates on the outside of the planking (taking great care to line them up with the shrouds-to-be) and hold the blocks in place with a couple of screws—until the ceiling covers them and is finally pierced with the through bolts from the chainplates. And if you plan to fit the plates inside the planking, real yacht style, you'll have to install blocking and chainplates at once (plate against the inside of the planking, usually, with blocking filling the space to the inner face of the ceiling) before you cover it all up forevermore. This means, of course, that the deck, or at least the covering boards, must be in place before the chainplates go on.

And if you don't think of anything else (except a good soaking with wood preservative), you may be able to resume work on that ceiling.

Start at the top with the first strip nicely spaced ½ inch below the sheer clamp, all the way from the forwardmost frame in the bow to the remote region of the lazarette. And another, and another, scattering the butts nicely, and fastening as you go with one bronze nail in each frame you cross until you've covered down to the heavy ceiling at the ends—and view a great gap amidships that tapers both ways to nothing (Figure 12-5). You can attack this area

figure 12–5

Ceiling above the bilge stringers

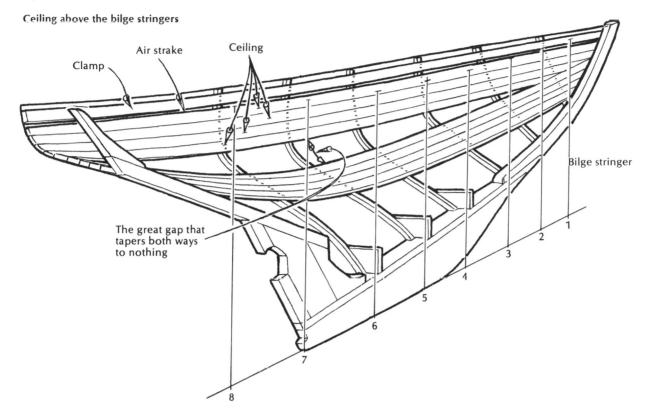

Clamp

Air strake

Ceiling

The great gap that
tapers both ways
to nothing

Bilge stringer

1
2
3
4
5
6
7
8

figure 12–6

Ceiling below the bilge stringers

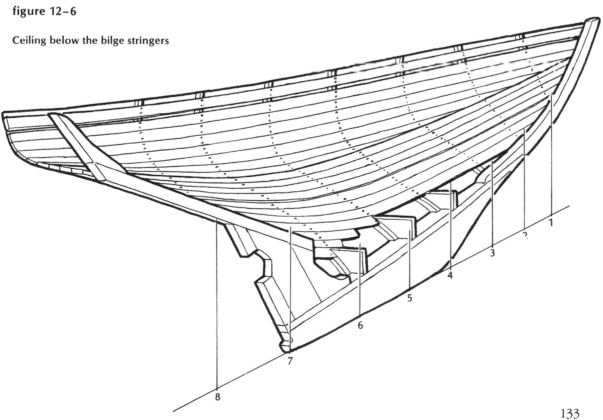

1
2
3
4
5
6
7
8

133

figure 12-7

Scribing the butt of a ceiling plank

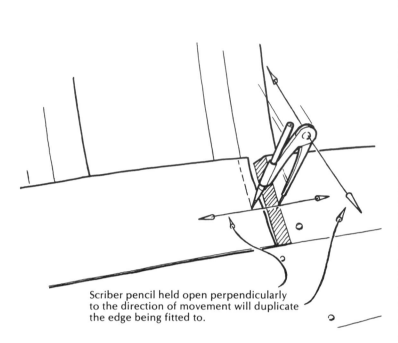

Scriber pencil held open perpendicularly to the direction of movement will duplicate the edge being fitted to.

with strips laid against the top line of the heavy ceiling and running out to points at the ends, or you can keep 'em coming down from the top, with points fitted to the heavy ceiling at the ends, until the hook becomes tolerable—at which point you scribe and fit (see Figure 12-6) a wider piece with its lower edge equidistant throughout from the top of the heavy band, and work up to it from below.

The area below the heavy band, down to the tops of the floor timbers (or to the plane of the underside of the cabin sole, which is probably the same thing) may deserve thicker stock, because of the likelihood that parts of it will be exposed to kicks and scuffs caused by stand-up walking on the lee side. (We used to drop the cabin floor down, like unto a shrunken channel between high banks, and assured the Owner that he'd be Glad, yes, Glad to have that area between bunk front and sole to walk on when she was driving into it with the rail down. Of course, if the vessel happened to be wide and flat-floored, with bunk fronts rising plumb

from the cabin sole, we were even more enthusiastic about that wonderful unencumbered width of dance floor.) Except for this possible increase in stiffness, the ceiling below the great divide should go on with less fuss than you faced in the upper region.

I trust that Figures 12-5 and 12-6 will make these schemes clear. You may get the feeling about now that all this switching of scenery and attack is needlessly complicated and even downright silly—and so it is in many boats, especially those that are long and lean, with much deadrise from garboard to bilge. Experiment with edge bending, and do the job the easiest way you can.

But a new problem rises to confront you here: What about all those holes through the planking, with their through-hull sleeves and seacocks? "Hah!" says you. "I'm too smart for that foolishness. There won't be any holes." Nope. Just two cockpit scuppers, water inlet, exhaust outlet, stack drain for the engine, transducer to starboard, sink drain to port, inlet and outlet for the toilet, outlet for the bilge pump, above-water vent for the gas-bottle locker—and so on. You can't, I think, dispense with all of these, no matter how primitive you're willing to go. And every one of these through-hull fittings (except the exhaust outlet, which usually goes through the transom) must be exposed in a gap in the ceiling, and not a tiny one, either. Figure 12-8 takes a close look at the process of making a through-hull fitting.

You've probably messed things up already, in your youthful exuberance. You have my sympathy, because I have never yet, in 55 years of fitting ceiling, ever once planned ahead for these openings. However, I have usually managed to drench the planking, butt blocks, and frames with a couple of coats of oil and poison, sometimes with red lead in the mix, before hiding them forever from human eyes; but I have always done this too late for drying, and have finished the ceiling job bruised, slippery, and smelling to high Heaven. In Ratty's immortal words, there's nothing—absolutely nothing—half so much worth doing as simply messing about in boats. Especially if you own a second set of work clothes and can spare the first for a week's airing. Be warned. And when you leave those openings in the ceiling, fit the reinforcing blocks as you go (and even bore for the through-hull sleeves) and make sure you don't interfere with the updraft, or let slide your jackknife or bevel gauge behind the fresh-laid lining.

figure 12–8

Through-hull fitting

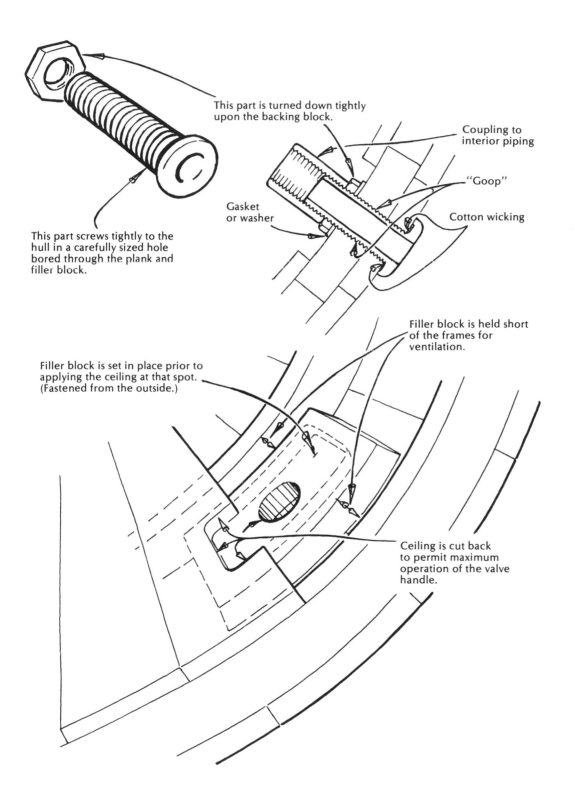

This part is turned down tightly upon the backing block.

Coupling to interior piping

"Goop"

Gasket or washer

Cotton wicking

This part screws tightly to the hull in a carefully sized hole bored through the plank and filler block.

Filler block is held short of the frames for ventilation.

Filler block is set in place prior to applying the ceiling at that spot. (Fastened from the outside.)

Ceiling is cut back to permit maximum operation of the valve handle.

Chapter Thirteen

Deck Framing

It's a great day indeed when you remove the molds. But don't be in too great a hurry; a few things need doing before you break them loose.

I assume that you've been properly cautious, with ties across from sheer to sheer in the middle third of the hull (to prevent spreading) and braces between frames below the future location of the sheer clamp in the ends of the vessel, where she'll try to come together. You should mark a true, pure line, representing the underside of the covering board, identical port and starboard, on the sheerstrake, with due allowance for the crown of the deck. The sheer marks on the molds will help you get this right. Dress off the sheerstrakes to this line.

Be sure to run a pencil line down the inside of the planking, along the business edge of each mold. If you haven't yet followed my instructions in Chapter 11, I wish you'd roll a strand of cotton into the topside seams, and even do some smoothing above the turn of the bilge, to calm the visitors, but I'm afraid this is too much to expect—so go ahead and yank the molds out. As soon as you've finished gawking at the vastness of that hold, we'll consider the problems of the deck frames.

In its simplest form, the deck frame consists of beams extending from side to side of the vessel, usually spaced about the same distance apart as the hull frames—with various openings left for houses, hatches, cockpits—and damned well fastened at both ends to resist the weight of years and boarding seas. This end fastening has taken various forms through the centuries, ranging from spruce-root lashings, hanging knees fastened to frame heads, mortise-and-tenon joints through the sheerstrake, to the system most of us now use, which I will describe here.

The sheer clamp

The first move is to fit and fasten a timber to the insides of the frames, with its top edge below the top of the sheerstrake by the depth of the beams, and extending from the stem to the transom. This is a simple enough proposition, with only two inherent pitfalls.

You'll notice the first problem (as I finally did about the third time around) when you lay your concave beam mold across the hull from sheer to sheer and mark on the inside of the frame for the top edge of the sheer clamp at that frame. If the vessel has tumblehome, plumb, or even slightly flaring topsides, that mark must be, below your mold, much less than the depth of the beam. The beam must hit the inboard edge of the clamp. In the forward sections,

figure 13-1

Square-edged clamp timber set to the height of the underside of the deckbeam without correction

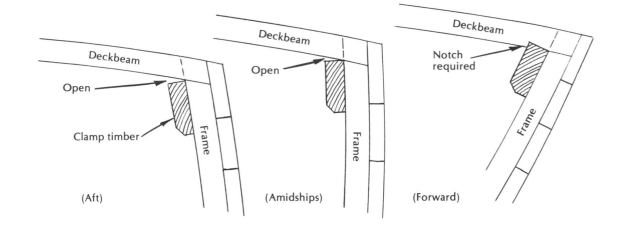

(Aft) (Amidships) (Forward)

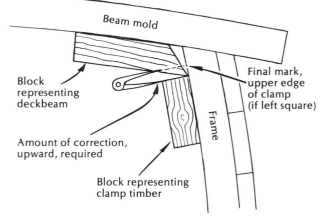

where the topsides very likely flare decidedly outward and the beams are short, the opposite effect occurs: the inboard edge of the clamp is higher than the outboard and must be notched to get full-width contact with the bottom of the beam. Figure 13-1 shows this effect better than I can describe it.

The second problem crops up in the forward part of the vessel. It's very likely that the flare of the topsides will demand a humped-up curve, which you may have noticed when you fitted the sheerstrakes. Since the clamp is to be a 1½- by 4½-inch timber, you are not likely to get this curve by edge-setting. Perhaps you'll have to steam it, or even saw it to shape; maybe you'll split it (horizontally, of course) with a saw cut, back to the point where the timber straightens out and starts curving in the other direction (see Figure 13-2a). The latter scheme works fine, and never mind what people say. By the time you bolt the beams to the split clamp vertically and bolt the frames horizontally every foot or so, it'll be plenty strong.

Cut the forward end of the sheer clamp to bear snugly against the back of the stem, make the scarf cut (2 feet long, horizontal cut; see Figure 13-2b) at the after end, slide it forward on top of your temporary cross-braces, and haul it out to the frames with all the clamps you can muster. You'll be happy you fastened the sheerstrake with screws, because you can now back them out and replace them with ⅜-inch galvanized carriage bolts. Up, down, up, down—counterbore the bolt holes to set the heads ½ inch into the sheerstrake (fill the holes flush to the planking with polyester putty if you're going to paint the hull).

Assuming you can't get stock long enough to make a one-piece clamp, cut a matching scarf on the after piece and spring it to the marks. Lock the scarf together, lay the after end out over the transom, and cut it to bear tightly against the transom frame. Bolt the clamp to the frames as above, and put four vertical bolts through the scarf.

Don't worry when the croakers say, "She'll hog, sure'n hell, 'thout that clamp's one piece!" Just you wait until we get a shelf into her.

Mid-station marks

Right now, with the deck plan in hand, you need a benchmark from which to plot your boundary stakes. Lay a straightedge across the hull from sheer to sheer, with one edge exactly centered above the 'midship station mark on the top of the keel. As shown in Figure 13-3, stretch a string from the center of the stem to the center of the sternpost to get the athwartships center of the straightedge. Measure from this point, port and starboard, to the outside of the planking, and be properly proud if she proves to be no more than an inch wider on one side than on the other. File this information in the back of your mind, or in your notebook if you must, and go on to your main objective, which is to spot two points on the straightedge exactly equidistant from the center, and as far out as is convenient—right at the sheer, probably. Now hook your 50-foot tape or nonstretching wire to the exact center of the after

figure 13-2a

Clamp timber at the bow

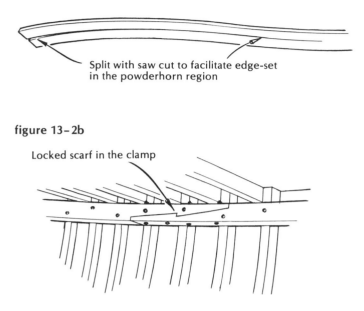

Split with saw cut to facilitate edge-set in the powderhorn region

figure 13-2b

Locked scarf in the clamp

figure 13-3

Mid-station marks established at the gunwales for purpose of laying out deck timbering

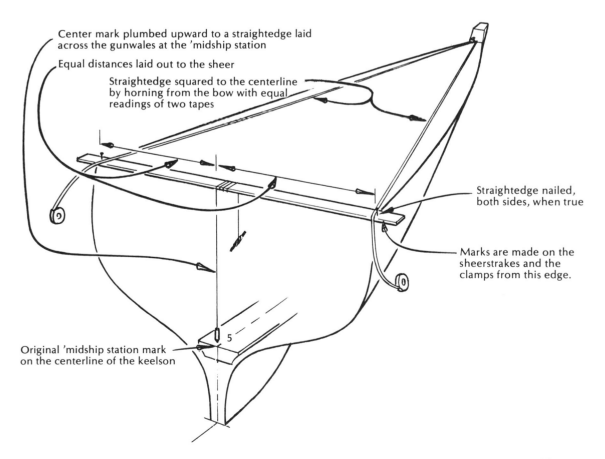

Center mark plumbed upward to a straightedge laid across the gunwales at the 'midship station

Equal distances laid out to the sheer

Straightedge squared to the centerline by horning from the bow with equal readings of two tapes

Straightedge nailed, both sides, when true

Marks are made on the sheerstrakes and the clamps from this edge.

Original 'midship station mark on the centerline of the keelson

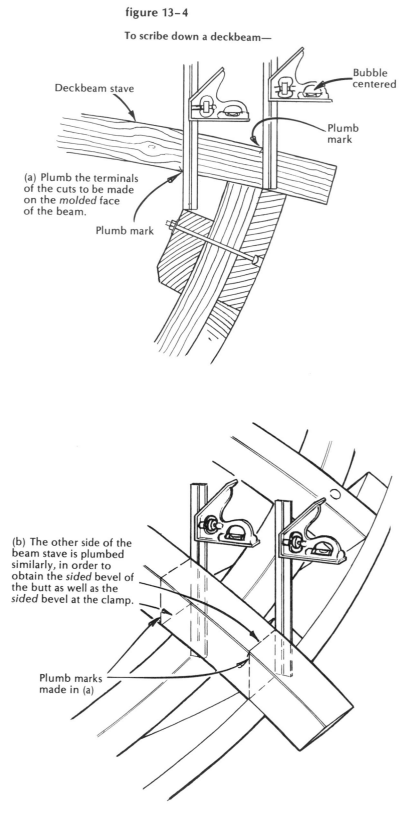

figure 13-4

To scribe down a deckbeam—

Deckbeam stave

Bubble centered

Plumb mark

(a) Plumb the terminals of the cuts to be made on the *molded* face of the beam.

Plumb mark

(b) The other side of the beam stave is plumbed similarly, in order to obtain the *sided* bevel of the butt as well as the *sided* bevel at the clamp.

Plumb marks made in (a)

face of the stem, and proceed to adjust the straightedge until the two points on it are equally distant from the stem, even as they remain equally distant from the center. Check your marks with a plumb bob, from the station mark on the keel; then nail the straightedge to the sheerstrakes, so that it'll stay put while you lay off all your longitudinal distances from it.

Mark these essential longitudinal distances—the ends of the cockpit, the ends of the house, the forward hatch, the centerline of the mast, the chainplates, all of the deckbeams—on the sheerstrake *and* on the top of the sheer clamp, being very careful to indicate on which side of the mark the beam is to be placed. It's embarrassing indeed, as I've found on several occasions, to discover that you've fitted, and fastened, a beam forward of the mark on one side and aft of it on the other. Ah, well—unless a bulkhead lands there, probably no one will notice.

Cutting and fitting the deckbeams

Now, armed with a tri-square with a bubble, dividers with a pencil leg, crosscut and rip saws, chisel and mallet, you are ready to mark, cut, and fasten the main deckbeams, if you have any handy. I blithely assumed a while back that you had a proper beam mold to use while dressing the sheerstrakes fair for the underside of the deck and for marking for the height of the sheer clamp. Use this pattern to mark those fine, sweeping planks you saved out, so that the grain follows the crown of the beam (5 inches of crown in 10 feet of length, or whatever your designer calls for).

I always saw out deckbeams with a light-gauge, well-set, sharp 10-inch table saw or (rarely) with the ubiquitous 7½-inch portable electric circular saw. Either of these tools does a smoother job than the bandsaw. Check the sawn beams carefully against the pattern, because they may change shape after sawing.

If you lack sweeping stock to make sawn beams, you can steam-bend straight stock on a form, over-bending enough to retain the proper crown when you take them off the form. Or you can glue-laminate the beams over forms with five plies of a wood that glues well—a process much loved in these times because, we are told, at last someone has come up with a way to make wood a satisfactory boatbuilding material. I almost wrote Viable Alternative instead of satisfactory; if I did, I would have put a trademark symbol after the term.... I druther saw them out, myself. Maybe they won't be compatible with the Space Age, but they'll be good oak or locust, and will hold fastenings forevermore, and won't delaminate, no matter what.

Set up staging inside the boat to match the outside staging to make the sheer about belly-button high when you climb aboard with your tool kit and one of your long beams. Lay said beam across the boat on top of the sheer planks, exactly over the spot it will drop to after you've cut it to length. Clamp the beam somehow, so it can't shift position.

Look at Figure 13–4 and proceed to mark for the end cuts: Plumb up from the inside edge of the sheerstrake to the top of the beam; plumb up from the inside top corner of the clamp to the bottom edge of the beam (and a little higher); set your pencil-bearing dividers ¼ inch less than the plumb distance from the top of the sheerstrake to the top of the beam; and scribe a line at this distance, above the top of the sheer clamp, on the forward and after faces of the beam. (The "¼ inch less" is not introduced to allow for errors, but rather to allow you to set the beam into a notch of that depth on the sheer clamp.)

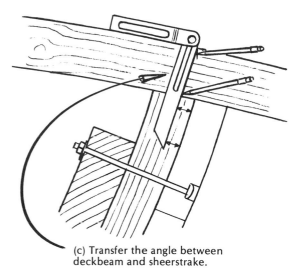

(c) Transfer the angle between deckbeam and sheerstrake.

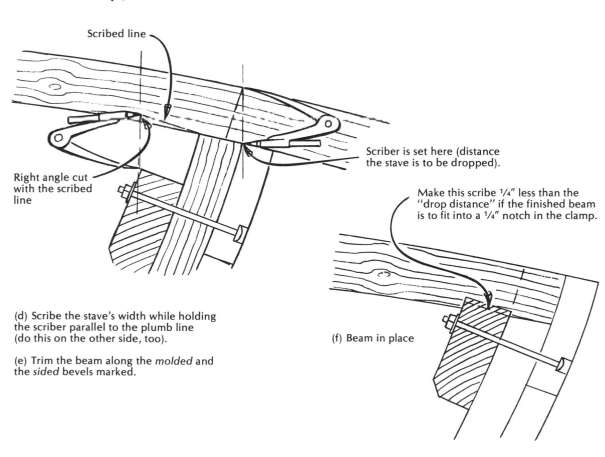

Scribed line

Right angle cut with the scribed line

Scriber is set here (distance the stave is to be dropped).

Make this scribe ¼" less than the "drop distance" if the finished beam is to fit into a ¼" notch in the clamp.

(d) Scribe the stave's width while holding the scriber parallel to the plumb line (do this on the other side, too).

(e) Trim the beam along the *molded* and the *sided* bevels marked.

(f) Beam in place

figure 13–5

To locate and hold a carlin—

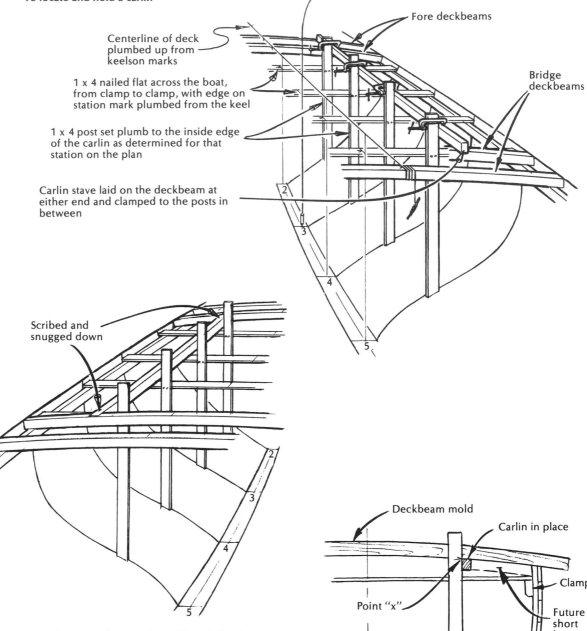

Centerline of deck plumbed up from keelson marks

1 x 4 nailed flat across the boat, from clamp to clamp, with edge on station mark plumbed from the keel

1 x 4 post set plumb to the inside edge of the carlin as determined for that station on the plan

Carlin stave laid on the deckbeam at either end and clamped to the posts in between

Fore deckbeams

Bridge deckbeams

Scribed and snugged down

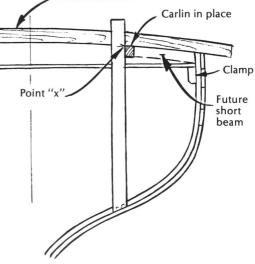

Deckbeam mold

Carlin in place

Point "x"

Clamp

Future short beam

Now mark, on the side of the beam, the angle of the end cut from the plumbed-up mark at the top, down and parallel to the inside of the sheerstrake. Then mark a line on the top of the beam, parallel to the top edge of the sheerstrake. Tread softly to the other side of the boat and go through the whole process on the other end of the beam.

Put the beam down on the staging, kneel on it, and make the following three cuts: (1) end cut with a crosscut saw; (2) underside cut with a ripsaw, working to the scribed lines on the fore and aft faces and stopping at the mark plumbed up from the corner of the clamp; and (3) a little sloping cut to free this piece.

You can now try the beam in place. It should stand 1/4 inch too high, and this amount you'll cut into the top of the clamp, so the beam will drop down just flush with the sheerstrake and with a little jog against the inside of the clamp.

I'm happy that's over with, and that I don't have to struggle through those directions myself; but you're lucky to have Sam Manning's drawings to go by. Please hark to my warning that there are no shortcuts, yet rest assured that you'll be able to mark one of these beams in two minutes, automatically, with one eye on the bubble, after you've done three or four.

Is this not dreary stuff? Fussy, tedious moves advancing little toward this fabric's final soaring beauty. But when the beams begin to drop into place—one, two, three, without a miss—you can be very full of joy for a while.

Go ahead and fit all the full-width beams: after and forward ends of the cockpit, after end of the house, middle beam in the bridge deck, forward end of the house, and all the beams in the foredeck. Use the beam mold to make sure you don't have a maverick in the bunch, and fasten them all to the clamps—one 3/8-inch bolt, each end, countersunk, dead center, down through the center, with nut and washer on bottom.

The breasthook, quarter knees, shelf, and blocking will come later. Right now you must install the fore-and-aft carlins that establish the edges of the cockpit and the house. This is the trickiest part of the deck-frame project, and takes some planning.

Your construction half-breadth plan should give the half-breadth of the house from the fore-and-aft centerline at every station. Nail a straight one-by-four on top and on the flat across the hull from clamp to clamp at each station. Stretch your string again and mark exact centers of all these temporary cross members—and while you're at it, the centers of all the beams you have so far installed. Lay off on the end beams and on these horizontal flats the widths to the inside of the carlin. Now at each of these marks fit and fasten a plumb post, inboard of the mark. Lay your beam mold against each in turn, as in Figure 13-5, and behold—the inner top edge of the carlin has to land exactly at Point X; you have a fine row of posts to spring the carlin around and clamp against.

figure 13-6

Carlin at deckbeam

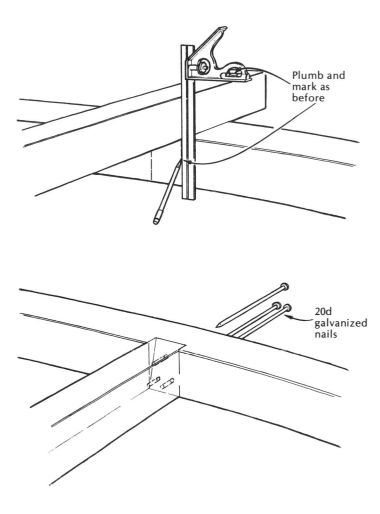

Plumb and mark as before

20d galvanized nails

Fasten blocks on top of the end beams where the *outboard* edge of the carlin will lie, and bend the timber around the posts and on top of the end beams. At this stage of the proceedings you'll want the *lower* edge of the timber to land on the crown marks. Use your tri-square to mark for the end cuts on this timber just as you did on the deckbeams: plumb up from the point where the top of the carlin will land. This point will be 1/2 inch into the face of the beam to allow for a sloping notch (see Figure 13-6).

Figure out the rest of the angles and cuts from the drawing, remembering always that this plumb business works at both ends, unfailingly, and that any deviation from it spells

143

figure 13-7

Sheer curve in the cockpit carlin

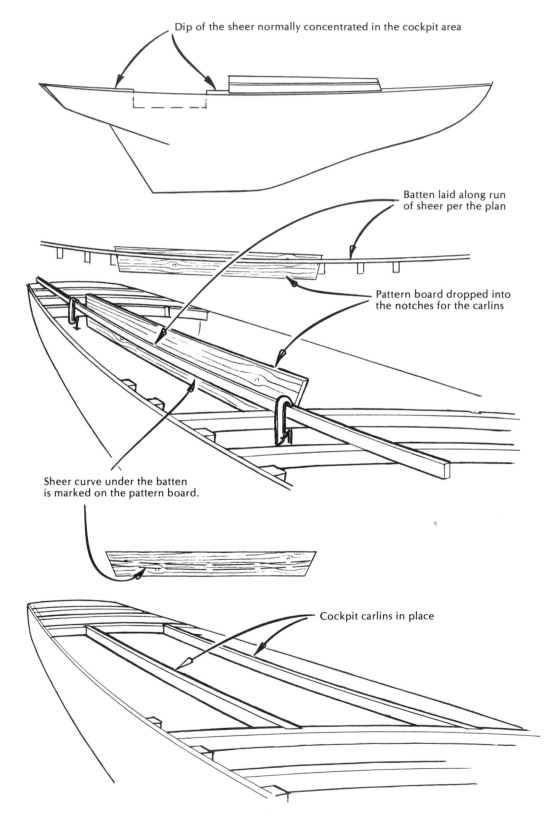

Dip of the sheer normally concentrated in the cockpit area

Batten laid along run of sheer per the plan

Pattern board dropped into the notches for the carlins

Sheer curve under the batten is marked on the pattern board.

Cockpit carlins in place

disaster. Cut the sloping notches in the beams, cut the ends of your carlin timber to match, and spring it in. Push the carlin down and clamp it with the top edge at the crown marks on your temporary posts; drill for and drive three galvanized 20d spikes at each end through the beam and into the end of the carlin (see Figure 13-6).

Go aft now and fit the carlins for the sides of the cockpit. These are usually straight fore and aft, but they must be dipped in profile to match the sheer. This shape can be determined by the same method outlined above; or you can run a batten on top of the bridge-deck and the after-deck beams, alongside a piece of pattern stock dropped into the notches in the main beams. Mark a fair profile on the pattern. Saw to the line, and mark your carlin timbers from it. Saw them out and install as above (see Figure 13-7). You are now ready to fit the short beams.

Lay out the short beams carefully, square to the centerline, exactly opposite each other port and starboard. You'll be happy you did when you install bulkheads, hanging shelves, and deck eyebolts. You will, of course, perceive that the top of the carlin must be dressed off to the crown of the deck. You can do this now or put it off until all the beams and tie-rods are holding the carlin against your attack, but if you choose to defer dressing off, you must be wary of one small effect: Unless you shim up the outboard end of the beam (at the sheerstrake while marking them) to match the incorrect height above the carlin, your marks will be wrong, because one end will have to drop that small bit more than the other to achieve its final resting place.

The boatbuilder's lot is hard enough without adding any avoidable complications, so let's dress off now. Saw off the posts to let your plane go by (you'll have to depress them before you lay the deck, so why not now?) and dress off the top of the carlin to match the deck crown.

As you fit all those short beams, remember to plumb up from a line ½ inch in from the edge of the carlin, the top of the sloping notch; from the inboard edge of the sheerstrake (to give the top of the beam at the outboard end); and from the inboard edge of the sheer clamp— and to scribe up from the clamp with dividers set ¼ inch less than the distance the beam must be dropped (see Figure 13-8). Fit half a dozen beams, tack them in position with 5d box nails, and drill and fasten them all at once. I like to use two or three 20d spikes from the carlin into the end of the beam, and a bolt through the sheer clamp, as you did on the ends of the main beams.

figure 13-8

Short beams joined to a carlin

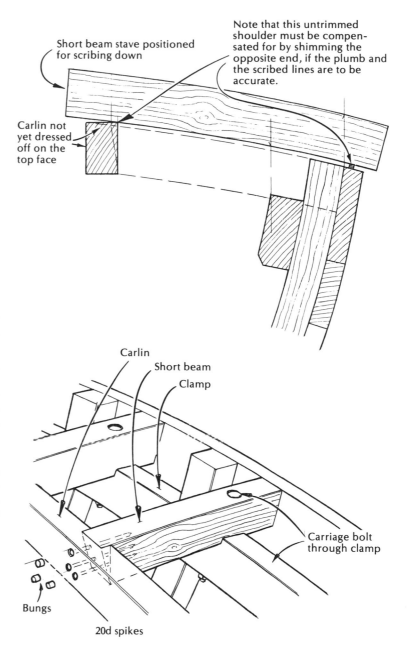

Short beam stave positioned for scribing down

Note that this untrimmed shoulder must be compensated for by shimming the opposite end, if the plumb and the scribed lines are to be accurate.

Carlin not yet dressed off on the top face

Carlin

Short beam

Clamp

Carriage bolt through clamp

Bungs

20d spikes

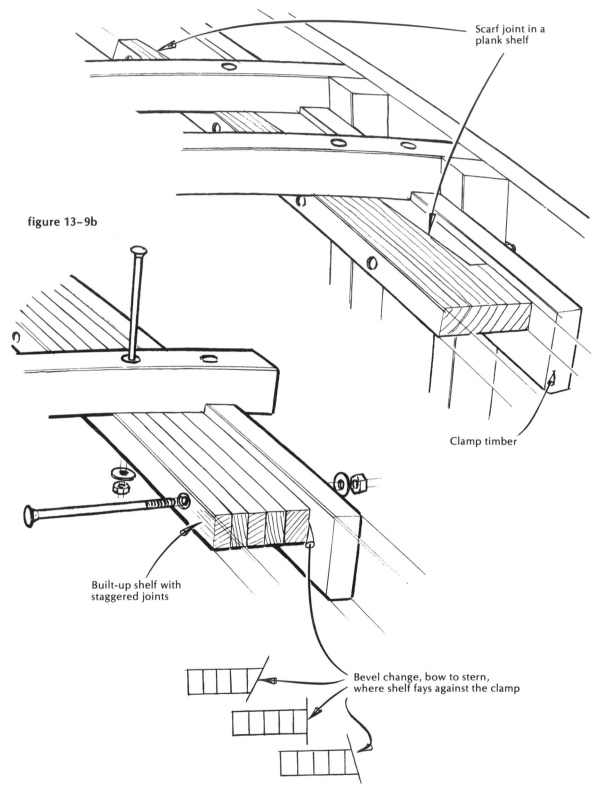

figure 13–9a

Beam shelf

Scarf joint in a plank shelf

Clamp timber

figure 13–9b

Built-up shelf with staggered joints

Bevel change, bow to stern, where shelf fays against the clamp

The beam shelf

Now let's consider the beam shelf. This bit of furniture is a flat stiffener fitted around the sheer under the deckbeams, against the clamp. It can be sawn to shape from several pieces scarfed together (Figure 13-9a), or it can be built up with four or five narrow pieces, say 1½ by 2 inches (Figure 13-9b), sprung into place, and through-bolted to the clamp and the deckbeams. The shelf may go the entire length of the boat, or it may extend only a few feet forward and aft of the main chainplates. Whatever its length, it must be fitted on its outboard edge to a constantly changing bevel on the inboard face of the clamp.

If you are working with fairly heavy timber for the shelf—for example, a plank 2 inches by 12 inches by 14 feet long, to produce a 2- by 5-inch shelf with a scarf at each end—you will be wise to take a spiling on a light, curved spiling board and note the bevels at 2-foot intervals. You can transfer the shape from the spiling board to the stock, and saw the shelf out and bevel it to a fit that is fairly close before you ever take it aboard the boat. Clamp the shelf in place, scribe for the final fit, remove it, dress to the marks, and bolt it solidly to the beams and the clamp. (There is, of course, the possibility that some adjacent beams might not be exactly the same depth. If you can't stand frustration and don't know how to use invisible shims, you shouldn't be in this business.)

With the beams and shelves in place, you can install the tie-rods. These are very important strength members, especially needed under a caulked deck, and especially valuable as the big guns against those sharp-eyed critics who fret about your cheap fastenings from the carlin to the beam ends.

Get out your long ⅜-inch drill, choose likely spots—about 18 inches from each end and no more than 3 feet apart through the rest of the length—and proceed to drill holes through the carlin, the shelf, and the clamp (Figure 13-10a). Countersink for the nut and washer, of course, on the inboard face of the carlin.

An alternative is to run the rod above the shelf and the clamp, out through the frame and the sheerstrake (Figure 13-10b). This system gives the tie-rod a better angle—one that will make the rod more closely parallel to the line of the deck, that is. This system will require more, and still more, higher bungs in the sheerstrake. It's a toss-up which way you do it. Just be sure the rods are square athwartships, or you'll be in trouble when you fit the bulkheads.

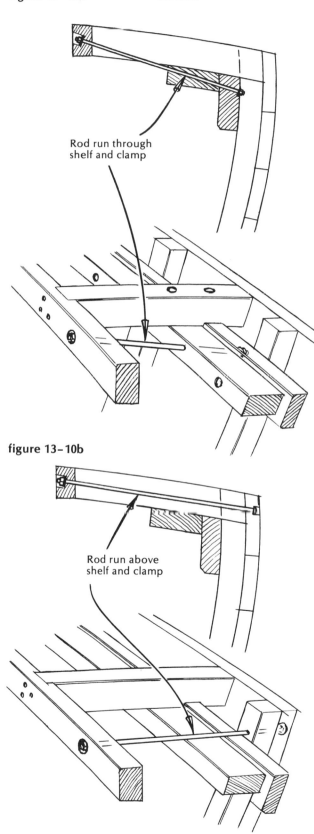

figure 13-10a   Tie-rods

Rod run through shelf and clamp

figure 13-10b

Rod run above shelf and clamp

figure 13-11

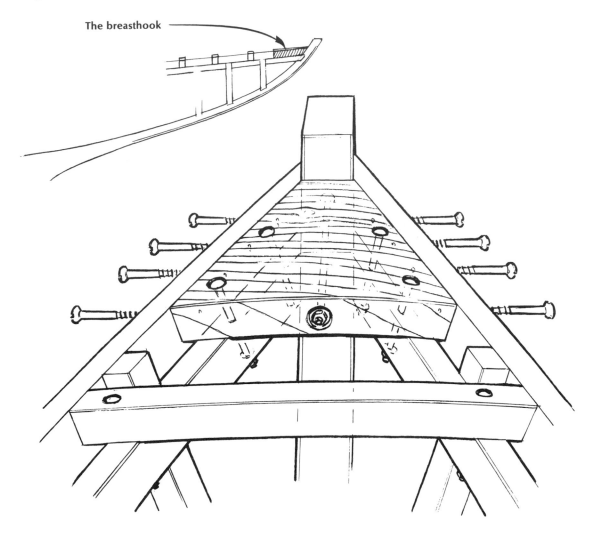

The breasthook

Finishing the deck frame

What more must be done before you can cover all this with something watertight? Not much, just the breasthook; quarter knees; centerline blocking between all the beams in the foredeck, the bridge deck, and the afterdeck; blocking to take bolts from the gallows frame, the mainsheet horse, and the quarter cleats; the under-deck bases for the lifeline stanchions, the anchor windlass, the mooring cleat, the backstay fittings, and the eyebolts—and a few more that you'd better pre-plan before you start laying the deck.

Start with the breasthook. This, in my lexicon, is a block of durable hardwood with its bottom surface fitted to the tops of the sheer clamps, the ends fitted tightly against the sheerstrakes, and the forward (short) side fitted against the after face of the stem. The breasthook grain must run athwartships. The top of the block must be dressed off to the line of the underside of the decking. I usually edge-bore this piece before installing it to take one bolt from the midpoint of the after edge through to the forward face of the stem. Drive two bolts on each side down through the sheer clamps, and four good screws on each side from the sheerstrakes into the breasthook—and you can be reasonably sure that the nose of the vessel will stay together (Figure 13-11).

With all your tools up at the bow, you might as well fit the centerline blocking back to the forward end of the house. This blocking need not be the full depth of the beams, and it may vary in width to accommodate whatever deck furniture will be sited over it: a wide-based windlass, the staysail boom pedestal, the king-

figure 13–12

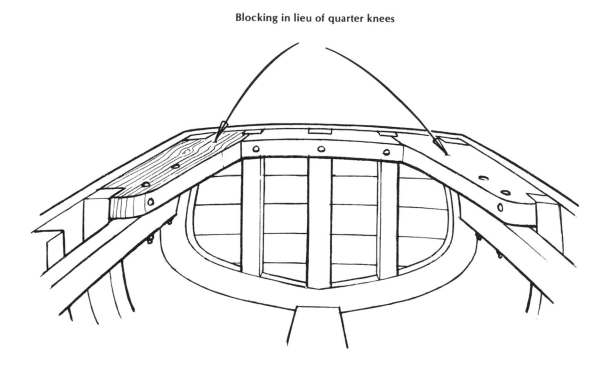

Blocking in lieu of quarter knees

plank, or the butt joint in plywood decking. Also fit a good plank, wide enough to take the widest-spaced bolts in the windlass, with the forward end against the stem, underneath all the beams and back to the hatch opening in the foredeck. Your big bolts from the mooring cleat, the bowsprit socket, and so on, will go down through this plank and tie everything together. Naturally you must fit chocking between the blocking and the plank so you'll have solid wood to tighten against.

Move your gear aft and install the quarter knees. These are invariably shown as beautiful grown crooks, dead-fitted to the transom frame and the inside of the sheerstrake, and presumably bearing upon and bolted to the after ends of the sheer clamps. I prefer to tie this corner together with a big hunk of fore-and-aft grained blocking, partly because I lack such crooks. As

shown in Figure 13–12, it must be bolted to the clamps, pinned to the transom frame, and screw-fastened from the sheerstrakes, and it must have enough area to take all the odd fastenings from the covering boards, the toerail knees, and all the other things that come together at this busy corner.

I almost dare suggest that the end is in sight.

Locate, fit, and fasten the blocking to take the lifeline stanchions. Ditto, ditto, ditto for the gallows frame, the mainsheet horse (tie this one under the beams, something like the mooring-cleat technique up forward), the backstay fittings, and the jib-sheet track—grain fore-and-aft on all.

Put some posts from the keel to the underside of the main beams, and smooth everything off ready for the decking. As for me, I'm going sailing.

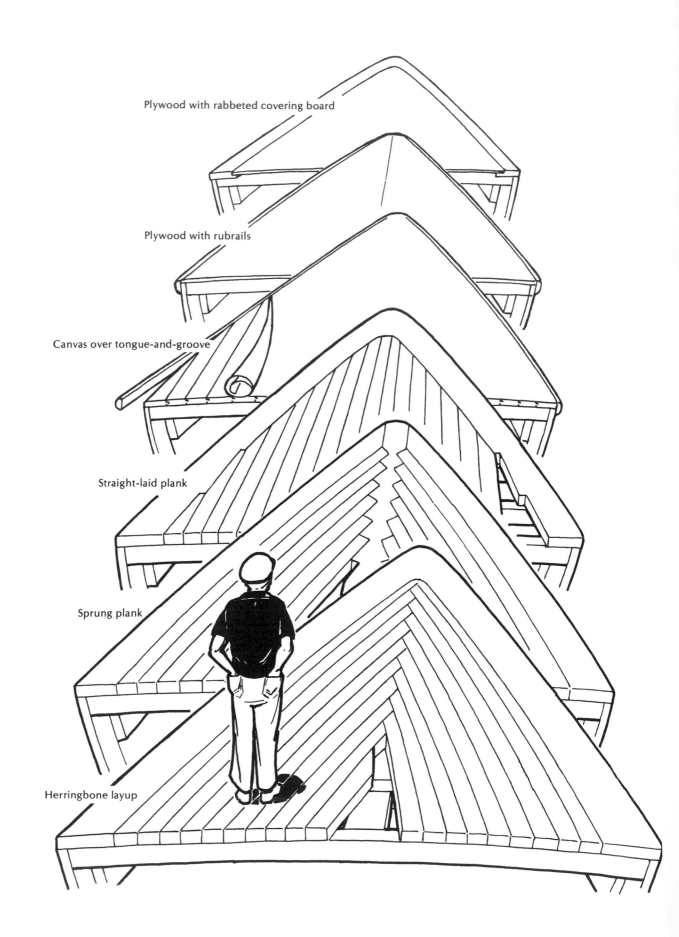

Plywood with rabbeted covering board

Plywood with rubrails

Canvas over tongue-and-groove

Straight-laid plank

Sprung plank

Herringbone layup

Chapter Fourteen

Laying the Deck

Sometimes I think that life must have been much simpler in days of yore—Life, of course, meaning Boatbuilding, which includes deck-laying, which was (and still is) the most important problem we have to face. Everything you needed was at hand, with no searching of soul or advertising pages. You would have saved out, for extra under-cover drying, enough of your best planking stock to do the whole deck. You'd decide, on the basis of size, form, function, and cost, which of two inevitable, classic patterns you'd use—and proceed to lay that deck. You fitted and fastened wood to beams in time-honored pattern, caulked the hell out of the seams, filled them with home-grown sticky stuff, and soaked the deck with salt water once a day. No miracle fillers, no costly coverings— and you could chop wood on it, shovel snow off it, run around barefoot on it. I've done this type of deck in redwood, cypress, cedar, pine, fir, and teak, with bits of mahogany at times for covering boards and margin planks. Some of them needed re-caulking after one year, or 12, and some didn't leak at all.

I think it's safe to say that this classic laid deck is the right one to use on a big workboat, the best-looking on a yacht big enough to stand the weight, and possibly the least expensive in materials (and most expensive in labor) of all the many choices now available. I'll state here the rash, biased, and probably foolish generalization that this classic deck should not be attempted in less than $7/8$-inch thickness, which means that it's not for small, light boats. I'll make the further observation that if you've got enough sense to come in out of the wet (a very good comparison in the present instance, and purely coincidental, I assure you), you'll leave this deck construction to us old relics from a bygone age, and you'll sell your soul for a mess of pottage that looks suspiciously like thin wood layers buttered with chewing gum.

We'll get to that later. At the moment, I'll share a secret with you: I hope to build the Perfect Singlehander this winter (I've already reduced the choices to only seven hull forms and four rigs), and the one item I'm sure of is the deck, which will be laid, and caulked, and cursed, and patched, and oh, so beautiful that my heart will leap up at the sight of it. And it'll be only $3/4$ inch thick.

Once upon a time I built a big boat for a professor, a solemn and learned man, and we sat in the main cabin beneath a splined-teak housetop discussing the next payment, always a fascinating subject. The boat was yet in the shop, under a splendid one-year-old tar-paper roof, and an April shower trickled through the shop roof, found a gap in the splined teak, and dribbled upon the professor's magnificent and

figure 14-1

Straight-laid deck

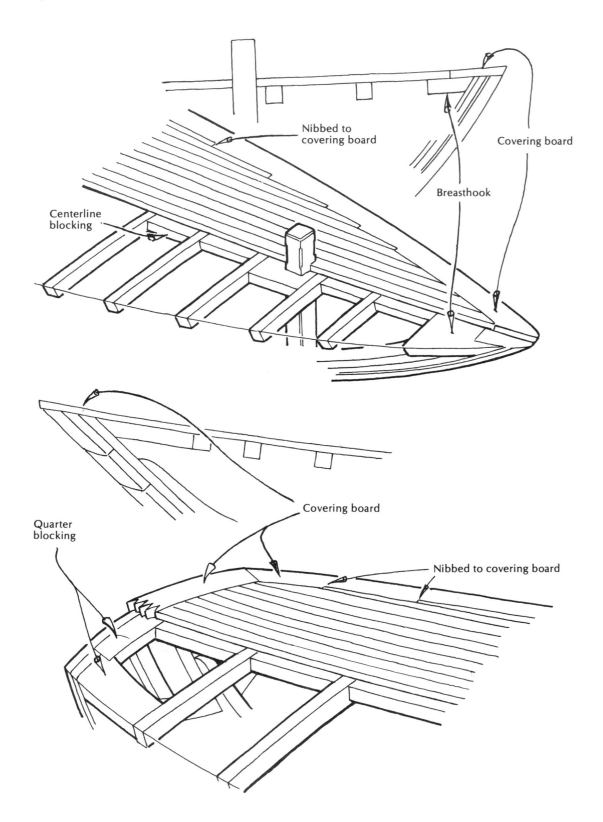

Nibbed to covering board

Covering board

Breasthook

Centerline blocking

Covering board

Quarter blocking

Nibbed to covering board

twitching nose, all to my considerable embarrassment. But he had assured me that Teak Can't Leak (see Claud Worth, pp. such-and-such, *et sequitur*), leaving me in a stronger position than I deserved. You can be sure that I made the most of it. Anyway, we decided that a canvas-covered housetop wasn't too bad an idea after all. I have steadfastly adhered to that belief ever since. As for the main deck, likewise in 1½-inch teak, laid straight fore-and-aft, nibbed into the covering board—that, too, leaked like a...sieve until we recaulked and refilled the whole business, devil seam and all. We (or I, anyway) decided that that teak must have been towed across from Burma; it couldn't have gotten so wet any other way.

So now, leaning heavily on Sam Manning's drawings, I'll try to describe some of the variations on the theme of the laid deck, with special emphasis on my final (to the moment, that is) conclusions as to how it should be done.

Straight-laid decking

As you undoubtedly know, you can lay this deck straight fore-and-aft, parallel to centerline and nibbed into covering board and margin planks (see Figure 14-1). With no edge-bending involved, the strips can be wide enough to take two good fastenings at each beam. The nibbing need not start until the angle between the deck plank and the covering board gets to be less than 20 degrees. I like to leave the absolute minimum of blocking under the joints; if the rain from heaven breaches the first defense, it's far better to let it dissipate its strength on the skipper's bunk than to confine it in a dark and savory rot pocket. I shudder at the thought of trying to keep the joints between the covering board, knightheads, and stem tight, and the hundred stanchions I've put through covering boards (though their substance was the best black locust) arise to haunt my memory. So I say, saw off the stem, run the decking right over it (and over the top of the transom, too), and do not pierce the covering board with anything except twice as many fastenings as you think necessary, into deckbeams and sheerstrake. When you caulk that devil seam, you want to feel confident that it will resist mightily any attempt to spread it. (Of course you know about the devil seam? It's the seam at the inboard edge of the covering board; and when you're between the Devil and the deep blue sea, with the water seething through the scuppers, you want to have a good grip on a shroud, and

you hope that the caulkers had some pitch hot when it came time to pay that seam.)

We have yet to decide what to do where the laid deck is interrupted by openings—house, cockpit, hatches. If these deck structures are parallel-sided fore-and-aft, you can lay the deck to the inside of the openings, caulk with infinite care, and even put in vertical stopwaters where the ends will be covered by the bedded, belted coamings. Or you can, as you nearly must do if your life is complicated by a curved house side, install margin planks on carlins and deckbeams, with light blocking and doubled-up beams, respectively, to take the ends of the decking, and keep all caulked seams in the open (see Figures 14-3 and 14-4). This is, of course, standard practice on big vessels. I have usually (after a brief struggle with my conscience, and with sublime confidence in whatever sticky stuff is at hand) brought myself to omit the athwartship margins and go for hidden seams under the ends of the house. You can always put stopwaters in them from the outside—round ones, in drilled holes, or cedar wedges with the caulking hard against them. (See Figure 14-2.)

What more should we say about straight-laid decking? If you want a rule of thumb, and the plans don't specify it, make the strips twice as wide as they are thick, the covering board

figure 14-2

Deck plank laid to the inside of opening

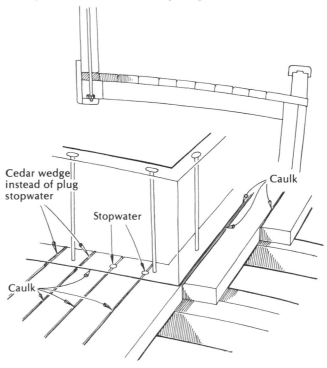

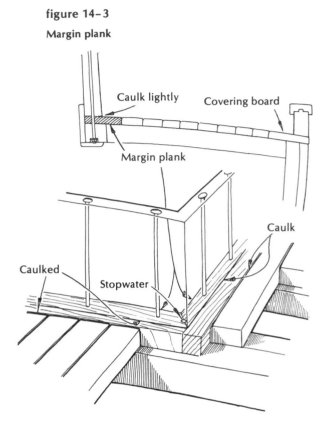

figure 14–3

Margin plank

Caulk lightly

Covering board

Margin plank

Caulk

Caulked

Stopwater

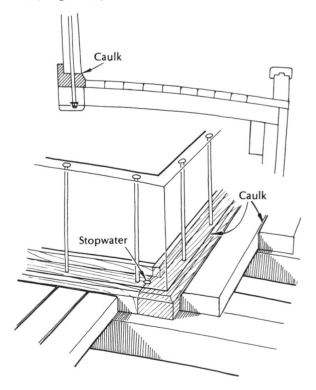

figure 14–4

Sill, or grub strip

Caulk

Caulk

Stopwater

about five times as wide as it is thick, of constant width except at the forward ends where port and starboard round in nicely to meet in a centerline seam on the breasthook and stemhead. (And before you install the bowsprit, caulk that seam, and poison it, and fill it, and bless it, and cover it with sheet lead or copper folded down the sides and face of the stem.) You can shape this covering board out of a harder wood than the rest of the decking. You'll saw it to shape, each side in at least three pieces scarfed or butted together. The butt joint is the easier of the two (done on a block between) deckbeams, the same as a plank butt, peppered with fastenings, saturated with poison, caulked and filled). And *don't* lay out and cut the nibs all at once, before installing the piece, or you'll get yourself in a hell of a mess. Mark and cut each strip of deck planking as you come to it, and mark from it the necessary cut in the covering board—done lengthwise with your smallest hand-held power saw almost to the 1-inch-square jog at the forward end. With no blocking underneath, the end cut can be made with a fine-toothed handsaw, and the corner cleaned out with a chisel. To support the nib end between deckbeams, hang a 1- by 3- by 6-inch piece of locust under it, screw-fastened from the covering board and the preceding strip of decking. (See Figures 14–5 and 14–6.) Thus you'll avoid the painful job of fitting a solid block between the beams, and achieve the same result with less work and more ventilation.

I once launched a new schooner, and the owner and the guests moved joyfully aboard to spend the first night afloat. Came the dawn, and the beams from the rising sun shone through a gap under the covering board and dazzled the eyes of the half-awake owner, so that he thought his bunk must be on fire. He came ashore without breakfast, not too damned pleased, and told us about it. And I say unto you, who are about to deck a boat: Plane the top of that sheerstrake smooth and fair, so that a fly attempting to light on it will slip helplessly off. Set the covering board in sticky goo and fasten it to the (hardwood) sheerstrake with a long screw every 6 inches. After you've fitted and fastened the toerail (with long drifts or continuous-threaded rod), then caulk the seam tenderly, and assume that it'll stay light-tight and mosquito-proof. Otherwise you, too, may awake with the sun in your eyes (or moonbeams, which are more dangerous).

I forgot to start you with bone-dry decking, cut to size and racked up in the hottest part of the shop overhead for at least two months

figure 14–5

Nibs in the covering board

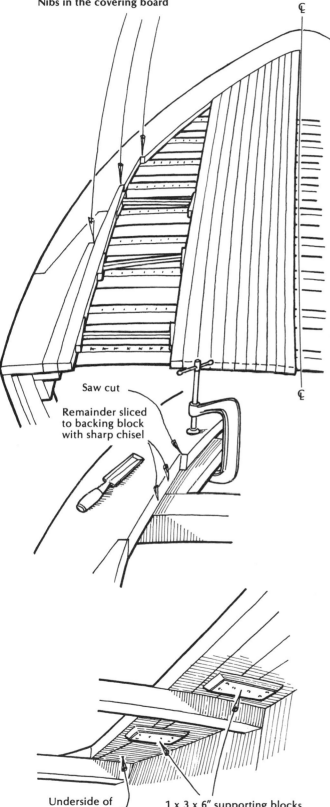

Saw cut

Remainder sliced
to backing block
with sharp chisel

Underside of
covering board

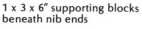

1 x 3 x 6″ supporting blocks
beneath nib ends

before you are ready to fit it. And after you've caulked the whole deck, maybe you ought to remember Pete Culler's advice and not be in too much of a hurry to fill the seams flush. Saturate them with paint and oil and poison; if they show signs of weeping at the end of the first season, harden down the cotton, and soak them some more. When they've all settled down, serene in their ability to protect your bunk, fill them with something old-fashioned that will soften in the sunlight and adjust forever to the width of the seam.

Fastenings for this straight-laid deck: I like galvanized blunt-pointed boat nails, about two and one-half times as long as the deck is thick. Drill and counterbore for them, of course; set them with a hollow-nosed punch made from ³/₈-inch mild steel or copper. Or dig deeper into your wallet and buy Anchorfast bronze ring nails, number 8 wire or even heavier. Make the kingplank wide enough to take the cleat, wind-lass, and bowsprit, and still leave no seam covered.

Let's leave this and consider the beautiful sprung deck and its problems.

Sprung decking

You know, of course, what this looks like: narrow strips bent edgewise to the line of the sheer, nibbed into a kingplank (Figure 14–6) or herringboned together on the forward and after decks. The system works best on a long and easy curve, and the strips of decking must

155

figure 14–6

Deck for 56′ schooner

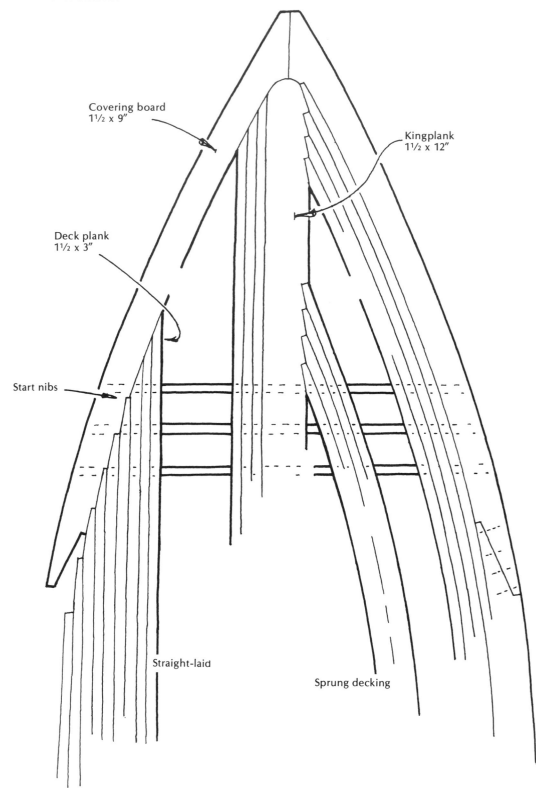

Covering board
1½ x 9″

Kingplank
1½ x 12″

Deck plank
1½ x 3″

Start nibs

Straight-laid

Sprung decking

be narrow, limber, and flawless. You can scarf pieces together to reach the length of the deck. You can blind-fasten them to the beams, run in a strand of cotton, fill the seams flush with color to show up well against the wood. You can oil it, and scrub it, and become a slave to the loveliest of all decks. Sometimes, in some cases, the effort is justified, and you can dwell with beauty and joy forever—if you can get some reliable party to sluice it down twice a day when you're not on board. And you can hedge your bet with the thought that this is the almost-perfect base for a canvas covering. Not so good as you could have achieved, with one-fifth the labor, in plywood, but still pretty good. And anyway, t'were better to have loved and lost than never to have loved at all. So turn your back on me and spring those strips. But *please* try to mill your stock to show edge grain on top, and dry it long and hot, and tunk it on end to snug it out to the covering board between clamps.

Consider these questions: Have you installed plenty of tie-rods from the clamps to the carlins? Have you sozzled the timberheads and beam tops with poison? Fitted blocking for the lifeline stanchions? Beveled for the caulking seams, and applied two coats of paint on the bottom and sides of every strip a week before you're ready to lay them? Have you weighed using blind-finished nails against the alternative of putting one good bunged bronze nail straight down the middle? *Really* convinced yourself that this is the way to go? (Remember what young W. Shakespeare said once: Lilies that fester smell far worse than weeds.) And remember that teak was once (a hundred years ago, in England) considered to be at best a reasonable substitute for Québec yellow pine—which is our noble white pine, *Pinus strobus*, complete with the King's broad arrow. For my money, cedar is better than either of them—and a laid, caulked deck, painted a light color, is a far better bet than the same deck left bare.

And finally: If you pay any attention to the doubts expressed above, you will cause me great disappointment. This involvement of ours, this almost passionate and slightly unreasonable feeling we have for wooden boats, does not welcome quantitative analysis in terms of man-hours, materials costs, and consumer demand. We're just ornery enough to think that we can take a few ancient hand tools and shape natural wood into a thing of great beauty and usefulness. No matter what you may think, I love that sprung laid deck.

Caulking

With that point settled, I'd like to say a few words about caulking. I usually avoid the subject because my mallet doesn't ring, and let's face it, I never apprenticed under a real pro, nor helped hawse the oakum into a real seam. I have even been known to use a wheel on hull and deck seams (about a thousand miles of them, in 70 or 80 fair-sized boats, over the past 60 years). You might as well say that I also advocate feeding every third baby girl to the crocodiles, or even outlawing apple pie. Ah, yes. The competent caulker feels the weight of final responsibility. However bad the planking or decking job (and they're usually pretty bad), he and only he can make them tight and save the ship from total worthlessness. That's all fine and probably correct. All I want to say is this: These strips of decking (especially single-fastened sprung strips, and skinny ends) are not too steady on their feet. You can caulk one side hard enough to push it off balance and get uneven results. So what you do is caulk both sides at the same time (see Figure 14-7). This may sound like a complicated process requiring at least four hands, but you'll get the idea in a very few minutes. Start the cotton in two seams (even in *all* the seams, clear across from the covering board to the kingplank), somewhat less than half as firm as it should end up, and work back and forth, side to side, ever tighter—until it's tight enough, and all even. How do you know it's tight enough? You hit it with your caulking iron, or lean on it with your wheel, of course. And then you soak it full of paint before darkness descends upon you. I used to caulk lightly, so that the owner couldn't peer up through the gaps, and never thought of priming the tightened seams till spring and putty time came round. I understand from recent reading that this dilatory attitude is almost sure to bring on ruin. So saturate that new-driven cotton with whatever it says on the can, and hope that you'll remember to get a seam filler that doesn't fight with it.

Canvasing

Outside the window as I write this sits the sloop *Micky Finn*, built in the year 1937, and a damned plain job at that. Iron fastenings, native pine plank (with a goodly proportion of sapwood), and the iron fastenings punched and puttied. For a deck, we nailed tongue-and-groove pine sheathing to deckbeams and sheer-

figure 14–7

Caulking

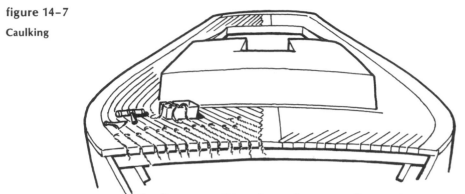

Simultaneous caulking of several seams, or all seams, from kingplank to covering board, prevents the plank strips from crowding or tumbling.

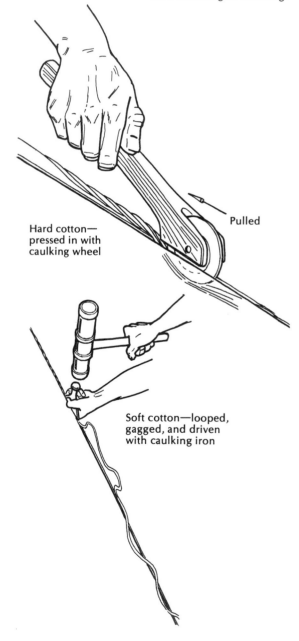

Hard cotton—pressed in with caulking wheel

Pulled

Soft cotton—looped, gagged, and driven with caulking iron

strakes, smoothed and trimmed it somewhat, primed it with one coat of lead 'n' oil, and stretched and tacked number 10 canvas over the whole business (as shown in Figure 14-8). At this point, of course, advice came in from all sides. "Too late!" said one. "Should have laid it in cement." And another: "Soak it with water, and paint it wringing wet; that way you'll save half the paint." A third: "Fill it with glue sizing, and get a *really* smooth surface!" Yet again: "Shrink it with airplane dope, or it'll never lie smooth." So we, in our perverse ignorance, mixed up all the odds and ends of leftover paint in the shop, strained it through a piece of burlap, and brushed it on the canvas until the cotton fibers were completely saturated. I'm afraid we did everything wrong. But there she sits, outside the window, sound aloft and alow, waiting for spring and another season afloat, with most of that original canvas still intact and keeping the water out. There's the reason, I think, that this plain and simple sloop has seen two generations of slick yachts come in glory and go in dust. Damp dust, that is, where the lovely deck joinerwork opened up just enough to admit the night dews and the busy little fungi. Canvas I have loved, and it has functioned predictably for me for slightly over half a century.

Plywood decking with covering board

So we come to fiberglass, which is here to stay. As far as I am concerned, it demands more patience, skill, money, and time than I am able to devote to it. A dedicated practitioner can spend 30 hours on a 30-foot deck and fortify it for the ages—if (they tell me) he works over flawless plywood, uses the Better Resin, and seals the raw edges with eight coats. I'm sure he

figure 14–8

Canvased deck—*Micky Finn* (1937)

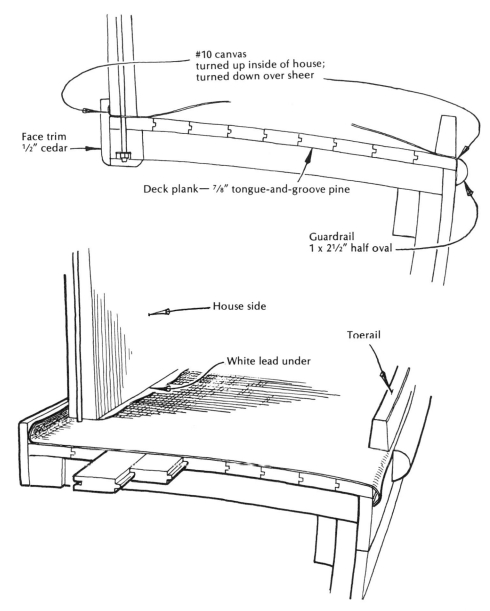

#10 canvas
turned up inside of house;
turned down over sheer

Face trim
½" cedar

Deck plank— ⅞" tongue-and-groove pine

Guardrail
1 x 2½" half oval

House side

White lead under

Toerail

wouldn't waste his time and substance over that tongue-and-groove pine deck. Not if he were smart, he wouldn't. The wood would let go or the glass would split, and the little bugs would flourish merrily in the gap.

But plywood is wonderful. It depends not on tie-rods to maintain its integrity as a glued-up rigid slab. You make butt joints, halfway between deckbeams, on plywood pads tightly fitted to the beams and the sheerstrake. Saturate all contact surfaces with waterproof glue and fasten together with screws in double rows 2

inches apart. No need to rout out and caulk. Just be sure that the deck paint lies smoothly, with no crack showing over the joint. You can cover this plywood, as mentioned above, with canvas or glass; you can use it as a base for a teak overlay, which is a kind of upside-down sophistry; or you can hide it under roofing paper, or tar and gravel, or deck paint loaded with sander dust. If you can get a good overlaid plywood, equal to the old Super Harborite (come to think of it, nothing is likely to be that good, but you can try), and seal it with super

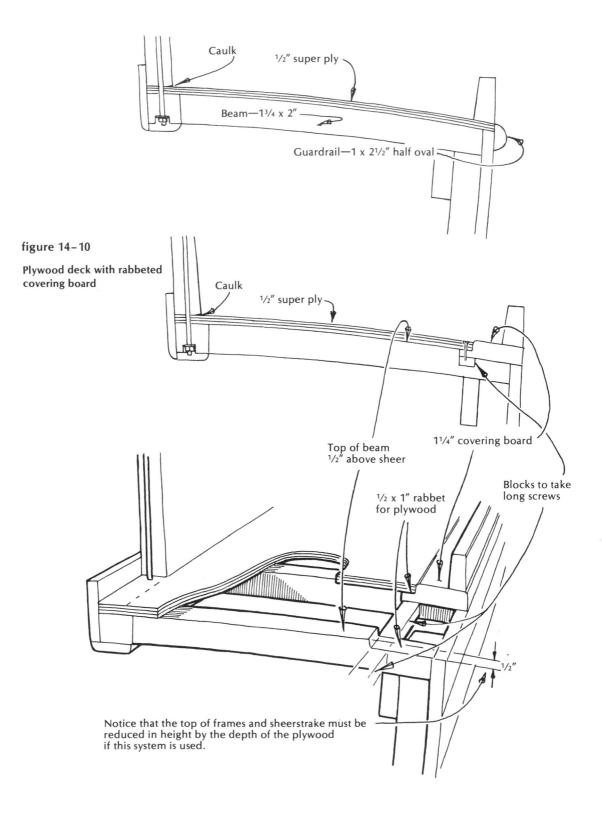

figure 14–9

Plywood deck with rubrail

Caulk

½" super ply

Beam—1¾ x 2"

Guardrail—1 x 2½" half oval

figure 14–10

Plywood deck with rabbeted covering board

Caulk

½" super ply

1¼" covering board

Top of beam ½" above sheer

Blocks to take long screws

½ x 1" rabbet for plywood

½"

Notice that the top of frames and sheerstrake must be reduced in height by the depth of the plywood if this system is used.

160

poisons, and then just paint it—over the proper saturation of special clear sealer, of course— then you'll have the best utilitarian deck I know of. I've used it thus over the past 25 years for decks, footwells, coal chutes, saw tables, and culling boards in my oyster boat. That overlay is tougher 'n a boiled owl, or a piece of old iron, and the plies stick together like musk oxen facing the wolf pack. But you've got to seal those edges and hide them where neither fog, nor dew, nor unclean thoughts can creep in and corrupt.

The obvious way is to carry this plywood out over the sheerstrake, bed and fasten it as directed back there for the covering board, dress it off and seal the raw edge with six coats of poisoned oil, and then cover it with a wide, tough molding, which you can call a rubrail, guardrail, or whatever (see Figure 14-9). Not a bad thing to have between the sheerstrake and a piling, incidentally, if you didn't manage to get fenders in place soon enough. But this molding must be above reproach, bedded and sealed absolutely watertight against the sheerstrake and the deck edge, leaving not the slightest gap for fresh water to enter, and screwfastened expensively, to be removable for inspection.

But perhaps you have good reasons for not using such a rail. Maybe it interferes with trailboards, a covestripe, chainplates, or your own idea of how a yacht should look—with no rubrail cheapening the sheerstrake, and a full inch or more of genuine covering board showing between the sheerstrake and the toerail. Sam's drawings—Figures 14-10, 14-11, and 14-12—will show you how to lay a plywood deck with a rabbeted covering board, after I get you thoroughly confused, as follows:

Go back two weeks and fit all those deckbeams *and* the breasthook block ½ inch too high (that is, ½ inch higher than the top of the sheerstrake). Now cut down those beam ends flush with the top of the sheerstrake, and far enough inboard to take the width of the covering board you plan to use. Cut out and scarf this covering board, and (as shown in Figure 14-10) cut a rabbet in its inboard edge ½ inch deep and 1 inch wide. (I'm assuming you'll use ½-inch plywood, which is strong enough for a 15,000-pound boat.) If you plan to bend this edgewise to the sheer, rather than cut it to shape, you are of course limited to a width that will take the bend (perhaps assisted by a whiff or two of steam). You'll cut the rabbet on straight stock on the table saw, and likely end up with the edge of the plywood under the

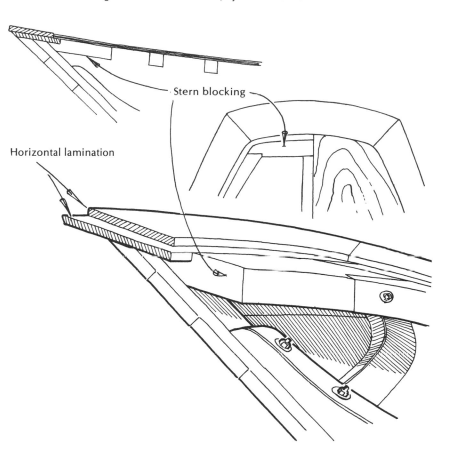

figure 14-11

Rabbeted covering board across crowned, cylindrical transom

Stern blocking

Horizontal lamination

toerail. Or you can saw the covering board to shape, at least 4 inches wide, using three or more pieces each side, scarfed together. You can cut the rabbet with your portable electric circular saw, before assembly, or you can do it with two passes of a router after the covering board is fastened in place. Either system, sprung or cut, is perfectly satisfactory, and each has its own slight advantages: The sprung piece is easier to fit, using less lumber; the wide-sawn covering board allows for a logical contrast in color or finish around the margin of the deck, and keeps the seam well inboard, clear of the toerail, where its integrity can be monitored without disturbing anything. With either system, you'll need to install heavy blocking between the beams to take fastenings from the stanchion sockets, ring bolts, cleats, and all the other vital pieces of hardware that grow around the edges of this deck.

You must also carry this covering board across the top of the transom, which has of course been cut to the crown of the deck and

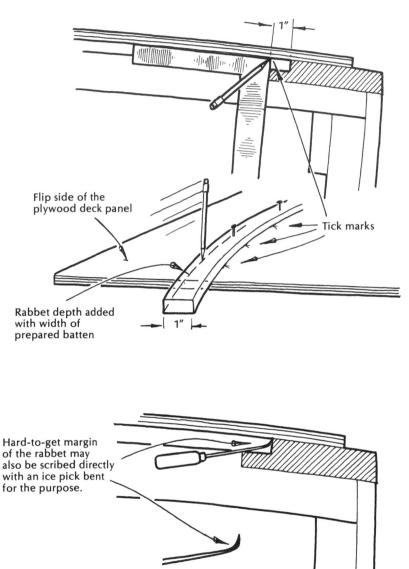

figure 14–12

Marking the underside of the plywood deck for the covering board

1"

Flip side of the plywood deck panel

Tick marks

Rabbet depth added with width of prepared batten

1"

Hard-to-get margin of the rabbet may also be scribed directly with an ice pick bent for the purpose.

flush with the sheerstrake. If the transom is a slice of a cylinder and set with much rake, this athwartships covering board may require the building up of three pieces and some heroic gluing and fastening over the poisoned blocking across the stern (Figure 14–11). Here's where trouble will start, if anywhere. Be forewarned: Try to out-think the raindrops now, and be on perpetual guard hereafter. Now fit, glue, and screw the ½-inch super-plywood over the beams, carlins, and breasthook, and

out into the rabbeted covering boards. Say this fast and it sounds easy; but the old piecrust system for marking the plywood is complicated by that rabbet. You can get at the inboard edge with your pencil, but there's a ½-inch gap above it and an inch more width needed on the outboard edge. So jam the slab down from above, mark a line or series of spots precisely above that inboard edge, flip the sheet off and over, and add the necessary inch with an exact 1-inch batten bent outside those marks (see Figure 14–12). Cut a bit full and dress with a block plane to get a perfect fit. Better use some light, tough blocking between beams to take longer screws and back up the joint where the plywood lies in the rabbet.

The cockpit

I've just now realized that there must be in this deck at least one depression, open to the sky, and needing, if possible, more sympathy and understanding than the main deck itself. This opening has had different names, such as "standing room," "footwell," "fish pen," or "cockpit," according to its use. We tender moderns have almost universally adopted the last one, ignoring its connotations (here labored the surgeon, in the heat of battle, cutting off legs and searing the stumps; and red was the color, even as in the pen where the fighting cocks tore throats out in the barn back home). We apply the name indiscriminately to vast, open work platforms and to tiny self-draining boxes, whether they occur aft, amidships, or forward. Each style has its virtues and weaknesses (and complications), perhaps in greater variety than we've faced in the deck itself.

Look at that footwell. Note that the top-edge-to-deck joint can be almost the same as the deck-edge-to-sheerstrake joint described earlier. Its upper rim must join tightly and strongly to the deck, and it must be able to sustain very heavy loads without starting a joint anywhere, top, sides or bottom. Fill it to running over with seawater, add a pair of 200-pounders standing there knee-deep, drop the boat out from under and catch it 5 feet down—and you'll see why you need some posts from the floor timbers and lots of tie-rods from the deck. You should also see why a straight-down, rigid scupper pipe, a consideration to be wished for devoutly for clean-out reasons, cannot survive the panting between the deck and hull. Sam has drawn, herewith, some variations on this footwell theme, showing how the creature can

figure 14-13

Footwell framed to the ceiling

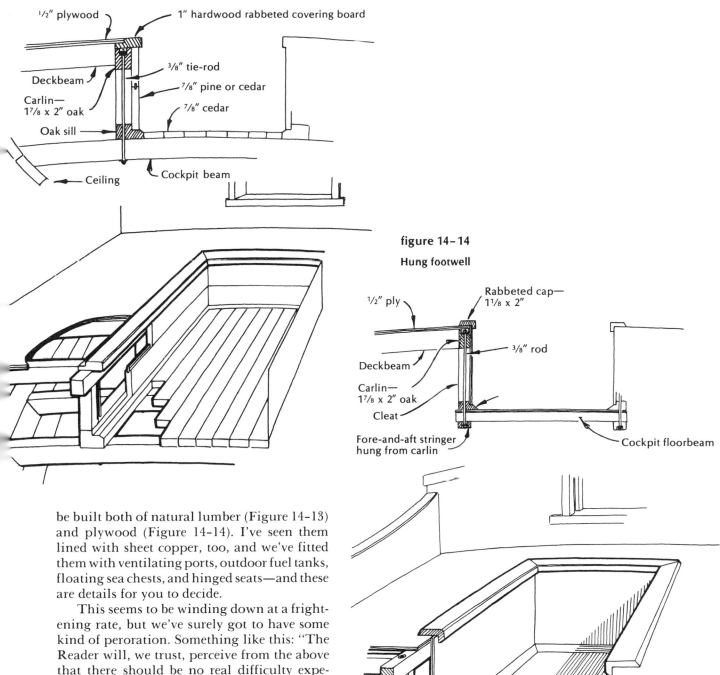

1/2" plywood

1" hardwood rabbeted covering board

Deckbeam

3/8" tie-rod

7/8" pine or cedar

Carlin—
1⅞ x 2" oak

7/8" cedar

Oak sill

Ceiling

Cockpit beam

figure 14-14

Hung footwell

1/2" ply

Rabbeted cap—
1⅛ x 2"

Deckbeam

3/8" rod

Carlin—
1⅞ x 2" oak

Cleat

Fore-and-aft stringer
hung from carlin

Cockpit floorbeam

be built both of natural lumber (Figure 14-13) and plywood (Figure 14-14). I've seen them lined with sheet copper, too, and we've fitted them with ventilating ports, outdoor fuel tanks, floating sea chests, and hinged seats—and these are details for you to decide.

This seems to be winding down at a frightening rate, but we've surely got to have some kind of peroration. Something like this: "The Reader will, we trust, perceive from the above that there should be no real difficulty experienced, even by the complete novice, in this matter of laying a deck." The hell there shouldn't, young feller. I think back to that day in 1938 when the drip came through two impenetrable barriers and landed on the professor's nose. 'Tis my sad experience that water, like Love, will find a way, and you'd better watch out real sharp or one or the other of 'em 'll get you.

163

Chapter Fifteen

Building the House

So you have the deck on, with two openings in it. The big one is to be covered with a structure (labeled, variously, trunk cabin, coach roof, deckhouse) that will provide headroom, admit air and light, keep out water, wind, and mosquitoes, and not detract unduly from the grace and elegance of the vessel.

Mr. Rudyard Kipling once remarked that there are nine-and-60 ways of writing tribal lays, and every single one of them is right. So it is with this structure. I've tried most of them in the last 50 years, and have finally settled upon a routine that works well for me. It even produces a result that fulfills most of the above-listed requirements. It demands no special aesthetic sense, inherited instinct, or awesome skill of hand and eye. The end product looks amazingly like the picture which shows a profile having a skyline at the top, a line where top meets side, and a third where side meets deck. It also shows an end view of the whole business, showing the amount of tumblehome (or lack of it) in the sides and ends, and the crown of the beams in the house top. But unless the designer is very good, indeed (and unless your work, to this point, in the matter of sheer, width of side decks, and consistency of main deck crown, is absolutely flawless), you will be faced with the need to make small adjustments—which take time and shake your confidence if done in a hit-or-miss manner, but which proceed smoothly and inevitably with the right technique and equipment.

The beam-crown pattern

The first thing you'll need to build the house is a beam-crown pattern, which in this case should be a light board slightly longer than the greatest width of the house, with a convex crown cut into one edge and matching concavity cut into the other (Figure 15–1). We'll assume for the moment, in charity, that your designer has been content to use a constant crown for the full length of the house. (I've known some designs that required every beam to be different from the one behind it; but I trust that the perpetrators of these horrors have now all been eliminated.) This crown is, very likely, described as an arc with a radius of 7 feet 3 inches (or whatever) and is, of course, easily marked by tacking one end of a slat to the floor, measuring from the nail the length of the given radius, and marking the path of that point along the length of your pattern. For a known radius (and if it is short enough to fit an uncluttered space on your shop floor), this is the sensible way to describe it.

But suppose the S.O.B. (this should, of course, read N.A.) describes the crown as hav-

figure 15-1

Beam-crown pattern

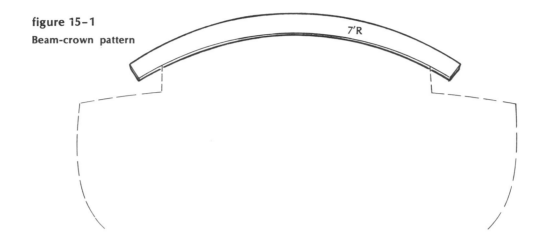

7'R

figure 15-2

To find the center of radius for a given crown—

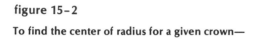

8¾"

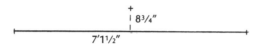

7'1½"

(a) Connect the endpoints and the center of crown with straight lines, or chords.

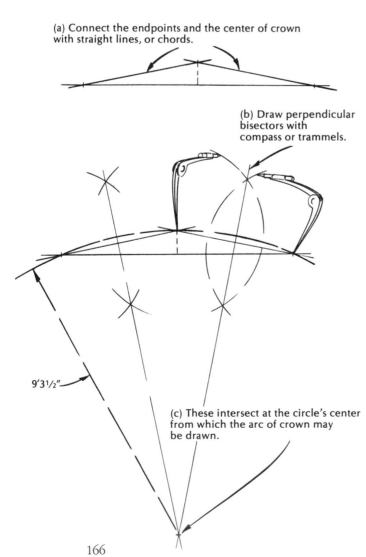

(b) Draw perpendicular bisectors with compass or trammels.

9'3½"

(c) These intersect at the circle's center from which the arc of crown may be drawn.

ing a height of 8¾ inches in 7 feet 1½ inches length. You can lay off this line on the floor and swing arcs of experimental radii until your knees and patience have both given out and you've achieved a curve that comes very close to hitting all those points. Or you can attack the problem as in the accompanying drawing (Figure 15-2, steps a,b, and c), which is self-explanatory and uses up what little I remember from my high school geometry lessons.

Then there's the textbook method, known to all students of naval architecture, whereby you draw a doughnut (which sits on a line like the sun on the horizon) and carve it into strange sections whose heights are spaced at ordained intervals along the lines. Spring a batten to these marks, and there you have it—the almost-perfect arc, flawed minutely, if at all, by the irresponsibilities of a less-than-perfect homogeneous batten. My head aches when I think of it.

Then there's the right way, which deserves a paragraph in itself.

You draw a line, the length of the beam. At each end of the line, stand a rubbing post in the form of an eightpenny nail (or any other size you have handy—I don't want to be too damned didactic), and halfway between these nails, measure up, from the line, the height of the crown you want in the beam. Find two straight-edged boards, each slightly longer than the longest arc you expect to need (4 inches sliced off the edge of an 8-foot sheet of plywood come straight and handy). Snip off a corner on each so that you can butt the points together at the mid-crown mark while the edges are pushed against the nails (see Figure 15-3). Tack some laths across to keep the two straightedges touching at the point and at a constant angle to each other. Now, if you slide the point from the

166

center mark to one nail and then to the other, *keeping the straightedges against the respective nails while sliding*, the path of the point will be a perfect, flawless arc reaching from nail to nail, and the arc will be exactly the right height in the middle. Run a pencil point, of course, at the end of the tip, to mark the pattern you want to cut. This truth machine can be readjusted in moments to fit any beam whose length and height of crown are within its scope. (Soon we'll be equipped to determine the length and crown of any beam in a tortured housetop, and we'll be happy we have this quick-and-dirty way to mark it out.)

Now, in sweet charity, let's assume that the design calls for constant crown, and that, about six days from now, you will need 16 beams, identical (except for length) in every respect.

If you have on hand some clear, sweeping planks that grew in a curve to match your pattern, then you may rest serene and go on to the next step, knowing that you can saw them out

when they're needed. But beware—such sweeps have been known to change shape after sawing. Don't plan to saw your beams out of straight-grained stock, because they'll be likely to check open and break where the grain runs across the curve. You could steam-bend the stock over a form built to a tighter curve, precisely calculated to produce the arc you want when the beams straighten out—ever so slightly, indeed, but inevitably, and not all to the same amount. In view of these difficulties, you'd perhaps best plan to make them of glued laminations, thus:

Build a gluing form (or two, or three, if you have the strength) by sawing out a 2- by 2-inch rainbow and mounting it on a backboard like a prize fish (see Figure 15-4). The radius of the top edge of the two-by-two should theoretically be shorter (by the depth of the beam) than the radius of the finished beam.

Saw out and smooth the stock for the laminations. The strips are too rough as they come from the saw and should be planed before glu-

figure 15-3

To draw a true arc without knowing the center of radius—

Crown specified

8-penny nail at endpoint of the crown

Distance between endpoints

Frame built to touch both endpoints and the midpoint of the crown

The arc is described by the pencil at the midpoint of the frame as the frame is worked along the nails.

Touching

Touching

167

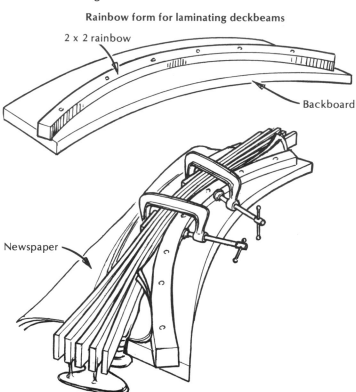

figure 15-4

Rainbow form for laminating deckbeams

2 x 2 rainbow

Backboard

Newspaper

ing. You must use a minimum of five layers to produce a beam that will hold its exact shape when the clamps are off. When we planked with mahogany (which was the least expensive wood, all things considered, that we could get), we sawed up the edgings for beams. We thereby impressed the owners with our dedication to fine craftsmanship, and doomed ourselves to sanding and varnishing the beams. Lacking mahogany, we used fir or spruce, with an occasional layer of oak or ash on the bottom.

Each morning, first thing, mix a coffee can of Weldwood glue (consistency of thick cream), line the gluing form with old newspapers, smear the strips, set one C-clamp to tie down the middle of the bundle, and clamp both ways toward the ends, placing the clamps no more than 6 inches apart. If you have two more forms to fill, you'll need a minimum of 30 clamps to squeeze three dinky little 5-foot beams. Take the clamps off next morning, ship on the lobsters, and set 'er again...and five days later you'll have enough beams to frame the length of your 15-foot house. And high time, too, because you'll be ready for them.

Without further arguments, preparations, or apologies, let's build this house.

figure 15-5

Ends of the house set into position with bar clamps

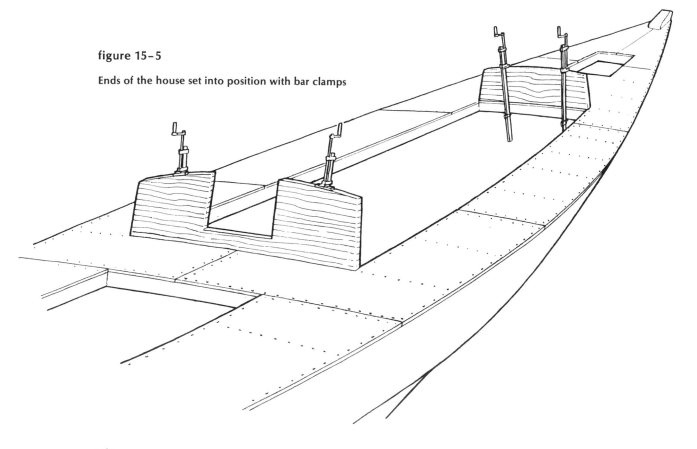

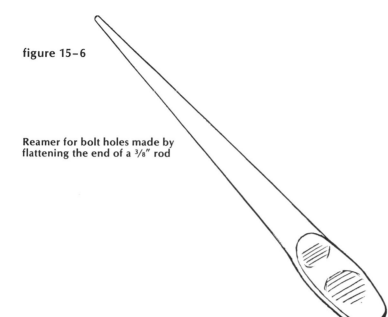

figure 15-6

Reamer for bolt holes made by flattening the end of a ⅜" rod

Fitting the house ends and cornerposts

First, cut out and fit the two ends. (I assume that you have boards wide enough, or that you have glued two pieces together to get the necessary width.) The construction drawing should give you the height at the corners; your deck-beam pattern should give you a fairly accurate line for the bottom edge of each end; and the housetop beam pattern should give you the top edge of each end (allowing for the thickness of the decking to lap over the beams and yet enough extra to allow for trimming and beveling). The ends will, of course, be cut with the correct amount of tumblehome, as shown in the construction section through the middle of the house. If the designer leaves such a detail to your judgment, which seems unlikely, and if you want my advice, slope them in 1 inch to the foot of height, or thereabouts. (Forty years ago we always set them plumb, and they looked horrible.) Make the ends square, and about ¼ inch short of the corners of the opening in the deck. Leave the bottom edges (which sit on the deck) square to start with. The after end will likely be plumb in profile view, and should need very little beveling after you have scribed and dressed it to a light-tight fit to make it stand. Unless the designer goes for a rakish look, the forward end of the house will very likely stand at about 90 degrees to the centerline of the forward deck—and therefore will need only scribing and trimming to get that perfect fit against the deck.

Cut the opening for the companionway in the after end, and set up both ends in position

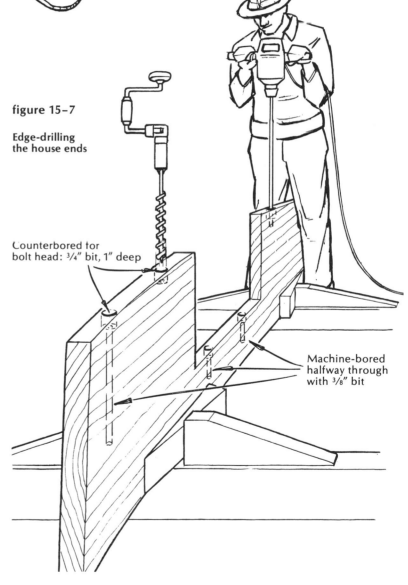

figure 15-7

Edge-drilling the house ends

Counterbored for bolt head: ¾" bit, 1" deep

Machine-bored halfway through with ⅜" bit

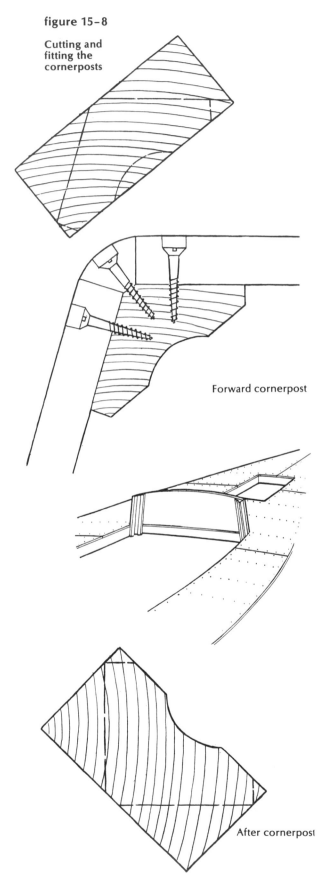

figure 15-8

Cutting and fitting the cornerposts

Forward cornerpost

After cornerpost

with two bar clamps on each, as shown in Figure 15-5. (Their inner faces will, of course, be exactly flush with the trimmed-off deck opening.) Mark for the bolts that will tie the ends to the deck frame—at least four in each. The outer bolts should be not more than 6 inches from the corners; put two through the sill in the after end, and perhaps two more 3 inches clear of the companionway opening. All these bolts should be plumb in the athwartships plane, and you might take a quick look to make sure none of them lands on a deck fastening. Now unclamp the ends, square across from the lines on the top and bottom edges, mark the exact center with a prick-punch, and get ready to drill for those bolts.

This drilling process may appear to be extremely difficult, if not hazardous, with the chance—nay, likelihood—of ruining a very expensive piece of wood. I once thought so, and felt smugly thankful that I was endowed with the skill to drill these all day long and never miss one—until I lent the gear and described the technique to a thickheaded, brash amateur, and sat back in ghoulish glee to await his report on wayward drills—only to have my pride fall in the shavings when he came back the next day, frankly puzzled that I should have had any doubts. What's supposed to be difficult about that? He did it just the way I told him. Since then I've advised a dozen more young boatbuilders, and only one needed to be threatened with the ancient and traditional aid of a pig turd hung on a string from the end of his nose, so he'd know for sure which way was straight down.

Take a scrap of 1- by 12-inch board, mark a half dozen straight lines on one side of it, clamp it on edge on the floor, and practice the business of edge-drilling. You need a 3/8-inch drill, 18 inches long. You can get one, labeled "bellhanger's drill," from an electrician's supply store, or you can weld a 5/16-inch shank to a "jobber's length" machinist's drill. (You will, of course, call this a *bit*, because you'll use it in a 1/2-inch electric *drill*, and you don't want to confuse the terms.) Start the bit exactly on center, where marked with a prick-punch; line it up by eye with the line on the side of the board, and proceed to bore down a little more than half the width of the board. Turn it over, aim as before, and bore down until your bit enters exactly into the hole you bored from the other edge, or almost exactly.

You'd best make a reamer by flattening with a hammer one end of a piece of 3/8-inch rod and then filing it (see Figure 15-6). Spin this up and down the hole, and you'll know for sure that the bolts will go through without binding. Practice with three or four holes, and you'll gain the necessary confidence and faith to tackle those that count. (Note, in passing, that this skill will be needed when you build an edge-bolted rudder, centerboard, mast step, or footwell.)

And here they are, those that count, to be drilled as follows: Clamp each house end to something so that it stands top edge up, lower edge on the shop floor (see Figure 15-7). Counterbore 1 inch deep with a ³/₄-inch bit for the bolt heads (which will be ³/₈-inch hex nuts) and stand astraddle of the victim with drill in hand and mind serene. Sight down the pencil line and both sides of the board (it helps if you can wall your eyes at will) and press the trigger. Don't bear down hard. Think of a hummingbird hovering over a blossom. Haul out the bit ever and anon to clear the clogged shavings. As in your practice sessions, bore halfway and a little more; tip the board over, clamp, and bore 'til the bit breaks joyfully into the tunnel you started from the other side of the mountain. Comfort yourself with the thought that there remain but 23 of these to be done ere the house is finished, and proceed, with no further help from me, until you have these ends all bored and reamed.

Clamp the house ends back in place, and run the long bit down each hole in turn through the deck and deckbeam. Measure for all the bolts—from the top of the nut at the top end to the underside of the beam, plus ¼ inch. Counterbore in the beam ⁵/₈ inch up, to take a standard ⁵/₁₆-inch washer, which will spin up the thread on your ³/₈-inch bolt. Make up the bolts, start them in their respective holes, unclamp again, ream holes through the deck and beam, lay a good bead of sticky stuff (butyl rubber, for instance) and maybe a half-strand of caulking cotton, looped cautiously around the bolt holes—and pick her up tenderly, lift her with care, and tap the bolts home. Put on the washers and nuts, but don't try to squeeze the hell out of the assembly just yet. You want the goo to harden a bit and adjust itself, so some of it will stay in the joint when you tighten up all around. Saw out and clamp a piece of scrap across the companionway opening to reproduce the crown you cut out of it. If you're satisfied with the way these ends stand in profile (and you'd better be, because you aren't going to change them much), brace each with a

figure 15-9

Junction systems—house sides to deck

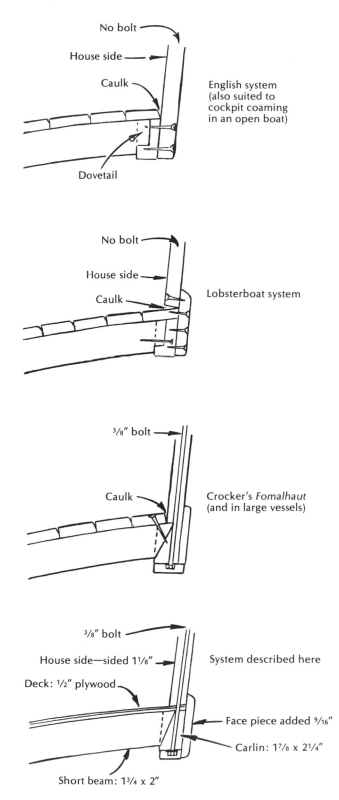

No bolt

House side

Caulk

Dovetail

English system (also suited to cockpit coaming in an open boat)

No bolt

House side

Caulk

Lobsterboat system

³/₈″ bolt

Caulk

Crocker's *Fomalhaut* (and in large vessels)

³/₈″ bolt

House side—sided 1⅛″

Deck: ½″ plywood

Short beam: 1¾ x 2″

System described here

Face piece added ⁹/₁₆″

Carlin: 1⅞ x 2¼″

figure 15–10

Framework
for the house sides

Beam-crown mold

Straightedge defining profile of
the house along the centerline

Top of the house side

Temporary uprights
set to the tumblehome
of the house sides

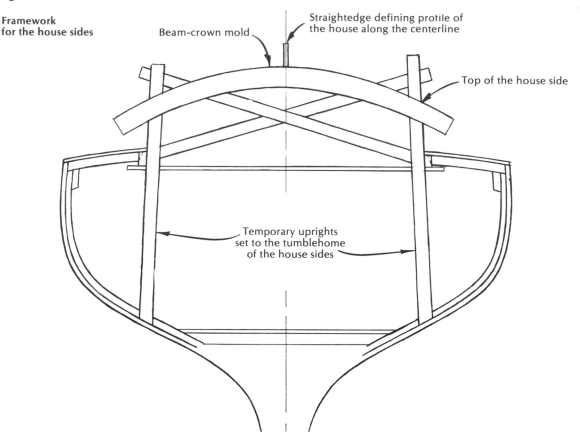

slat from the deck, and prepare to put in the cornerposts.

I differ from most yacht designers. They draw a perfectly fitted, one-piece rabbeted cornerpost. I make it in two pieces, for the following reasons: (1) It's much easier that way; (2) where the hell am I going to find a piece of mahogany that thick? (3) if a leak develops, I can always remove, resmear, and replace the outer piece, just as I would a beat-up outer stem on a dory; and (4) it's easier my way.

With that point settled, saw out a piece of mahogany, locust, black walnut, or whatever, about 2 by 5 inches and long enough to make the two forward corners, with a little extra to spare. Set your bevel square to the angle between the end of the house and the side-to-be. Mark this angle on the end of your two-by-five (see Figure 15-8), and cut each of those corners with a bandsaw or a tilting-arbor table saw (or even by hand, if all else fails). Now cut the piece in two, and fit each half to its corner—tapering from the deckline down on the outside and forward faces—until it is snug to the deck frame and fits tightly against and follows the tumblehome of the house end. Finish shaping

the post to your heart's desire. I always run a groove down the inner face, and cut the edges square, so the face pieces and beam ledges can butt against them, as shown in Figure 15-8. Glue and screw-fasten the post to the house end, but do not fasten the lower end to the deck frame.

The cornerpost at the after end will be treated in just the same fashion, but will come out of a narrower piece of stock.

The house sides

You now have, with these cornerposts, a bearing surface for anchoring your clamps when you are springing the house sides around the temporary framework. This last, which you are about to install, is the key to the entire business of shaping, fitting, clamping, and fastening the house sides. Here is how you make the framework:

Saw out about a quarter of a mile of 1- by 4-inch straightedge stock. Climb aboard, pick likely spots that are roughly one-fourth, one-half, and three-fourths of the distance along the length of the house. Tack a piece of your one-

172

by-four to the under edges of the fore-and-aft carlins (and exactly square across the centerline of the vessel) at each of these spots. Clamp a vertical piece, its bottom resting on the inside of the hull planking, sloped inward to match, roughly, the tumblehome showing in the already installed after end of the house. Scribe and cut the bottom end so it can be tacked to the planking; fit it in the way of the carlin to bring its outer edge to the deck edge; set it exactly at the right amount of tumblehome; and nail it to the crosspiece and the carlin. Fit and fasten the identical twin on the other side, cross-brace the two as shown in Figure 15-10, and go on to install the other three sets.

You will notice that the actual tumblehome on the forward end of the house is greater than at the after end—this effect is the result of the slight rake aft in the profile view. So split the difference when you set up the framework at the three-quarter distance—that is, give the

framework a bit more tumblehome than the middle one shows and a bit less than is apparent when you sight past it to the forward cornerposts. Don't worry too much about this, but try to make the two sides alike.

Now you need only a centerline (profile) along the middle of the house, and you'll be ready to mark the exact shape of the house sides. This centerline may, in your construction profile, show as an old-fashioned sway-back dip, the look-of-tomorrow hump, or a straight line parallel to the waterline. The last, I think, usually looks right and is certainly the easiest to work with, especially if you plan to deck with plywood. (The dipped or humped profiles inevitably generate compound curves, which plywood abhors.)

Stand, therefore, on edge, from the mid-crown of the aft end to the mid-crown of the forward, a 1- by 6-inch straightedge, clamped solidly in place. (You can obtain the same ref-

figure 15–11

Measurements on the spiling board that determine the whole shape of the house side (the interior face)

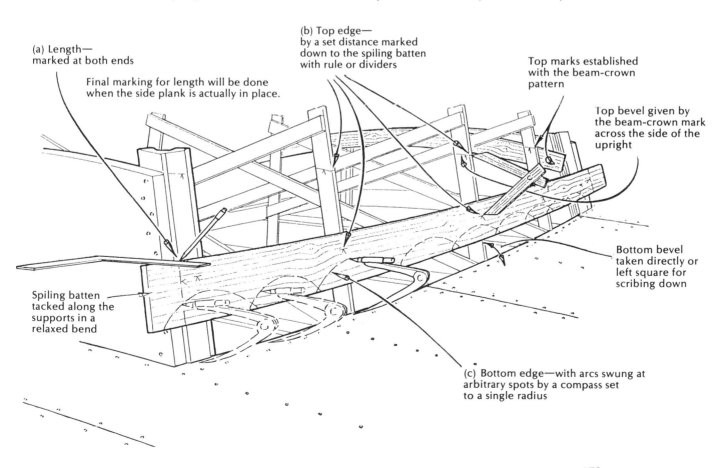

(a) Length—
marked at both ends

Final marking for length will be done when the side plank is actually in place.

(b) Top edge—
by a set distance marked down to the spiling batten with rule or dividers

Top marks established with the beam-crown pattern

Top bevel given by the beam-crown mark across the side of the upright

Bottom bevel taken directly or left square for scribing down

Spiling batten tacked along the supports in a relaxed bend

(c) Bottom edge—with arcs swung at arbitrary spots by a compass set to a single radius

173

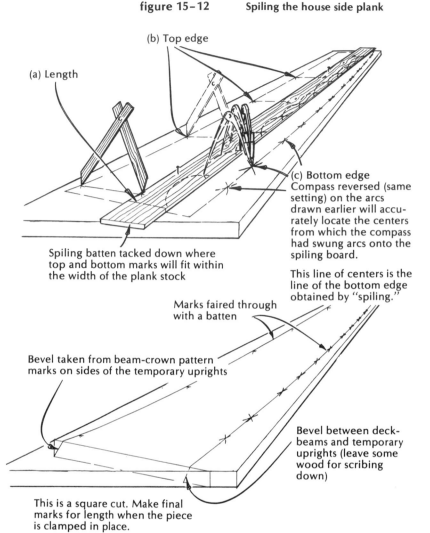

figure 15-12   Spiling the house side plank

(a) Length

(b) Top edge

(c) Bottom edge
Compass reversed (same setting) on the arcs drawn earlier will accurately locate the centers from which the compass had swung arcs onto the spiling board.

This line of centers is the line of the bottom edge obtained by "spiling."

Spiling batten tacked down where top and bottom marks will fit within the width of the plank stock

Marks faired through with a batten

Bevel taken from beam-crown pattern marks on sides of the temporary uprights

Bevel between deck-beams and temporary uprights (leave some wood for scribing down)

This is a square cut. Make final marks for length when the piece is clamped in place.

erence line with a tight string, but you'll be forever pushing it out of true and waiting for it to stop humming.)

The next operation is the payoff for all the effort described above. Take your beam-crown pattern, lay it against one of your temporary uprights, with its top edge against the bottom of the fore-and-aft straightedge. Adjust the pattern ends up or down (above the deck edge, on the outside of the vertical uprights) until the heights are exactly the same both port and starboard. Mark a fine, bold line on the athwartships face and the outboard edge of each upright (see Figure 15-11)—and go on to do likewise on the other two sets. As surely as night must follow day, these points (five in all, counting the ends) must delineate the inner top edge of the house side, at the under surface of the housetop.

You must now mark for the lower edge of the house side, which is to fit the deck with a watertight joint. This line is most easily obtained by scribing the line on a spiling board and then transferring it to the board that will form the house sides, as shown in Figures 15-11 and 15-12. (I assume that you know how to take and transfer a spiling; my only warning in this case is that you take special pains to assure that your spiling board is comfortable and relaxed before you mark it.) Now, while the spiling board is in place, mark each of your five height-reference points, and lay off the respective heights above the line of the lower edge. Run a batten through the points for a fair line. These heights are for the inside of the house side, and must be increased at the top by the amount you'll lose when you bevel the bottom edge to fit the crown of the deck.

Proceed now to saw it out and bevel the bottom edge of the side to fit the slope of the deck. Clamp the side in place, around your uprights and to the cornerposts. If your spiling was accurate, the side should lie comfortably, with its lower edge touching the deck all the way. Snug it down with three bar clamps, note that the top edge is high enough, mark for trimming the lower edge for fit, mark for the end cuts at the cornerposts, and climb aboard.

Now is the time to mark for the edge bolts. (See Figure 15-13.) As in the house ends, there should be one bolt not more than 6 inches from the corner. For the rest, you need only to bear in mind that they should be roughly at right angles to the carlin, and they must not land where a deckbeam ends, nor where a tie-rod comes through the carlin, nor less than 2 inches from a portlight hole, nor more than 20 inches apart, nor in the way of fastenings in the deck, nor on a strength-bulkhead at the mast partners. You may make two false starts and squander several minutes before you arrive at the perfect pattern.

Anyway, unclamp, correct the fit on the bottom edge, cut the ends where marked from the cornerposts, and *mark out an identical twin*, complete with the bolt locations and a little extra length on one end (you'd be surprised to know how many boats are a bit longer on one side than the other; and it's always the shorter side you measure first). Now set 'er up on edge, and counterbore the holes through the carlin; smear with Wonder Cement; drive the bolts and screw-fasten to the cornerposts. Pluck out all that temporary framework, and prepare to install the beams.

Fastening to the beam ledge

As usual with any job you start in a boat, there are a half dozen things to be done before you begin the serious business. Right now you have to fair off the tops of the house sides (to the exact heights obtained from that temporary framework) and install a beam ledge. Use the concave edge of your beam pattern, or one of the beams themselves, laid across, to give you the angle...and be very glad, indeed, that you countersunk the bolt heads deep enough. The beam ledge, probably made from the same stock as the house sides, and 1/2 inch deeper than the beams, can be sawn to the correct bevel (the same on both the top and bottom edge) and sprung into place inside the top of the house side. When you fasten the ledge (with glue in the joint, and screws from the ledge into the house side), try to keep the screws clear of the spots where the beam ends will land. This beam ledge, or a reasonable facsimile of it, sawed to shape, will of course be carried across the tops of the house ends.

By the time you have fitted all the above, and the beams, and the companionway frame, and the mast partners, and the face pieces, you may think back with sadly won wisdom to the day when you were fitting planks, and foolishly thought that the hull was the big problem.

So what type of joint do we make where beam meets ledge? Your designer very likely shows exquisitely fitted dovetails (Figure 15-14), the mark of the master craftsman who Really Cares. (We are probably safe in assuming that the man who calls for full dovetails is at least twice as conscientious as the slipshod fellow who is content with the half version. In my youth, I encountered three designers, whose awesome talents enabled them, respectively, to draw a full-sized toilet in a sailboat not much bigger than said fixture, to draw quarter-beam buttocks straight as a string, and even to specify Philippine mahogany for planking—on a lobsterboat, mind you. Needless to say, each of these giants of the trade could have drawn full dovetails with absolute precision wherever wood met wood.) I say, to hell with dovetails, except in the corners of a sea chest, or any other place where they're fully exposed and will draw oohs and aahs. I think they are holdovers, in a very conservative trade, from the days when

figure 15-13

Boring the carlin

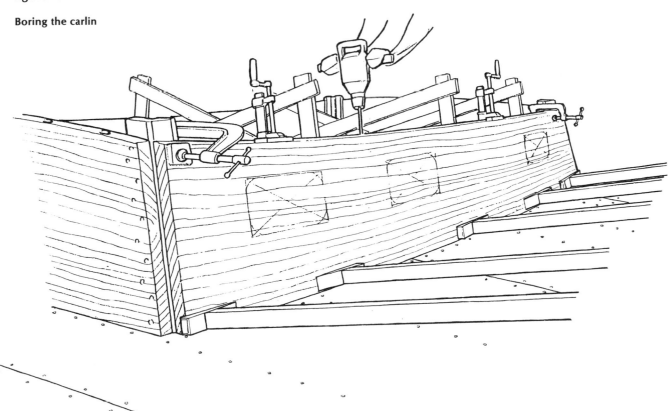

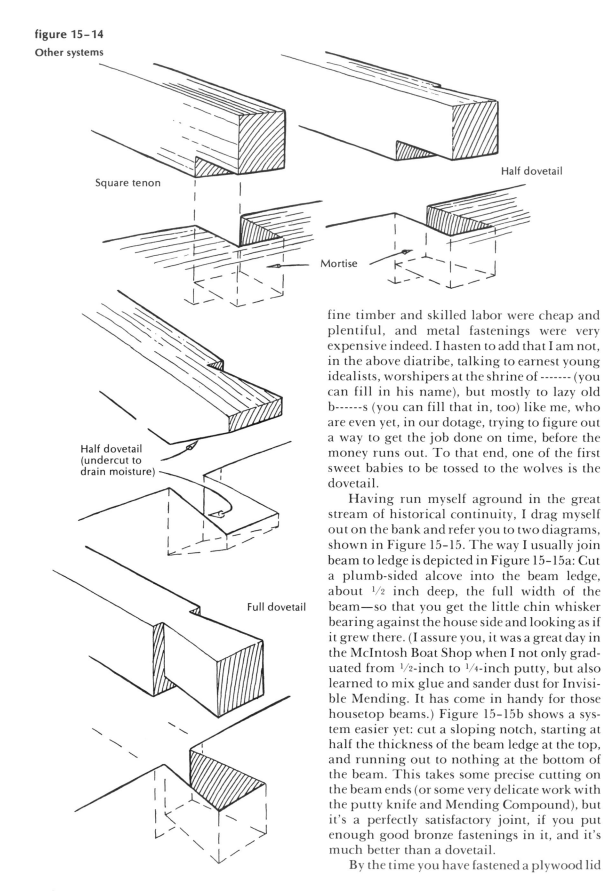

figure 15-14

Other systems

Square tenon

Half dovetail

Mortise

Half dovetail
(undercut to
drain moisture)

Full dovetail

fine timber and skilled labor were cheap and plentiful, and metal fastenings were very expensive indeed. I hasten to add that I am not, in the above diatribe, talking to earnest young idealists, worshipers at the shrine of ------- (you can fill in his name), but mostly to lazy old b------s (you can fill that in, too) like me, who are even yet, in our dotage, trying to figure out a way to get the job done on time, before the money runs out. To that end, one of the first sweet babies to be tossed to the wolves is the dovetail.

Having run myself aground in the great stream of historical continuity, I drag myself out on the bank and refer you to two diagrams, shown in Figure 15-15. The way I usually join beam to ledge is depicted in Figure 15-15a: Cut a plumb-sided alcove into the beam ledge, about ½ inch deep, the full width of the beam—so that you get the little chin whisker bearing against the house side and looking as if it grew there. (I assure you, it was a great day in the McIntosh Boat Shop when I not only graduated from ½-inch to ¼-inch putty, but also learned to mix glue and sander dust for Invisible Mending. It has come in handy for those housetop beams.) Figure 15-15b shows a system easier yet: cut a sloping notch, starting at half the thickness of the beam ledge at the top, and running out to nothing at the bottom of the beam. This takes some precise cutting on the beam ends (or some very delicate work with the putty knife and Mending Compound), but it's a perfectly satisfactory joint, if you put enough good bronze fastenings in it, and it's much better than a dovetail.

By the time you have fastened a plywood lid

over the entire business, it will be strong enough to jump on from 10 feet up—and you can be sure that some joyful 200-pounder will do it some day. (Or some night, if it's the dark of the moon, and he doesn't realize that the Eastport tide has dropped 8 feet since he went ashore. I hope he breaks a leg.)

Back to the construction plan to get the beam layout. This will be complicated only by the length of the companionway opening, the location of the mast partners (if the mast steps through or on the housetop), and, usually, a skylight aft of the mainmast and an escape hatch forward of it. Each of these openings will require the fitting of half-beams to fore-and-aft carlins, stringers, or whatever you want to call them. Locate, fit, and fasten the beams at the ends of these openings; stretch a tight string from the stem to the transom, and mark the exact centers of these main beams. Fit and fasten the fore-and-aft members (including the mast-partner blocking, if any), and install the short beams two on each side, usually, in the way of the companionway, one on each side at the partners, skylight, and forward hatch. I always make the fore-and-aft members somewhat deeper than the beams, with a simple butt joint against the beam, and the extra depth extending under it, for the owner to bang his head on (see Figures 15-15a, 15-16).

The blocking between the mast-partner beams is, of course, no deeper than the beams—and when I install it, is likewise a simple butt joint against the beam, pinned in place with plenty of spikes, and tied together athwartships with edge bolts before and abaft the mast hole. No rebates, lodging knees, or keylocks. Fit the short beams to the fore-and-aft members with the same end joints as described above: into the alcove in the house side, and with the simple sloping notch at the inboard end (Figures 15-15a, 15-17). If the design calls for hanging knees at the companionway and partner beams, fit these now, before the rest of the long beams are installed and cramp your work space.

You will forgive me, I hope, if by making the following recommendations I seem to doubt your ability to mark and cut so simple a thing as a deckbeam. I only fear that in your youthful exuberance you'll try some shortcuts (in a figurative sense, that is) and wind up with some beams that don't quite reach.... I, too, have oft been told of the Inscrutable Oriental Craftsman who needs only look intently at the gap to be filled, and goes to the lumber shed and cuts a piece that falls exactly into place. It's

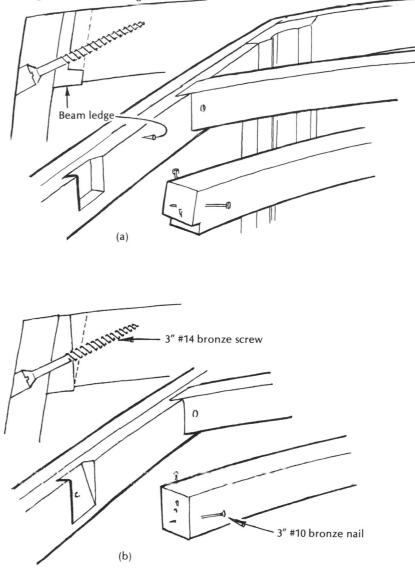

figure 15-15

Joining beams to beam ledge

Beam ledge

(a)

3" #14 bronze screw

3" #10 bronze nail

(b)

an instinct, they say, totally lacking in us Westerners, who can't do half as well with all our steel tapes and bevel squares. (And astrolabes and prolapses, as one critic said.) All right, I admit it; but I don't think you are any better at this business than I am. So, study Figure 15-17, *then* cut.

Be bold, cut to the mark. Start with a long beam, and move forward to a shorter length if you mess it up. Tack them all in place with a fivepenny box nail at each end; anchor a slat to the forward end, 5 inches clear of the centerline; and space (and tack to the slats) the centers of the beams exactly as they are spaced at their ends. Mark and cut 1- by 4-inch blocking to fit

177

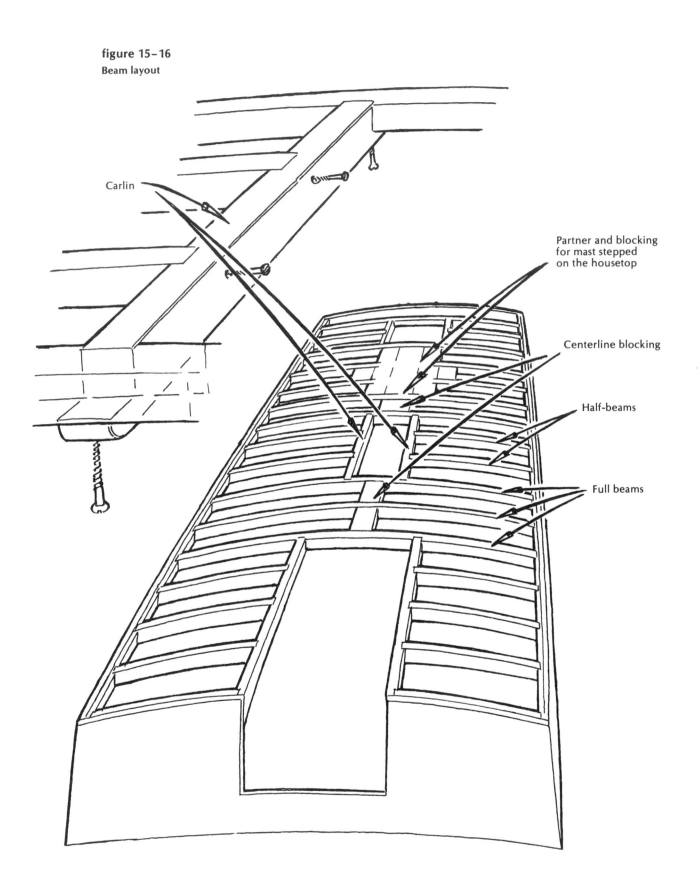

figure 15–16
Beam layout

Carlin

Partner and blocking
for mast stepped
on the housetop

Centerline blocking

Half-beams

Full beams

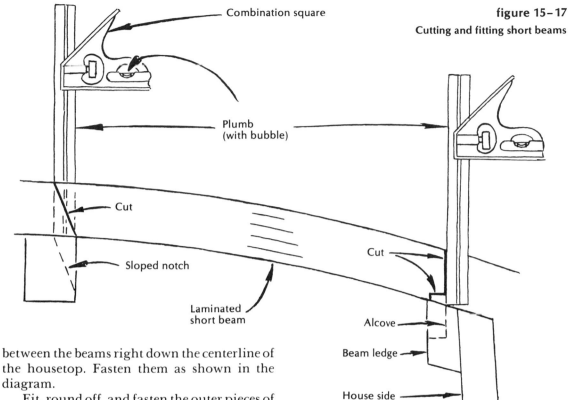

Combination square

figure 15–17

Cutting and fitting short beams

Plumb
(with bubble)

Cut

Sloped notch

Laminated
short beam

Cut

Alcove

Beam ledge

House side

between the beams right down the centerline of the housetop. Fasten them as shown in the diagram.

Fit, round off, and fasten the outer pieces of the cornerposts, with plenty of sticky stuff in the joints. Fair off everything smooth as a smelt. Lay the deck (housetop, that is), consisting of doubled plywood with joints staggered and glued between, or matched pine or cedar in narrow strakes, or single-thickness plywood butted on centerline blocking, or whatever else you fancy. You can even put white Formica on the underside, if you want. Fasten well, especially around the edges. Trim off, and glue-and-screw a $3/8$- by $2\frac{1}{2}$-inch piece of trim molding all around. (See Figure 15–18.)

Fill all the punched-down fastenings with polyester putty, the boatbuilder's friend. Cover the top with canvas, loaded with paint, if you're old-fashioned like me; but I'll forgive you if you use that smelly stuff—though not on matched pine, unless it's plenty thick and independently strong. Bring this cover down around the edges, and seal the edge of the canvas with half-oval molding, hollowed out to hold sticky sealant. Remember that any exposed canvas underedge will act as a wick to draw sweet water into the joint, and the rot spores will devour your fine work before you realize what's going on.

When you fit bronze portlights with a sleeve (called a "spigot" in the trade) that lines the opening in the wood, be sure to leave plenty of clearance at the top and bottom, because the

house sides will inevitably shrink, and you will have to tighten the hold-down bolts. But you can't squeeze these ports, and the house sides will inevitably split to relieve the strain.

You aren't entirely out of the woods yet (perhaps we should switch the figure of speech, and say you still may need some guidance across the bar)—so read on for more details.

figure 15–18

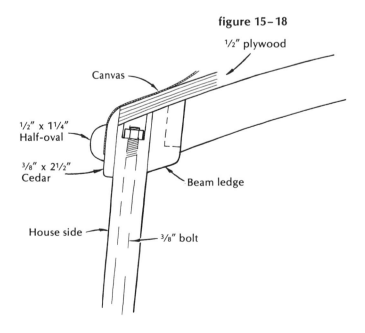

$1/2''$ plywood

Canvas

$1/2'' \times 1\frac{1}{4}''$
Half-oval

$3/8'' \times 2\frac{1}{2}''$
Cedar

Beam ledge

House side

$3/8''$ bolt

179

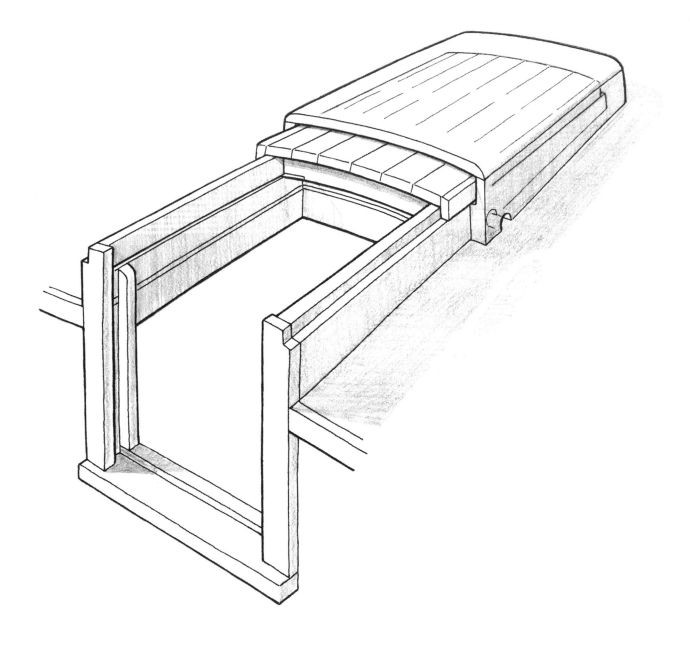

Chapter Sixteen

Hatches and Other Deck Joinery

We once built a big clipper-bowed cutter, designed by Sam Crocker, and handsome beyond words to describe. It was a painful job from start to finish. The owner had haunted the great yacht yards on City Island, and had arrived at some standards of excellence (mainly in matters of fine teak-and-mahogany brightwork on deck) that were beyond our experience and, I regret to say, talents. They were especially beyond the contract price. The really important thing, he felt, was this: You tie up alongside, somewhere, and people walk along the wharf and look down on your deck. That's the view that counts. It establishes you as the owner of a real yacht, or it points up the melancholy fact that you patronized a backwoods boatyard somewhere east of Long Island. There are, admittedly, farmers in those dark regions who can build a strong hull, but....

So, to provide us with a sample that we could strive to equal, he made up (in his own shop) a complete set of companionway rails and sliding hatch cover, splined, glued, sanded, and finished with 10 coats of varnish. Unfortunately, the damned thing didn't fit by a mile, and we spent days beveling, scribing, narrowing, and straightening before we could get it fastened in place. By that time it had a somewhat battered look, but the owner was proud of

it. We went on to fit his colossal railcaps (milled from straight stock, to be steamed, edge-bent, and scarfed together) and his classic skylight and a great hatch in the foredeck—and a housetop laid in gleaming natural wood. I'll bet it shrank to a sprinkler system that would put out a general-alarm blaze.

And, you know, the man was right about the importance of this deck furniture, though not entirely for the reasons he lived by. A wooden hull is a simple thing. Keep it wet, and it takes care of itself. A companionway hatch cover lives a more difficult life. It must open and close almost at the flick of a finger, thousands of times a season. It must cheerfully support the weight of stamping feet. It must repel water that hits it violently from all sides and above. It must do all these things (and look good besides) in spite of sun and salt. Other deck openings—hatches in the fore- and afterdecks, water-trap ventilators, skylights—must meet and overcome some of the same problems. And when I add toerails, deadlights, and mast jackets to the list, I almost wish I'd stuck with dugout canoes. However, here we are, Sam Manning and I, having lured you thus far through the sweet and simple parts of boatbuilding, and honor demands that we try to finish the job.

figure 16–1

Companionway slide

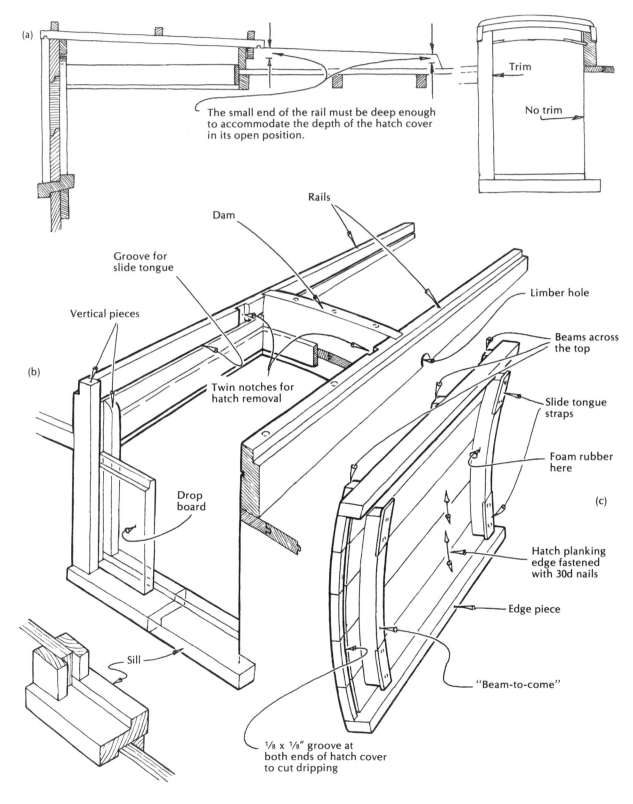

(a)

The small end of the rail must be deep enough
to accommodate the depth of the hatch cover
in its open position.

Trim

No trim

Rails

Dam

Groove for
slide tongue

Vertical pieces

Limber hole

Beams across
the top

(b)

Twin notches for
hatch removal

Slide tongue
straps

Foam rubber
here

(c)

Drop
board

Hatch planking
edge fastened
with 30d nails

Edge piece

Sill

"Beam-to-come"

⅛ x ⅛" groove at
both ends of hatch cover
to cut dripping

figure 16-2

Hatch-slide systems

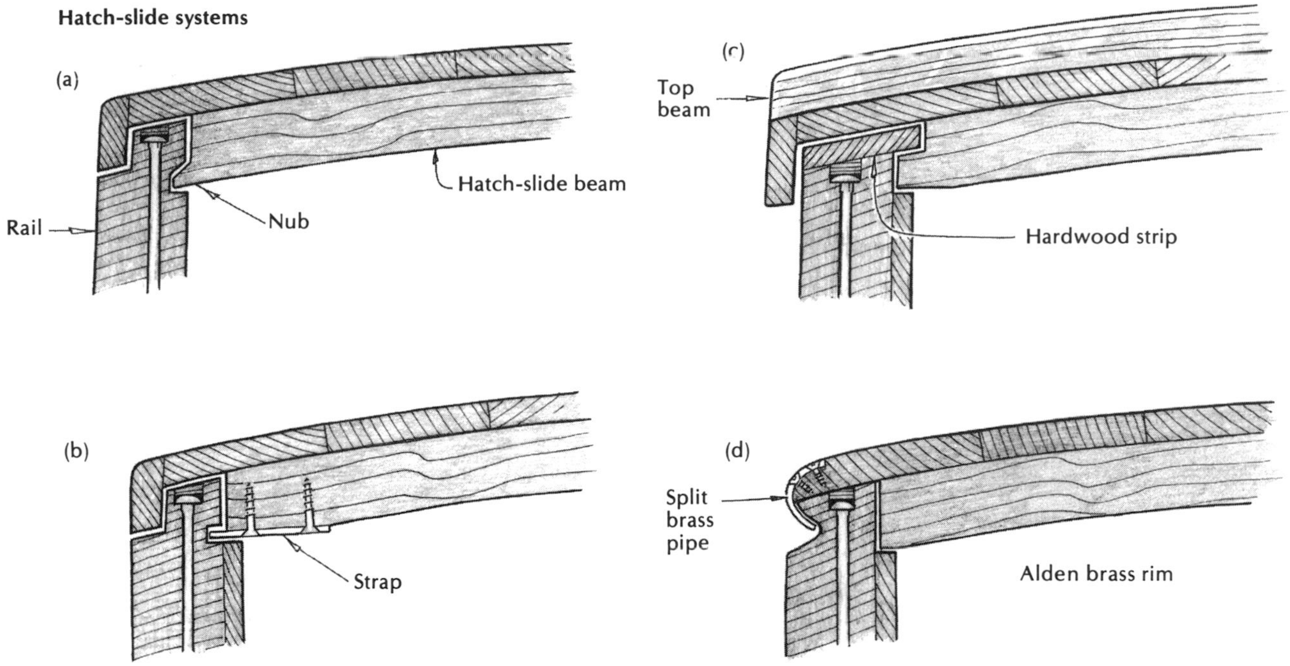

(a)

Rail —

Nub

Hatch-slide beam

(b)

Strap

(c)

Top beam

Hardwood strip

(d)

Split brass pipe

Alden brass rim

Companionway rails

Let's consider the companionway opening and its cover. This is a tricky bit of furniture, with details that can vary in minor ways, and is frequently left to the ingenuity of the builder. I can understand why, as I attempt to describe my own way of doing this job. Here's where Sam takes over (see Figures 16-1 and 16-2). I'll lead you from one drawing to the next, with briefest comment on each.

The first move, of course, is to shape and fasten the rails, a bit more than twice the fore-and-aft length of the opening in the end of the housetop which forms the companionway (Figure 16-1a). The rails must, obviously, lie exactly parallel and perfectly straight, stand plumb on their inner faces, and fit the 'thwartships crown of the house. They will be bridged at the forward end of the opening by a dam that stands flush with the tops of the rails and is crowned top and bottom to match that 'thwartships crown of the housetop (see Figure 16-1b). The rails must further incorporate some means for locking the cover down, while still allowing it to travel smoothly fore and aft. Provide for this by making a full-length groove along the inside face of each rail, exactly parallel with the top. (I have an ancient ¼-inch dado cutter which has done this job for me countless times.

You can do the same thing by making four passes on your table saw.) A projection from each beam end, either a nub left sticking out (see Figure 16-2a), or a flat piece of bronze screw-fastened under the end (see Figures 16-1c and 16-2b), will ride the groove and prevent the cover from rising up.

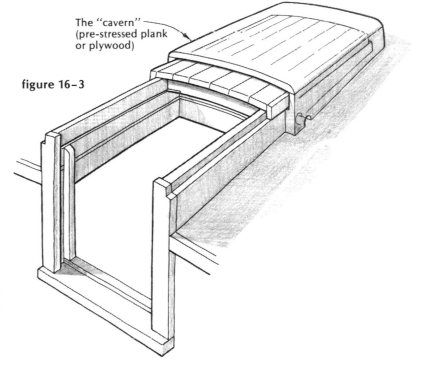

The "cavern" (pre-stressed plank or plywood)

figure 16-3

figure 16–4

Dorade-type skylight

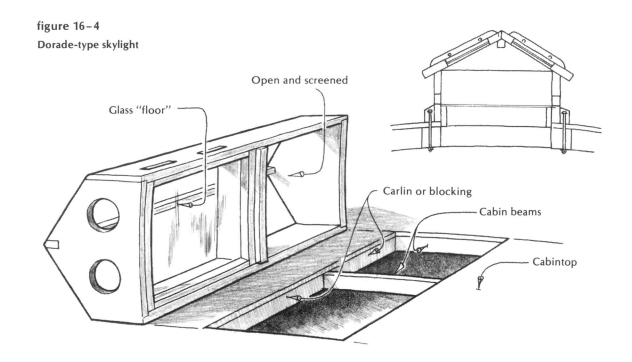

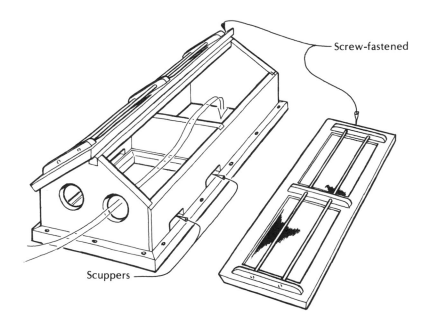

You might also note that the hold-down job can be done in a number of other ways, two of which are shown. The first (Figure 16-2c) uses an extra flat strip, screw-fastened to the top of the rail, and projecting inward over the notched beam end. Make this of dense, hard wood, wax it with the butt end of a candle, and replace it with ease if it breaks or weathers. Or, if you want to stagger in the footsteps of the great

(Herreshoff? Alden? Concordia? What boat was it that darkens the mists of my memories?), you can do it as in Figure 16-2d. It looks simple enough, once you get that 1¼-inch i.p.s. brass pipe split precisely down the middle, but it involves some delicate shaping of curves and rabbets. If you've got the time and patience, go to it. One more detail: I always make these rails about twice as high aft as forward, for no good reason except that they look better to me that way. Suit yourself, or even follow the designer's drawing, if he deigns to detail this bit of furniture.

Bore the limber holes, just forward of the dam, right at the bottom edge, as shown in Figure 16-1b, and line the holes with flared copper tubing, to seal the exposed end grain.

Now you can fasten these rails in place. Use bolts made from ¼-inch continuous-threaded brass rod through carlins and beams, and add screws, up from the underside of the housetop, between beams. Don't forget the bedding compound.

And what about the after ends that stick out over the bridge deck? Yacht designers and other idealists do wondrous endings here. I go through a brief struggle with my conscience, and then saw them off (tenderly, and with trembling hand, I assure you) flush with the end of the house, ready for the vertical pieces that will confine the drop boards.

figure 16–5a

Flat hatch

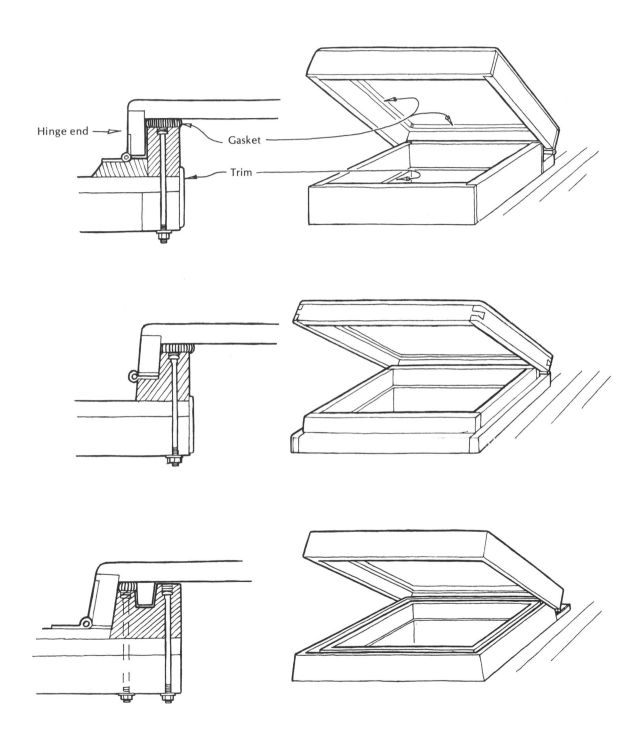

Hinge end →

Gasket

Trim

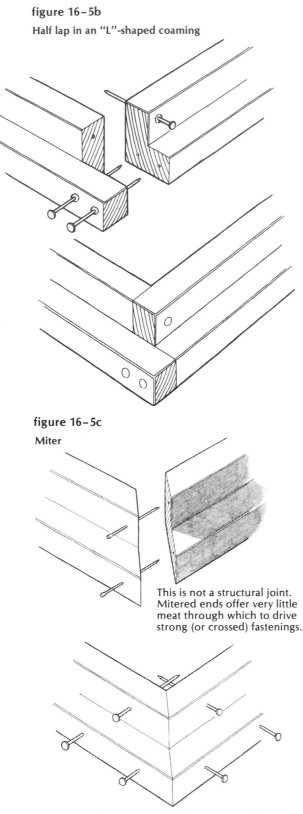

figure 16–5b

Half lap in an "L"-shaped coaming

figure 16–5c

Miter

This is not a structural joint.
Mitered ends offer very little
meat through which to drive
strong (or crossed) fastenings.

As a trim joint, as with decorative moldings,
a miter can be kept closed with substantial
fastenings set into structure behind the joint.

Companionway sill and frame

Before we tackle the sliding cover, let's finish around the vertical part of the companionway opening in the after end of the house. Start with the sill. This is a piece of teak, locust, or dense oak, rabbeted as shown in Figure 16–1b, notched at both ends to extend inches beyond the opening. Fit vertical pieces, stepped on these sill ends. The after (outside) ones will reach exactly flush with the top of the rails; the forward ones will be shortened by the depth of the beam-to-come at the after end of the sliding cover. These vertical pieces will, of course, lap inward, past the inner faces of the rails and the house end, and thereby provide slots to confine the drop boards. You can, if you wish, make this front, back, slotted assembly out of one solid piece, rabbeted and grooved as necessary. Elegant, and more nearly meeting City Island standards. I salve my conscience and justify my simple two-piece construction with the thought that it is cheap and easy to do in the first place, and easily repaired thereafter.

Companionway sliding hatch cover

And now to the sliding cover itself, which we trust will stay watertight for the next 30 years and glide o'er the rails as smoothly as skis in wintertime. (And not a bad thought, at that; it's all in the wax, they say.) If you have accompanied me thus far without complaint, you are stuck with two beams, shaped to the crown of the housetop, flush with the tops of the rails, and jammed respectively against the forward face of the uppermost drop board and the like face of the dam. Your mind's eye will likely be dazzled now with a vision of gleaming mahogany or teak, laid lengthwise, with splines and glue between planks. If you choose to go this way, be sure the stock is bone dry, and be prepared to varnish it twice a year. (If, in spite of everything, it shrinks and opens up, you can always cover it with canvas.) You can do a more reliable and much less expensive job with cedar or white pine heartwood, glued edge to edge *without* splines, and painted as light a color as your eyes can stand. You may even consider plywood—one piece, seamless, impregnable and everlasting—but if you do, make your own carapace by gluing at least three layers of 1/4–inch ply over a crowned form. You'll have edges to seal, though, and plywood to look at. I'd rather go for tongue-and-groove boards, with canvas over. Observe, of course, that this cover extends past the after beam and over the

figure 16–5d
Half lap

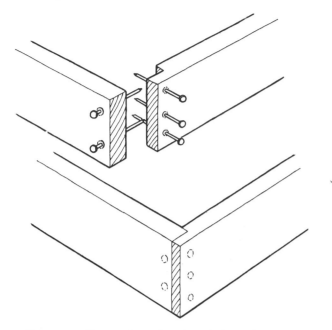

Common nails, countersunk and puttied, are shown. Bunged screws might be used, or finish nails. All these fastenings are in shear.

The strength of this joint is in the crossed fastenings. The longer and slimmer they are, the better they hold in the end grain.

figure 16–5f
Dovetail

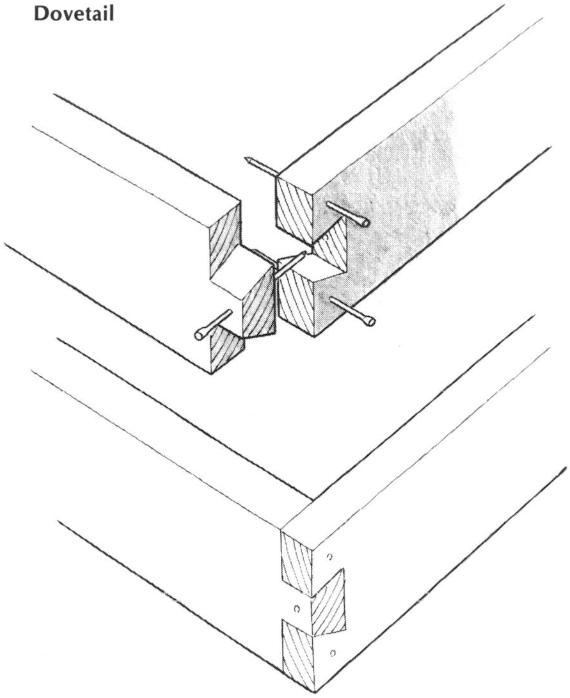

figure 16–5e
Tenon

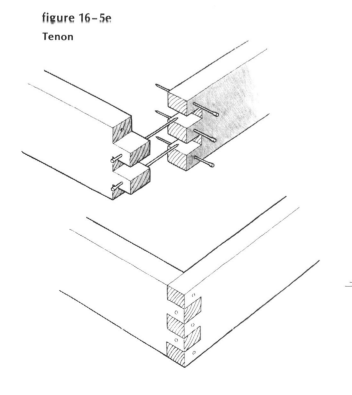

figure 16–5g
Hatch stick and hold-down line

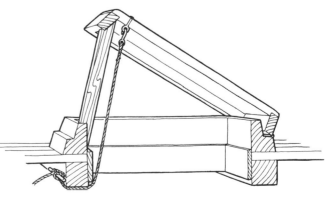

figure 16–6

Toerail

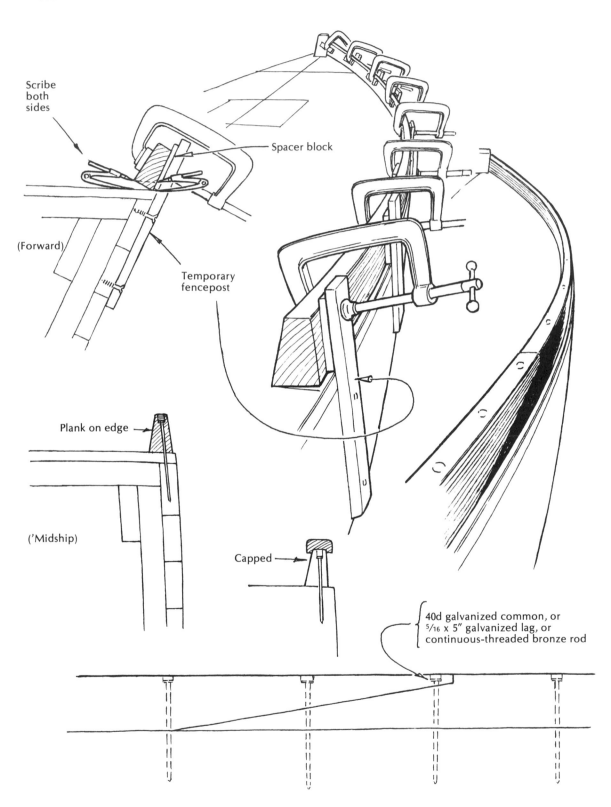

Scribe
both
sides

Spacer block

(Forward)

Temporary
fencepost

Plank on edge

('Midship)

Capped

40d galvanized common, or
5/16 x 5" galvanized lag, or
continuous-threaded bronze rod

drop board. I like to fit and fasten three beams, as shown in Figure 16-1c, across the top: one at the after end, to support the overhang and provide a hand grip; one in the middle, to give strength where needed; one over the forward beam, for chafing gear and symmetry. And if you are wise you'll install drifts (30-penny spikes, 6 inches apart) to stiffen the edge grain against the splitting effect of weight on top. Bed and fasten the edge pieces, fitted as close as you dare, to shed water clear of the slides. Cut those twin notches, 2 inches aft of the dam, up from the routed groove, so that you can lift the after beam up and over the dam and work the cover off the forward end of the rails. Stick a strip of foam rubber weatherproofing on the after face of the forward beam to help seal against water coming aft along the housetop and jumping over the dam, and also to absorb the shock when the sliding cover is slammed shut—I hope it opens as promised.

One last addition, if you wish. Build a cavern, forward of the dam, big enough to swallow the sliding cover when you shove it ahead (see Figure 16-3). This will stop water that might otherwise wash back along the housetop. It will provide a fine base for an airtight dodger. This stout roof can be topped with chocks to take the transom of an overturned dinghy. It's a fine thing if you plan to cross oceans, a cozy home for wasps in wintertime, and a nuisance when you paint the housetop. We've roofed it with 1/4-inch aluminum plate, rolled to the proper crown, and we once fastened the aluminum with bronze screws, which ate away the metal in one short summer. We sacrificed, with sorrow, my beams across the top of the slide, to keep the height of this cavern as low as possible. All in all, a pretty thing, and you can decide for yourself whether it's worth the extra bulk and labor. I think it is, and sometimes wish I'd done it on our own boat. But then I think of the wasps and live crabs scuttling to safety in the far end.

I hope the drawings make all this comprehensible. I hope you're as happy as I am to get it over with, and go on to drop boards and skylight.

Companionway drop boards

Drop boards usually come in sets of two—the upper one crowned, of course, to fit snugly under the overhang when the cover is closed, and with a ship-lap joint where it sits upon the lower board. Make them with hardwood cleats on the ends, sloppy fit endwise, with 45-degree horizontal louvers cut through them, if you wish. Make a set of screens to match. Make a secure stowage place for them under the deck-beams, and don't tell me you'd rather have cute little twin doors on hinges. They are even more of a nuisance.

Skylight

My down-gazing client of the first paragraph, having ticked off the companion slide (probably with a low mark), would next assess the skylight, which might well be considered the crowning glory of a proper yacht. I suppose I have built a dozen of them in the classic style—and they all, at some time, have dripped rain upon the cabin table. I much prefer the construction shown in Figure 16-4. This is simply a large version of a Dorade-type ventilator, shaped and trimmed to look exactly like the opening skylight, but without the complications of hinges, adjustable openers, seals, and gutters—and the tight canvas cover that you lash about it as a last resort. It is strong, cheap, durable, and it has one great virtue: it keeps on working all the time, moving air into or out of the cabin, at the mooring or driving into a head sea, in fair weather or foul. Look to the drawings, therefore, and don't expect any more apologies from me.

Think of a Cape Cod cottage with a glass roof, and with a solid partition, midway in the length of it, tight to the floor and walls, but extending no higher than the eaves. Lay a watertight glass floor in one room (with drains, at floor level). Carefully omit the floor in the other room. Cut two large round holes in the north end, the room with a floor. Air and, inevitably, water will enter the cottage through these openings; the air will flow over the partition and down into the cabin, and the water, knocked down by the glass baffle, will drain harmlessly away. You can fit cowl ventilators to the end opening; and you can install the skylight with the opening aft, to draw air out rather than to drive it in. (You will, of course, fit removable insect-stopping screen to the big opening.)

Make the sides and ends of the stock at least 3/4 inch thick. Dovetail the corners for a fancy job, or jog sides past ends as shown, made tight with glue and screws. The glass floor must be bedded and glazed watertight on a ledge just clear of the foundation, with (scuppers) limber holes above it to drain away invading water. The roof, with its four glazed panels, ridgepole, overhanging eaves, and brass-rod protectors, must be bedded to the walls and ends in sticky stuff so it can be removed as a unit. You will, of course, use shatterproof glass throughout. You'll make the opening long enough to span two bays between the beams of the housetop (leaving the middle beam intact) so that you can bolt it solidly to the housetop frame. And you can say about now, as I do, "Why not fit a fine, flat-opening hatch, with hinges fore and aft on the cover, and a transparent roof to let in the light?" But you'll lose that constant flow of sweet air in and out, and the hearty if misplaced approval of the wharf brigade. So study Figure 16-4, make your own adjustments, and decide for yourself.

Hatches and covers

As for that flat hatch, you'll need one, very likely, in the after deck, and another, certainly, up forward in the top of the house or in the foredeck. Consider that this one may be an escape route, or a passageway for bunched sails and spare anchors. It may be buried under solid water at times, and must be strong enough so that no conceivable accident can tear the top loose and overboard. Strong hinges should be bolted or riveted to the the coaming and cover. And, finally, you must provide some means to hold the cover tightly closed against water and thieves. I have always shunned the beautiful brass quadrant-style hatch openers because they clutter up the opening and snag anything going in or out—and they cost a lot more than two notched sticks and strong hold-down lines, which belay on cleats on the far sides of the deckbeams.

Figure 16-5a shows three cross sections through coaming-and-cover configurations; Figures 16-5b through 16-5f show details of joint options. The first construction is simple and obvious, and does very well if you provide a foam-rubber gasket between the lid and coaming. The second construction is perhaps neater, and not difficult to do if you have the means to rabbet stock for a perfect match between the coaming and rim. Halve the corners together, as shown in Figure 16-5b, and do not be tempted to join them with a picture-frame miter (Figure 16-5c). The third construction, with double coamings and deck-sweeping skirts on the cover, is probably worth doing in a forward hatch for offshore work. A wave-top that breaches the first defense still has to climb a

wall, penetrate a gasket, cross a chasm, and surmount another wall. Somewhere on this journey it should get tired.

So how shall we cover the cover? In our early and primitive days, there was no question: roof it with tongue-and-groove boards and stretch canvas over all. Came more yachty ideas, with varnished mahogany companionway slides, and we went to glued-up natural-finish tops—and inserted larger and larger plexiglass rectangles until the entire top was translucent, and the quiet gloom of the forepeak was no more. That bit of sunlight below did much to dry the air and discourage mold.

Right about now you may weigh respectfully the advice of your hard-headed experts, who point out that (for a petty few hundreds of dollars) you can buy precision-made cast-aluminum hatches, complete, and save yourself two days' labor and future grief. So you can, and a good thing too. But if you've come this far with your dream, on blood, sweat, scrounging, and pennies, you're a hopeless case anyway, and may as well continue to do things the hard way.

Toerails and bulwarks

And so we come to the toerail, that simple rim around the outside edge to keep you and various items of gear from going overboard. This fence comes in a great variety of shapes and sizes. The simplest form is a square strip; its most elaborate is a bulwark, supported by top timbers or bronze knees, and finished with a fine wide cap on top. Most often it will be a plank-on-edge piece, edge-fastened to the covering board and sheerstrake, usually tapered from bottom to top, and beveled to match the flare or tumblehome of the sheerstrake. A simple thing indeed. Armed with bar clamps, props from the underside of the shop roof, and timbers up the topsides, I managed, for the first 20 years of my career, to fit and fasten this toerail in a week's time. It was a process somewhat akin to stuffing a live boa constrictor into a garbage bag, and I groped ever for a better way.

And this is the ridiculously simple solution, which you would likely have arrived at in a much shorter time: Screw-fasten a row of fenceposts ($^5/_8$- by 2-inch oak, a foot long, say) to the sheerstrake, as shown in Figure 16-6, with the top ends peeping up 3 to 4 inches above the deck edge. Space them no more than 3 feet apart. Spring and clamp your rail stock

figure 16–7

Bulwark, in a West-country merchant schooner (c. 1880)
(Drawing courtesy of Basil Greenhill, *The Woodshipbuilders*)

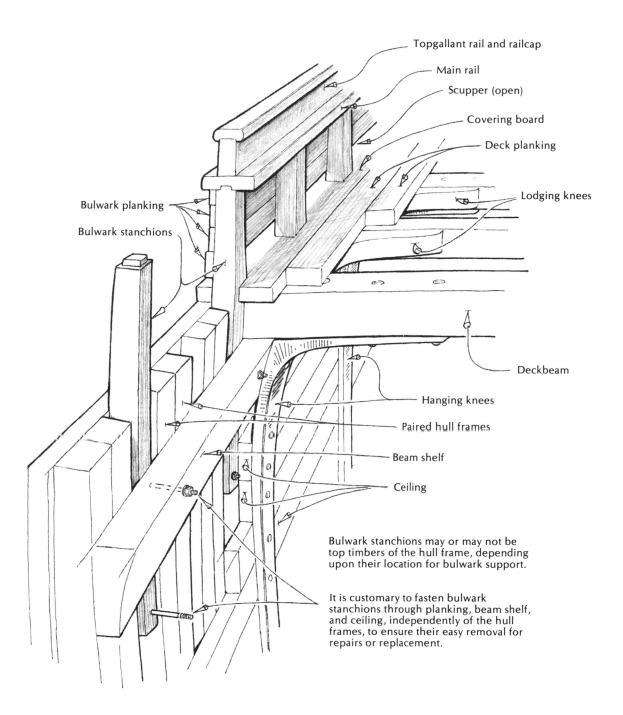

Topgallant rail and railcap

Main rail

Scupper (open)

Covering board

Deck planking

Lodging knees

Bulwark planking

Bulwark stanchions

Deckbeam

Hanging knees

Paired hull frames

Beam shelf

Ceiling

Bulwark stanchions may or may not be top timbers of the hull frame, depending upon their location for bulwark support.

It is customary to fasten bulwark stanchions through planking, beam shelf, and ceiling, independently of the hull frames, to ensure their easy removal for repairs or replacement.

figure 16–8

Cabintop grabrail

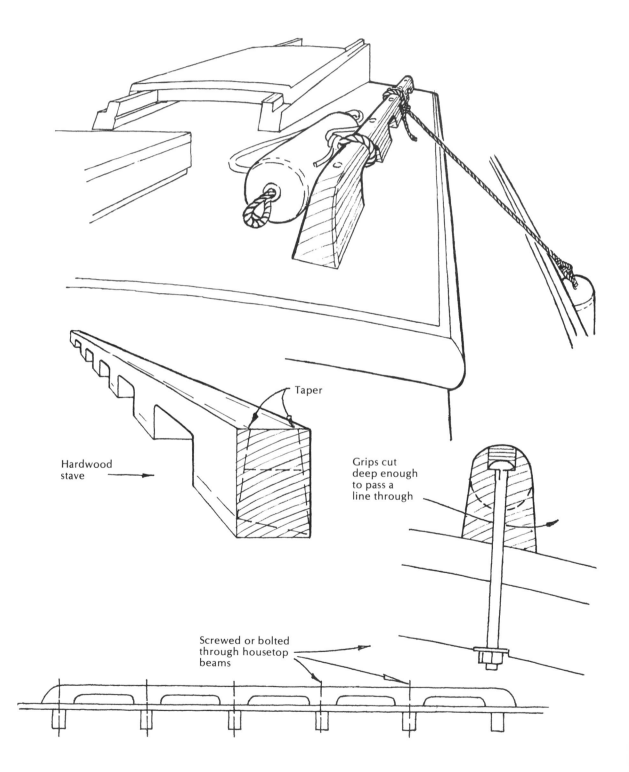

Taper

Hardwood
stave

Grips cut
deep enough
to pass a
line through

Screwed or bolted
through housetop
beams

down to the deck, inside this line of posts (with maybe a $1/8$-inch shim on each, to move it in from the edge), set your scribers to the greatest gap, and mark the whole length, inside and out. If your boat has a full bow, and much flare forward, you may need posts forward at 18-inch intervals to hold that end down (or, if the rail refuses to hook down to the stem, you may even have to cut it to shape out of a wider piece), but at worst you have the nasty thing under control. So take it to the bench and plane the bottom fair and tenderly to the lines you have scribed on the two faces. Clamp it back in place again (the forward end let into the rabbet in the stem—or jogged into the heavy block just aft of the stem—and the after end cut for the scarf, as shown). Scribe once more if the fit is less than perfect, but drill for fastenings now before you remove it for the final shaping. As for fastenings, you'll be shocked to hear that we have used flathead galvanized spikes, from 30-penny in $3/16$-inch holes up to $3/8$- by 10-inch spikes on 4-inch-high rails over $1^{1}/2$-inch hardwood sheerstrakes. You'll probably be happier with long bronze screws or, best of all, long and skinny galvanized lag screws. For these you will, of course, counterbore to take the thin-walled socket wrench that fits the square head of the lag.

If you have more patience than I have, you'll soak the contact surfaces with oil and poison, and wait a day before fastening down in a fine smear of sticky stuff. Fastenings should be two to the foot, deeply countersunk, sealed with a slug of oil before the bung goes in. Fit the next piece to the scarf joint shown; clamp, scribe, bevel, fasten; true the whole length to the proper profile and either level or parallel to the deck crown across the upper face if you plan to cap it. (A cap is expendable and easily repaired—and you can smooth it and shine it to match your heart's desire.) Look at Figure 16-6, and make up your mind.

If yours is a real little ship with a proper laid deck and covering boards, you may be tempted to build this fence big-ship style, with top timbers, knightheads, waist plank, wide cap, kevels—a bulwark that is strong and beautiful, but requiring constant vigilance against leaks around shrinking top timbers. (Shape these timbers from the best black locust, or bone-dry hard pine, or even teak; soak the mortises with a week's worth of oil and poison; caulk around the timbers with cedar wedges in the traditional way, or fill the gaps with an old-fashioned pitch-based seam compound that will soften and expand when the sun hits it.) You understand, of course, that the top timbers in big vessels are extensions of the main sawn frames, rather than extra pieces. Our small ones are mortised through the covering boards, one at a time, to extend down at least two planks below the sheer. You'll fit them between frames, fasten a light plank around them, and cover them with a flat cap. This will likely be sawn to shape, in three or four lengths scarfed together, and grooved and mortised to sit tightly over the bulwark and top timbers. The wharf brigade will approve, even if you question whether it was worth all that effort. I hope Figure 16-7 will clarify some details that I have treated lightly.

Handgrabs

When we were very young (and perhaps possessed of more enthusiasm than knowledge), we considered stanchions and lifelines to be something for old men and small children. We reserved one hand for ourselves, and sailed in an intoxicating mood of dare-deviltry. But we did have sense enough to provide one more item of deck furniture. This, of course, was a pair of grabrails, running the length of the housetop, port and starboard, shaped to fit the hand, and fastened beyond reproach. These grabrails immediately become anchorage for boathook, rolled-up awning, deck mop, dinghy, sail bags, and anything else that needs to be kept up out of the wet. If they are to sustain, with elegance, all this gear (and you, too, in times of peril), they deserve some careful planning.

As you probably know, you can buy (or cast from your own pattern) a set of bronze brackets, fasten one over each beam, and thread a round wooden dowel or bronze tube through them. You can even buy short sections of rail, shaped from solid teak, ready to drill and fasten. The castings are expensive, and the ready-made rails never come with the correct spacing of gaps, or the right bevel to stand plumb on the sloping housetop. I therefore suggest that you look at Figure 16-8 and cut your own to fit—with gaps deep enough to take big hands, or $3/4$-inch lines, and looking as if they belonged to this particular boat. Fasten them with a bolt or big bronze screw through each beam that they cross. Your wharf-side critic will approve of scoured teak here, or mahogany shining under 10 coats of varnish. You'll be wiser to put your faith in black locust or tough oak.

193

Chapter Seventeen

Fitting Bulkheads

You won't believe it, but you'll have to go through this bulkhead-fitting routine exactly 11 times as often as you now think likely; therefore, you'd better learn how to do it right now. I can think of four major systems, or techniques, for fitting a bulkhead. I'll end up trying to describe, with the help of Sam Manning's drawings, the method I use. It works well for me and can be twisted 90 degrees to do bunk flats and dish shelves. But before I get to this last one, I'd like to touch upon the other three.

The first and most common technique is what I call the Attrition Method. Armed with that most wonderful of precision instruments, the scriber (dividers, pencil-leg compasses), the craftsman holds a piece of lumber in his left hand and with the other makes a sweeping pass that would do credit to a Scotsman attacking with his *skean dhu*. Thanks to the infallible nature of his marker, the resulting pencil line is everywhere equidistant from surrounding obstructions, and bears a certain family resemblance to the spot it is destined for.

But this workpiece, as we shall call it hereafter, having been sawn to the line, comes out a bit short and bumps in the middle, while the ends are discouragingly distant from their final resting place. Well now: scribe her again, and cut, and try—and after the third or fourth trip to the bandsaw, the remaining half of the piece begins to look pretty good...and a bit of molding and some putty will fix it beyond reproach. (But by this time the inboard edge is by no means plumb and will need recutting and regrooving before the next one goes against it.)

You think I exaggerate? Not at all. I can show you some quick bulkheads I've done when I couldn't be bothered to go through all the proper moves. Attrition works on stone walls and armies, but you don't need it as a way of life.

A second system, developed independently by numerous practitioners, can be called the Staff and Feeler Method (Figure 17-1). It's a good one, too, especially valuable for marking a large slab of plywood. In its crude and simple form, the staff and feeler consists of a plumb post like a flat tree trunk at the innermost edge of the bulkhead-to-be, with pointed branches reaching out and touching strategic points on the perimeter of this little world: bottom corner of the carlin, top and bottom edges of the sheer clamp and the shelf, eight or ten spots along the curve of the vessel's side below the clamp. Use as many more as you think you'll need. Tack these branches to the trunk; remove the great tree intact, if possible; lay it on the plywood;

figure 17-1

The "Staff and Feeler" system

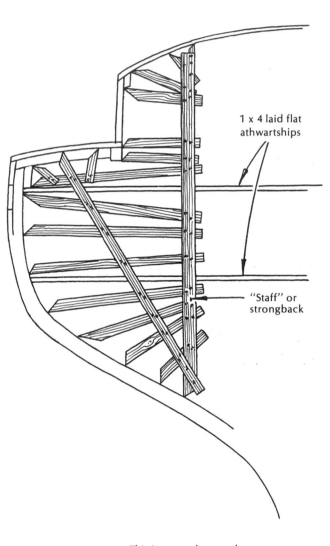

1 x 4 laid flat
athwartships

"Staff" or
strongback

This is a template made up
of pointers fastened to
a strongback.

and mark the outline. If you've worked carefully, allowed for bevels, and have remembered correctly which branch meant what, you should be able to saw out a piece that needs very little trimming to make it fit.

A third system, which might be called the Skeleton in the Closet, is really a fleshing out of the last method. Scribe and fit small pieces (soft pine or cedar, ¼ inch thick, easily shaped with a jackknife) to all the flats and curves that the bulkhead will fit (see Figure 17-2). Tack them lightly in their places and join them with more of the same pattern stock—anchoring all of this fragile outline to the vertical staff at the innermost edge of the location. (Some tiny "quilting" clamps are very handy helpers in this assembly business.) Unhitch the assembly, lift it out tenderly, and mark the stock for cutting.

This skeleton pattern system works better than any other to fit the thwarts to a skiff, a one-piece flat for a bunk platform, a floor timber, or an engine bed. Don't be ashamed to use it even under the scornful eye of a Master Builder. He probably goes for the Explorer's or Surveyor's Method, which I won't pursue any further at the moment. Then there's the Linoleum Layer, or Joe Frogger, Method, excellent in its way, but which I will likewise spare you.

And so we come at last to the simple, logical way to fit a bulkhead. You should be able to probe to the bottom of this great mystery in about five minutes, and never again need to worry about it. If Sam Manning and I can't make it all clear by the end of this chapter, it's our fault, not yours.

I don't know yet how many moves we'll make, so I'll just say, *First*—Decide where that bulkhead is going and take proper steps to guarantee that it starts, continues, and remains there throughout your struggles. You may think this is a silly warning, but I assure you that it's very easy to mark for one spot and then discover it isn't exactly the right one. You must therefore establish a tangible athwartships plane, precisely located at one face of the bulkhead-to-be, and rigid enough to support the staves, by clamps and temporary fastenings, until the fitting is complete and you can install fashion pieces and cleats to tie it all together. This backward approach (something like buying a horse and then building a barn around him) may lead you to suspect that I, too, am about ripe for pasture. This I hotly deny, and ask you to proceed thus:

Cut a straightedged 1-by-4 and nail it to the under edge of the sheer clamps, port and star-

figure 17-2
The "Skeleton in the Closet"

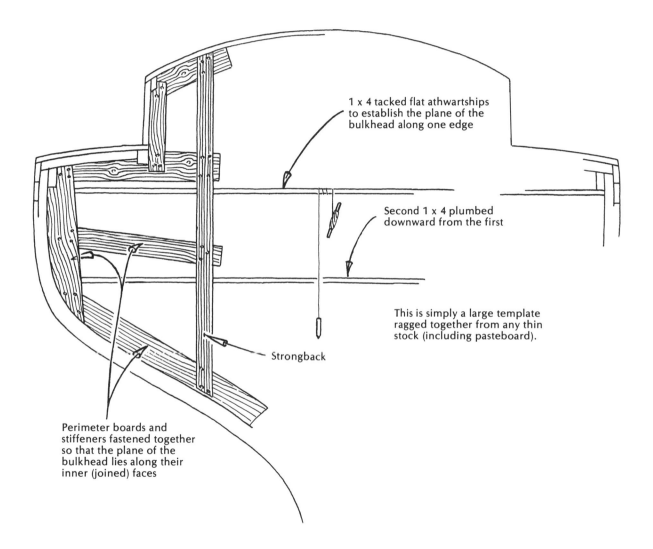

1 x 4 tacked flat athwartships to establish the plane of the bulkhead along one edge

Second 1 x 4 plumbed downward from the first

This is simply a large template ragged together from any thin stock (including pasteboard).

Strongback

Perimeter boards and stiffeners fastened together so that the plane of the bulkhead lies along their inner (joined) faces

figure 17-3

"Bud's Favorite"

Use of a spirit level to guide the scribing of a locus of points accurately across a wide distance

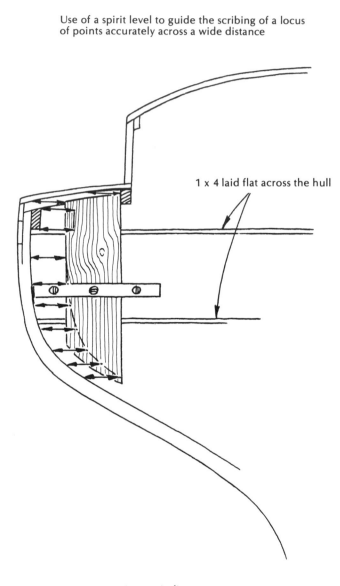

1 x 4 laid flat across the hull

Arrows indicate a constant divider setting (or ruler measurement, or marks on a stick) in determining the distance horizontally that this piece must be trimmed to fit the ceiling tightly.

board, exactly where the bulkhead is to go. (If you or the designer managed to locate a deck-beam at this magic spot, so much—so *very* much—the better, because otherwise you'll have to pad out the nearest one or insert an extra.) Now get out your trusty plumb bob, and spot for another athwartships 1-by-4, to be fitted and tacked to the inside of the ceiling a foot or so below, and exactly plumb under—and therefore parallel to—the upper one. There's your inviolable plane, nicely delineated and strong, to assist when you clamp up your first piece for marking. This piece, in case you may wonder, is a length of clear white pine heart-wood, 12 inches or more wide, with a groove in the inboard edge to take a ¼-inch spline. You may plan to use something else, but I'd rather you didn't tell me about it. (I feel that I'm as broad-minded as Henry Ford, who didn't care what color the customer wanted, as long as it was black. Or Nat Herreshoff, who admitted that there are two colors—black and white—that you can paint a boat, but only a dam' fool would go for black. It's interesting to contemplate the diametrically opposite attitudes toward the buying public of our two greatest manufacturing geniuses—one opting for black, and the other for white.)

So you've got this fine piece of lumber, rough cut as in Figure 17-3, moved outboard as far as it will go, and in place. Let's indulge in a little fantasy here: If that board were a flat sheet of wax, and all the parts of the boat were hot enough to melt wax on contact, you could slide that slab of wax exactly horizontally, melting as it went, until it reached the distantmost corner under the sheer clamp. (You will kindly assume instant cooling of boat mass, so that the edges remain sharp and tight.) The key to the success of this maneuver is that the slab moved, without wavering, exactly horizontally, as far as, but no farther than, it needed to go. So all you've got to do to your piece of pine is predict, mark, and remove any parts of it that would prevent its reaching that corner under the sheer clamp. You can't, by any stretch of imagination, expect to do this marking job accurately enough with scribers alone, freehand. You need, in addition, your sliding-blade tri-square, a good level, and a bevel square.

Look at the picture. That inboard edge is exactly plumb, a bit taller than the height required when it has moved outboard to its final resting place. Now, with sliding-blade tri-square level, mark lines exactly horizontal, on the face of your workpiece, from all salient points in the profile of the cave: two or three arbitrary spots on the roof; top and bottom corners of the clamp; top of the hull ceiling under the clamp; a dozen different spots down the curve of the ceiling. And now your dividers become useful. (You can get the same result with a folding rule or a thin stick with a pencil mark on it.)

Set your dividers to (or measure) the distance from the outboard edge of the workpiece to the remotest point under the sheer clamp. Mark this exact distance out, on each horizontal line, from its point of origin (corner of the clamp, the spot on the under surface of the roof, whatever.) Join these points, as proper, with straight lines or fair curves—and saw to the marks at the proper bevels.

And that's all there is to it. This direct marking technique works horizontally, as above, or vertically, as for a deckbeam, or diagonally, for that matter, if you lay off all your identical distances exactly parallel on the line of travel. Get this principle firmly fixed in your mind, and you are fully equipped to handle almost every problem that arises. After all, there are only three moves in boatbuilding: mark a piece, cut it to shape, fasten it to another piece. Keep doing this 'til there she sits, looking as if she were alive....

Which brings us to the second piece in that bulkhead. You can measure the length of the plumb edge, lay off the angles at the top and bottom on your stock, make some slight, educated allowances, cut and trim to fit—no great job, with no jogs or other intricacies.

Or you can make a skeleton pattern, like a hockey stick with a blade at each end. And fit another, and another—under the carlin, up the inside of the house coaming, marching inboard to the door frame. Tack the bottom ends to the ceiling, remove the lower athwartships 1-by-4, fit the fashion pieces (1 1/2 by 1 1/2 inches, screw-fastened to the ceiling and bulkhead staves)—and take the whole damned thing apart to insert the splines. If you remembered to mark a mirror duplicate of the first piece, you've got a good start on the twin bulkhead on the other side of the boat. Don't worry if they look frail at this stage. They'll have horizontal cleats all over them, front and back, to hold bunk tops, galley benches, bookshelves, chart table—and they'll be stiff enough, under this mutual aid program, to support all the rest of the joiner-work in the boat.

So what are you waiting for? Get in there and fit those bulkheads.

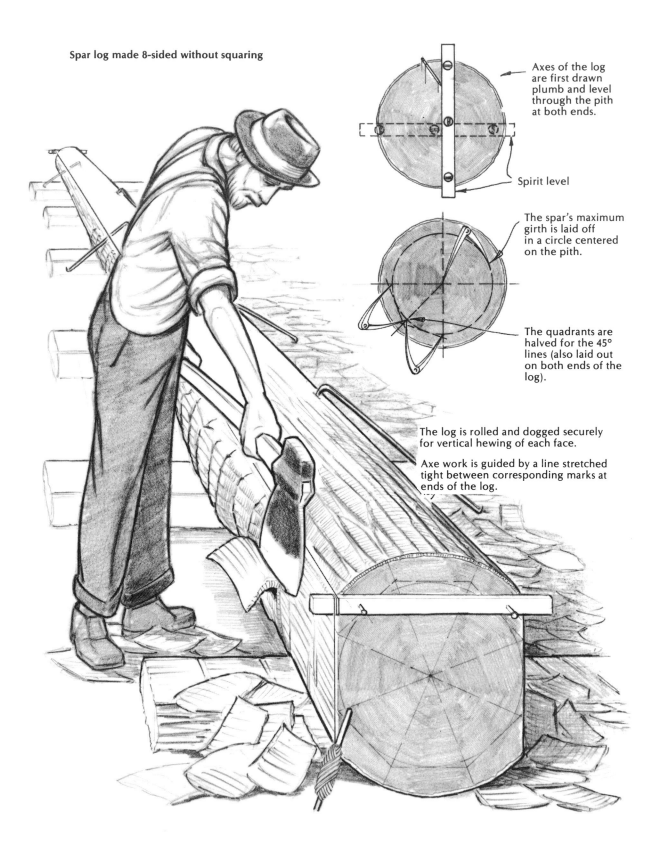

Spar log made 8-sided without squaring

Axes of the log are first drawn plumb and level through the pith at both ends.

Spirit level

The spar's maximum girth is laid off in a circle centered on the pith.

The quadrants are halved for the 45° lines (also laid out on both ends of the log).

The log is rolled and dogged securely for vertical hewing of each face.

Axe work is guided by a line stretched tight between corresponding marks at ends of the log.

Chapter Eighteen

Spars

When we were very young, and wished to give wings and magic to our skiffs, we'd go deep into a spruce swamp to find a tree that had died standing. Trim off the small dead limbs, smooth it with a drawknife, keep the taper that came naturally, maybe fit a sheave at the top for a halyard, step it in a hole in the forward thwart, fit it with some kind of sail (made from a discarded bedsheet or a painter's drop cloth)—and the winds of Heaven were our companions in a glorious voyage to the Happy Isles. These were four miles (and half the World away) downwind. If the tide didn't favor, we might have to row a spell on the return voyage. It was worth it. That little spar was the ultimate key to romance and adventure.

Now, some 60-odd years and perhaps 400 spars later, the same feeling flows from a new one, half-shaped on the bench. We've learned ways to build it to any size or shape we want, and we can make it lighter in weight, more enduring in the frost and fog and heat of the sun; but we haven't improved its purity of form and purpose. It's still a fine, natural thing that aspires to the clouds.

(And do you remember Herman Melville's most beautiful spar in all the world? I think her name was Fayaway, and she lived in the Vale of Typee. She stood in the bow of his canoe and spread her raiment to the benevolent trade-wind, and they sailed across the lagoon with no thoughts of the evil in a great white whale.)

I suppose I should say something about materials for wooden spars, even if I thereby damn myself as one grateful for second best. I have known men who, despairing of getting Sitka spruce, have given up the whole project as impossible. I have small sympathy for them. They'd as well starve in the presence of food too plain for their educated taste—which is to say that you can make splendid spars of slow-grown Douglas-fir, Eastern spruce, and dozens of other woods around the world. Elijah Kellogg's fisher boys stepped hemlock masts in their Chebacco boat, and I think some of the Block Island cowhorns, like the fabled *Roaring Bessie*, sailed with natural unstayed cedar masts from Block Island's Great Swamp.

Back in the '30s, when we first learned about box-section masts and casein glue, we could buy, at the local lumberyard, a clear fir timber 6 inches by 8 inches by 26 feet long. We'd slice it, painfully, on the big table saw, scarf and taper the four staves, and glue them together. This was long before epoxy, even before resorcinol glue, but the joints still held—and so far as I know, are still holding in some of those masts, now nearly 50 years old. And we learned (or thought we did; answers came more easily and less dusty in that fresh dawn) that if you had enough spruce and glue

figure 18-1

Taper in a solid spar

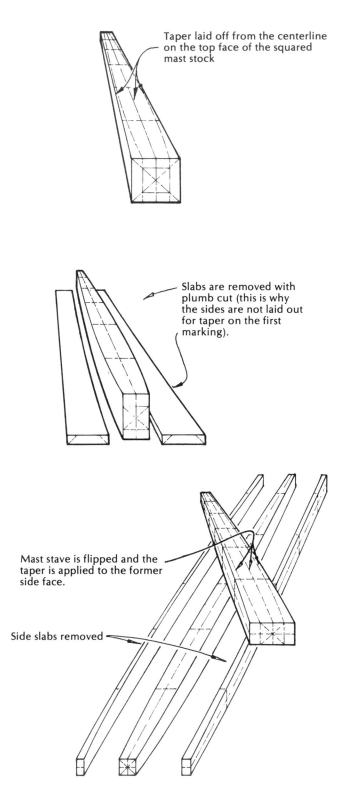

Taper laid off from the centerline on the top face of the squared mast stock

Slabs are removed with plumb cut (this is why the sides are not laid out for taper on the first marking).

Mast stave is flipped and the taper is applied to the former side face.

Side slabs removed

and clamps and time, you could build a spar that would reach the moon.

But until the great breakthrough, which happened less than a hundred years ago, mastmaking was not much more complicated in theory and practice than that foray into the swamp to find a tree. If the mast was to be free-standing, as in a catboat, you kept the taper of the grown stick and cheerfully accepted a very loose fit of the gaff jaws when the sail was hoisted. If the vessel was a sloop with shrouds, and reason told you that the mast was now a strut in pure compression, you still knew that constant taper saved weight aloft and certainly looked better. (And furthermore, you avoided with clear conscience the tedious and painful job of squaring and re-rounding a bigger trunk.) I went through all this—with broad-axe, drawknife, spar planes, special soft fillers for the inevitable deep checks—until I discovered that I could buy a square timber of Douglas-fir, perfectly clear, cut from outside the heart of the tree, in almost any size I might want. Of course, the price was shocking—as much as 10 cents per board foot on the wharf in Portland—but even I could see that life was simpler, the end result better, if I needed only to taper and round this precise piece of heart-free timber.

Shaping a mast or spar

This is how it's done—on a solid or hollow mast, the loom of an oar, a handle for a boat-hook, or a flagpole for the front lawn—in progressive steps, as follows:

First, taper the end or ends exactly to the dimensions given, exactly square at all points. (On most spars, such as masts for a jib-headed rig, and for booms and gaffs, the side next to the sail should be kept straight, with all the tapering done on the other three. Elementary, of course.) You'll mark for these taper cuts (with an honest batten) on the top face of your timber, as shown in Figure 18-1, and make precisely plumb cuts with bandsaw or tablesaw— or with portable power saw or even an axe and an adze, if the timber is too big to be brought to the mill. Turn it, then, 90 degrees and make the remaining cut or cuts, always remembering the need to keep all cross sections exactly square. Any sloppy work at this stage will persist to the end of the job; you'll have lost control, and the final product will be something less than perfect. (And don't roll self-righteous calipers around a spar that I shaped last year. My hand slipped.)

figure 18–2a

Layout of 8 and 16 sides on a tapered spar stave

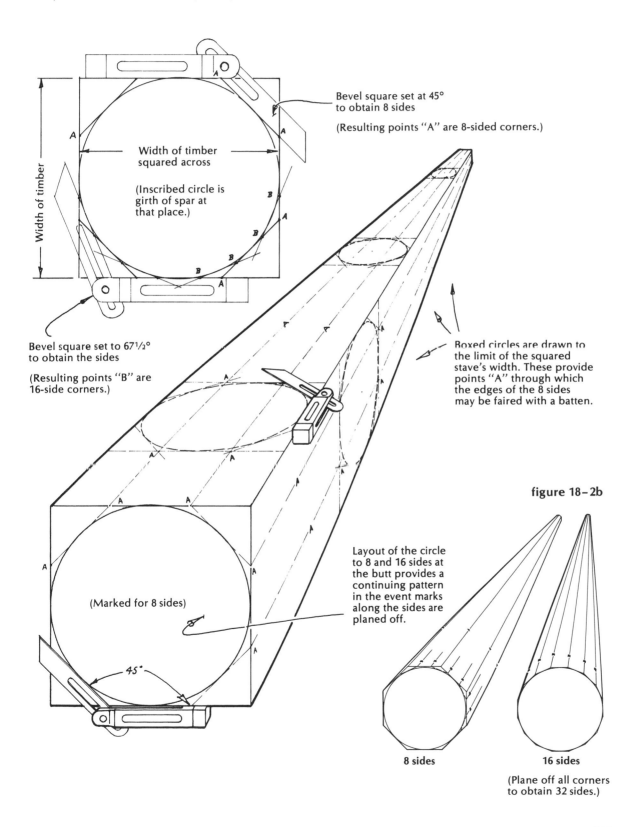

Bevel square set at 45°
to obtain 8 sides

(Resulting points "A" are 8-sided corners.)

Width of timber
squared across

(Inscribed circle is
girth of spar at
that place.)

Width of timber

Bevel square set to 67½°
to obtain the sides

(Resulting points "B" are
16-side corners.)

Boxed circles are drawn to
the limit of the squared
stave's width. These provide
points "A" through which
the edges of the 8 sides
may be faired with a batten.

figure 18–2b

Layout of the circle
to 8 and 16 sides at
the butt provides a
continuing pattern
in the event marks
along the sides are
planed off.

(Marked for 8 sides)

45°

8 sides

16 sides

(Plane off all corners
to obtain 32 sides.)

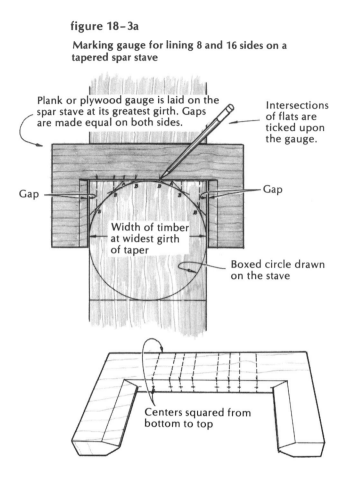

figure 18–3a

Marking gauge for lining 8 and 16 sides on a tapered spar stave

Plank or plywood gauge is laid on the spar stave at its greatest girth. Gaps are made equal on both sides.

Intersections of flats are ticked upon the gauge.

Gap

Gap

Width of timber at widest girth of taper

Boxed circle drawn on the stave

Centers squared from bottom to top

The next move is to mark for the cuts that will make this stick 8- and then 16-sided. Figure 18–2 shows the process clearly: You draw a circle the exact diameter of your square stick (preferably on the side of the stick itself), and confine it with lines tangent to it and square across the timber. Then mark tangents at 45 degrees, to intersect those 90-degree tangents, as shown in the drawing. The final operation in this exercise is to draw yet another tangent, this time at 67½ degrees, to locate the line for the 16-side cuts. If, now, you repeat this entire process at convenient intervals along your tapering spar, you will have a series of points to be joined by batten-faired lines, which you will duplicate on each side of the other three sides of the stick. Cut off the four big corners to make the stick 8-sided, with a power saw, drawknife, or hand plane, whichever best suits the size of the job. Freshen the marks and cut the 16 flats on it, then 32 (by eye, this time)—and it's ready for final finishing, which will be done with the aid of an inside-out power-driven sander belt, to be described later.

In the meantime, let's make a simple tool that will do automatically all the marking de-

scribed in the above paragraph. Figure 18–3 shows it all, better than I can describe it: the notched board, with an opening slightly larger than the greatest diameter of the spar-to-be; the beveled ends of the notch, to maintain a center-line bearing against the side of the square timber; finally, the sharpened markers, threaded through the board's backbone. The only tricky bit is to get these markers located at exactly the right spots. If you are a lot smarter than I am, you can do this spacing by percentages. As for me, I lay the tool across that circle, with beveled ends snug against the sides of the timber, and note where the 8-side and 16-side lines cross the centerline of the underside of the board's backbone. Drill for the markers, which may well be ³⁄₁₆-inch screws, ground to a point and threaded through a ⁵⁄₃₂-inch hole. If the scratches they make are too dim, run a soft pencil along the groove afterwards.

As for the wonderful finishing tool: a rubber-covered drum (Figure 18–4), spun by a slow-speed electric drill, nestles in the bight of a sander belt that has been hung, inside out, over the 32-sided spar. Hang the spar up eyebrow-high. Start the drill, walk the length of the spar, turn it over, and do the other half; go over it once again with a fine-grit belt. Don't expect this marvelous machine to correct gross inequalities. Remember always that this tool is but a poor thing to save some labor. It can't do your thinking for you.

So what more do we need to say about solid, one-piece spars? Mostly praise. They made possible the exploration of the world and all overseas commerce for a thousand years, and for lack of them, empires tottered. But that perfect tree is not always easy to come by, nor even a sawn timber of the right size and quality. And the solid mast is heavier than it needs to be, and it will develop checks. So....

The hollow spar

We discovered good glue back in the 1930s and very quickly learned that it's easy, quick, and (usually) less expensive to build a mast out of several small pieces. No more need to agonize over imperfections in the one big piece, no need to pickle it in the salt pond, or dry it for a year before it's fit to use. In the 1930s, the jib-headed rig was fast displacing the gaff-headers, permitting (and requiring) the more elaborate staying after the style of Marconi's radio masts. The four-board, box-section mast suddenly became beautiful. The great breakthrough had come.

figure 18-3b

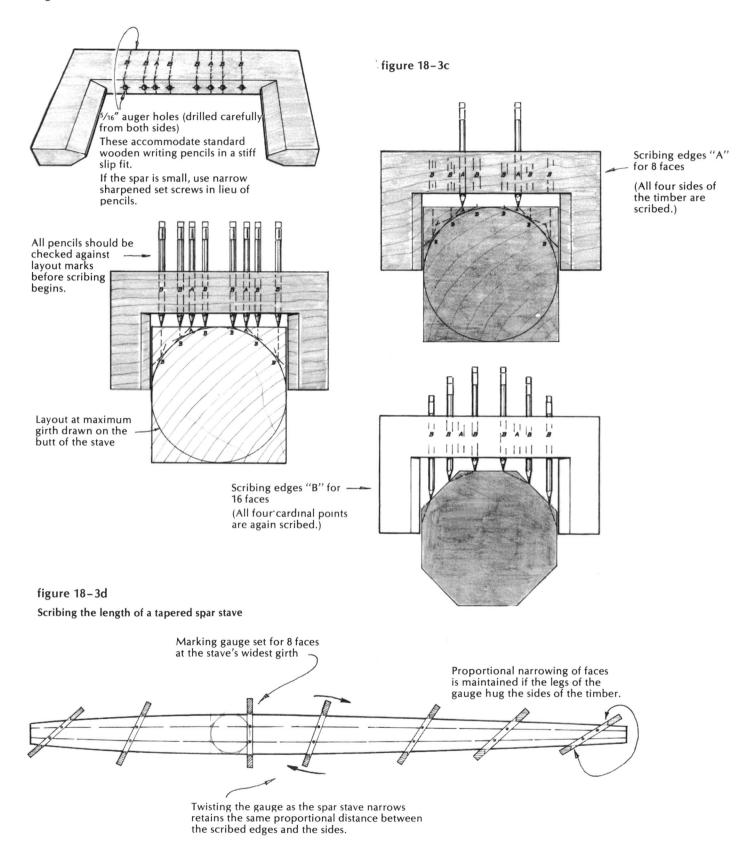

$^5/_{16}$" auger holes (drilled carefully from both sides)

These accommodate standard wooden writing pencils in a stiff slip fit.

If the spar is small, use narrow sharpened set screws in lieu of pencils.

All pencils should be checked against layout marks before scribing begins.

Layout at maximum girth drawn on the butt of the stave

figure 18-3c

Scribing edges "A" for 8 faces

(All four sides of the timber are scribed.)

Scribing edges "B" for 16 faces

(All four cardinal points are again scribed.)

figure 18-3d

Scribing the length of a tapered spar stave

Marking gauge set for 8 faces at the stave's widest girth

Proportional narrowing of faces is maintained if the legs of the gauge hug the sides of the timber.

Twisting the gauge as the spar stave narrows retains the same proportional distance between the scribed edges and the sides.

figure 18-4

The marvelous spar-finishing machine

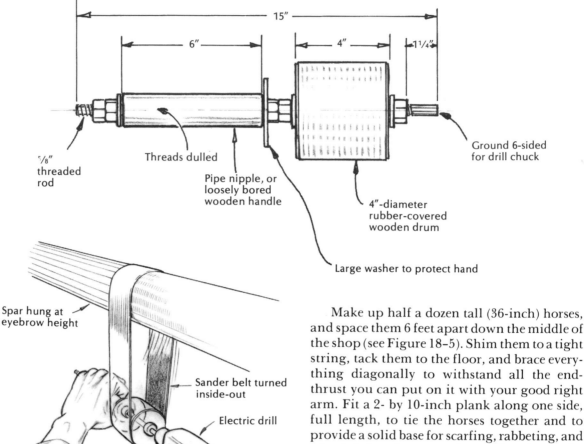

15"

6"

4"

1¼"

⁵⁄₈"
threaded
rod

Threads dulled

Pipe nipple, or
loosely bored
wooden handle

4"-diameter
rubber-covered
wooden drum

Ground 6-sided
for drill chuck

Large washer to protect hand

Spar hung at
eyebrow height

Sander belt turned
inside-out

Electric drill

We made scarfing jigs and spar clamps, and convinced ourselves that the glued joints were the strongest parts of those assemblies. We decided that the making of hollow spars is probably the easiest part of boatbuilding. With enough dry spruce (or fir, or other light and tough wood) of any available size, we could add length to existing spars, mend broken booms, or build new light masts that would stay straight forevermore. We had taken yet another step toward controlling our destiny—and had lost the primitive joy of seeking out that perfect tree in the depths of the swamp.

Therefore, we'd better get to the business of gathering the few, simple bits of equipment you'll need.

Make up half a dozen tall (36-inch) horses, and space them 6 feet apart down the middle of the shop (see Figure 18-5). Shim them to a tight string, tack them to the floor, and brace everything diagonally to withstand all the end-thrust you can put on it with your good right arm. Fit a 2- by 10-inch plank along one side, full length, to tie the horses together and to provide a solid base for scarfing, rabbeting, and edge-joining the staves that will make up the completed spar. Note that this spar bench can be disassembled, to sleep peacefully under the shop for 50 weeks of the year. It's slightly more elaborate than you'd need to shape and glue a solid boom, and it could be improved to handle all the possibilities in a full-time spar shop. Use your own ingenuity, but keep it true and uncluttered so that you can march up and down both sides, and around the ends, and spread glue at a dead run.

And on this bench you'll clamp a scarfing jig, which is a very simple device for marking and controlling chisel-like matching cuts. (See Figure 18-6.) Two identical wedges, with a slope of 1 inch in 12 inches, are screw-fastened to a short plank—exactly abreast of each other, separated only enough to accommodate the widest pieces you'll be joining. The wedges will, of course, be deeper than the work-piece you're about to slide between them and out to the jumping-off place. To fit an end, you'll

206

clamp as shown, make cuts across, split off most of the wood between cuts, and finish with a long jointer, precisely to the slope of the wedges. You could, of course, cut these slopes almost to size on a bandsaw, or do the whole job with a high-speed router and a special jig, or even work them down with repeated passes on a movable ramp in a surface planer. Just be sure that the ends match perfectly.

Unless you own or can borrow vast numbers of C-clamps, you'd best make up a set of special spar clamps, as shown in Figure 18-7—two pieces of hardwood, two continuous-threaded $^3/8$-inch steel rods, with nuts and washers above and below. You'll need one every foot for the longest spar you'll make. You can distribute the pressure (on staves less than an inch thick) by inserting a 6-inch pad above and below, as shown. You can even squeeze the staves together with giant hose-clamps, or rope and wedges, or spiral wrappings with strips of rubber or nylon line, but you won't have the good control of pressure that you get with these homemade clamps.

(And you may say at this point, "Who needs pressure? Doesn't the old...fossil realize that epoxy has changed all that? At last made wood a reasonable substitute for the more commonly accepted materials for boat- and spar-making? Fills the gaps, seals against fungus forevermore, makes joints stronger than welded iron? *No* pressure needed?" —Sure enough. But I still prefer cold-water-mix Weldwood, which does not require controlled temperature or humidity, costs very little, and forgives my incompetence as a chemist. And anyway, we grew up together.)

One more bit of soul-searching. What about this caution to scatter scarfs, the weak spots, as widely as possible? If you hark to that implied doubt and accept it, you'd best stop right here. Glued wooden spars are not for you. But if you believe, as I do, that the glued-scarf sections are always the stiffest and strongest parts of the stave, then you'll be happy to see them all cheek-by-jowl, or however else chance and available lengths may dictate their spacing.

So here we are with a bench, a scarfing jig, some clamps, glue, and a pile of 18- and 20-foot spruce planks—2 by 6, which actually measure about 1½ by 5½ inches. We need a mast for a moderately powerful jib-headed cutter, which we'll sail in the track of the *Spray* to the Straits of Magellan. Nothing special, but it's to be as light as we dare make it. It must be strong enough to take a hundred knockdowns in a row

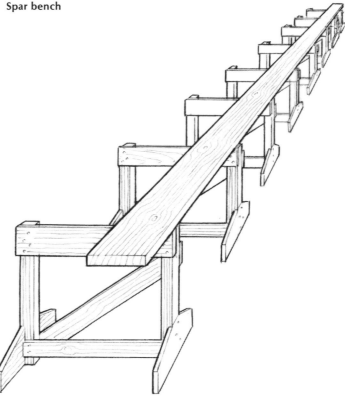

figure 18–5

Spar bench

with the spreaders in the water, and never the slightest doubt that it can take another hundred without a worry in the world. It must, of course, be able (with once-a-year maintenance) to cope with the tropical sun and northern winters through the next 30 years. Nothing very special, as you can see—no controlled bending, or internal halyards, or engine exhaust up the hollow. Since time is not of the essence, we can afford to spend all of six days on this job. (Let's pray for cool and cloudy weather for gluing, hot and dry for the cure.) We'll make it round, for the natural look, and because we might decide to switch to a gaff-headed rig at the last moment. We'll need to scarf an 18-foot piece to a 20-foot one to make, comfortably, the 35-foot overall length of each stave, with some left over to trim back on the butt end of the finished spar. We'll do all the tapering in the upper section of each stave, before gluing the scarfs. And when we clamp these scarfs together, with slippery glue on both faces, we'll be agonizingly aware of their desire to skid lengthwise and out of line when the clamps are tightened. So we'll squeeze them between perfectly straight cauls, a foot longer

figure 18–6

Scarfing jig—1:12 slope for all spar-stave scarfs

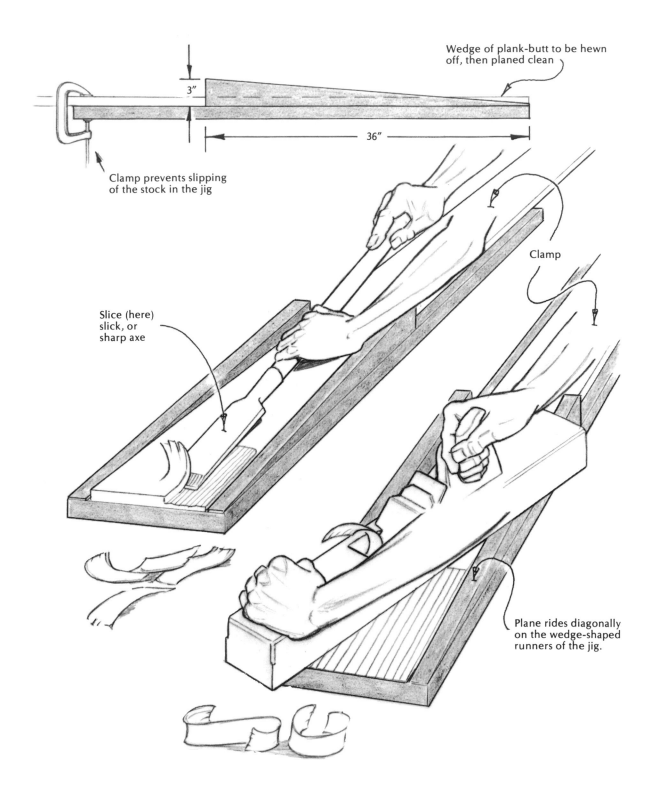

Wedge of plank-butt to be hewn off, then planed clean

3"

36"

Clamp prevents slipping of the stock in the jig

Clamp

Slice (here) slick, or sharp axe

Plane rides diagonally on the wedge-shaped runners of the jig.

than the scarfs, exactly the width of the stave, and with waxed paper between caul and scarf (see Figure 18-8). And we'll use plenty of clamps: four C-clamps on each scarf to hold the joint in line, and four of your special spar clamps to spread the load. Leave them for now. You can do no more until the morrow, when the thumbnail test will tell you if it's safe to release the clamps. (If the oozed glue is brittle, the bond is safe to handle.)

Good enough. Off with the clamps, clean off the glue, joint the matching staves exactly alike and perfectly square on the edges. Cut that rabbet, as shown in the cross section in Figure 18-9, full length of the forward and after staves, to stop inward movement and help with alignment of the side staves during the final assembly. (Or, if you wish, you can attach temporary cleats to the side staves to stop that inward and uncontrollable skid.) Fit a solid plug, 2 feet long, at the top end where the main halyard sheave and all the masthead rigging tangs come together; fit another at the butt end, long enough to reach above the halyard cleats, winches, and main-boom gooseneck. Run through a dry dress rehearsal; rally your helpers, trained in the ways of clamps and brushes; mix two quarts of glue, and go to it. Wet both surfaces, work fast, set up those clamp bolts as if you had a built-in torque gauge in your right arm—and let it set for 24 hours. While you wait, you can soothe your impatience by gluing stock for a 3-inch-diameter solid boom, or a tapered mast for your peapod.

When you can wait no longer, strip off the clamps and taste pure joy. You've got all the time in the world, now, to clean, shape, and round that beautiful thing, and every move can be sheer delight. And when you've got this one done (except for the sheave, spreaders, tangs, sail track, and a few other things the plans call for), you'll know about all I can tell you about sparmaking. Stay with that one-in-twelve slope for all scarfs; smooth surfaces to join; keep wall thickness no less than one-fifth of the diameter, whether round or box-section—and that's about it.

Figure 18-10 shows various cross sections using four staves, or two thick ones hollowed out and glued together. You can, of course, build up that thickness by gluing two and two together, and then dig out the valley in each of these built-up halves. Use your adjustable-depth circular saw to make nicely calculated lengthwise scores, close together, four passes

figure 18-7

Homemade spar clamp

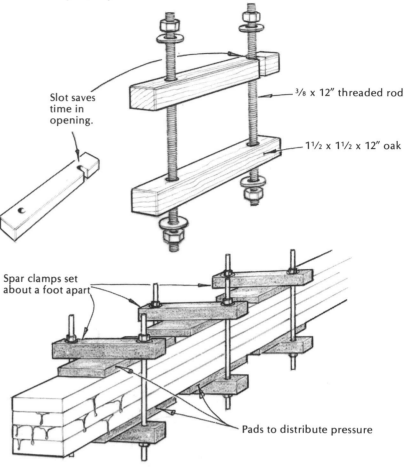

Slot saves time in opening.

3/8 x 12" threaded rod

1½ x 1½ x 12" oak

Spar clamps set about a foot apart

Pads to distribute pressure

for each setting, down the steep sides and across the bottom of the fjord. Break out the wafer-thin leaves with a gouge, and smooth the hollows with a round-faced plane. You will, of course, have stopped the hollowing short of the ends, for built-in plugs, and you could also leave a solid section where the spreaders will thrust and shroud-tangs will bolt. Glue these two troughs together, and round off the outside in the usual way.

If you have tools and patience to handle the scooping-out process, you may decide that this is the simplest and most satisfactory way to make a hollow spar. And if, in the glory of your new-found confidence you decide to try an eight-stave construction—go right ahead, but don't expect me to help you. I have trouble enough handling four. (I will, though, pass on a rumor I heard that saddles and giant hose clamps are the answer.)

209

figure 18–8

Scarf-joining a spar stave

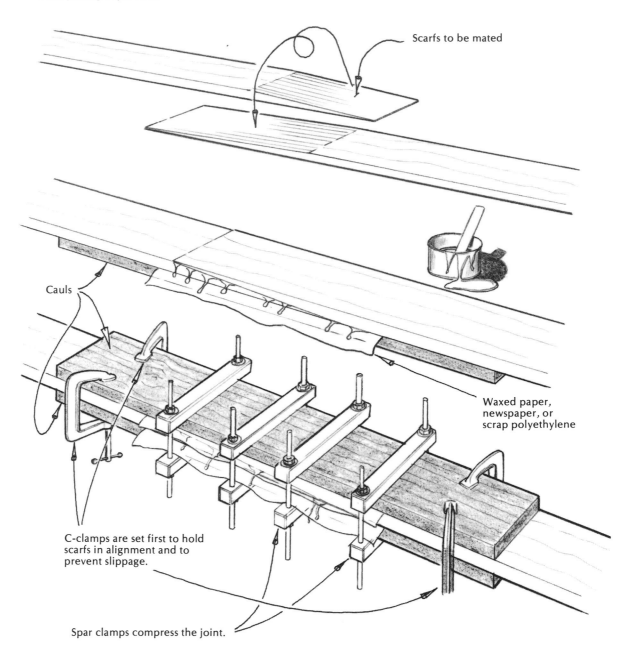

Scarfs to be mated

Cauls

Waxed paper,
newspaper, or
scrap polyethylene

C-clamps are set first to hold
scarfs in alignment and to
prevent slippage.

Spar clamps compress the joint.

Lengthening a spar

Once upon a time, a man I knew shaped a magnificent round spar for a new catboat, and he measured off the length from the top (the stick was several feet too long) and cut it off—on the wrong mark, so that it was 2 feet too short. Some appropriate words were spoken, and another member of the crew, under better emotional control, cut the remains into 6-foot tapered rolls, which are always handy around a boatyard. No great harm done, you may say. You'd be wrong. That man told me with tears in his eyes that he'd never since been able to pick up a crosscut saw without his hand trembling. The pitiful part of this is that it was completely unnecessary. Had he known what

figure 18–9

Making up a hollow spar

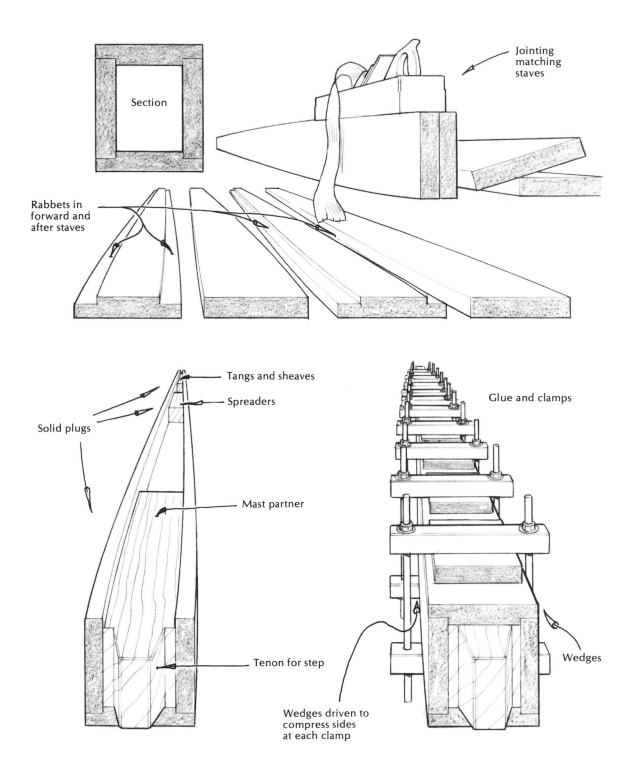

Section

Jointing
matching
staves

Rabbets in
forward and
after staves

Tangs and sheaves

Spreaders

Solid plugs

Mast partner

Tenon for step

Wedges driven to
compress sides
at each clamp

Glue and clamps

Wedges

211

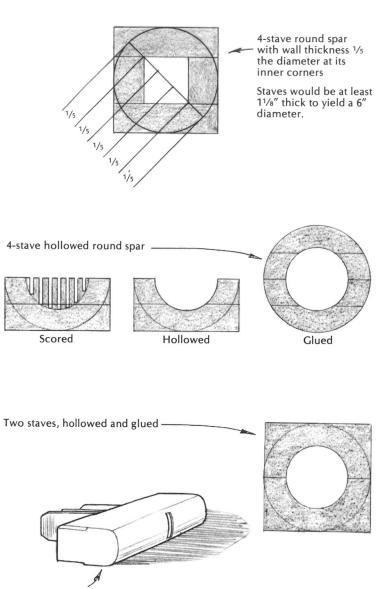

figure 18-10

Cross sections of hollowed spars

4-stave round spar with wall thickness ⅕ the diameter at its inner corners

Staves would be at least 1⅛″ thick to yield a 6″ diameter.

⅕ ⅕ ⅕ ⅕ ⅕

4-stave hollowed round spar

Scored   Hollowed   Glued

Two staves, hollowed and glued

Hollowing plane

we know now (and had he thought he could convince the owner that we, uh, *he* had meant to do it that way), he would have laughed off that little mistake almost as a childish error, and instructed one of the gang to lengthen her out as called for. Just one more instance of the New Freedom in the post-glue era, more useful even than the elliptical patch, which brings forth exclamations of wonder and delight from casual observers, and hides a hideous knothole

from the owner's eye. And yet one more: someone comes in with a splendid boom broken clean in two, and the sad story that it will take six weeks to get a new one from the factory— what then? Let's first lengthen that mast.

Look to Figure 18-11. We'll dress the butt to a flat wedge with our standard one-in-twelve slope exactly the same on both sides. This is most easily controlled and accomplished with the aid of another scarfing jig, one slightly deeper than the diameter of the mast with a fairly snug fit along its sides. Clamp the butt in the jig, as shown. Make saw cuts across, whack off the chunks, and dress the result down with a long plane that rides toe and heel on the wedges. Turn it over exactly 180 degrees, exactly at the same fore-and-aft location in the trough, and do the other side likewise. Now saw out (or build up of two pieces glued together) two slabs, rectangular in section, each about ¼ inch wider than the diameter of the spar, and ⅛ inch thicker than the half-diameter (and, of course, long enough for the desired extra length). Cut a chisel-style scarf on one end of each, using the same jig and technique. Clamp them together, and try them for fit to enclose that wedge on the butt of the mast. Finally, glue the works together, taking extraordinary precautions against endwise sliding and creeping out of line. Dress down the new part in the square to the proper size and taper, then round and smooth it to match the rest of the spar. If you paint it, nobody'll ever know what happened. (We've lengthened out a gaff-headed mast as much as 8 feet, to convert to jib-headed, and we've replaced 3 feet of masthead that went soft beneath the eyes and sheaves. In every case, the operation was successful, and it sure beat making a new mast.)

As for that broken boom: simply do the same joint twice, as shown in Figure 18-12, scarfing your two side pieces to the wedges cut on the two broken ends—with a flat between scarfs, of course, calculated to restore the original and proper length of the boom. Or maybe you'd like to make it a bit longer this time, while you're at it. Use this method if you've broken your best spruce oar, or your boathook handle, or your beautiful 7-foot curved tiller—scarfing and gluing can get to be a mania.

And one last thing. To hide and seal that porous knot, to restore wood to the spot where your broadaxe has sliced too deep, you proceed thus: Scoop out a depression in way of the defect, smoothly curved from end to end and perfectly flat across. A compass plane, set to the

212

figure 18–11

To lengthen a spar—

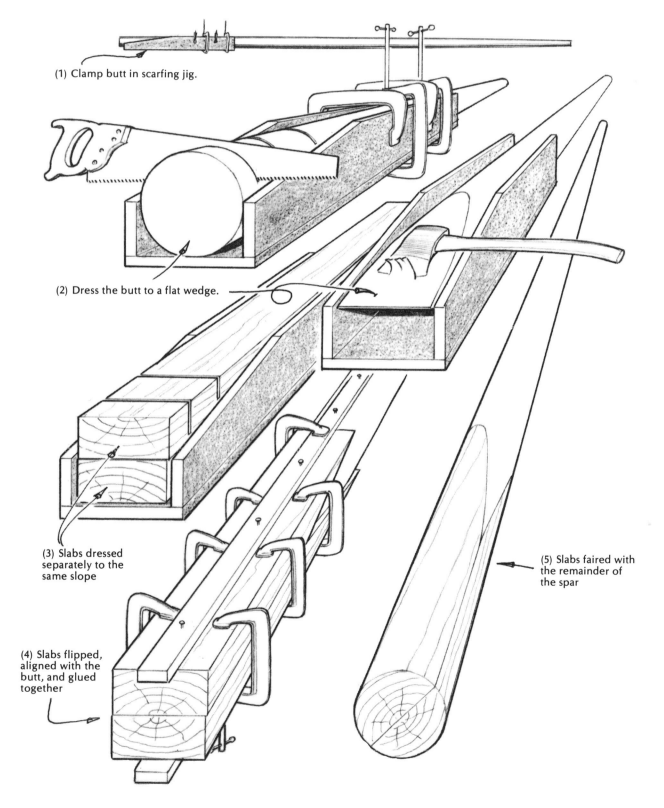

(1) Clamp butt in scarfing jig.

(2) Dress the butt to a flat wedge.

(3) Slabs dressed separately to the same slope

(4) Slabs flipped, aligned with the butt, and glued together

(5) Slabs faired with the remainder of the spar

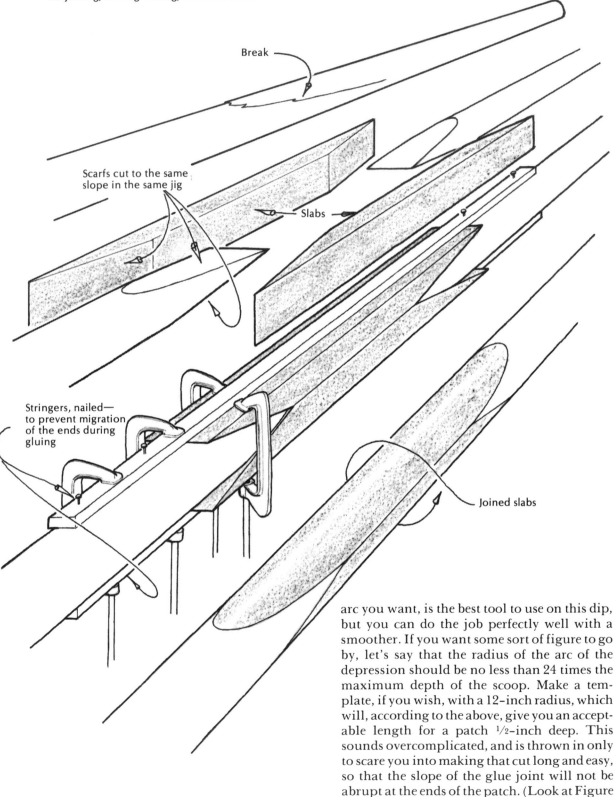

figure 18–12

Re-joining, or lengthening, a broken boom

Break

Scarfs cut to the same slope in the same jig

Slabs

Stringers, nailed—to prevent migration of the ends during gluing

Joined slabs

arc you want, is the best tool to use on this dip, but you can do the job perfectly well with a smoother. If you want some sort of figure to go by, let's say that the radius of the arc of the depression should be no less than 24 times the maximum depth of the scoop. Make a template, if you wish, with a 12-inch radius, which will, according to the above, give you an acceptable length for a patch ½-inch deep. This sounds overcomplicated, and is thrown in only to scare you into making that cut long and easy, so that the slope of the glue joint will not be abrupt at the ends of the patch. (Look at Figure 18-13, and ignore most of this wordiness.)

214

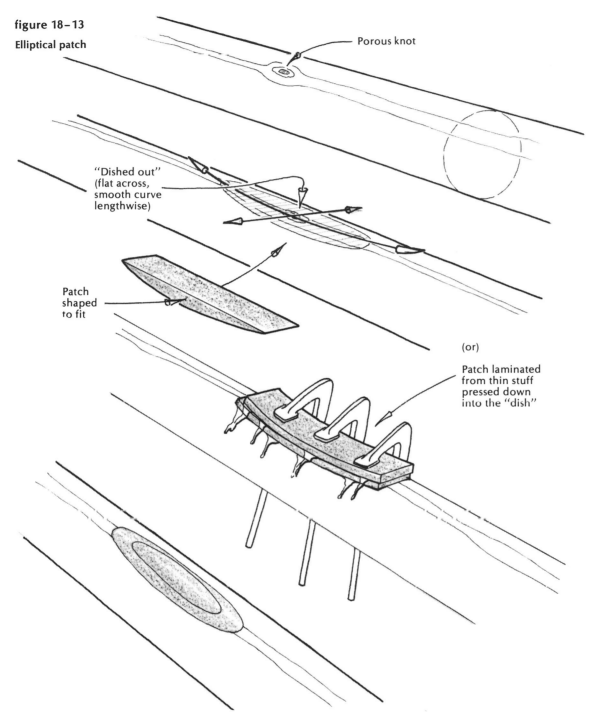

figure 18-13

Elliptical patch

Porous knot

"Dished out" (flat across, smooth curve lengthwise)

Patch shaped to fit

(or)

Patch laminated from thin stuff pressed down into the "dish"

The next move, of course, is to fit and fasten a patch that can be rounded off to look as if it had grown there. You can cut this to fit, if you wish, or you can bend it in—in one piece, or in several laminations. Whichever you do, you'll appreciate the long and easy shape of that curve.

Clamp as shown, with careful spreading of the pressure. Dress fair, with a drawknife, plane, and sander—and be smugly modest when the audience marvels at the perfection of those joints. "Nothing to it!" says you. "Any craftsman can do as well." And between you and me, that's the hell of it; he doesn't even have to be a craftsman.

And that, I think, is my final word on spar-making. All you need is a jig, some clamps, glue, a hand plane, and a little confidence.

215

Chapter Nineteen

The Rudder

You may find it hard to believe that there are hundreds of ways to make and hang a rudder, and about as many ways it can go wrong—to bind, or break, or jam, or fall off, or twist the stern of the boat out of shape. In some ways, the rudder is the most complicated and important part of your new vessel. I'll attempt to describe, with the help of Sam's drawings, how I have made and installed just two types of rudder, as I have done them dozens of times. (I'll skip the pop-ups, the balanced spades, the Viking steering-oars, the aimable jets—all of which simply move the stern of the boat sideways, and aim the bow where you want it to go.)

The first type, then, is the classic inboard rudder. It is hung on the sternpost, usually with a jog in its forward edge to make room for a propeller; the stock enters the counter through a watertight tube and stuffing box. It is controlled by tiller, or quadrant with cables, or one of the various worm-gear, rack-and-pinion, or hydraulic push-and-pull mechanisms. In olden times (before I started making rudders, that is), this stock might have been made of wood, an upward continuation of the rudder's leading edge, housed and turning in a planked-up rudder trunk or port. I have rebuilt such an installation in elderly Friendship sloops and catboats (and have listened to bitter complaints about how the damned ports always leaked),

but I am happy that we later builders, with access to better and cheaper metal, have managed to do a neater and possibly more reliable job in our little boats. Bear with me, then, while I try to describe my way of building, hanging, and controlling this inboard rudder.

Shaping the rudder stock (inboard)

I usually start operations by making a skeleton pattern, showing the location and angle of the propeller shaft, the propeller aperture, the exact angle of the jog in the stock, and the locations of the pintles. All this information is marked on or tacked to a straight lath that represents the forward edge of the rudder-to-be (see Figure 19-1).

The first and apparently most formidable job is to shape that stock—either by making a pattern, and casting it in bronze (as we've done several times, in agony and at vast expense), or by bending a good piece of propeller shaft to the correct angle. The latter is the simple and, if I may say so, the right way to do it. A good bronze propeller shaft (we usually managed to find a secondhand one, cheap) is a reliable piece of gear, while a casting is sometimes suspect; I've known of a couple of rudder stocks that wrung off at a bad moment.

So—to bend this shaft to the exact angle,

figure 19–1

Rudder pattern (inboard)

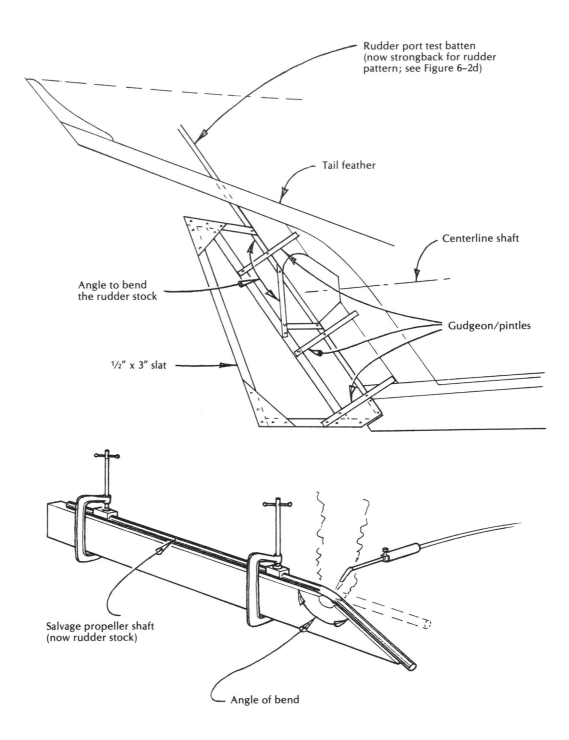

Rudder port test batten (now strongback for rudder pattern; see Figure 6–2d)

Tail feather

Centerline shaft

Angle to bend the rudder stock

Gudgeon/pintles

½″ x 3″ slat

Salvage propeller shaft (now rudder stock)

Angle of bend

you clamp it atop something solid, with the short end overhanging the edge of the platform. Arrange a stop to catch the end when it droops to the proper angle, and proceed to heat it at the bending point with a big, blue flame from your borrowed torch. Mind not the color of the heat, nor grow impatient and doubting. Maybe apply a very light pressure out on the end, and wait until it droops gently of its own sweet will, and stops just where you planned. Leave it to cool. Drill it precisely fore-and-aft for the $1/2$-inch bolts. (This is best done on a drill press, of course, and the holes will require some tapered reaming and countersinking to take the forged heads of the bolts.) You will rejoice at the thought that the dogleg in this rudder stock handles the main part of the turning load, and the bolts are thus relieved of a great deal of stress.

The blade itself

So now we need a blade to wave behind this stock. I have always shaped this of wood, usually in two pieces—the main part fitted precisely to the bronze stock, and the after piece drifted to it, tapering to a fine edge aft. That's a simple proposition, but some care is needed in the selection and shaping of that wood. If you have had to cope with a few warped rudders, you'll understand the problem—which arises from wood's tendency to change shape with every change in moisture content. It is therefore reasonable to suggest that the wood, when shaped, should be as wet as wet can be, because that's how Old Ocean will keep it. You don't want something "perfectly seasoned"; you want, if possible, a piece from the middle of the log, with the annual rings square across it. You may also want to install a cleat on the bottom—and two sets of flat bronze bands, through-riveted, if all else fails. You must, of course, groove the rudder's forward edge to accept almost half the diameter of the stock in a light-tight fit, and then drill dead-center for the bolts.

(It might be worthwhile at this point to consider what happens if this rudder can be made without the bend in the stock—for a boat with an off-center propeller, Herreshoff style, or for no propeller at all. This pleasant state would seem to allow a simpler, more efficient rudder; but its strength would depend almost entirely on the edge-bolts' resistance to bending, without the great power of that crooked stock to apply pressure to the blade.)

Hanging the rudder (inboard)

Let's assume that you've bolted the main (forward) piece of the rudder blade to the stock, as in Figure 19-2, and are ready to hang (or hinge) this rudder in place. I like to support it on four bearings: a stuffing-box of some sort on top of the tail feather, one bearing above the propeller aperture, and two more below it— with the bottom bearing as low as possible. To you who have gazed long at modern spade rudders, this may seem a needless excess of good bronze castings; but I will not begrudge the extra cost. Look at Figure 19-3, and prepare to make the patterns.

The bearing above the propeller aperture must fit, of course, around the main stock, and must be such that you can install it with the rudder in place—and, incidentally, remove it with no great trouble in case of damage. The great Nat Herreshoff used a two-piece fitting, riveted together and to the sternpost. I have meekly and thankfully used the same device since I first encountered it on a Herreshoff boat, and have not known it to fail or even wear to a sloppy fit. One pattern, of course, will do the two halves. Use $3/8$-inch hardened copper rivets through the sternpost, with perhaps a $1/2$-inch-bronze rivet where the two halves come together.

And as for the bearings below the propeller aperture: I use one-piece castings, as shown, on the sternpost, with long straps let in flush and through-riveted. The mating half, on the rudder, slides in and is secured by the floating pin. (I assume that you can handle the simple patternmaking involved, and I hope that your foundry will pour good, old reliable naval bronze, which will bend, and stretch, and hang in there long after the supermetals have perished from an excess of strength.)

Let's go clear to the top, now, and arrange for the stock to lodge inside the boat. This requires a hole through the tail feather that is aimed exactly down the line of the sternpost, and had best be lined with everlasting metal to keep the worms out. (They love dark, unpainted rudder-stock holes.) We usually achieved this ideal by boring for a threaded-pipe rudder port, of best red brass, screwed down through the timber. The right clearance for our standard $1 1/2$-inch-diameter rudder stock was provided by $1 1/2$-inch I.D. pipe, and a pipe cap, drilled out to shaft size, served to jam flax packing around the top of the stock to keep the port watertight. This installation required some precise work—boring a hole exactly in line, of

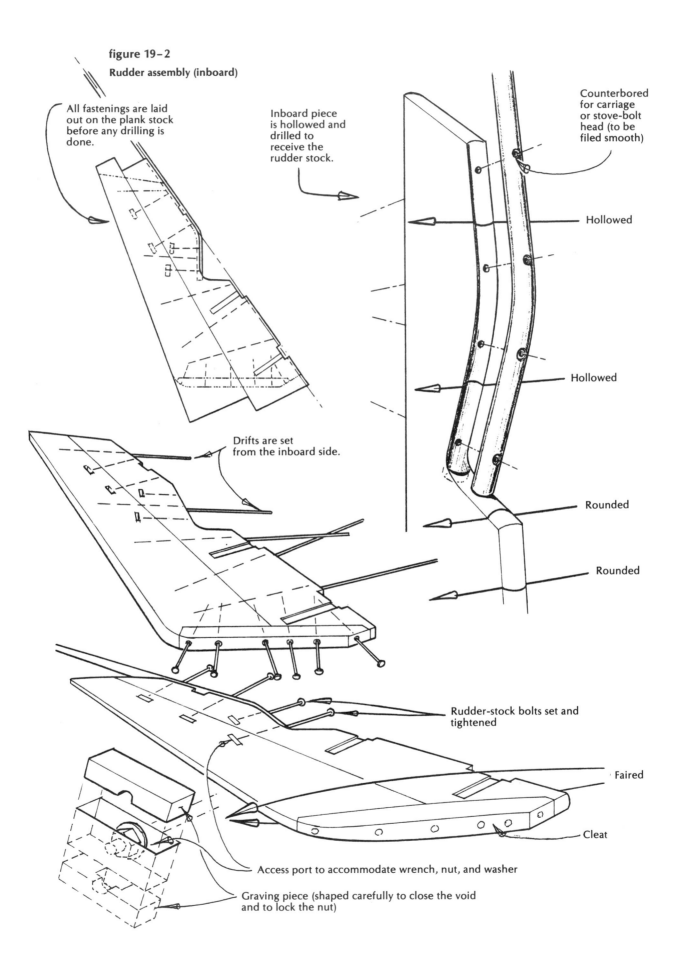

figure 19–2

Rudder assembly (inboard)

All fastenings are laid out on the plank stock before any drilling is done.

Inboard piece is hollowed and drilled to receive the rudder stock.

Counterbored for carriage or stove-bolt head (to be filed smooth)

Hollowed

Hollowed

Drifts are set from the inboard side.

Rounded

Rounded

Rudder-stock bolts set and tightened

Faired

Cleat

Access port to accommodate wrench, nut, and washer

Graving piece (shaped carefully to close the void and to lock the nut)

correct diameter to take the thread on the pipe for a perfect fit, tight enough to allow no working or leakage. (We put bolts horizontally through the timber, above the planking both forward and aft of the port, to guard against any split that might develop.) We used this simple system on dozens of boats, with the approval of the designers and our own consciences, and with no catastrophic failures, but we finally chose a more complicated arrangement—a custom-made casting to fit each particular boat, which was better in several ways. As shown in Figure 19-3, this is a heavy casting, with a wide base, angled to bolt on top of the tail feather, and fitted with a packing gland. This casting provides a stronger support for the rudder stock, and can always be re-seated if any leak develops under its flanged base. (It's a very pretty piece of patternmaking, too, and fine practice for the work you'll be doing someday on goosenecks and hawsepipes.)

You'll core for the hole, and clean the casting itself out to a smooth clearance for the rudder stock; and you'll wait, for the final fitting and bolting, until you've swung the rudder into place (having, of course, lined the rudder port with copper tube or lead sleeve, and the grooved sternpost with sheet copper.) Drop the lovely casting down over the stock, shave the top of the horn timber (tail feather) to correct for any tiny errors in angle, and fasten it down—preferably with naval bronze bolts, to match the metal in the casting. And I mean bolts, four of them, all the way through the tail feather. Bronze screws are not good enough. I've seen one of these castings, screw-fastened, all adrift and leaking torrents, and the boat was only 40 years old.

Two more warnings. First, the heel of the rudder must sit tightly upon an extension of the deadwood, or in some sort of heel bearing, with no gap to catch your overridden anchorline or a lobster-pot warp. Second, the stock should, if possible, extend upward through a strong bearing at the deck, with an exposed fitting to take an emergency tiller. This upper bearing helps to withstand the severe side-load generated by the lever arm of the steering device working against the pressure of the rudder—and note that the load approaches infinity as the tiller length approaches zero. This sounds like a desperate way to describe the situation. Your knowledgeable friends will point out, patiently, that the torque on the rudder head remains constant, whatever the length of the lever arm, and that a hydraulic ram with a 100-pound thrust against a 1-inch tiller has the same turning effect (torque) as a 1-pound thrust on a 100-inch tiller—or words to that effect. But these experts always ignore the side-thrust, which is the cause of much rudder trouble. Therefore, if you choose a worm-screw steerer (and a very good choice it is, if you can find one), get the double-arm style, as shown in Figure 19-4. If you can grab the brat by both ears, you can twist its neck without breaking it off. That hydraulic ram looks like a perfect solution, but its power must be countered by strong bearings, above and below, or it can wring the stern right off.

An outboard rudder

I trust that the above has put you in a proper frame of mind to appreciate the other kind of rudder—hung outdoors for all to see, vulnerable to attack by pirates, and terminating the length of the vessel in a no-nonsense lack of overhang. There are some (myself among them) who feel that after overhang in a vessel is worth its cost and weight when that vessel is running downwind in a big following sea; but that is a matter of opinion only, and fares poorly against the obvious and numerous virtues of the sawn-off stern and its outboard rudder: No holes through the hull; a cinch for a self-steering setup; cheap, strong, all-wood construction. Beauty is, after all, in the eye of the beholder, and most of the present-day beholders are too young to have been corrupted by the seductions of ancient classics; so let's get at it, and build an outboard rudder. (See Figure 19-5.)

Begin with the technique as described for the inboard rudder, first making a skeleton pattern from a thin board for the main piece, marked with the line of shaft, the propeller aperture, the top of the transom, the location of the pintles, the angle of the bottom in profile. Now find the best piece of oak that ever grew on the cold hillside—a plank sawn from near the center of the butt log, blue in color, with interlocked grain and a tough, mean look about it. Joint one edge of this plank absolutely straight, and lay it in, waiting until you've installed the gudgeons on the transom and the sternpost.

Hanging the rudder (outboard)

It's unlikely that you can locate off-the-shelf hardware for hanging this rudder, so you'll do well to make patterns and get castings before proceeding any further. Note that the gudgeons

221

on the sternpost are one-piece castings, and that one pattern will do for all three—the upper one, shorter in the arms and wider in the spread, can be bent wider and sawn shorter. (If the bronze won't stand that much bend, you'd better take the whole batch back to the foundry, and demand something better. Your rudder hardware must be above reproach.)

The fitting high on the transom must obviously have a flat base, to take bolts fore-and-aft through the transom knee; the other three are let into the sternpost, above and below the propeller aperture and at the lower end of the post, and riveted through with 3/8-inch copper. And bear in mind, while you are fitting these, that one slight misalignment will lead to strained fastenings, worn bearings, noise, and the expenditure of about 50,000 unnecessary foot-pounds of energy over the next 30 years. So take care, and get them in line. Install the top and bottom gudgeons, and align the others to a tight string between centers; or, easiest of all, use a length of cold-rolled steel shaft (borrowed, of course, and perfectly straight) to work to, for the final, delicate fitting.

All you need to do now is line up and rivet the pintles on the rudder, to match the gudgeon spacing; cut the aperture for the propeller, if any; fit the cheek pieces at the top, to take the tiller; and shape, drill, and drift the second (aft) piece to this main one. Taper this trailing edge of the rudder blade as much as you dare, so that the wake will close in around it, slick as off a mackerel's tail. (Many years ago I was told, separately and at length, by two of the most revered of all authorities, that this after edge should be left thick and square. One of the sages claimed that those bubbles and swirls were actually pushing the boat ahead; the other maintained that this area of confused currents increased the turning effect of the rudder to the extent of doubling its area. I delved into the theory of perpetual motion to strengthen my distrust of the first sage; and I eventually added another tapered plank to the rudder designed by the second that seemed, somehow, to lack authority in the likelihood of having to coax the vessel onto the other tack. I won't tell you the names of these two, lest I be scourged to a dungeon by you who worship the True Word. But I advise you to make that blade big enough, and taper it down very thin.)

That cleat on the bottom edge may look somewhat amateurish, but it covers end grain, and helps wonderfully to withstand warping.

The tiller

And now, to control this outboard rudder: the simplest, cheapest, strongest, and most reliable means is a tiller (the longer, the better) that comes inboard above the top of the transom. It need not allow for swinging more than 40 degrees from center amid sheet blocks and gallows frames, and it should fetch up against a positive stop when hard over. You can add controls to it in a dozen different ways—lines on tackles from both sides, with quick-jam locking devices on them; or a notched comb, as in the old lobster sloops; or removable pegs in a crossbar, to stop the swing (and never in exactly the right place)—and even that wonderful system, unbelievable, called the Shin Cracker (described by Frank Bullen in *Cruise of the Cachalot*, incidentally) which mounted a steering wheel, with drum, on the end of the tiller, and wound itself back and forth across the deck like a spider trying to make up its mind. The helmsman got a peek at the compass whenever his travels brought him past it. (Bullen's initial horror, I'm happy to state, softened to a grudging admiration for the system before the cruise was long underway.)

Let's suppose, now, that your design (or desire) calls for conventional wheel steering, with stub tiller or quadrant entering through, rather than over, the transom. A quadrant, whether grooved for cable or toothed for gear, will fetch up against the inside of the transom when hard over, and make you wish it would go another 10 degrees. A straight tiller (plenty long, to keep low the strains on cable and rudderhead) can be arranged to give you an easy 40 degrees or more, and still fetch up against a positive stop clear of the transom; but you will have to accept uneven tension on the cables as the tiller goes from center to hard over. This effect is not as bad as it may sound; we've done dozens of rigs like this over the years, and they all worked. Inevitably, cables wore out and broke, and we learned the hard way that the finest stainless steel is the least durable material for steering cables. Plain steel, well greased, seems to last twice as long. Bronze tiller rope, if you can find it, is better yet—and then, there's chain, and hard-laid Dacron. Design the parts of this system to give you at least three revolutions of the wheel from hard over to hard over, and be sure that you've provided for quick attachment of your emergency tiller, and have done something to bar insects and wavetops from entering your vessel through that tiller

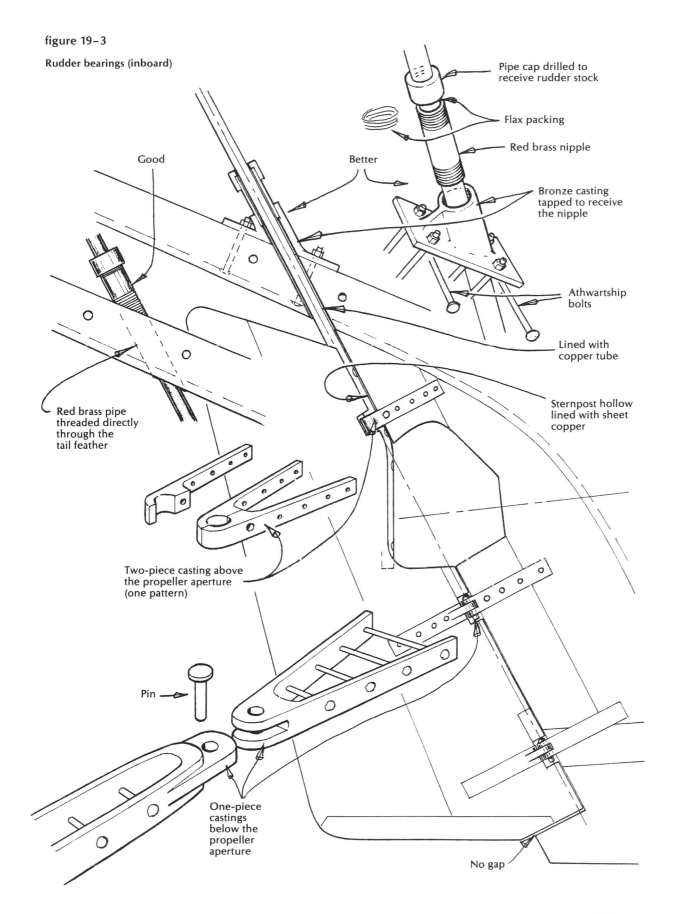

figure 19–3

Rudder bearings (inboard)

Pipe cap drilled to receive rudder stock

Flax packing

Red brass nipple

Bronze casting tapped to receive the nipple

Good

Better

Athwartship bolts

Lined with copper tube

Sternpost hollow lined with sheet copper

Red brass pipe threaded directly through the tail feather

Two-piece casting above the propeller aperture (one pattern)

Pin →

One-piece castings below the propeller aperture

No gap

223

slot. We have used a rubber tube, seized around the inner neck of the tiller, and fastened tight to the circumference of the transom opening. An inner tube out of a truck tire (if there is yet such a thing available) does very nicely, and endures the flexing for a long time.

And, finally, this warning: Ignore the advice of those who tell you to install all these sheaves, cables, and push-rods while they are easy to get at, with no deck and cockpit in the way. That is bad thinking. Some distant day, a sheave will

figure 19-4

Worm-screw steerers

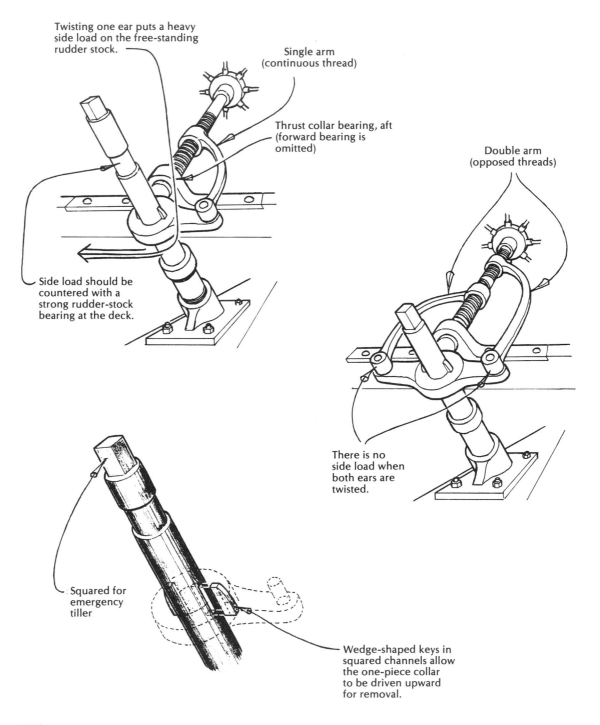

Twisting one ear puts a heavy side load on the free-standing rudder stock.

Single arm (continuous thread)

Thrust collar bearing, aft (forward bearing is omitted)

Double arm (opposed threads)

Side load should be countered with a strong rudder-stock bearing at the deck.

There is no side load when both ears are twisted.

Squared for emergency tiller

Wedge-shaped keys in squared channels allow the one-piece collar to be driven upward for removal.

224

figure 19–5

Outboard rudder

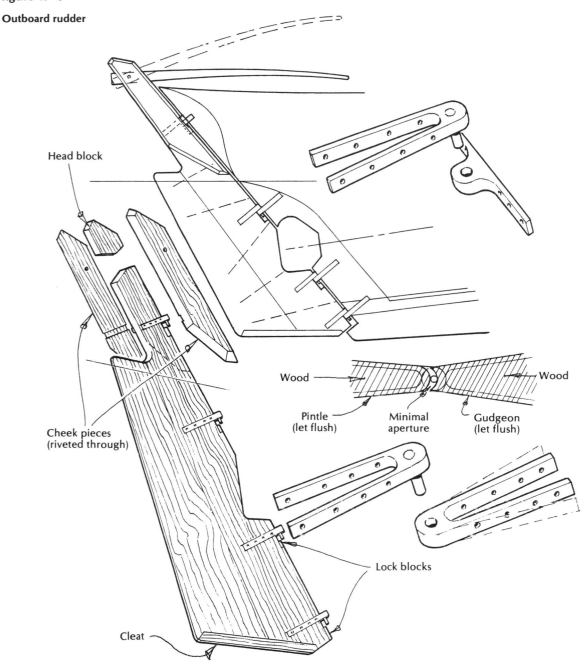

Head block

Cheek pieces
(riveted through)

Wood

Wood

Pintle
(let flush)

Minimal
aperture

Gudgeon
(let flush)

Lock blocks

Cleat

freeze, or a cable break, or a key wiggle loose, and you'll have to crawl in and repair the damage, before you get blown onto a lee shore. When that day comes, you'll be glad you planned and installed these parts, originally, with everything in the way. If you did it once, you can do it again; but if you did it the sensible way, with the hull wide open, and then buried your steering installation behind handy shelves and impregnable bulkheads, you'll be sorry indeed. In the meantime, plan everything so that it can't possibly break, or corrode, or jam. Grease those sheaves, check the cables, and be sure the ash tiller hasn't rotted at the rudderhead. Should have been black locust, anyway. Happy steering to you.

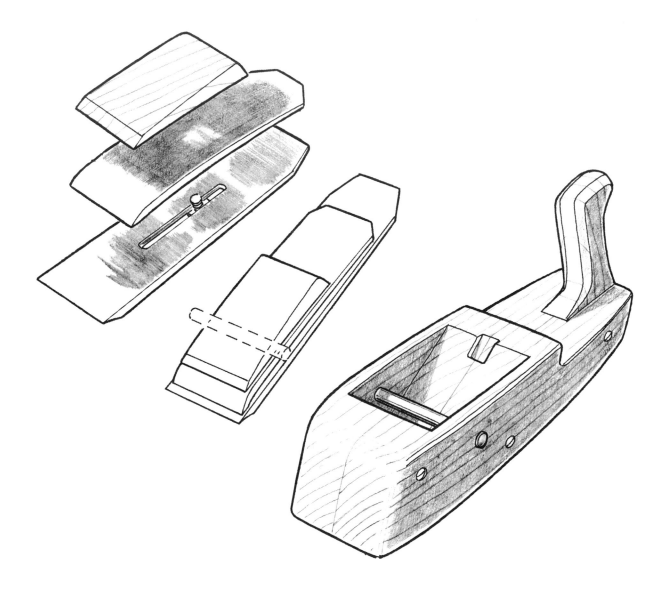

Chapter Twenty

Tools and Devices

Long years ago, we built a boat for a designer who yearned to be Poet and Artist at once; and in his search for the eternal verities, and any other justification for his 35-a-week-and-found, he once propounded as in a vision his concept (that's an unfortunate choice of words) of our separate roles—his and ours, that is. He was the father of this lovely thing that we were creating. Guess where that left the boatbuilders. We thought about it...and thought about it. As good red-blooded Republicans, we certainly were in favor of Motherhood, but even then we had a pretty fair idea as to how the work got divided. And there was something else about the setup that was vaguely disquieting.... And if you are beginning to wonder what all this has to do with the problem of How to Build a Steam Box, I'll tell you: absolutely nothing.

Steam box and bending forms

Every book on boatbuilding tells you how to make a steam box. You can use infinite lengths of stovepipe, truck-tire innertubes, 6-inch drainpipe leaning over a campfire, open troughs with hot water circulating through, wooden chests—and on to Bill Simm's ultimate steam box, which was a torpedo tube from a defunct submarine. I like one that's deep and narrow, built of thick pine boards (to keep the heat in, and stand rough treatment), and equipped with an adjustable partition, which you push in with a long stick—no sense heating the whole 20-foot box for a batch of 6-foot frames. Make it about 7 inches wide and 14 inches deep (inside dimensions), and fasten plenty of hardwood cleats to the outsides of the wide boards before you assemble the box. (Fastenings go *from* the softwood *into* the hardwood whenever possible; this is a good rule to remember.) Lay on the steam through a 1¼-inch pipe nipple, threaded through one side, down low, 2 to 3 feet in from the open end. Set the far end of the box 1 foot or so higher, so the steam will go up back, and the water will run down front—and into the pail you have waiting for it. The best door is a short length of padded board, nailed at its mid-height to the end of a leaning prop. Make a slide-in rack to keep things an inch or two off the bottom of the box. You can get real fancy, if you want to, and pipe the condensation back to the reservoir that feeds the boiler.

Steam: You want it hot, wet, and plentiful, so that the temperature inside that box will go up close to 212 degrees and stay there. You won't get it from a teakettle on a hot plate. You need a rig that was used to heat a small house in a Northern winter. If you can't find anything ready-made, lower a 10-gallon drum through a snug hole far off-center in the end of a 55-gallon drum; install crossbars to support the boiler, and more crossbars below it for a grate; cut an oval hole in the top to take a 6-inch stack; fit hinged doors to fire-box and ash-pit openings; fit a 1¼-inch floor flange to the top of the boiler for a steam outlet, and 1-inch pipe through the top and halfway to the bottom, for fill pipe. (When this last starts to blow, you know it's time to refill.) This rig is nicely portable, for those sister-frame and plank-repair jobs on remote river banks. Yank out the boiler, and you've got the world's most efficient heating stove and trash burner.

You'll need various built-up forms, for pre-bending cockpit coamings, transom planking, toboggans for the neighbor's children, and the like. You can use some of your crooked box-boards for building forms. Assume that the piece you are forming will halfway straighten out when you free it, and allow for this when you lay out the form. Such members as house-top beams, which are made up of glued laminations (see Figure 15–4), will hold their formed shape if made with five layers; no fewer. Use cold-water-mix glue, a caul (or continous strips) to spread the pressure of the clamps, and plenty of newspaper between the form and the oozing glue. Build one form a day, whenever you can spare the clamps, and they'll be ready when you need them.

A basic kit of hand tools

These pages have shown you some specially adapted tools, jigs, and devices to be used in various steps of boatbuilding. Of course, you'll also need an assortment of basic tools.

Make your own mallets. If you have a half-dozen of them around the shop, you may be able to find one when you need it. Use the heaviest and toughest hardwood you can find; turn the heads and handles on a lathe, if possible. Flatten the sides of the handles, which should be ⅞ inch in diameter through the heads, and 1¼ inches at the grip. The biggest mallet should have a head that is 9 inches long and 4 inches through the middle, and have a handle that is 14 inches long overall; this is the tool for driving frames into their sockets, and subduing shutter planks. Everyday mallets might have heads 7 inches by 3½ inches, and 12-inch handles. Experiment, and find out what fits your hand. Shun the rubber mallets; theirs is not the true music.

Roam widows' attics and waterfront dives in search of wooden planes—small ones, not the great, long jointers—that have some life left in their irons. You can shape their soles to the peculiar curves you meet in boatbuilding. Remember that a 9-inch round-faced plane with a sharp dumb-iron will cut fast across the grain of the hardest oak, when no other tool in your kit will touch it. Also remember that good fitting depends upon that last pass with a small plane in a skilled hand; all the elaborate power tools you can buy won't do it as well—although they certainly speed up the approach to the final moment.

Therefore, get yourself four standard metal planes: first, a 9-inch smoother, with a 1¾-inch blade; second, a fore plane that is 18 inches long, with a 2¼-inch blade; third, a low-angle block plane; and fourth, a rabbet plane. Get good ones. These are the tools that make that final pass. They'll last a lifetime, and earn their keep every day.

Chisels: You'll need the standard set, from ¼-inch chisels through at least 1½-inch ones. I like the long, heavy framer pattern, with big sockets. Get one gouge, of 1-inch radius. If possible, get a 3-inch (or wider) slick, to supplement your adze. And, of course, as with planes, get as many more types, shapes, and sizes as you can acquire without pain.

Handsaws: One standard "ship" pattern, 6-point crosscut; one ripsaw; one fine-toothed panel saw; one keyhole saw. And wherever else you may skimp, don't skimp here. Ask the men who live by the saw, and don't pay any attention to the consumers' guides. Learn to joint, set, and file, but not on these new blades. Take them to an expert. Remember that you can borrow a man's horse, shirt, hideaway, or last remaining $10.00, but you can't borrow his handsaws. These are somehow personal.

Sailing yachts have been defined variously as magic carpets, jealous mistresses whose rigging costs more than the hull, and depressions in the water into which you pour money. To the boatbuilder, they sometimes seem to consist mainly of an infinite number and variety of fastenings, for each of which he is expected to bore a hole of exactly the right size, taper, depth, and smoothness—and then cut a recess for the head, which will eventually be bunged. He therefore needs some assorted drills, bits, and augers, most of which cannot be found in the local hardware store.

Start with the standard set of "jobber's length" high-speed drills, from $^1/_{16}$-inch to $^1/_2$-inch. Keep this set complete at all times; buy extras, in quantity, of the size you find right for the big jobs such as plank fastening, decking, and ceiling. Order two each of "extra length" twist drills (6 inches long) in $^1/_8$-inch, $^5/_{32}$-inch and $^3/_{16}$-inch sizes. These cost about twice as much as the regular drills do, but you've got to have them for long fastenings. For twist drills larger and longer yet, ask for electricians' bits, which are 18 inches long, and come in sizes from $^1/_4$-inch to $^5/_8$-inch. Get one of each. Cut the square shanks off, and grind flats to fit the three-jaw chuck of your $^1/_2$-inch electric drill. Order Fuller counterbores, with at least two tapered drills for each, to fit numbers 10, 12, 14, and 16 wood screws. These are the only combination drills and counterbores we have found that will stand up to really hard wood.

Twist drills are not good for the long holes. When you bore the big timbers in the backbone, the floor timbers, and the mast partners, you'll need long ship augers, which haul themselves

through the wood, and push out the chips behind them. The old-fashioned "barefoot" pattern (see Figure 4–8c) is the best, for speed and ease of cutting, and especially for keeping to its course in spite of diagonal grain in the timber. You can withdraw it easily, to clear the chips (and be sure you do, much more often than seems necessary, lest you break it and your heart at the same time), and you can resharpen it with a small file. But beware of the old "barefoot" twist drills you may find in antique shops—most of them have been filed too many times. Your ship chandler will get you good new ones. You'll need $^1/_2$-inch, $^5/_8$-inch, and $^3/_4$-inch sizes (at least) in barefoot augers, and $^3/_8$-inch, $^7/_{16}$-inch, and $^1/_2$-inch sizes in single-spur augers with a center worm. Perhaps you can borrow the one big tool you'll need for the shaft alley and rudderport, and never need again; these holes will be $1^3/_4$ inches in diameter, and very difficult indeed to bore with anything except a barefoot auger.

Finish this list with a full set ($^1/_4$-inch to 1-inch) of solid-center, double-spur, standard-length wood augers, a set of the new flat bits, and a good expansive bit, with cutters to do every diameter from $^1/_8$ inch to 4 inches.

Before getting to the power tools, let's add a few more tools to your hand kit. You'll need a lip adze (see Figure 3–3), and some hammers: two or three assorted nail-driving, curved-claw hammers; one good ball-peen hammer, for riveting; and a shipwright's pin maul, or small sledge, for heavy driving. You'll also need a steel square, 24 inches on the long arm; a good sliding-blade 12-inch try square, with a bubble in the handle (see Figure 15–17); as many bit stocks as you can get, one of them good; screwdriver bits, one $^5/_8$-inch wide, two about $^7/_{16}$-inch, and one $^3/_8$-inch wide. Cut the shank off one of the medium bits, and use it in your big electric drill. Make your own nail sets out of $^3/_8$-inch hard (but not brittle) steel rod—ground to a slight taper, cupped on the end if possible. (We used to make them of hardened copper, for setting round-headed galvanized boat nails. I won't ask you to believe that those nails are holding very well 30 years later, or that some of those boats are still keeping old Ocean at bay with their original caulking, too—which is a frightening thought indeed, if you read the advertisements.) Remember the words of the old boatbuilder who confessed that only 45 years of his life had been spent actually working; he'd spent the other five years (well spread out) looking for his bevel gauge. Buy one of the thick, clumsy, awkward things that lock with a lever on the side (see Figure 5–3), or you can make a compact gauge out of flat brass (see Figure 9–12). If you are very deserving indeed, you may find, in a dark corner of what was once a genuine hardware store, a glazer's bevel. This has a 12-inch boxwood handle and thin brass blades at each end, and was made by Stanley in the days before everything came packaged in clear plastic. If you find one, keep looking: maybe, even farther back in the store, there'll be a box of plane irons made by Buck Brothers. (This is roughly equivalent to unearthing from a kitchen-midden incontrovertible evidence that Leif the Lucky slept here in the year 1000—and not much more likely, I'm afraid.) To continue: Get a good drawknife; an eggbeater drill big enough to take at least ¼-inch shanks; assorted hand screwdrivers, one with spiral drive; wood rasps, Stanley Surform rasps; a good spokeshave, preferably the old wooden-handle type; a sharpening stone, of aluminum oxide or equal, coarse on one side and fine on the other; and, if possible, an adjustable-bottom "compass" plane by Stanley, which you can set to the curves of knees and deckbeams. (Mine was patented in 1877, but not made until later in the century.) Get soft "framer's" pencils; a claw wrecking bar; a 12-foot steel tape; a plumb bob; a good level, at least 24 inches long; and carpenters' compasses that take a round pencil for one leg, and open to at least a 6-inch span.

Tools for working in metal

You will spend much time from now on making up odd-length bolts, cut from lengths of rod, threaded for nuts at both ends. Use a good hacksaw frame, with 12-inch blades. Buy the high-speed grade, even at three times the cost of regular blades. They last three times as long in mild steel and bronze, and will cut stainless steel, Monel metal, and the shanks of your new augers and screwdrivers. The same reasoning applies to dies for cutting the threads. The 1-inch-diameter, non-adjustable ones are not good enough. You'll need ¼-inch through ½-inch dies, adjustable, in National Course thread, as a minimum set. Take the bigger rods to a machine shop, or perhaps buy thread-cutting nuts of those sizes. Automotive supply stores usually sell them.

You will, of course, need a good machinist's vise, various files, wrenches of all kinds, Vise Grips and regular pliers, and lubricant for thread cutting. (We use poured-off bacon fat on iron and steel, and a thin, pale liquid called "Rapid Tap" for threading bronze and hardened copper.)

When you drill copper, bronze, or aluminum, or attempt to enlarge any hole already drilled, you will find that the regular cutting angle on the spiral flutes of most drill bits has too much lead, causing them to grab and break. Cure this by stoning a flat along the leading edges of the flutes so that they become vertical scrapers, with no remaining tendency to screw themselves through the metal. And when you drill stainless steel, go through with constant pressure, at the full-load speed of your big drill, and never let the chip break—one free spin, and the drill is finished. Only the best high-speed drills will stand this work—and you won't get them at a bargain price in a handy plastic folder.

Power tools

Power tools are much like governmental bureaus, in one respect: Once you've got the power, it's fatally easy to add another; but you'll never do away with one. When I built my first big boat, I had one small circular saw, driven by a ⅓-horsepower motor. This was a great luxury, after years of building skiffs entirely with hand tools. Two years later, having decided that I was about ready to revolutionize the boat-building industry, I acquired a good Stanley ¼-inch drill, and a very small bandsaw. (That drill is still working very well, after 37 years of hard service; I wish I could say as much for myself.) I discovered at the same time that I could get big keel timbers from a sawmill, instead of cutting a tree down and hewing it square by hand. (As I have mentioned previously, I never was much of an axeman.) I built more big boats...and I bought a 3-foot bandsaw for $20.00, and a big tablesaw for $10.00. I got a surface planer, a drill with a ½-inch chuck, and—mixed in with the building of more big boats—power sanders, portable electric saws, a drill press, router, more drills, power screwdrivers, a table saw with tilting arbor and dado-cutters, and even a power-operated hand plane, which is a lovely tool indeed. And now I couldn't do without a single one of these. The government would collapse.

What's the point of all this? I'm not sure, but

I think it indicates that (1) you can do a lot of boatbuilding without being fully mechanized; (2) I am not in a secure position to tell you exactly what power tools you need; and (3) having cut the shanks off all those augers, you'd better get yourself a pair of electric drills, and not the cheapest ones, either. Get a saw arbor, and build a wooden table around it. Get the biggest bandsaw you can manage. Look into the possibilities of renting tools by the day, or the weekend. You can cut the keel, the sternpost, and most of the stem to shape, in a day, with a big portable circular saw, which would be of very limited use to you afterward. A good saber-saw will save you some labor in fitting plywood bulkheads, but don't believe the man who tells you that it will handle every cut you'll ever have to make. You can live without a jointer, a radial saw, or a spindle shaper; I can count my fingers and thumbs, all the way to 10, and suggest that you may even live longer and more happily. You can buy a lot of bronze, oak, and good red mahogany for the price of these elaborate machines, and not one of them is smart enough to build a boat.

Last, but not least...

You'll need clamps. Even working alone, you can easily (and profitably) tie up 30 C-clamps at one moment when planking; and if someone is helping you bend frames, you'll use 50. They need not be the best clamps in the world, and most of them can be small, with 5-inch and 6-inch openings. You should have two 8-inch clamps, two 10-inch clamps, one 12-inch clamp, and three or four sets of the fittings that go on ³/₄-inch pipe or wooden bars to make up any length you need. You can cut that figure of 50 down to 20, and still manage, but there'll be moments of frustration. Seek them in secondhand shops and junkyards, and even buy new ones if all else fails. Oil the threads, and learn to spin them open and shut. Get the simple solid clamps, rather than the sliding-bar type (these let go when you jar them with a close hammer blow). Finally, get a half-dozen tiny "quilting frame" clamps, to use on the skeleton patterns you'll need to make for bulkheads, floor timbers, and such.

Scout around and acquire two 10-ton jacks, one of them hydraulic (see Figure A–5), and the other with a low lifting toe. Cut 3-inch steel pipe to 4-foot lengths (four of them) for moving the ballast casting around.

Appendix A

Fitting a ballast keel to an already built hull

Suppose you are like most of the young folks nowadays, and just couldn't wait, but set up housekeeping before you could afford Baby. That is to say, you have the boat all built, and now the casting has finally been made to—you hope—the right size and shape to fit the hull. Now it's time to face up to things, and act as if you'd meant to do it this way right from the beginning. This manner of building a boat may seem somewhat confused, but I'll tell you what to do next. I've been through this rigama-role many a time—the matter of the late, late casting that is unavoidably delayed because I couldn't afford the time, or the money, or both, to get it done at the start of the job. So the problem is not, Will it fit? but rather, How can I locate and bore the holes in the keel, to get the best possible compromise?

Marking for bolts

Elementary. Instead of clamping the wood keel to the recumbent casting and marking directly, you clamp it onto a board that is big enough to cover the whole area, mark the out-line on it, and bore all the bolt holes through it, right up the cores. All but the aftermost of these holes are square to the top of the casting, and therefore the top surface of the board gives a true pattern of the relative keelbolt locations—except for that aftermost one, which is the meanest of the lot, anyway. The safest treatment for that one is to bore for it after the casting is in place—which requires that you dig a pit under the sternpost deep enough to take the long auger and the big drill. (Do the job when you are ready to slide the rudder stock up through its port in the tail feather, and thereby get double value for your efforts with the shovel.) And oh, my friend, when you bore that hole—start it with a twist drill, just enough to center the barefoot auger—think clean thoughts as your finger trembles on the trigger, and clean those chips ever and anon, for if you get this one stuck, or Fate leads it astray, you have trouble.

We seem to be ranging far into the future. Let's get partway back, and consider the problem of the board with the holes.

figure A–1a

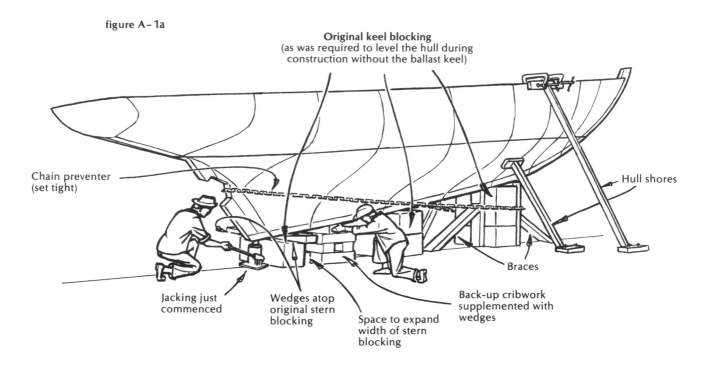

Original keel blocking
(as was required to level the hull during
construction without the ballast keel)

Chain preventer
(set tight)

Hull shores

Braces

Jacking just
commenced

Wedges atop
original stern
blocking

Space to expand
width of stern
blocking

Back-up cribwork
supplemented with
wedges

Jacking up the hull

The boat is sitting on three sets of blocking, as shown in Figure A-1a, all of them interfering with the pattern board and the casting that will follow it. She's got to be raised higher, and suspended with the bottom of the keel com-

pletely exposed, except at the extreme forward end. This will take some careful doing, for if she falls over in the process, you might be underneath, and you would make an awful mess on the shop floor. You want one helper, who is scared but calm. (Shoo the eager ones away.) Have at hand plenty of 6-inch by 8-inch

figure A–1b

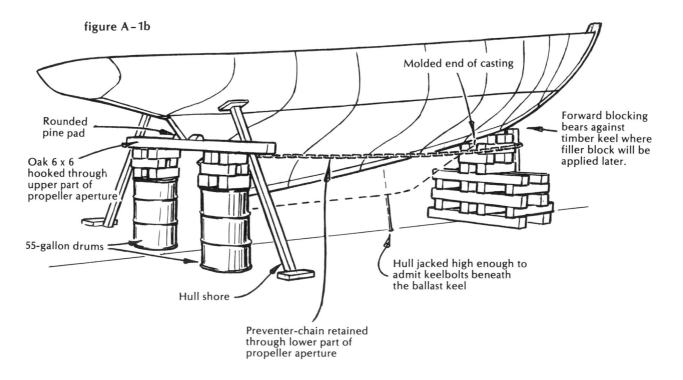

Molded end of casting

Rounded
pine pad

Oak 6 x 6
hooked through
upper part of
propeller aperture

55-gallon drums

Forward blocking
bears against
timber keel where
filler block will be
applied later.

Hull jacked high enough to
admit keelbolts beneath
the ballast keel

Hull shore

Preventer-chain retained
through lower part of
propeller aperture

234

by 4-foot blocking, and a dozen big wedges. Brace the forwardmost keel block strongly, and run a chain from its top, aft and through the propeller aperture (see Figure A-1b), and back on the other side. Set it up with a load binder. Set shores on each side, exactly abreast of the pivot point of the keel on this forward block. (Note that if these shores are forward of the pivot point, they will tighten intolerably as the stern is raised; and if they are aft of it, the hull will lift away from them, and be unsupported.) Set another pair, just for my sake, above or below the others, in the same vertical line. Now go down, aft, and prepare a foundation for your hydraulic jack under the keel. Make it wide, firm, and absolutely level athwartships and fore and aft. Install your helper just forward of the jack. His job is to keep a firm cob of blocking and wedges rising as the keel rises, so that she can't drop more than 1/2 inch, no matter what happens. Start jacking. You'll go up about 7 inches at a lick, and will of course keep what you gain each time (and while building up your jack foundation for the next try) by wedging tightly from both sides, on top of your helper's cob pile. Keep going until the keel is high enough. Imagine the casting as it will be when in place under the keel, and the room you'll need to start the long bolts up through it.

And now for a skyhook. If you have been so foolish as to install a propeller shaft and stuffing box, remove them. Place a heavy 55-gallon steel drum on each side, abreast of the propeller aperture 2 feet out from the center. Block up from these to support a mean, tough 6- by 6-inch oak timber 6 feet long, through the aperture, with a nicely rounded soft pine pad on its top where the sternpost rests. Take the load on the jack, tighten the crosstimber upward with twin wedges on each block pile, remove 2 inches from your safety blocking ahead of the jack, and lower away. Push it, shake it, bounce it, sight for sag, make sure it's resting easy, with plenty in reserve. Fit another pair of shores under the bilges, from the floor. Go forward now, jack clear, and block up to the keel, ahead of the spot where the casting will terminate. And there she is. Remove the loose blocking from underneath, and replace it with a pair of horses built up to leave just enough space for sliding your pattern board under the keel.

Saw the pattern right to the line, and slide it under the keel, remembering that the marked face is the one you should be looking at from where you lie on your back under the boat.

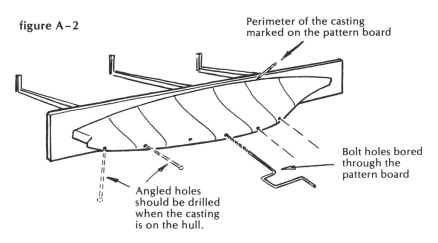

figure A-2

Perimeter of the casting marked on the pattern board

Bolt holes bored through the pattern board

Angled holes should be drilled when the casting is on the hull.

Center it exactly, get the after end (top surface) precisely 3/16 inch forward of the line of the forward edge of rudderport, and tack it firmly in place. Let us hope, pray, and even assume that the pattern at this point appears to represent a casting that was intended for this boat—with the proper amount of plumb-sided wood keel overlapping each edge, and the port overlap showing at least a family resemblance to the starboard.

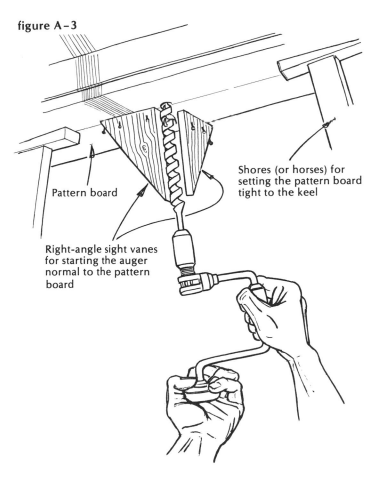

figure A-3

Shores (or horses) for setting the pattern board tight to the keel

Pattern board

Right-angle sight vanes for starting the auger normal to the pattern board

figure A-4

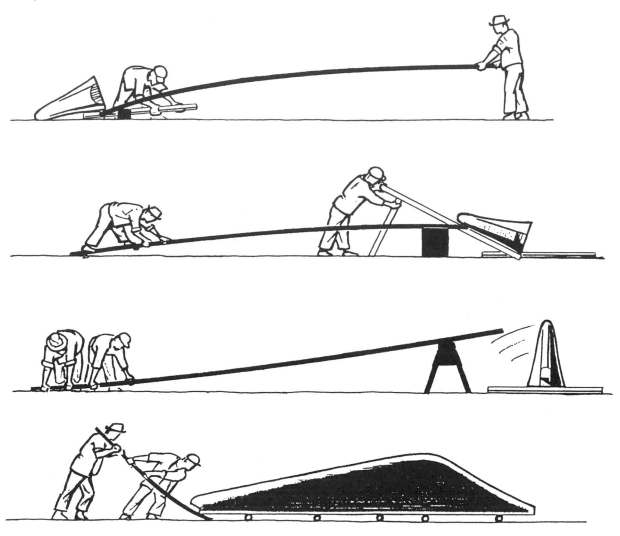

Boring the holes

Sharpen your double-spur auger and bore the bolt holes through the keel, using every means you can think of to guide them square to the surface, both fore and aft and athwartships. (See Figures A-2 and A-3.) Remove the pattern, and gird yourself for the next operation.

Coping with the casting

Many years ago, in the days of housejacks, we used to stand the casting upright, out in the open, and build a fine cradle under it. This was pretty work. A 12-foot timber, chained to the side and lifted by tackle, provided the power to raise it in one smooth motion. (Because of the length of the lever arm, the casting had small desire to slide sideways. Figure that one out, by moments and forces, and you'll be equipped to smack down the patient expert who smiles gently and tells you that length of tiller arm can have no possible effect on the rudderhead and its supporting bearing.) On its cradle, the casting rolled easily into position, and was pushed up the last inch with screw jacks. Then we acquired a toe-jack and a hydraulic jack (known as Sears and Little Joe, respectively) and decided to try the Easter Island technique of standing the thing up, right where it belongs.

That's the way to do it. No cradle—just roll it in on its side, defenseless. Start it up with Sears; block it; wedge it; and finally roll it against braced stakes on the far side. Get room for the hydraulic, and the battle's won. But operate everything at arm's length, with your feet behind you.

So there it stands, on two wide blocks, its top 6 inches below the keel, centered about right aft but 3 inches off to one side at the forward end, and a bit too far aft. Now, here's where you demonstrate your finesse and confound the onlookers. Build a firm foundation under the forwardmost bolt cavity, to take the hydraulic jack. Set it crosswise with its head in the hole, but tipped at a crazy angle (see Figure A–5) as if to push the casting yet farther off center. (Note, however, in a sly way, that the top of the jack is still well to your side of a plumb line from the far edge of its base.) Look at the athwartships bracing at the pivot point on the after support, move the forward bracing well clear, and start to pump. The casting will stir, tremble, and then move majestically toward you as the jack picks it up and proceeds to stand erect. This is all you need to know. Repeat as necessary. If it needs moving forward, remember, Atlas, that you can move the Earth if you have something to butt a hydraulic jack against—but be sure the blocking cannot teeter and undo your efforts when you relax the pressure. Also, read the directions on the jack: there's only one position in which the valves will work when it's horizontal.

As the casting rises, vertically, one end at a time, choose and smear on whatever magic bedding compound and preservative you think best. If the top of the casting is very rough indeed, I would give it a mushy fairing coat of Portland cement and fine sand, and apply black, asbestos-filled, roof-patching cement to the underside of the keel. Get the casting up there, and the bolts in place, while the filler is soft; wedge up the casting to take all the weight of the hull above it. Set up the nuts on big washers, with oakum grommets and sticky stuff underneath. Oh, I got so excited back there that I forgot to warn you to ream the holes in the wood keel to a moderately easy drive fit for the bolts—which you should have coated, thoroughly, with the grease used for mothballing machinery in idle steamships. And don't try a canvas or felt gasket between wood and iron. You'll have trouble enough if you do it the easy way. Fill the bolt-head sockets flush with a thick Portland cement mixture, rich. Hold it in place while it's drying with little wooden pads, propped with sticks from the ground.

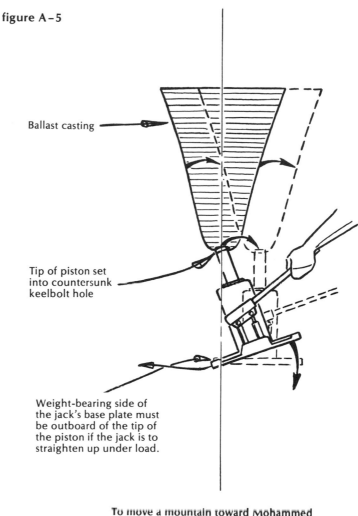

figure A–5

Ballast casting

Tip of piston set into countersunk keelbolt hole

Weight-bearing side of the jack's base plate must be outboard of the tip of the piston if the jack is to straighten up under load.

To move a mountain toward Mohammed by means of a hydraulic jack—

Finishing up

Fit, fasten, and fair off the small chunk of deadwood at the forward end of the casting. Then fair off the sides of the wood keel, between the rabbet and the top of the casting. Use a quick-turn adze here, and expect to re-grind it every time you hit the iron. Finish with round-sole plane and disc sander. Clean the iron with the disc grinder and a wire brush, and build up a surface with whatever anti-rust and barrier coats you believe in. We have tried everything from red lead to super-epoxy and would hate to guarantee any one of them. I would probably use two coats of ZRC, which stands for zinc-rich coating, and insulate it with some kind of inoffensive barrier paint before the final anti-fouling goes on. Ask your experts what to use.

237

Appendix B

A ballast keel filled out with deadwood

Suppose your design calls for a ballast keel scarfed at its after end that must be faired out with deadwood to the sternpost. This is the usual construction, for good and sufficient reasons which I will ignore right now. The problem is, of what do you make this deadwood, how do you fit it, and how do you fasten it?

Let's go through the various moves to be made. Suppose we build this deadwood right-side up, working from the top down. This plan poses two small problems: first, what to hang it to above, and second, how to get under it in order to bore up through the scarfed end by way of the cored holes in the casting. The latter problem can be solved by setting the casting high up on blocking, or by supporting it over a narrow trench. For the first, the obvious answer is, of course, to hang the deadwood from the boat's actual (wood) keel, whether at this point it is bare or already fitted with stem and sternpost.

Let me assume that the ballast keel casting is now upright, adequately supported on strategically placed crosstimbers to allow access from below to all bolt holes, braced to keep the flat top precisely level athwartships, and approximately level fore-and-aft. (See Figure B-1). This care is necessary so that you can determine the true centerline of the casting, from its forward end to the aftermost end of the

figure B-1

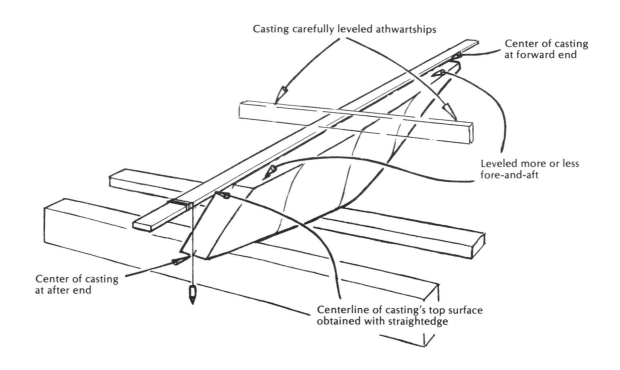

Casting carefully leveled athwartships

Center of casting at forward end

Leveled more or less fore-and-aft

Center of casting at after end

Centerline of casting's top surface obtained with straightedge

scarf, which is, of course, below the plane of the flat top. Do this with a straightedge, centered at the forward end of the casting, and located by a plumb bob over the aft end. The point at which this line leaves the after end of the flat is not necessarily the mathematical center at that point (because of possible irregularities in the top of the casting), but it is the one that must coincide with the true centerline on the underside of the wood keel.

Place the keel carefully in position on the casting now, and bore up through it, in the way of the flat, at least two holes for keelbolts. It would be advisable to use temporary bolts at this stage, a bit undersized so as to be easily removable. The overhanging after end of the keel will tend to sag downward of its own weight. Lay a timber across its top and block up the ends, and thus keep everything wide-open underneath. You now have a large vacancy, about as shown in Figure B-2, to be filled with a block of deadwood that tapers in profile, in plan view, and from top to bottom. This must be fitted worm-tight, if not watertight, to the end of the ballast casting, and it must be strong enough to withstand severe abuse in the event of a grounding. And if you

can work it so that the bottom surface is sacrificial (like the after end of that mythical snake that steamed away with pilothouse and engine room intact, leaving only gristle between the pursuing jaws), so much the better. Your designer very wisely draws an outline, labels it "oak," and leaves you to your own devices.

Let's make it of timber with high moisture content, so that it won't swell and overhang the metal casting, nor yet build up an intolerable load on the bolts that tie it to the keel. Let's make it in layers, each of which can be cut to shape (in plan view) with the saw that you used on the keel. Finally, let's finish off at the bottom with an especially hard piece, 3 inches thick, spiked or screw-fastened to the main body of the deadwood, and independent of the main fastenings, rudderpost, and gudgeons—in short, a shoe piece that is easily replaceable if it gets chewed-up, worm-eaten, or otherwise obnoxious.

We'll use oak flitches, sawn clear of the heart, 4, 5, or 6 inches thick as necessary to build the pile and come out even. A friendly and patient sawyer can taper one of these in profile to your pattern with the big board saw; otherwise, you'll have to do it with your small

240

figure B-2

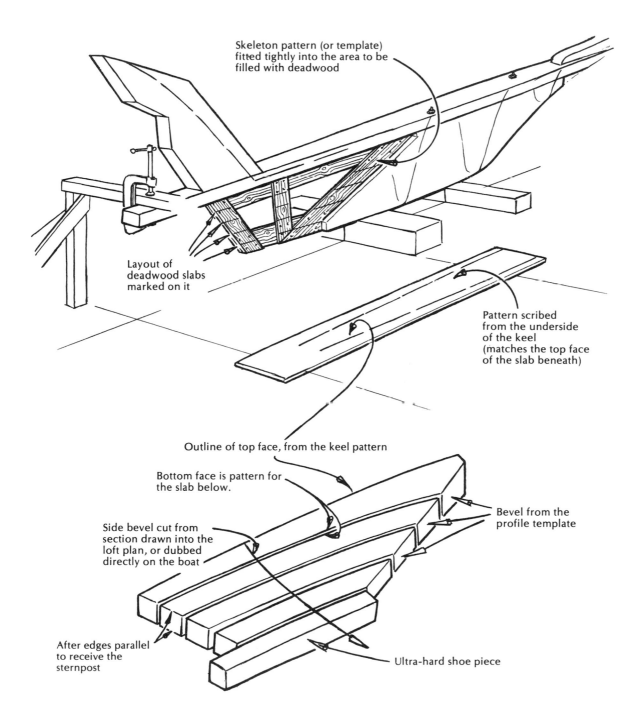

Skeleton pattern (or template) fitted tightly into the area to be filled with deadwood

Layout of deadwood slabs marked on it

Pattern scribed from the underside of the keel (matches the top face of the slab beneath)

Outline of top face, from the keel pattern

Bottom face is pattern for the slab below.

Side bevel cut from section drawn into the loft plan, or dubbed directly on the boat

Bevel from the profile template

After edges parallel to receive the sternpost

Ultra-hard shoe piece

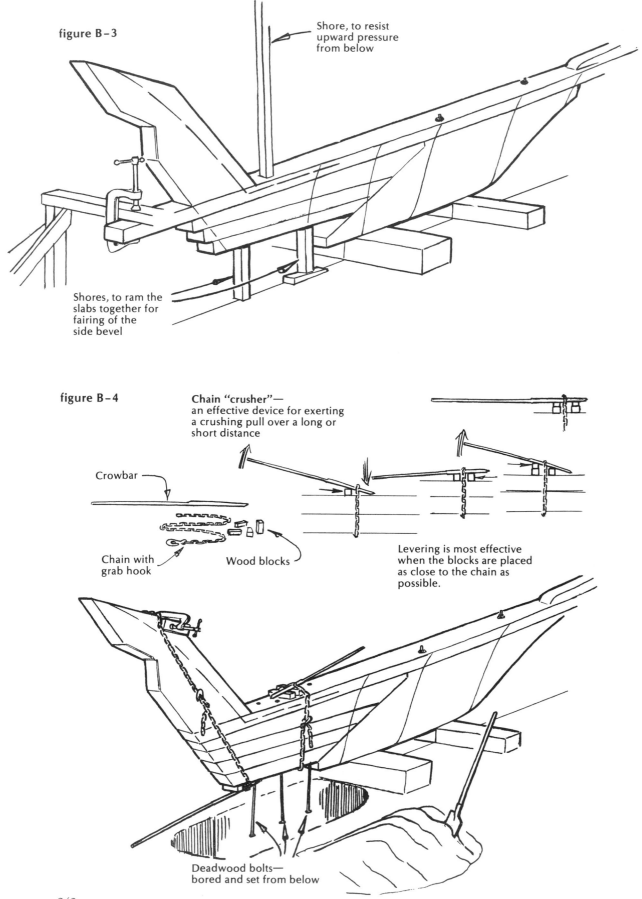

figure B-3

Shore, to resist upward pressure from below

Shores, to ram the slabs together for fairing of the side bevel

figure B-4

Chain "crusher"— an effective device for exerting a crushing pull over a long or short distance

Crowbar

Chain with grab hook

Wood blocks

Levering is most effective when the blocks are placed as close to the chain as possible.

Deadwood bolts— bored and set from below

tools, just as you will have to cut the slopes at the scarf.

Make a skeleton pattern of the profile, as in Figure B-2. Make a pattern (to match the underside of the keel) for the top surface of the uppermost slab. Apply the skeleton pattern of the profile to the stock you've selected for this top piece of deadwood. This will give you the angle of the scarf cut as well as the outline of the piece in profile. Mark around the skeleton pattern on both sides of the stock, directly opposite from each other, and cut down to these lines. The easiest way to remove most of this wood is to make saw cuts crosswise and down to the line about 3 inches apart, and then split off the small blocks in between with a big chisel. Smooth it with an adze and plane, shove it forward and up the slope of the ballast casting's scarf, and hang the after end by clamping it to the keel. Taper the sides, cautiously, and remove this first piece of deadwood to serve as a pattern for the top of the second slab. Keep this system going for all the deadwood pieces, fitting them one at a time, rough-tapering each, then going on to the next. Note, of course, that the fixed width at the after end (representing the siding of the rudder stock or rudderpost, as the case may be) moves progressively forward, according to the rake of the rudder, as you work downward. When you have filled the space down to but not including the 3-inch expend-able shoe, ram the pile tight against the ballast casting (Figure B-3) and proceed to bore for the bolts. Treat this deadwood as if it were part of the ballast, and fasten accordingly, with big bolts, staggered off center and planned to be clear of future floor timbers. Score the sides of the pile with adze cuts, so that you can reassemble with precision. Take everything apart (including the keel of the casting), coat all contact surfaces with worm-repellent waterproofing sticky stuff, and put the deadwood back together with bolts (Figure B-4). I assume that the sternpost was in place before this final assembly. Make the cut, on a line parallel to the rudder stock, to take the forward face of the outer sternpost, rudderpost, or whatever you want to call it, which should properly extend from the propeller aperture, past the end of the keel, to the top of the 3-inch shoe. Fit, round off, and fasten the shoe (using 60-penny galvanized spikes, which follow a $1/4$-inch drill, or 4-inch number 16 bronze screws, set way in—see Figure B-5). You can sandwich tarred felt between it and the deadwood as a worm stopper, if you like. Fit the outer sternpost (with a groove for the rudder stock) and fasten it to the deadwood, end of keel, and sternpost with bronze drifts, remembering to keep them clear of the two pairs of big gudgeon straps that are to come later—and proceed to adze and plane everything fair.

figure B-5

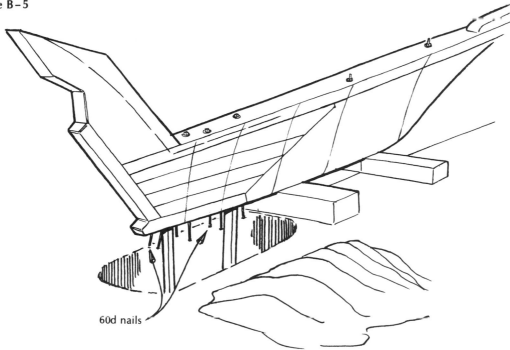

60d nails

"You've done a real good job, boys... but who the hell put in that centerboard trunk?"

Appendix C

Centerboards and Trunks

Certain crafty old boatmen will greet the word "centerboard" with bitter derision, and a cynical scorn they'd otherwise reserve toward a proposal of a good buy on the Brooklyn Bridge. They've had experience with centerboards. They know maybe not *all* of the troubles you can have with that foolish invention, but they know enough of them.

Centerboards and trunks can have problems, as you'll probably be told—at length, with heat, and in lurid detail. Your informant, wise in the ways of boats, will list a few of the problems he's had with that invention of some Cape Codder, or English shipwright, or the Foul Fiend, whichever came first. The trunk will inevitably leak and can never be cured; it splits the boat in two, and makes it creep together to jam the foolish board up or down; or it chokes with pebbles when you ground out, and the pennant breaks, the pin wears out, and the board drops to the bottom of the sea, which is a good place for it. Besides that, the centerboard and trunk take up room in the best part of the boat, and create an antisocial barrier in an otherwise friendly cabin.

Your informant will likely hold you with his glittering eye and tell once more an ancient, classic centerboard story that goes something like this (you've probably heard it twice already): Old George, the boatbuilder, had gone to his reward, and the gang gathered in sadness at the close of working hours to build him a proper coffin, shaped with the loving craftsmanship that the subject deserved. They fetched down boards from overhead that George had been saving for 40 years past—teak, mahogany, and black locust, fit for a hell-of-a-lot-better customer than he'd been getting all that time. And each of the boys brought his own jug, to ease the pain and sustain him through the dark hours of dedicated labor. There was no overall plan, although the foreman assigned jobs in a general sort of way. So there were a couple of dovetailed corners, and one half-lapped, and the fourth mitered—and each man did his best, in the dim lantern light, as he had been taught in his youth. Finally, the lanterns faded, come the dawn; and the foreman, waking with a start, said, "You've done a real good job, boys." Then he raised the lid, and looked in,

figure C-1

Wooden centerboard trunk, for a dory or a sharpie

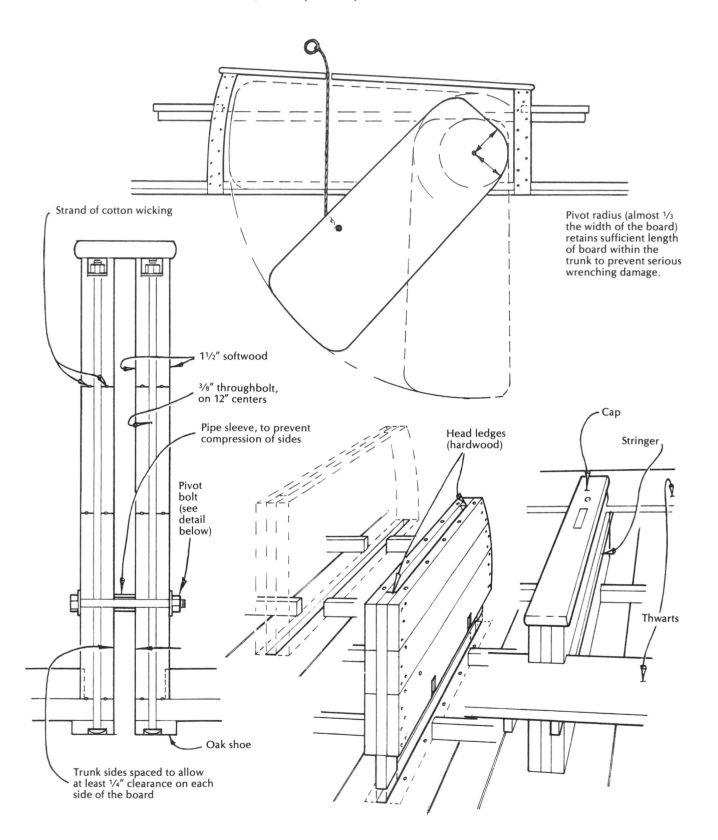

Strand of cotton wicking

Pivot radius (almost ⅓ the width of the board) retains sufficient length of board within the trunk to prevent serious wrenching damage.

1½" softwood

⅜" throughbolt, on 12" centers

Pipe sleeve, to prevent compression of sides

Pivot bolt (see detail below)

Head ledges (hardwood)

Cap

Stringer

Thwarts

Oak shoe

Trunk sides spaced to allow at least ¼" clearance on each side of the board

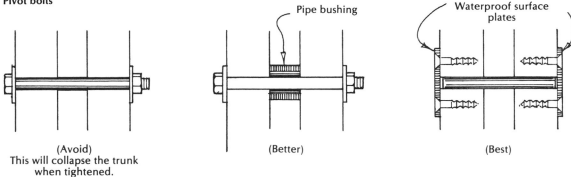

(Avoid)
This will collapse the trunk
when tightened.

(Better)

(Best)

and said, "But who the hell put in that center-board trunk?"

On the other hand, centerboards are wonderful. Countless thousands of them have been installed, to last the life of the boat without trouble. Consider what they'll do for you: They'll let you explore the peace of shoal waters, and sit upright when the tide leaves you aground; they'll bump you aware of shoals; they'll slide easily onto trailer or railway; and they'll let you ride the ninth wave high up the beach when there's no other escape in an onshore gale.

But they *do* need understanding of their problems, or they'll warp, and bind, and leak most cruelly.

A matter of mechanics

It's safe to say that most of the trouble comes from failure to provide a good lateral support. If you're slamming into a steep chop (or maybe slamming onto a sandbar, rail down), the board will exert a great wracking pressure against the sides of the trunk, which must therefore be strongly supported by thwarts, or by knees from floor timbers, or by attachment to a bulkhead. Any movement from side to side will inevitably loosen joints. And if the board pivots at a point that is low and far forward, so that it can hang, straight down, with almost all of its area clear of the bottom—its prying action against the trunk is so great that you'd better provide a positive stop to prevent its going more than halfway, or you can expect real trouble.

The simple solution, of course, is to move the pivot point up and aft, so that a goodly portion of the board remains in the trunk when the hoisting pennant breaks or runs wild. Lose a bit of area, gain a bit of depth, and the center-board will end up just the way the designer intended—except, of course, if the boat devel-

ops an ugly weather helm, or makes leeway at a yaw angle that is greater than 7 degrees, in which case it's your tampering that has ruined perfection.

But, right or wrong, high or low, you've got to provide a pivot pin for that board (unless, that is, you have in a cowardly moment decided on a daggerboard instead). In olden times, we used a plain galvanized bolt, through trunk sides and board, with a flat washer and ring of cotton under the head and the nut, respectively. This bolt would loosen and start to leak, and we'd tighten the nut, and gradually squeeze the trunk sides together, to jam the board, and start yet more leaks. So we learned to install a sawn-off pipe bushing in the board, to take the wear of the pin and the compression of the bolt against the trunk sides (see Figure C-1). The final development was a floating pin, ends flush with the trunk sides, capped at each end with a watertight pad. And we learned, the hard way, the most important thing of all: arrange this pivot business so that you can get at it without tearing the boat apart.

Perhaps it's time to consider the design and construction of the trunk, and some of the variations that have been developed to fit different boats and different conditions.

The centerboard trunk

The simplest trunk of all (for a flat-bottomed skiff, for instance) consists of two wide boards separated by vertical posts at the ends, strongly through-fastened, to form a narrow, parallel-sided slot—with an opening to match, through the boat's flat bottom. In our innocence of 70 years ago, we sawed off the posts (or head ledges) flush with the bottom of the trunk, fastened the sides with screws or long nails up from the bottom, and assumed that we'd have to tuck a bit of caulking cotton under the ends of the head ledges after the sides had swelled. Then we got the brilliant idea (probably from an older and wiser builder) of extending the head ledges through the bottom, so that we could caulk around stopwaters from the outside, and thus avoid any wait-and-see period. This helped our image with our customers, who felt, rightly, that having paid nigh onto a hundred dollars for a new sailboat, they shouldn't be expected to have to bail it out every week.

And then came bigger boats, with such complications as outside ballast shoes (slotted, of course, to let the centerboards drop through), which forever prevented access to the bottoms of the head ledges, or to the lower ends of the fastenings that held the trunk sides tight to the top of the keel. This was a sobering thought indeed. Lose the mast, run out of money, have the crew quit ship in Tahiti—these minor misfortunes could be coped with; but if that centerboard trunk loosened up, you were in real trouble. And therefore, I say, keep it simple: do not attempt to copy some wonderfully ingenious system (Figure C-2) of rabbeted bedlogs, splined side planks, angled drifts—which may have been necessary and desirable in a cargo schooner, or Commodore Munroe's *Presto*, but it is too complicated for me. I have always put my faith in throughbolts—plenty of them, in one length from the bottom of the wood keel to top of the trunk side, and easily tightened by the threaded nut on the upper end; and, especially, plenty of transverse bolts through the head ledges, installed with the thought that I might have to remove pieces of the garboard plank to get at and replace the lowest ones. Beware of using bone-dry hardwood (oak, or longleaf Southern pine), which can swell with enormous power and break a fastening that attempts to confine it. It's far better to use weak copper, which will stretch 10 percent of its length without breaking, rather than a super-bronze, which will stretch not at all. And consider that cedar will swell very little, will crush under the bolt head to relieve an intolerable strain, and will make fine-smelling trunk sides.

Another thing we learned—when fate or our own stupidity made it impossible to get at the bottom of that keel, and the trunk sides were not yet fastened to it, or tragically floating on decayed or broken bolts—was to cut a great, long thread on one end of a bronze or stainless-steel rod, lock two nuts on the upper end, and turn that lower end 3 inches into a hole in the keel, sized to the root diameter of the thread (and a slip-fit through the timber that was to be pulled down.) What joy was ours when continuously-threaded rod appeared, in all sizes and metals, and we no longer needed to struggle with a dull die and exact measurements! When we assembled these parts—trunk sides to head ledges, the entire works to the top of the keel— we did *not* use miracle epoxy, which we had never heard of (and would have distrusted anyway); we laid a strand of caulking cotton in sticky goo, carefully clear of the bolt holes, and reminded ourselves that barrels managed to stay tight with unembellished wood-to-wood joints. Sometimes the trunk sides warped inward when the wood swelled, and reminded us, unfeelingly, that we should have fitted stiff vertical cleats, fastened from the inside faces of the trunk sides, before we bolted it all together. So we used infinite wood screws from cleats into trunk sides, to straighten the warp and free the board once more.

We need a cap on this trunk—preferably watertight, pierced by a tube to lead the pennant to winch, tackle, or cleat—and another sealed opening, such as a deck plate, strategically located to allow shoving the %&$#! board down after an unfriendly oyster has wedged itself into the bottom of the trunk. And you can hang a lovely, two-sided dropleaf table to this cap, but be sure you can get the whole thing off, easily, intact, in time of need. (We once drained the sink into the centerboard trunk, in a big sloop, and were gratified, and even somewhat shaken up, at season's end, to discover no tiniest trace of marine growth on the board or inside the trunk. This bit of research may make you even more aware of the effect of detergents on our watery environment, but it will also arm you with brave confidence in the face of the teredo peril. The little so-and-sos need clean water, or they get a tummyache. And if the sink drain disgusts you or clutters the galley, you can absentmindedly pour fuel oil in through the pennant hole until it has displaced most of the water in the trunk. The oil will stay there, through rough water and smooth, until hauling-out time, when you will, of course, collect and dispose of it properly.)

From drop keel to centerboard

Once, some years ago, we installed a magnificent welded-steel, galvanized centerboard trunk in a big Crocker-designed ketch (see Figure C-3). The trunk alone weighed about 700 pounds, and the board it housed (a streamlined weldment, loaded with boiler punchings) weighed even more. The sides of this trunk

figure C-2

Rabbeted bedlogs and vertical stiffening cleats

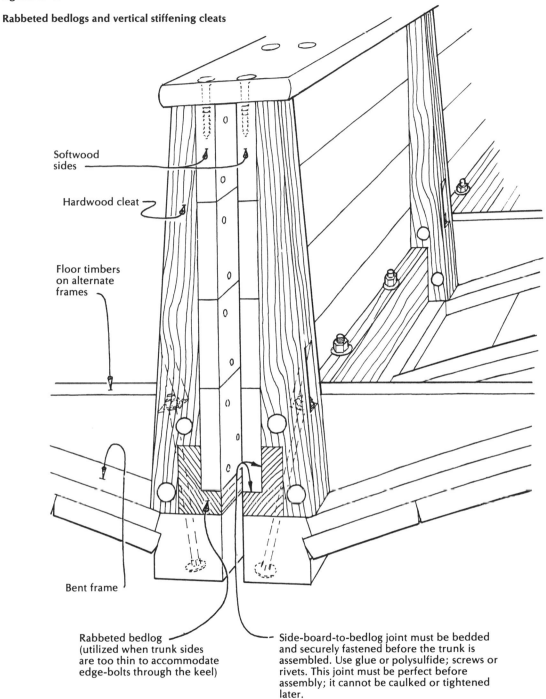

Softwood sides

Hardwood cleat

Floor timbers on alternate frames

Bent frame

Rabbeted bedlog (utilized when trunk sides are too thin to accommodate edge-bolts through the keel)

Side-board-to-bedlog joint must be bedded and securely fastened before the trunk is assembled. Use glue or polysulfide; screws or rivets. This joint must be perfect before assembly; it cannot be caulked or tightened later.

extended down through the slot in the wood keel to the top of the ballast shoe, and thrust out great flanges, above, to marry with the ends of the floor timbers. This was a drop keel that added considerably to the vessel's sail-carrying power. It was a fine piece of engineering—so long as the winch and cable survived the load,

and rust was held at bay by the galvanizing. (I wonder what 30 years in warm water has done to that boat?) And we designed and built three smaller boats (25′ long, with 18″ draft) with very heavy boards. They stayed tight and carried sail nobly; but the hoisting winches were a hazard to incautious hands, and the boards, thrust upward on a shoal and dropping violently into deeper water, would snap even a very strong pennant. So we went to lighter boards, ballasted just enough to overcome any buoyancy left in the water-soaked wood. These boards were fitted with flexible pennants, usually a springy line, over a sheave in the trunk cap, and leading to a cleat in the cockpit.

But before then, some 65 years ago, when we had not learned about laminar flow, or developed much skill or patience, we would haunt blacksmith shops and junkyards in search of a slab of ¼-inch steel plate that could be shaped and drilled for a centerboard in the new dory, or in the ancient catboat that had dropped its original board somewhere at the entrance to the cove. We'd pay 12 cents a pound, out of our clam money, for a lucky find, and sail away forever and a day with never a thought of rust or chafed-off pivot bolts. In our innocence, we thought they were very good centerboards indeed, and the pennants thrummed a noble orchestration when we slid down the front of a wave at a breathtaking six knots.

figure C-3

Steel centerboard trunk for a 40′ Crocker ketch
(centerboard 3′ × 9′; hollow, ballasted, weldment)

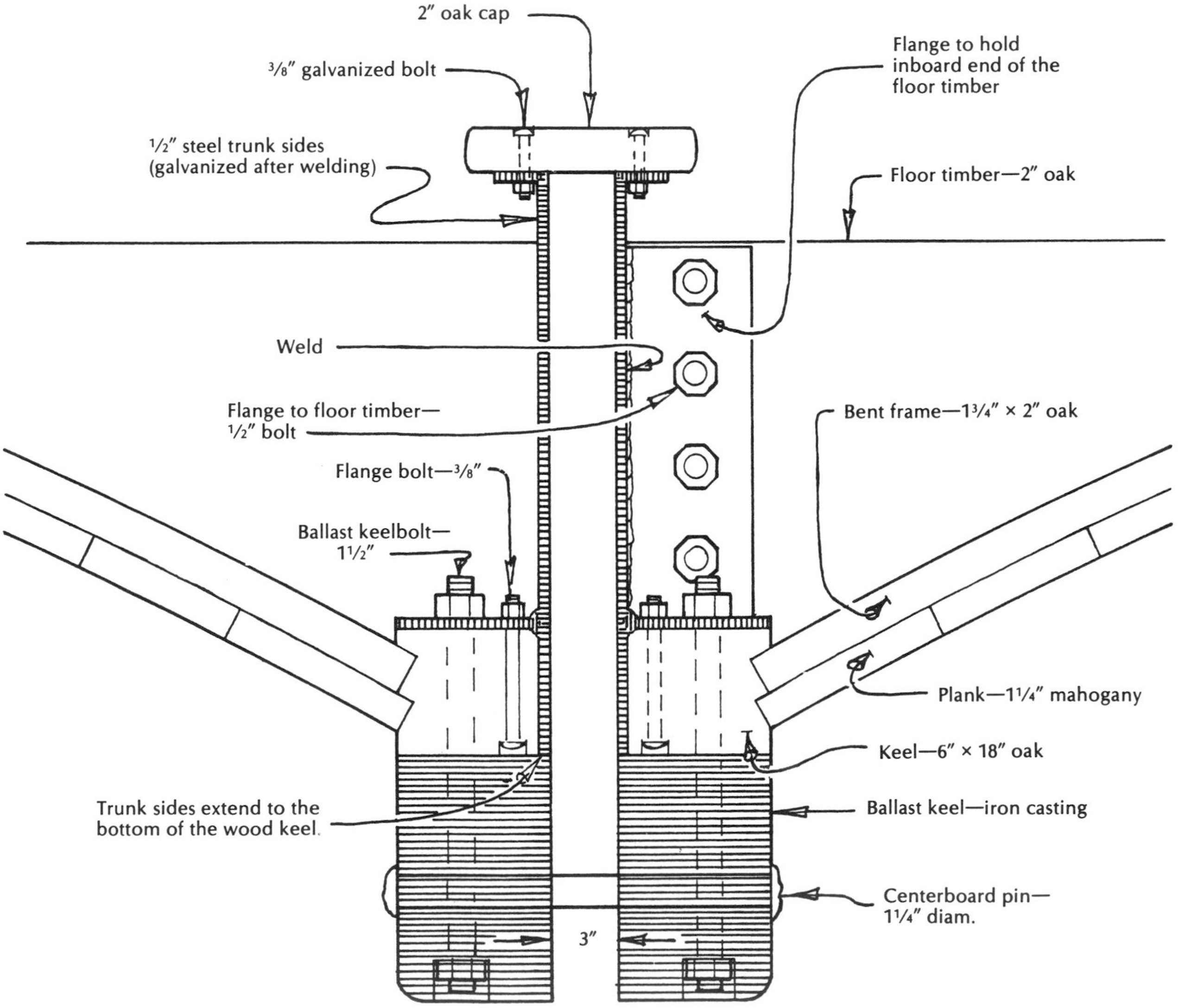

250

figure C-4

Centerboard options, for a dory or sharpie

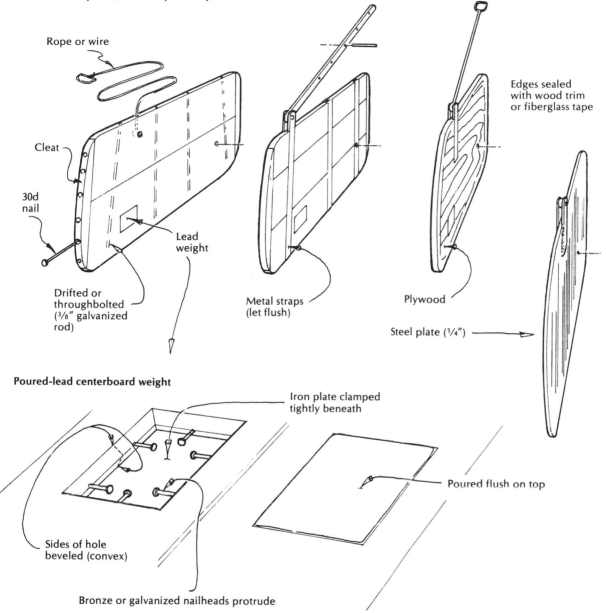

Rope or wire

Cleat

30d
nail

Drifted or
throughbolted
(3/8" galvanized
rod)

Lead
weight

Metal straps
(let flush)

Edges sealed
with wood trim
or fiberglass tape

Plywood

Steel plate (1/4")

Poured-lead centerboard weight

Iron plate clamped
tightly beneath

Poured flush on top

Sides of hole
beveled (convex)

Bronze or galvanized nailheads protrude

So, to make a simple wooden centerboard: Proceed with the thought that it's likely to warp, slightly, at some time in its career, and therefore should be fitted with what may seem a ridiculous amount of clearance in the trunk—perhaps a slot 50 percent wider than the thickness of the board. Build it of green lumber, quarter-sawn; fit vertical cleats on both ends; and, if the board is thick enough, install one-piece drift- or throughbolts, top to bottom. Cut out that cavity in the after end, perhaps, and pour it full of lead to give just the right amount of negative buoyancy (see Figure C-4). Sharpen the leading and trailing edges—and ignore sophisticated alarmists who know all about chords, and laminar flow, and what you can fabricate in aluminum or fiberglass. You can also save your money for a couple of years and buy a very nice new sailboat that doesn't have a bit of that nasty wood smell. So you can, but it wouldn't be half as much fun as building your own—complete with centerboard.

251

Index